EVIL AND THE AUGUSTINIAN TRADITION

Recent scholarship has focused attention on the difficulties that evil, suffering, and tragic conflict present to religious belief and moral life. Thinkers have drawn upon many important historical figures, with one significant exception – Augustine. At the same time, there has been a renaissance of work on Augustine, but little discussion of either his work on evil or his influence on contemporary thought.

This book fills these gaps. It explores the "family biography" of the Augustinian tradition by looking at Augustine's work and its development in the writings of Hannah Arendt and Reinhold Niebuhr. Mathewes argues that the Augustinian tradition offers us a powerful, though commonly misconstrued, proposal for understanding and responding to evil's challenges. The book casts new light on Augustine, Niebuhr, and Arendt, as well as on the problem of evil, the nature of tradition, and the role of theological and ethical discourse in contemporary thought.

CHARLES T. MATHEWES is Assistant Professor of Religious Studies at the University of Virginia, where he teaches theology, ethics, and religion and culture. He has published in *The Journal of Religious Ethics*, *Modern Theology*, *The Journal of Religion*, *Anglican Theological Review*, and *The Hedgehog Review*.

EVIL AND THE
AUGUSTINIAN TRADITION

CHARLES T. MATHEWES

Department of Religious Studies
University of Virginia

CAMBRIDGE
UNIVERSITY PRESS

PUBLISHED BY THE PRESS SYNDICATE OF THE UNIVERSITY OF CAMBRIDGE
The Pitt Building, Trumpington Street, Cambridge, United Kingdom

CAMBRIDGE UNIVERSITY PRESS
The Edinburgh Building, Cambridge CB2 2RU, UK
40 West 20th Street, New York, NY 10011–4211, USA
10 Stamford Road, Oakleigh, VIC 3166, Australia
Ruiz de Alarcón 13, 28014 Madrid, Spain
Dock House, The Waterfront, Cape Town 8001, South Africa

http://www.cambridge.org

First published 2001

Printed in the United Kingdom at the University Press, Cambridge

Typeface Baskerville MT 11/12.5 pt.   *System* QuarkXPress™ [SE]

A catalogue record for this book is available from the British Library

Library of Congress cataloguing in publication data
Mathewes, Charles T., 1969–
Evil and the Augustinian tradition / Charles T. Mathewes.
p.   cm.
Includes bibliographical references and index.
ISBN 0 521 80715 8 hardback
1. Good and evil.   2. Augustine, Saint, Bishop of Hippo.   I. Title.
BJ1406.M28 2001
214–dc21   2001025558 CIP

ISBN 0 521 80715 8 hardback

Henry Hill Mathewes
January 1, 1930 – July 14, 1996

imus autem non ambulando sed amando
St. Augustine, *Epistula*, 155.4

Ουκουν, εφη, εγω . . . των γε σων κληρονομος;
Plato, *Republic* 1.331d.8

. . . Indeed some of these new writers, at the same time that they have represented the doctrines of these ancient and eminent divines, as in the highest degree ridiculous, and contrary to common sense, in an ostentation of a very generous charity, have allowed that they were honest well-meaning men: yea, it may be some of them, as though it were in great condescension and compassion to them, have allowed that they did pretty well for the day which they lived in, and considering the great disadvantages they labored under: when at the same time, their manner of speaking has naturally and plainly suggested to the minds of their readers, that they were persons, who through the lowness of their genius, and greatness of their bigotry, with which their minds were shackled, and thoughts confined, living in the gloomy caves of superstition, fondly embraced, and demurely and zealously taught the most absurd, silly, and monstrous opinions, worthy of the greatest contempt of gentlemen possessed of that noble and generous freedom of thought, which happily prevails in this age of light and inquiry. When indeed such is the case, that we might, if so disposed, speak as big words as they, and on far better grounds . . .

Jonathan Edwards, *The Freedom of the Will*

The generally accepted view teaches
That there was no excuse,
Though in the light of recent researches
Many would find the cause

In a not uncommon form of terror;
Others, still more astute,
Point to possibilities of error
At the very start.

W. H. Auden

Contents

Acknowledgments

This book first took form as a dissertation at the University of Chicago Divinity School, and first thanks must go to members of my dissertation committee, who labored through it with grace and fortitude. Jean Bethke Elshtain contributed her acumen and intelligence, and perpetually pressed me to make my prose more punchy, or at least less turgid; she remains a treasured teacher and friend. Kathryn Tanner shared her theological acumen and philosophical meticulousness with me, not only during the composition of the dissertation but also before and after it, and my gratitude is profound; she is my model of a theological – that is, a mathematical – mind. Most of all, William Schweiker, as my main advisor and *Doktorvater*, exhibited a superabundance not only of all the intellectual virtues but also of the moral ones, particularly forbearance and fortitude; it has taken me years to learn some of the lessons he has tried to teach me and, while he has always been my teacher, I am only slowly learning the extent to which I am his student. It is an honor to thank him here.

Others at Chicago were also essential. The Institute for Advanced Study in Religion at the Divinity School provided some financial support and a lively intellectual community for the final year of dissertation writing, and I thank Frank Reynolds, then the Institute's director, for being the catalyst for that community. Conversations with many others were crucial, especially with Maria Antonaccio, Todd Breyfogle, Kelton Cobb, Paul DeHart, Heidi Gehman, Kevin Hughes, Derek Jeffreys, Lois Malcolm, Mark McIntosh, Aristotle Papanikolaou, the Reverend Sam Portaro, Rick Rosengarten, Jamie Schillinger, Jim Thompson, Darlene Weaver, and Brett Wilmot. Neither Chris Gamwell nor Paul Griffiths was on my committee, but both of them made indispensable contributions to this work, directly and indirectly, and I am grateful for their wise counsel; Paul Griffiths especially deserves recognition for a heroic and speedy read-through of a penultimate draft of the book, followed by a most helpful written commentary upon it.

In the University of Virginia Religious Studies department, I have been greatly aided by my colleagues in the "Theology, Ethics, and Culture" area, stimulating and helpful conversation partners all; in particular, conversations with Larry Bouchard, Jim Childress, Jamie Ferreira, Langdon Gilkey, John Milbank, Peter Ochs, and Gene Rogers have significantly advanced this argument. I also thank Anne Monius, Ben Ray, Abdulaziz Sachedina, Augustine Thompson, Robert Wilken, and my department Chair, Harry Gamble. Students in several of my courses, particularly those on "Evil in Modernity," "Inflicting and Suffering Evil," and "The Augustinian Tradition," have suffered through my attempts at grappling with the issues treated here; their questions, and also their confusions, helped me greatly. Several students in particular – Brian Moriarty, Jason Smick, Gordon Steffey, and Danna Weiss – have helped in particularly significant ways. Beyond the Religious Studies department, Talbot Brewer, Jon Haidt, James Davison Hunter, and Joshua Yates have been indispensable, and delightful, conversation partners. Last but not least, the Institute for Advanced Studies in Culture at UVA – which James Davison Hunter directs – has provided welcome financial support, and, more importantly, bracing intellectual camaraderie.

The transformation of the dissertation into a book was greatly aided by a grant for the summer of 1999 from the Wabash Center for Teaching and Learning in Theology and Religion, and I thank the Center, and especially Lucinda Huffaker, for their financial and other support. Support of a different sort was provided by colleagues outside UVA, who have been excellent conversation partners: I think especially of Lewis Ayres, John Bowlin, John von Heyking, Darlene Weaver (again!) and James Wetzel. All – especially Jim Wetzel – have shared their intelligence, suspicion, wit, and considerable erudition with me. D. M. Yeager's editorial voice – more accurately, her pen, and mythic yellow "stickies" – has never been far from my mind in the composition of this book; I have written it, thinking of her, with fear and trembling.

Grateful acknowledgment is made for permission to use in this book materials from the following essays:

"Operationalizing Evil," in *The Hedgehog Review* 2:2 (Summer 2000), 7–17;

"A Tale of Two Judgments: Bonhoeffer and Arendt on Evil, Understanding, and Limits, and the Limits of Understanding Evil," in *The Journal of Religion* 80:3 (July 2000), 375–404;

"Reading Reinhold Niebuhr Against Himself," in *The Annual of the Society of Christian Ethics* 19 (1999), 69–94.

Gratitude to one's family in a book seems misplaced: it is impious to localize their influence. But to make a start: my sister, Jennifer Lennox, and her husband, Randall Lennox, have both been sources of support and warmth like the sun. My mother, Martha Mathewes, has read parts of this and talked with me about it over meals, during trips, and on walks; without her persistent love, hugs, and kisses I doubt it would have ever been finished.

My wife, Jennifer Geddes, has lived with it for as long as she has known me, and at times I fear that she has lived more with it than with me; she has read drafts of it, she has argued with me about it, she has been honest, infinitely patient, and always absolutely loving. This book would not exist without her. Now that it is completed, I am eager for life with her, without it.

The dedication is to my father. The completion of this book marks an obligation long ago undertaken, and too long left undone. All my life we debated the matters treated in this book, and when I sat down to write it, I imagined him as the reader. I imagine him so still. I have written it for him.

Charlottesville, Virginia
August 28, 2000
Feast Day of Saint Augustine

Abbreviations

Conf.	*Confessiones*
DCD	*De civitate Dei*
DDC	*De doctrina Christiana*
DeMor.	*De moribus ecclesiae catholicae*
DeMus.	*De musica*
DLA	*De libero arbitrio*
DNB	*De natura boni contra Manichaeos*
DUC	*De utilitate credendi*
DVR	*De vera religione*
Ep.	*Epistulae*
IoEp.	*Tractatus in epistolam Iohannis,*
OpImp.	*Contra Julianum opus imperfectum*
QAS	*De quaestionibus ad Simplicianum*
Retr.	*Retractationes*
Sermo	*Sermones*

Introduction: reaching disagreement

Evil as such, which [allegory] cherished as enduring profundity, exists only in allegory, is nothing other than allegory, and means something different from what it is. It means precisely the non-existence of what it presents. The absolute vices, as exemplified by tyrants and intriguers, are allegories. They are not real, and that which they represent, they possess only in the subjective view of melancholy; they are this view, which is destroyed by its own off-spring because they only signify its blindness. They point to the absolutely subjective pensiveness, to which alone they owe their existence. By its allegorical form evil as such reveals itself to be a subjective phenomenon.

Walter Benjamin 1977, 233

SOME FACTS

Here are some facts:

In the beginning God created the heavens and the earth, and God saw that all was good, and so all is good. Among God's many creations was mankind, whom God gifted with freedom in order that they may love, both one another and God, as God loves them as well as God's self. The cost of this gift is risk; for a free being is by definition never wholly under another's control, and their actions can never be perfectly determined by another's will. In creating free beings in order to enter into relationships of love with them, God risked the possibility that they would resist that love. And so we have.

Sin came into the world through the first humans, and by that act all after them are placed under its yoke. Now sin spreads its stain far and wide, and the whole world groans under its weight, but the bare fact that all creation *suffers* sin reveals that there is an underlying goodness to being which can be destroyed only by destroying being itself. So our sin does not end creation but mars it, echoing down through history, crippling all

I

humanity in its always futile, because never more than partial, revolt against its source of being in God.

As God's will demanded the final perfection of communion between human and divine, and as humans had refused that perfection, the redemption of humans required divine intercession. Christ's life, death, and Resurrection have secured that intercession, and the Incarnation has consummated God's relation to the world; through Christ, God's absolute involvement with the world secures the possibility of human salvation, and thus the fulfillment of the divine will. God in Christ comes in time, to redeem time, and so time, while still in part our prison, becomes also the theater of our redemption, and a vehicle for grace – the arena of our repentance, our slow, painful, turning back, in Christ and through the Spirit, to God. We suffer in the interim – indeed we suffer the very interim itself – until his second coming, when sin and death shall be no more. But now, in this in-between time, sin most emphatically does exist.

For Christians, this is our condition; and Christians rightly call these "facts," events accomplished, whose reality is evidenced in the lives we live today. Christian theology begins with these facts, and attempts to construct an account of the human situation which comprehends them all. But theology also begins where we are, in the middle of our muddied lives, so it must interpret those facts, and our understanding of our lives, in such a way as to reconcile them – in such a way that one explains the other, and that, vice versa, one exemplifies the other. In such attempts, questions naturally arise about the sense – both the specific meaning and the potential meaninglessness – of these theological claims. This book is concerned with one set of such questions: what light can this account throw upon our existence as moral creatures, particularly as *flawed* moral creatures? How are we to understand ourselves, and how *can* we understand ourselves within this account? What illumination can it bring to our experiences of fallibility, failure, and fault, and what illumination can such experiences bring to the account?

Sometimes reflection on our experiences can make this narrative seem deeply implausible, indeed possibly harmful, even to those (perhaps *especially* to those) who know the narrative best. Here, for example, is the theologian James M. Gustafson, reflecting to his old friend Paul Ramsey on the (in)adequacy of the Christian tradition's typical response to evil:

I think the tradition has sold people short, Paul Ramsey. It has led them to expect things in the primary language of the tradition that failed over and over again. There are experiences of suffering in the world, Paul. There are experiences of suffering of the innocent in the world, and traditional religious language has a way of just putting syrup on that stuff – and not suffering with the suffering, and not being in pain with those who are in pain! (Gustafson in Beckley and Swezey 1988, 239)

This book is meant especially for those who both feel the power of the Christian moral vision proclaimed above and yet remain painfully aware, with Gustafson, of its "Pollyannaish" perils. It is also meant for anyone who cares to think soberly and practically about the phenomena of evil; for I judge that anyone so interested would be wise to heed the Augustinian tradition of reflection on these matters. But the book does not resolve this tension for believers, or provide a tight solution for more skeptical inquirers. It means instead to show how the Augustinian tradition seeks to help humans accept this tension as inescapable in our world, and thus to help us more fully inhabit it, by learning to live with both claims simultaneously. By returning to one of the primordial sources for much Christian thinking about suffering and evil – Saint Augustine of Hippo – and by thinking through his thought, we can recover the lessons that he and the tradition he inaugurated – the Augustinian tradition – aimed to teach about understanding and responding to evil.

MODERNITY AND EVIL: SUBJECTIVISM AND ITS LIMITS

This is especially important now, because our culture seems to lack the ability, and more particularly the moral imagination, to respond usefully to evil, suffering, and tragic conflict. Indeed the whole intellectual history of modernity can be written as the story of our growing *in*comprehension of evil, of our inability adequately to understand both the evils we mean to oppose, and those in which we find ourselves implicated. Most philosophy, ethics, and even theology proceed magnificently, as if at the center of all our lives there did not squat this ugly, croaking toad.[1] We have largely forgone attempting to comprehend evil, and choose instead to try to ignore or dismiss it through some form of ironic alienation, muscular moralism, or (if you can imagine it) some combination of the two. This problem cripples our thinking about how to respond to evil, and leaves us trapped in a stuttering inarticulateness when faced with its challenges. Andrew Delbanco puts it well: "A gap has opened up between our awareness of evil and the intellectual resources

---

[1] Exceptions include, in different ways, Berkouwer 1971, Midgley 1986, C. Plantinga 1995.

we have for handling it" (1995, 3). We know neither how to resist nor how to suffer evil, to a significant degree because we do not understand it: it bewilders us, and our typical response to it is merely a theatricalization, a histrionic which reveals no real horror at the reality and danger of evil but rather our fear of admitting our incomprehension of what we confront, what it is we are called to respond to, when we encounter evil. We oscillate between what Mark Edmundson calls a glib optimism of "facile transcendence" and a frightened, pessimistic, "gothic" foreboding (1997, xiv–xv, 154–5); this oscillation exhibits the guilty conscience of modernity.

In this setting, any attempt directly to reflect upon evil is already also, and simultaneously, an attempt to deconstruct the modern project's most grandiose self-understanding – not in order to renounce modernity's achievements, but rather to detach them from the perilously Promethean triumphalism within which they are so frequently embedded. It is no surprise, then, that the greatest modern self-critics, namely, Sigmund Freud and Friedrich Nietzsche, reflected in sustained ways on our difficulties in coming to grips with what we have traditionally called "evil", Merold Westphal aptly calls them "the great modern theologians of original sin" (1993, 3). And it is no surprise that their reflections led them, in different ways, to the conclusion that the root cause of modernity's failure adequately to conceptualize evil lies in the prototypically modern understanding of human being-in-the-world. Freud's philosophy of mind, and Nietzsche's philosophy of agency, both challenge the coherence of pictures of the self as a strictly autonomous being, precisely because such pictures cannot handle the full complexity of our situation before, and implication with, evil and tragic conflict. And they were right: our confusion before evil is due to modernity's general commitment to what I call "subjectivism," the belief that our existence in the world is determined first and foremost by our own (subjective) activities – that the sources of power and control in the universe are our acting will and knowing mind, before which the world is basically passive.

Subjectivism has disastrous consequences for our attempts to understand and respond to evil because it obscures our complex implication in the difficulties we face; it ignores how we are "always already" implicated in evil and mistakenly suggests that the challenge is straightforwardly (if not easily) soluble by direct action. It leads us to picture evil as fundamentally an *external* challenge to ourselves (hence making our basic moral claims ones of innocence and victimhood). Furthermore, even those contemporary positions that explicitly resist assent to subjectivism – most typically, significantly enough, prompted by reflection on evil and tragic conflict – imply that vulnerability to such vexation is simply our "natural" situation, brought on by our failure to be perfectly subjectivistic agents, thereby offering us (as a consolation prize, as it were) a "wisdom" which threatens to plunge us into despair. In both cases, evil's challenge goes missing, and becomes redefined as either the simply contingent difficulties of our time and place, or the insuperable natural conditions of human existence.

Evil's problematic status to us is deeply debilitating – not because we need our noses rubbed in evil out of some juridically perverted urge to make us morally housebroken, but because we need to find a better way to respond to evil. Unfortunately, most of those who write on these matters, few as they are to begin with, rest content with speaking of our need to be perpetually "open" to "the tragic." I cannot speak for you, but the last time catastrophe happened to me, it did not knock and ask to be let in. We need not be told to be "open" to tragedy; such talk is actually an attempt to mitigate tragedy's damage to us, like leaving the front door unlocked so that the burglars will not break the frame when they come to rob and kill you. We do not need merely to hear the bad news, nor do we need a more intimate *acquaintance* with evil; we need to know *what to do about it*. Indeed without knowing what to do we will be psychologically incapable of acknowledging the depths of our depravity. To despair sufficiently, we need to hope. And until we transcend subjectivism, we cannot even know what real hope is.

THE AUGUSTINIAN TRADITION: PROSPECTS AND PROBLEMS

This book argues that the Augustinian tradition can help us better to understand and respond to evil. In a world riddled by conflict, cruelty, and suffering, a world which seems daily more vexed by these questions, renewed study of Augustine, who so famously brooded over these matters throughout his life, would seem to be a wise move. But this is a surprisingly controversial proposal, as Augustine is more often a spectral presence haunting the debate than a participant within it; he appears most often, in Goulven Madec's felicitous phrase, as the "evil genius" of our heritage (1994). Most contemporary thinkers mention his name merely to dissociate themselves from him, or to blame him for our own puzzlements before these issues. The reasons these thinkers give for this shunning of Augustine are interestingly different, and indeed even contradictory: some claim his picture of evil as privation is too "aesthetic," too consoling and optimistic, others claim his account of sin is too "juridical," too repressive and pessimistic; some claim he legitimates violence against demonized opponents, others claim he makes us passive victims of others' assaults; some claim he is too otherworldly, others claim he is all too worldly, indeed even "Constantinian." While these critics' diagnoses of and prescriptions for our problems may differ, they share a common aversion to any attempt to return to Augustine; for them, progress in answering these questions is measured by movement away from all Augustinian resonances.

This book argues the reverse: despite contemporary prejudices to the contrary, Augustine's program, appropriated and extended by others – in particular, Reinhold Niebuhr and Hannah Arendt – offers much that we can still use. Even in our "demythologized" twentieth century there have been authentic Augustinians. (It seems odd to call the century with Nazism, Communism and consumerist advertisement-culture a "demythologized" age; but let that one lie for now.) This claim – that a "tradition" of Augustinian thought persists in modernity – faces criticism from two sides. "Modernists" argue that past thinkers such as Augustine are defunct, while "anti-modernists" argue that modern thinkers such as Niebuhr and Arendt are failures. But both are far too simplistic in their posturing. Contemporary prejudices against the tradition are largely due to misrepresentations of the Augustinian proposal as grounded most basically on a negative insight into – sometimes more dramatically portrayed as a disgusted recoil from – the realities of sin and evil. In fact, however, Augustine's project is grounded most basically in his positive account of love (and correlatively freedom) rather than pessimism (and correlatively enslavement). And that account continues to inform some of the best work done in modernity on human existence. Hence, we can meet the challenges to the Augustinian tradition by showing how its insights, in both Augustine's own thought and in the thought of several of his recent descendants, remain vital to understanding our own ethical and religious situation.

To summarize those insights: the Augustinian tradition interprets evil's challenge in terms of two distinct conceptual mechanisms, one ontological and the other anthropological. Ontologically, in terms of the status of evil in the universe, it understands evil as nothing more than the *privation* of being and goodness – "evil" is not an existing thing at all, but rather the absence of existence, an ontological shortcoming. Anthropologically, in terms of the effect of evil on a human being, it depicts human wickedness as rooted in the sinful *perversion* of the human's good nature – created in the *imago Dei* – into a distorted, misoriented, and false imitation of what the human should be. *Privation* and *perversion*: together these capture the conceptual contours within which the tradition proposes its practical response to evil. Against worries that these concepts are archaic, relics of a superstitious pre-modernity, the book shows how they continue to inform moral and religious reasoning in modernity, by tracking their role in modern thought. And theirs is a major role: Niebuhr's "Christian realism" develops Augustine's account of sin as perversion, and implies the normative account of human nature that that account assumes; similarly, Arendt's work on totalitarianism and "the banality of evil" develops an Augustinian account of evil as privation, and entails the normative metaphysic of creation from which that account derives. Two of the twentieth century's most important thinkers on evil and sin – perhaps *the* most important thinkers on this topic – are distinctively Augustinian in their accounts of evil and sin. This is no accident.

Then again, both accounts require substantial revision, for each is flawed by a partial adherence to subjectivism. Subjectivism can manifest itself *epistemologically*, in the belief that humans alone must construct their intellective relations to the world, or *agentially*, in the belief that humans act in ways that rely for their determination, wholly and finally, on the free and spontaneous choice of the human will. Niebuhr's "epistemological" subjectivism underlies his account of the roles "general" and "special" revelation play in shaping humans' interpretation of themselves, their world, and God; Arendt's action-subjectivism underlies her account of the human's capacity for action which is essentially non-teleological in form. For both of them, the self remains the primary actor: for Niebuhr, "in the beginning was the question," so to speak, the question that the self finds itself compelled to ask and answer; for Arendt "in the beginning was the deed." But the key subjectivist assumption both share is that in the beginning is *the self*.

Neither of them consciously endorsed subjectivism; on the contrary, the programs of both thinkers are sharply critical of particular manifestations of it. (Indeed, ironically enough, each critiqued the form of subjectivism the other suffers from.) And their critiques rely on insights that each appropriated from the Augustinian proposal. The subjectivist leaven in their thought is precisely what is *not* idiosyncratic to them, but part of their common modern inheritance, and even more precisely, that part of their inheritance that they did not themselves critically evaluate, but instead unreflectively assumed. Conversely, their real value lies in how they partly escaped these subjectivist commitments, a partial escape that was due to their partial appropriations of the Augustinian tradition's insights. Niebuhr, impressed with the Augustinian tradition's analysis and critique of the various dogmas of voluntaristic freedom, avoided the voluntaristic valences of subjectivism; Arendt, educated by Heidegger and Jaspers to appreciate the agent's experiential situatedness within an environment and a "world" which orients the self, avoided the reflective form of subjectivism. So both were fundamentally opposed to some versions of subjectivism, and for reasons which are fundamentally related to their partial appropriation of an Augustinian proposal, both were able partially to escape this subjectivism. The difficulty with their positions lies in the *partiality* of their escape.

Because of this, neither account can wholeheartedly warrant our hope for the world, and both contain elements which work against that hope; hence neither can illuminate our response to evil's challenges in terms of a basic response of increased *commitment*. In explaining the necessity of faith as a support for sustaining hope in the face of the challenge of tragedy, Niebuhr "naturalizes" evil by positing evil as a preexisting and primordial force which we meet in interpreting our world, and so undermines our confidence that God is wholly good. Meanwhile, in unpacking the power of freedom to overcome evil in the world, Arendt ends up rendering us episodic beings, and so subverts our ability to talk about our relation to the world as one of deep commitment. The axiological ambivalence of Niebuhr's proposal subverts our rationale for why we should be committed to the world, while the anthropological voluntarism of Arendt's account cannot explain *how* we are committed to the world. By seeking to secure the primacy of the subject, Niebuhr and Arendt are led to imply that the subject is victimized by something not themselves – either (as in Niebuhr's case) an external determination to sin, or (as in Arendt's) an internal fountain of natality that determines the agent's action. In seeking to secure the subject's freedom, both instead enslave the self all the more firmly to forces it can never control. Their subjection to subjectivism turns out to be nothing more than a modern form of what Augustine diagnosed as the *libido dominandi*, the lust to dominate that is itself the dominating lust.

Each of these failures is rooted in a deeper failure to understand our relations to the world as essentially relations of love. Niebuhr's account insists that humans meet God most primordially in experiencing the absence of God, not in a fundamental experience of love which sustains and directs their existence even before they are aware of its operation; similarly, Arendt's account insists that action is strictly autonomous, independent of any interests or goals, so action is essentially an *ex nihilo* reality happening within humans, a reality which cannot be understood as a loving response to the *mundus* which sustains our existence. Neither thinker wants wholly to do this; both, at other moments in their thought, conceive our relations to the world as basically erotic. But both are led by their residual subjectivist assumptions to undercut these more central motivations in ways which render their proposals incoherent. How can we advance beyond them?

In resolving the problems faced by both accounts, we are helped by a more thorough *ressourcement* of the work of St. Augustine. It is precisely those aspects of Niebuhr's and Arendt's thought in which Augustine's influence does not penetrate their modernist shells that were most vulnerable to subjectivist temptations; on the other hand, those aspects of their thought that were most Augustinian were most secure from such temptations – and indeed served them as the launching pads for powerful critiques of each other's subjectivist commitments. Thus our interest in offering a less subjectivist account than they admit may be materially advanced by offering a more thoroughly Augustinian proposal than they do. Augustine's theological anthropology resists our subjectivist temptations, and offers a well worked-out alternative to them: against subjectivism, a properly Augustinian anthropology understands human agency as always already related to both God and the world, so it chastens modern predilections for absolute autonomy while still affirming the subject's importance. To do better in grappling with evil, we must avoid subjectivism; and to be less subjectivist, we must be more Augustinian – or so this book argues.

REACHING DISAGREEMENT

This work makes this argument in three parts. Part 1 delineates evil's challenge to us, and drafts its understanding of the Augustinian tradition. Chapter one sketches the general contours of modernity's present perplexity before the challenge of evil, and diagnoses what in our situation makes it difficult for us to bring evil clearly into focus, locating our fundamental difficulty in our implicit commitment to subjectivist understandings of human existence. Chapter two describes the Augustinian response to evil, summarizes the concerns that the proposal typically elicits, and defends the Augustinian account against common claims that it develops from a negative insight into evil and sin, arguing instead that it derives from a more primary and fundamental positive vision of the universe, the human, and God, built upon Augustine's account of love. Part II rehabilitates the conceptual fundaments of this Augustinian position, by tracking its role in the work of Reinhold Niebuhr and Hannah Arendt – both (as is often recognized) in terms of their accounts of evil and sin, and (in a manner less well known) in the frameworks in which they place those accounts, frameworks which build upon Augustine's account of love. Yet neither Niebuhr's nor Arendt's formulation is fully adequate as it stands, for their Augustinian insights are undercut by subjectivist commitments which a fuller appropriation of the Augustinian proposal helps us expunge – a task greatly aided by their own partial apprehensions of (or at least openness to) the Augustinian insight into love's primordiality. Chapter three details Niebuhr's revision of Augustine's psychology of sin, beginning from his "Christian realist" account of original sin, and illuminates how his account, while crippled by subjectivism, still offers a hope we can mobilize practically, and so shows us how to acknowledge sin without collapsing into cynicism. Chapter four details Arendt's revision of Augustine's ontology, beginning from her account of "the banality of evil," and illuminates how this "banality of evil" thesis, while (again) hindered by her subjectivist assumptions, entails her "political ontology" and her practical proposal of *amor mundi*. Given these conceptual developments, Part III details the practical program following therefrom, arguing that the Augustinian tradition is ultimately a way of life offering a vibrant and world-affirming response to evil, in ways that its critics do not recognize. Against critics who accuse the tradition of otherworldly escapism and/or reactionary pessimism, Chapter five argues that the tradition demystifies and "demythologizes" the discourse of evil, refusing it any ultimate place in our cosmology by practices of forgiveness and "dirty-hands" action which allow humans to acknowledge the this-worldly inescapability of evil, suffering, and tragic conflict while still fully participating in worldly life. The book concludes by insisting that this response is not finally a *solution* to the problem of evil, but a resolute way of facing life vexed by that problem – a way of living in a world where evil will never be wholly defeated by human action, and yet a world where faith proclaims evil has already lost.

This argument is not likely to meet with general assent. But that is part of its value; its dissent from the contemporary consensus is not frivolous, a sort of diatribe from a crazy back-bencher made precious by its powerlessness. Today, when the confabulation and ritual demolition of straw men is quite common in normative inquiry, articulate and intelligent disagreement can be enormously profitable. At this point in time, debates about evil, tragedy, and sin do not need another formal attack on the idea of theodicy, nor another material defense of it, nor an appeal to "truths found in suffering that have been long repressed by the authoritarianism of orthodox Christianity." Contemporary theological and ethical research concerned with these issues has often remained unhelpfully general and vague in terms of positive proposals; while we can understand what it is that thinkers condemn, it is hard to see precisely what it is that they commend.

My complaint here is not essentially aesthetic or ethical; it is pragmatic. The project is strategically necessary: one of this book's main methodological assumptions is that we must understand thinkers rhetorically, as attempting to "push" conversations in particular directions. Books – perhaps especially academic books – are not finally aesthetic artifacts; they are interventions in ongoing debates. And those debates are constrained, operating within an "intellectual field" of potential "moves" (see McCole 1993, 24–8). The most appropriate intervention in the contemporary debate is not direct but indirect, not an attempt to address some single interlocutor, but rather to take a step back and call attention to what risks being obscured. We need a careful and detailed articulation of the tradition of thought that many contemporary works on this topic take themselves to be rejecting. To do this is an act of charity (in the sense of Augustinian *caritas*) for those outside the tradition, as at least then they will be clear about what they dispute. This is what this book seeks to offer. It aims to "reach disagreement" with its interlocutors – clarifying what issues separate us, and why they do (Elshtain 1995b, xi). It is not meant to be *charming*, but provocative; without real interlocutors to offer resistance, the debate risks falling into a frictionless whirring that goes nowhere.

The book's central task is to offer just this sort of resistance; by providing a detailed and pugnacious counter-position, it seeks to raise the standards (and perhaps the stakes) of the debate a notch or two. The opposition being so unclear, representatives of the Augustinian tradition must articulate the position they propound as clearly and forcefully as possible. The work does not centrally engage in a defensively apologetic project, fending off all possible challenges to the Augustinian proposal, nor does it attempt irrefutably to prove the truth of the Augustinian tradition, obliterating its opponents; rather it welcomes the challenges as opportunities more fully to rearticulate the tradition's fundamental insights, in the conviction that those insights still have much to say to us

today. While it is prompted by criticism, it attempts to turn that criticism
to positive use by elaborating the Augustinian tradition's "moral ontology," paying special attention to its account of suffering, evil, and sin, in
order to investigate the tradition's understanding of, and proper
response to, perils that always threaten, and often vex, our lives.[2]

This project is liable to be misread by different audiences in different
ways. I would like to head off those misinterpretations as best I can here.
Some want a thoroughly particularistic language, one wholly in the first-
order terminology of Christian theology, and they are suspicious of
attempts to talk in general philosophical abstractions, as if I am speaking in some sort of "public" or "lowest common denominator" language. For such "particularists," the language of sin is a distinctly
Christian language, and non-Christians have nothing to say about it –
and it has nothing to say to them. (Barth once said "only Christians sin,"
and I imagine he meant something like this.) My response to such
worries is simply that their concerns are misplaced. Nothing in this book
precludes a finer-grained, more particularistic discourse on evil and sin
(though I think mine is fairly fine-grained as it stands), and the kind of
linguistic purity they desire is inappropriate. I will not just preach to the
choir, however much the choir may need the preaching; I want to reach
as many people as possible.

Second, it is all too easy for a book like this to be read as simply the
latest in a long line of sour messages, "hellfire and damnation" sermons
delivered by tight-lipped preachers, a sermonizing to which, the culture
assumes, we all ought to give momentary nodding respect, and then go
about our business as before. But in fact both Niebuhr and Arendt give
the lie to this ideology of the once-born, those who believe in the power
of positive thinking. Their more "pessimistic" and their more "optimistic" visions are all of a piece, and are meant together to transcend the
simplistic dualism into which we are tempted to read them. Hence, I
spend time underscoring with each thinker the way that a real appreciation of their thought shows against the typical dismissive criticisms of
their work as pessimistic (in Niebuhr's case) or despairingly nostalgic (in
Arendt's). The Augustinian tradition, that is, is often read in modern
America as essentially focusing on things we ought not think about so
much. I want to resist this reading. But that, as Albert Hirschman has
said, is "[p]robably all one can ask of history and of the history of ideas

---

[2] See C. Taylor 1989, 41: a moral ontology is a framework that "lies behind and makes sense of
[our] intuitions and responses."

in particular: not to resolve issues, but to raise the level of the debate" (1977, 135). I do not want so much to deliver a message as to open a box of problems for the reader.

As neither thoroughgoing prolegomena nor comprehensive apologetics, the book attempts neither to defeat all comers *tout court*, nor to establish the Augustinian proposal on invulnerable foundations; of the making of critiques there is no end.[3] Rather, it uses the opportunity offered by the critical suspicions about the tradition to deepen our understanding of both evil and the Augustinian tradition. In Augustine's own terms, it uses the polemical occasion of defending the position as an opportunity for further, and deeper, constructive inquiry: it responds to commonly formulated worries about the tradition's account of evil – worries which it sees as arising as questions within the tradition itself, and not just imported into it from outside – in order to help us understand both the tradition and the challenge. To address these challenges, then, is to attempt to grasp the deepest roots of the Augustinian tradition, and to bring those roots to light.[4] In doing so, the work helps us better understand both the tradition's insights and the challenges we face.

FREEDOM, LOVE, AND THE AUGUSTINIAN TRADITION

One can legitimately describe this book as an investigation into the nature of human freedom. What is freedom's nature and extent, its capacities and limits? How should our understanding of it shape our understanding of our moral endeavors? How should it shape our understanding of God? Conversely, how should our understanding of God shape our understanding of human freedom? In a way, it uses the problems that evil presents to us as an opportunity to ask these questions.

"Freedom" has not gone undiscussed in modernity, but all too often the concept has been treated with more enthusiasm than thought, as if

---

[3] Thus Augustine, *DCD* II.i (based on 1972 translation, p. 48): "will we ever come to an end of discussion and talk if we think we must always reply to replies? . . . You can see how infinitely laborious and fruitless it would be to try to refute every objection they offer, when they have resolved never to think before they speak provided that somehow or other they contradict our arguments."

[4] Thus, while this account does not explicitly engage in a negative (and perhaps defensive) apologetic project, it does suggest that criticisms such as these, which such an apologetic would have to address, have little merit. (This does not imply, of course, that there are more pressing concerns than this, more genuine worries about Christianity.) Thus it engages extra-traditional challenges only implicitly. Explicitly, it is centrally concerned with exposition of the tradition, and by so being a positive account, it has negative implications; in being properly constructive, it is apologetic. In Augustine's own terms, it uses the occasion of defending the faith as an opportunity for deeper inquiry into the true character of the faith. See Mathewes 1998.

the sheer assertion of human freedom, vocalized with enough gusto, would in itself resolve, or dissolve, all obstructions to the progress of human happiness. This sort of "just do it" voluntarism proclaims the human's capacity to achieve any goal over any and every obstacle by the simple power of self-will. But the volume of the speakers' voices is equaled only by dimness of their vision. It is hard to believe that any sensitive moral agent would reflectively affirm that all obstructions to her or his own highest aspirations are essentially external to her or his own will. And, in fact, it is unlikely that any of us really believe it; for at the same time that our egotistical fantasies are fattened up by shoe advertisements, our moral self-understanding starves on a thin gruel of victim language – a diet able to sustain us only with heaping helpings of naive optimism, generated by the promise of "get happy" psychotropic substances with no relevant differences from other drugs, to offers of which we are told to "just say no." The problem with this moral worldview – what we may call the "just do it/just say no" account – is the simplicity, the "just"-ness, which it imputes to human agency, a simplicity possible only for a creature with a capacity to act in a wholly unconditioned manner, a way entirely self-determined. This vulgar voluntarism meets no one's needs, but, when coupled with a despairing pharmacological fatalism, it may staunch the hemorrhaging of our self-understanding just enough to create the (semi-)permanent illusion that, to borrow another recent mendacity, "I'm OK and you're OK."

This voluntarism has as its *doppelgänger* an equally profound nihilism, the faith that all can be embedded within a fundamental framework of necessity. All will fall back into the abyss of nature; all is part of the ongoing cycle of death and rebirth. We want to live, but we also want to die.[5] The shrill cries of marketeers cannot drown out this *basso profundo* which, no less than they, informs the tenor of the age. Because for us moderns our opposition to reality, and reality's ultimate triumph over us, are equally absolute, the absoluteness is an absolution; it offers us fatalism as the resolution to the problem of evil. This fatalism is merely the most superficial of nihilism's implications; more threatening, again because more basic, is the implicit understanding of the human as standing against reality, condemned to be in absolute opposition to it, until we finally absolutely submit to it. These two, optimistic voluntarism and pessimistic nihilism, constitute the Janus faces of our age; mod-

[5] See Ricks 1993, 1: "Most people most of the time want to live for ever . . . But like many a truth, it is a half-truth, not half-true but half of the truth . . . for, after all, most people some of the time, and some people most of the time, do not want to live for ever."

ernity is able to manage the travails of reality only by repeatedly (and schizophrenically) switching from one mask to the other.

In contrast to this cultural schizophrenia, Augustinians offer a calmer and more integrated vision. It is not surprising that we moderns understand evil centrally in terms of the exercise and restriction of our freedom and agency (terms which render invisible important aspects of the challenge), for this conceptualization seems the only one available to us. However, from an Augustinian perspective, the problem does not most basically concern our freedom, but rather our loves. As Heine said, freedom is a prison song, ultimately only of instrumental value; the bare fact that we are free to choose is meaningless if what we can choose offers us no satisfaction or happiness. Our contemporary anxieties about our freedom suggest something about our dissatisfaction with what material ends we can achieve, and in general with the overall happiness of our life. We must realize that our concern with freedom is ultimately not the most adequate formulation of our deepest cares.[6]

Love is crucial because it directly opposes the picture of ourselves that we typically assume – that we are fundamentally autonomous, fundamentally independent, isolated monads who must work to be connected to anything outside ourselves. Augustinians think this is a perniciously false self-image. The self is not fundamentally alone, nor is the world fundamentally a constellation of discrete atomic individuals; we are all in our lives intimately related with one another, so intimately indeed that this relation is in part *constitutive* of what and who we are. This is true not simply on a mundane level, but also – and indeed more primordially – on a theological level: God, as Augustine says, is "closer to me than myself," and the presence of the otherness of God at the bottom of the self is the fundamental energy moving the self to flower outwards toward otherness. This openness toward otherness is the core and primordial basis of what we call "politics," though our contemporary understanding of this term is so debased that it bears only the most attenuated connection to this deeper sense of politics. So Augustinian accounts place a great deal of pressure on our understanding of this term, insisting that we stretch our understanding to accommodate this broader sense.[7] Both Niebuhr and Arendt help us gain this broader

---

[6] This argument draws on C. Taylor 1989, especially chapter 25, "Conclusion: The Conflicts of Modernity."

[7] This insight is not restricted to Augustinian accounts; other, quite different programs have begun in recent years to think about the positive significance of politics beyond its typical (for our world) negative task of negotiating privacy for us. See Gutmann and Thompson 1996 and Sandel 1996.

understanding, and part of their attraction for this study is how their work challenges our typical understanding of politics. That their work does so has been recently recognized, and this recognition has been in part responsible for a return to their texts, and for the increasing number of calls for a *ressourcement* of our understanding of politics from their work.[8]

It is important to admit the real significance of questions of political freedom, and the absence of such freedom for almost all human beings on the planet today. Apart from a small group of highly "advanced" Western societies, most humans exist in conditions of severe abasement; inside those democracies, considerable fractions of the population live on the edge of poverty, to service the whims of the wealthy few. While the quality of life of the globe seems to have improved in several critical respects because of modernity, vast numbers of people suffer immiseration for the sake of the wealthy – and intellectual – elite. Central to this immiseration is the denial or restriction of the agency of these people. In these contexts, a philosophical or political emphasis on the importance of agency can be an intelligent, and indeed necessary, tactical move.[9]

Still, such tactics should remain tactical, and not eclipse the strategic import of emphasizing the purpose of freedom. It seems as incontrovertible as it is typically ignored: human agency *qua* human agency – in short, freedom – cannot be construed as the exclusive or even the central good of human existence. We must resist the tendency to slip from defending the immediate instrumental importance of freedom to defending it as the ultimate good. The problem is that the former looms so large as a concern that many feel it appropriate to focus solely on that project (e.g., Raz 1986). Programs that emphasize agency as the basic constitutive good of human existence often lose sight of the paucity of such an articulation of the human good, and can end up reinforcing the debasement of agency, and in particular its transformation from agency into *consumption*, into the activity of "creating a self" by purchasing various goods and services. Some might argue that these newer forms of self-enactment remain "legitimate" (whatever that means) ways of

[8] For Niebuhr, see the essays collected in Lacey 1989. For Arendt, see Margaret Canovan's suggestion that we need to rethink "politics," and that Arendt gives us much assistance in this project: "It is politics . . . that gives us the possibility of humanizing the lawless wilderness" (Canovan 1992, 277).

[9] Such moves are central to the arguments of, for example, Benhabib 1992, Lovibond 1983, Hurley 1989, and Nussbaum and Sen 1993.

enacting agency, not least because they do not differ fundamentally from earlier manifestations of agency (as all are fundamentally palimpsests, working over the multiform layers of our cultural inheritance). This debate is too large to enter into here, so I will only note that such arguments implicitly beg the question by relying on an unthematized understanding of legitimacy and authenticity, which seems to entail some criteria or norm by which to evaluate our manifestations of agency (see Mathewes 1999). Thus even our grammar relies on some sort of implicit picture of right and wrong agency.

This work addresses this issue in particular only indirectly, by investigating the connections between freedom and love. Niebuhr and Arendt are excellent figures to study here as model modern Augustinians – up to a point. At their best they share the (Augustinian) belief that proper human freedom is both profoundly significant and yet significantly constrained, oriented by what Augustinians identify as the reality of our loves. But both Niebuhr and Arendt also reflect the difficulties we moderns face in coming to appreciate this Augustinian vision, as both, at important moments in their thought, invest freedom with a sort of absolute independence from love that subverts their proposals. The Augustinian proposal articulated here argues that the essence of the errors of both Niebuhr and Arendt lie in their residual subjectivist inversion of the order of freedom and love, and that these mistakes are best dealt with by rejecting their foundational subjectivist assumptions – their belief in the primacy of human agency – and replacing it with an account of the human as *responding* (see Schweiker 1995). On such an account, our beginnings are understandable only as secondary to the absolute beginning of God's action in creation; we neither establish our epistemological framework nor inaugurate our agential projects *ex nihilo*.

In doing this, we are not simply repairing the particular errors of Niebuhr and Arendt; more basically, we are offering the rudiments of an interpretation of the Augustinian tradition which runs importantly counter to the usual modern interpretation. Indeed modernity's intellectual roots are found, to a significant degree, in important *mis*readings of Augustine's works; the roots of rationalism can be found in Descartes' misreading of Augustine's arguments about the *cogito*; and the roots of voluntarism can be found in late medieval misreadings of Augustine's account of the will. The Augustinian tradition is misconstrued if it is construed as fundamentally a pessimistic tradition, one emphasizing limits or sin; any appropriation of Augustine's negative insights must be understood as resting upon their deeper appropriation of his positive insight that the world is organized around love. Both Niebuhr's and Arendt's mistakes have roots in such typically modern misreadings of Augustine's thought, misreadings that grasped only part of Augustine's whole vision. It should thus come as no surprise, then, that Augustine, properly read, provides resources for an account more successful, because less subjectivistic, than much earlier philosophical anthropologies.

But the Augustinian account here proposed is not renunciatory of these earlier accounts. On the contrary, it seeks to incorporate the genuine insights of these positions into a broader, more capacious synthesis, even while transcending their errors. This work employs a hermeneutic of charity, *caritas*, and hence attempts as much to manifest in its method as it asserts in its arguments its fundamental claims about the centrality of love in our lives – both in our actions and in our inquiries. Too much work today is written in the service of what we may call a hermeneutic of exclusion, the interpretive version of identity politics. While such an approach may indeed be appropriate at times, the Augustinian proposal forwarded here seeks to challenge the exclusivity this approach all too often – both in the classic texts of modernity and in some of the more recent ones of anti-modernity – claims. Precisely what this means is more readily shown than said, and doing so will be one purpose, though not the central one, of the remainder of this work.

As I have said, this book is neither thoroughgoing prolegomena nor comprehensive apologetics. The arguments throughout are neither absolutely comprehensive nor totally satisfactory; I am not in the business of satisfying all such worries. While these arguments do hint at more fine-grained arguments which could be developed, even those arguments will still not satisfy everyone. I want to investigate the deep meaning and systematic implications of the Christian doctrine of sin – in both its directly anthropological (or ethical) and indirectly theological (or soteriological) aspects – guided by insights given classic formulation in the thought of St. Augustine. To this task it now turns.

PART I

Preliminaries: evil and the Augustinian tradition

CHAPTER ONE

Modernity and evil

And it is this battle of the giants that our nurse-maids try to appease
with their lullaby about heaven.

Sigmund Freud 1961, 77

Sigmund Freud's *Civilization and Its Discontents* is one of the few twentieth-
century works which attempt to grapple with the phenomenon of evil,
and of those few it is one of the most profound. It is also exemplary in
its dismissal of much previous thinking on evil: this chapter's epigraph
is Freud's epitaph for previous thought about evil, which he saw as little
more than a collection of mythologies symptomatic of our own ingrown
self-destructiveness. In the wake of the First World War, Freud suggested, we needed to "grow up" about evil – to recognize, beyond all
mythological consolations, that it is an ineliminable fact about us. He
offered a "scientific" analysis of our predicament, which built upon his
postulate of a primordial "death drive" attending all living creatures; it
was this death drive, working in darkness and silence, which fuels, both
directly (through acts of aggression) and indirectly (through repression)
the seething anarchy at the base of the human psyche. And it is this
drive's "titanic" struggle with the principle of love which Freud
described as "this battle of the giants" – and which, he thought, when
understood with cold objectivity, reveals the essential uselessness, indeed
infantilizing consequence, of religious "lullabies." In contrast, Freud
promises no happy endings. He ends his work with the hope that perhaps
now, when we as a species have begun to realize our full powers of self-
destruction, "eternal Eros will make an effort to assert himself in the
struggle with his equally immortal adversary. But," he concludes, "who
can foresee with what success and with what result?" (1961, 104).

Freud's account is among the most noble moments, intellectually
speaking, of an otherwise almost uniformly shabby century: it speaks,
with blunt honesty, of the very slender hope that the century can make

available to us regarding our future prospects. But Freud is wrong in his dismissal of previous thought and wrong about the amount of hope we can properly affirm. In this chapter I want to lay the groundwork for reaffirming this hope, by tracking down precisely what it was about Freud's context that made it very hard for him (and us) to appreciate the sources of hope we need to have.

To begin with, go back before the event that sparked Freud's rumina-tions regarding evil; go back to the beginning of World War I:

> Black and hideous to me is the tragedy that gathers and I'm sick beyond cure to have lived on to see it. You and I, the ornaments of our generation should have been spared this wreck of our belief that through the long years we had seen civilization grow and the worst become impossible. The tide that bore us along was then all the while moving to *this* as its grand Niagra – yet what a bless-ing we did not know it. It seems to me to *undo* everything, everything that was ours, in the most horrible retroactive way – but I avert my face from the mon-strous scene. (James 1987, 421)

These are the words Henry James used, in a letter he wrote to a friend on August 10, 1914, seeking to describe the impact of the onset of World War I upon his contemporaries and himself. And he was not alone in this assessment: Leonard Woolf wrote that the effect of the Great War, which killed ten million people and wounded thirty-six million others, was catastrophic: "It destroyed, I think, the bases of European Civilization . . . In 1914 in the background of one's life and one's mind there were light and hope; by 1918 one had unconsciously accepted a perpetual public menace and darkness and had admitted into the privacy of one's mind or soul an iron fatalistic acquiescence in insecur-ity and barbarism" (1967, 9). Woolf unpacked this claim by comparing the international public outcry against the massacre of Armenians in 1894, and the Dreyfus affair of that same year (in which the French Army in a blatantly antisemitic act tried, convicted, and cashiered a Jewish mil-itary officer), with the atmosphere in the late 1930s, when the European democracies were indifferent to Hitler's ever greater atrocities. Woolf saw a (to him) shocking resignation before and indifference to the pres-ence of horrendous evil: "The world had reverted to regarding human beings not as individuals but as pawns or pegs or puppets in the nasty process of silencing their own fears or satisfying their own hates" (1969, 28). One might imagine that Woolf would speak not very differently today. Those fortunate enough today to be not yet cynical, still live in a situation of perpetual moral astonishment.

Coming as it did, after a century of (in retrospect) stability and apparent progress towards greater and more universal civility and prosperity, World War I did seem, as James writes, "to *undo* everything . . . in the most horrible retroactive way." What is worse is that "the war to end all wars" was, with all its disastrous consequences, just the beginning; for us, in fact, its memory has largely been obscured by the horrors that followed it. And those memories seem to us equally impossible to grasp – not only because they have been buried in ever more recent horrors (as Kosovo eclipses Rwanda which eclipses Bosnia which eclipses the Kurds, *ad infinitum*), but also because the possibility of "grasping" any of those horrors – of grasping the essence of the twentieth century in thought or language – seems in itself impossible; the imagination has no capacity to comprehend, nor language any powers to represent, the horrors of our world.[1]

So the century's catastrophes have left us with a great many questions: what *is* an adequate account of the world, and how should such an account acknowledge and address evil? What is evil's nature and source? How can we, how *should* we, respond to it? Is there even such a thing as evil, or should we jettison the whole vocabulary as dangerously demonizing of others and so in part responsible for the crimes we commit against them? One would expect that the events of our traumatized century would compel reflection on these and similar questions. And many did expect this. In an essay published just after the Second World War, Hannah Arendt noted that "the problem of evil will be the central problem for all post-war intellectuals" (1994, 134). But Arendt's prediction did not prove accurate. Most people have followed James's advice, and averted their faces from the "monstrous scene."

But it is not only that there has been precious little serious sustained reflection on the problem of evil, what is worse is that we rarely realize this; indeed our intellectual energies seem to have been spent more on avoiding thought about evil than on confronting it. (As will be seen later in this chapter, the best evidence to the contrary – the "theodicy" debates in contemporary analytic philosophy – are more symptoms of this avoidance than attempts to overcome it.) "We lack a rhetoric of criticism for social evils," the sociologist Stanford Lyman says; but, ironically, we seem simultaneously "overwhelmed by evil and yet obscured from sin" (1978, viii, 269). But we misformulate the problem if we say

---

[1] This is why so much of twentieth-century literature, from Conrad's *Heart of Darkness* forward, has been dedicated to the impossibility of representing the extreme experiences most distinctive of the age; and the mention of Conrad's book, published in 1900, gives the lie to James's proclamations of exculpatory ignorance.

simply that modernity's failure to handle evil cripples it *tout court*; for what is this "modernity"? Any world that humans inhabit is far too complex to be characterized by a single totalizing concept. All sorts of things we would allow to be "modern" are in profound tension with, and some-times in outright contradiction to, all sorts of other things with equal claim to being "modern."[2] Nor is the problem modernity's disbelief in sin, its faith in technology, or its essential optimism and progressivism. On the contrary, modernity's very "progressivism," its belief in the utopian perfectibility of human life, is essentially an expression of deep despair; for it seeks some justification for the way things currently are, in the hope that they will lead to a future of real happiness. Our common optimism about the future has a desperate quality to it, because it is in fact simply the flip side of a deep despair about the past and present.

Most basically, the crisis of intellectual comprehension we face about evil has been brought on by our growing adherence to too simple a picture of the human, which I call subjectivism. These subjectivistic anthropological assumptions underpin all the faults enumerated above. While these assumptions are not unique to modernity, they suffuse the contemporary mindset. They undercut our ability to respond to evil's challenge because they blind us to the full complexity of that challenge, and to our ineradicable implication in it. We cannot handle evil's com-plexity because these subjectivistic assumptions make it impossible to see our entrapment in evil – our inability to escape it. (Hence by escaping modernity's problems, we will not be escaping evil's challenge; indeed, the opposite is more accurate: by overcoming these problems, we come to *appreciate* the challenge in a way we could not before.) We moderns have a hard time understanding and responding to evil's challenges because we do not believe in sin; and we do not believe in sin because we do not believe in hope; and we do not believe in hope because we believe that we are whatever we make of ourselves. So far from self-confidence, our faith in ourselves stems from our belief that we are aban-doned.

The "we" needs explanation. Throughout this chapter I talk rather promiscuously about "us." I take it that the "we" to whom I speak are actually a fairly narrow group – largely (alas) academics in anglophone universities and colleges – and that we are all decisively marked by the "modern" beliefs that I attempt to isolate and propose that we replace. But the "we" may extend beyond academics to many reflective people

---

[2] See Harvey 1989, Perl 1989, Jameson 1990, Giddens 1991, Pippin 1991, Latour 1993, and Yack 1997.

in the modern West. Following Bernard Williams, my use of "we" "operates not through a perilously fixed designation, but through invita-
tion . . . It is not a matter of 'I' telling 'you' what I and others think, but
of my asking you to consider to what extent you and I think some things
and perhaps need to think others" (1993a, 171 n. 1). I am not saying that
"we" share *all* our beliefs (though I do think that we share many of these,
at least much of the time, and that they are reflected in our lives fairly
regularly). But many of us do appeal to many of these beliefs, at least
when we need to appeal to some such beliefs. Many of us who call ourselves Christians hold these beliefs, and do so unreflectively (and with less
excuse than do non-Christians). Here I merely highlight some problems
latent in our present beliefs, in order to reveal how they tempt us towards
thinking that the challenge of evil is a problem which we can solve. For
now it is enough to make us sensitive to these temptations and their
implications for thinking about our situation.

EVIL

The challenge with which evil confronts us has historically been a popular
challenge for thoughtful people to confront. Labeling it a "popular"
problem intentionally avoids claiming it is "universal," as if we were all
always thinking about these perennial problems in some "latent" way;
rather, I am merely arguing that it is not uncommon for people to be troubled by it. More specifically, it is "popular" in two senses. First, it is historically very common; many people, at many different times and in many
different places and cultural contexts, have struggled with these concerns.[3]
Second, such concerns arise from ordinary life and trouble ordinary
people. This is in no way an abstruse or *esoteric* puzzle, concocted by scholastic elites with a lot of time on their hands and nothing better to do; it
is a challenge that troubles many thoughtful people much of the time.

But calling our difficulty "*the* challenge of evil" obscures the fact that
there is no one obviously proper identification of the challenge itself.
From the first personal recognition of suffering and evil, people move
backwards and forwards, both further specifying the problem behind
such experiences, and constructing a response to the problem so specified. Naturally such a project is circular, a "feed-back loop" in
which one's picture of our rightful relationship with reality inevitably
shapes one's picture of our current situation, and vice versa. Naturally

---

[3] Bowker 1970, Parkin 1985, Levenson 1989. I intentionally avoid the phrase "the problem of evil"
because that phrase typically encompasses only one sub-form of inquiry of the larger challenge.

also such a project is intimately related to other issues with which we struggle, so any provisional understanding, as Christopher Gowans says, "cannot be assessed fully apart from certain fundamental beliefs about the world" (1994, 77). While most reflective people acknowledge that there *is* a messiness, different positions disagree about how to describe it, and what to prescribe for it. Some think it is a genuine problem, while others see it as illusion; some describe it as part of the basic structure of things, while others say it is due to human error. Every great tradition of moral and religious thought must account for it, but hardly anybody agrees on just what "it" is. The actual attempted resolutions to the challenge once specified, can be, and are, resolutions to very different, indeed incommensurable, formulations of that challenge. Thus the most basic difficulty is a *meta*-difficulty, the problem of how to identify the difficulty in the most adequate, because most comprehensive, way.

Furthermore, the difficulty is not only about evil, about why it exists, its nature, and what it means for the moral nature of the universe; the challenge is also to our understanding of the good. Indeed, if we think about our fascination with the truly great evildoers of history, and our fascination with the truly great saints, we discover a disturbing asymmetry in our understanding: wickedness seems in some way more imaginable to us, more of a "live option," than sainthood. The holiness of a perfectly good person seems, well, *holy* – alien, otherworldly, perhaps divine, almost certainly boring.[4] To modify one of Wittgenstein's aphorisms, if a saint did exist, it seems we would not understand them. In contrast, the greatly wicked are all too familiar, and seem much more of a kind with ourselves, as much at home in the world as we are – perhaps even more. Indeed, the wicked may very well be in large part indistinguishable from the rest of us; as Albert Speer, chief architect and war industrialist for Hitler, once said, "it is hard to know the devil when his hand is on your shoulder." Evil – both within and without ourselves – is a reality whose felt recognition seems a precondition for, and at times definitive of, membership in the human race. How then can that not have implications for the good?

The challenge of evil has, that is, a *tragic* dimension to it. "Tragic" here refers not basically to a literary genre, but more fundamentally to the ontological conditions which ground the possibility of "tragic" events and invest them with meaning and significance. The tragic dimension of evil is that humans, in doing or becoming evil, can somehow be fundamentally at odds with (the rest of) reality, in some almost unimaginable

---

[4] For an interesting example of how saints seem strange to us, see Wolf 1982; for a response see Adams 1984.

way opposed to it – their beliefs shown to be fundamentally "out of kilter", "out of sync" with the world, their fellow humans, and themselves, and still be held, or still hold themselves, somehow at fault and thus responsible for so being wrong. Since Plato, what the West has called "philosophy" can be understood as an extended meditation on the implications of our experience of the tragic dimension of evil, for it reveals basic metaphysical problems inherent in the relation of human agency to the world. As Michael Peterson has suggested, this is "the 'existential problem of evil'" in all its richness (1997, 400–1).[5]

So evil troubles two distinct aspects of our theoretical framework. It challenges our *moral ontology*, our understanding of the moral nature of the universe, as it can suggest that the universe is characterized by fundamental moral conflict.[6] Faced with the reality of legitimate moral dispute and apparent conflict between incompatible goods and at times, in hard cases, seeking to understand the apparent necessity of choosing between evil choices, many are tempted to argue that there are irreconcilable moral dilemmas, and that the challenge of tragedy reveals the fundamentally inhospitable nature of our conflictual universe to our more monistic and synthetic ethical aspirations.[7] Is it not the case, such thinkers argue, that the presence of moral conflict is *prima facie* evidence for a moral incommensurability that goes all the way down? But even if we want (as I do) to deny the reality of ultimate moral dilemmas and the absolute incommensurability of goods, we should still acknowledge the presence of moral conflict and the present incommensurability of goods.[8] Given this, the present reality of evil threatens our understanding of our moral environment, and in particular the ultimate place of our moral convictions in the world. Most basically, it challenges what we may call "the moral agency of nature," where "nature" is defined in the

---

[5] See A. O. Rorty: "Tragedy reveals that there is, as it were, a canker in the very heart of action" (1992, 11). See also Wiggins 1980, especially his remarks about the "heterogeneity of psychic sources of determinism" (262). My use of "tragedy," though broader than its "technical" sense, is not simply a vulgarization, and it may be closer to Aristotle's use; see Kelly 1993. On tragedy and philosophy, see Cavell 1979, Barbour 1984, Nussbaum 1986, and Statman 1993. For a helpful account of the tragedians and sophists against whom Plato polemicized, see Goldhill 1986 especially chapter 9, "Sophistry, philosophy, rhetoric."

[6] See Steiner 1996, 129: absolute tragedy reveals a "negative ontology" in the world: "That crime attached by definition to the fact of birth. Thus even the unborn had to be hounded to extinction. To come into the world was to come into torture and death."

[7] See Kekes 1990, Stocker 1990. In theological circles, the most thorough and thoughtful discussion is found in D. M. Mackinnon 1968; Stanley Hauerwas seems at times to suggest something similar (see Hauerwas, Bondi, and Burrell 1977, esp. 12, 69, 201), but he does not systematically work out the insight.

[8] For discussions of this issue, see Santurri 1987, Scheffler 1992, and Donagan 1993.

broadest possible sense, as the encompassing environment of our exis-tence.[9] As James Wetzel has argued, "tragedy relates catastrophe to what humans will for themselves, but it also indicts the order that is ultimately responsible for the exploitation of human vulnerability" (1992b, 359). How do we respond to those realities, met in existence, which threaten to subvert our faith in the fundamental goodness of the world? This problem is all the more pointed for those who wish to affirm that this "moral order" is fundamentally rooted in a loving, personal, and omnip-otent God, the Triune God whose presence is proclaimed in and through the Gospel about Jesus Christ. How especially, that is, should Christian reflection be shaped by such considerations?

Secondly, evil also challenges our *moral anthropology*, because it reveals that human agency – and in particular human autonomy – is a much more problematic concept than many believe, and more dubiously attrib-uted to people than we usually assume. Classical tragedies famously suggest that our lives are not firmly or finally or really under our control – that something other than the "I" rules the "I"'s fate. But such suspi-cions seem hard to understand; for what would it be for us to not be self-governing? In conceptual terms, this is a question about our concept of autonomy. How should we understand ourselves as being *in* a world? And how can we understand ourselves as able, in some sense, to transcend it? We seem in some sense incommensurable with the world, able to be agential "loose cannons," unpredictable causal outlaws roaming an oth-erwise nomic world. Bernard Williams suggests that a proper apprecia-tion of tragic conflict teaches us "that the world was not made for us, nor we for the world" (1993a, 166). But that seems to leave us with one foot in the world and one out; for what does it mean to be such creatures?

This issue is further complicated by the curious fact that the possibil-ity of evil has ennobling anthropological implications; it suggests that humans have a more complex relationship with reality, one more poten-tially agonistic, than do other creatures. Certainly the Christian doctrine of the human as created as *imago Dei* expresses something like this, and other viewpoints suggest something similar. The experience of evil and tragic conflict reveals our ability to experience what transcends our full capacity to understand, while yet remaining an experience we know we cannot completely comprehend, and thereby offers us a significant but

---

[9] We must avoid a reductive naturalism here. For helpful advice on how to do this, see McDowell 1998, 167–97. See also Lear 1990. See A. Plantinga 1992 for a good typology of these options in contemporary thought as "Naturalism" and "Creative Antirealism." For a helpful investigation of the uses of nature in theology, see Murphy and Ellis 1996.

ultimately unsatisfactory glimpse into the powers we might have. In tragedy, as Walter Benjamin put it,

There is no question whatever of a restitution of the "moral order of the universe," but it is the attempt of mortal man, still dumb, still inarticulate – as such he bears the name of hero – to raise himself up amid the agitation of that painful world. The paradox of the birth of genius in moral speechlessness, moral infantility, constitutes the sublime element in tragedy. (1978, 307)

The Chorus's speech in *Antigone* on the human as *deinon*, "strange" or "wonderful," expresses a similar idea – "With some sort of cunning, inventive/beyond all expectation/he reaches sometimes evil,/and sometimes good" (Sophocles 1992, lines 400–3; see Heidegger 1959, 146–57). This suggests that the inevitable possibility of evil and tragedy is inextricably intertwined with recognition of the inestimable potential of humans – that, as Karl Jaspers says, "*there is no tragedy without transcendence*" (1952, 41). However, the reality of evil and the possibility of tragic conflict suggest that there are severe limits on our control – not only on our control over the "external" world, but even over ourselves. Here the self is not simply buffeted by forces beyond its own control, but can be internally corrupted and even destroyed by them. Indeed the destructive capacities suggest that the very dichotomy between "internal" and "external," on which the possibility of evil and tragic conflict apparently relies, itself relies on a thin membrane of good fortune – for in tragic events the "outside" has come "inside," and an otherness is discovered to lie at the bottom of the self.[10]

The reality of evil thus troubles the place of human agency in nature, in the world.[11] The fact of tragic conflict does not simply delimit the realm of human capacities, and thereby reveal to us that there are things beyond our control; it further reveals that that very realm is itself vulnerable to destruction. Human agency is not an inner citadel of protected autonomous decision, an inviolable *sanctum sanctorum* of subjectivity; rather, human agency is one more part of nature, of creation. But then what sense can we make of claims about our self-control? How *do* we matter in the world, and in what might such mattering consist? The possibility of tragedy not only reveals the limited extent of our power; it also reveals the fragility of what power we *can* have. The reality of evil and tragic conflict is thus not just a brute fact but a *threat*, a truth whose very existence challenges our own.

[10] See Gowans 1994: while tragedy "concerns *what happens to us*," and makes "no reference to the agency of the person who suffers the tragedy" (225), moral tragedy, as a distinct form of the larger category of tragedy, concerns "*what we do* as much as what happens to us" (226). See Nagel 1982, especially 176, 184, 186.   [11] See Lear 1998, 167–90.

There are two sorts of questions here. On one side there are questions about "the agency of nature," about the ontological and theological context within which humans operate; but equally important are questions about "the nature of agency," about the place of human agents in the world. Conceptually speaking, evil challenges our understanding of the deep structure of our being, and the deep structure of the world in which we live. As such, it is a route into concerns about the most basic and profound issues of existence. Why is it, then, that modernity finds thinking about evil so difficult?

THINKING MODERNITY UNTHINKING EVIL: MONSTROSITY AND THEODICY

The answer is simple. Modernity has a hard time thinking about evil because we moderns lack ways to acknowledge its persistence and pervasiveness, its intimacy and intransigence, so lack the resources by which we might bring the challenge of evil into reflective focus. Modernity's failure here is due most basically, conceptually speaking, to the fact that it takes a wrong attitude towards evil (not to mention to existence as a whole), understanding evil as something to be overcome, and attempting to *fix* it, to remove the problems and perfect reality. But in understanding evil as an external problem to be solved, an error to be repaired, we moderns treat evil as outside ourselves, waiting to be worked upon; in doing so, we fail to acknowledge our implication in it.

Yet this lack of acknowledgment is not the last word; there is a "return of the repressed." Evil – which implicates us whether we admit it or not – returns to vex modernity in monstrous guise, as represented in the imagination of modernity as the "fantastic" or the "gothic," a spectral figure that haunts the modern imagination. Here I want to explain the spell of "progress" that conjures up this spectral and disabling representation of evil; then I will detail the physiognomy of this specter, and finally, in the last subsection, I will explain why we find it so hard to escape this haunting.

PROGRESS AND THE GOTHIC

The reflexive faith in "progress" is the central practical *mythos* of modernity. By "progress" I mean the assumption (and its supporting assumptions) that humans are capable of, and hence responsible for, making the world into an increasingly better, and ultimately perfect, place. By calling this a "reflexive faith" I am trying to suggest both its pervasiveness and its remarkable implicitness, the way it "goes without saying" for so many people, precisely *by* going without saying, without being made explicit – if only because whenever it is raised as a matter for articulate deliberation, some people immediately, and most people eventually, can see its dubiousness. It is something like the "collective mentality" of our age, but it is such in important part because it operates so tacitly that it rarely, if ever, surfaces for critical examination.[12]

Hans Blumenberg has well described what I am gesturing at here in *The Legitimacy of the Modern Age*. He sees the history of western thought since antiquity as two successive attempts to overcome "the Gnostic challenge," which was "the problem of the quality of the world for humanity" – that is, our faith in the goodness of the world (whether thematized theologically or naturalistically) in the face of the problems of evil and suffering (Blumenberg 1983, 142).[13] Medieval Christianity, which is essentially (for Blumenberg) an extended elaboration of the Augustinian program, attempted to "ward off" Gnosticism's challenge (which appeared to it as the attempt to separate the God of Creation from the God of Salvation) by imputing responsibility for evil to humanity, and thereby imputing to humans (as a "side-effect" of the desire to acquit God of responsibility for evil) a power of free agency heretofore unimagined, but a power also, ironically enough, which humanity possessed only under the condition of having always already lost it:

The price of this preservation of the cosmos was not only the guilt that man was supposed to assign himself . . . but also the resignation that his responsibility for that condition imposed upon him: renunciation of any attempt to change for his benefit, through action, a reality for the diversity of which he had himself to blame. (1983, 136; see 133–4)

This project collapsed in the late Middle Ages, because of problems with the contingency of creation and the absolute power of the Voluntarists' God; a new approach took over, one which responded to Gnosticism not by justifying God through blaming humans, but by attempting to defeat the first premise of Gnosticism by improving the world: instead of a theodicy, modernity offers an "anthropodicy," and an anthropodicy based on "the world's lack of consideration of man, on its inhuman order" (1983, 142). This anthropodicy promises to justify us through an "existential program" of "self-assertion":

If the "disappearance of order" that was brought about by the disintegration of the Middle Ages pulled self-preservation out of its biologically determined normality, where it went unnoticed, and turned it into the "theme" of human self-comprehension, then it is also the case that the modern stage of human technicity can no longer be grasped entirely in terms of the syndrome of the anthropological structure of wants. The growth of the potency of technique is not only the continuation – not even the acceleration – of a process that runs through the whole history of humanity. On the contrary, the quantitative increase in technical achievements and expedients can only be grasped in relation to a new quality of consciousness. In the growth of the technical sphere there lives, consciously facing an alienated reality, a will to extort from this reality a new "humanity." Man keeps in view the deficiency of nature as the motive of his activity as a whole. (1983, 138–9)

Modernity defines itself by "the growth of the potency of technique," the promise of ever-increasing human power to shape nature, with the ultimate aim of transcending the deficiency (and deficiencies) of nature in order to realize an ever greater, ever happier, state of human flourishing. And so all forms and realities that hinder human power are to be overcome. As Reinhold Niebuhr summarized the modern faith, "historical progress gradually changes the human situation, delivering man from the ambiguity of his freedom over, and subordination to, the temporal process . . . [and] finally makes him master of historical destiny" (1949, 79). Certainly this position is less loudly expressed today; but it still seems the background idea in most people's understandings of history, and it still remains alive in the thought of many who reflect on problems of suffering and evil today. Examples of this are easy to find: they often simply say there is a way to solve the problem of evil, and all our energies ought to be dedicated towards this aim (see, e.g., Goldberg 1996).

The existential program of modernity has enormous implications for how it attempts to deal with evil – and, in turn, its attempt to deal with evil has enormous implications for the sustainability and shape of its existential program. In brief, by making progressivism the central program of modernity, modern thinkers have forsworn the possibility that evil may not be simply "fixable" in this manner, but may be more profoundly intertwined with human achievements. This can vex thinkers and lead them to despair of realizing their hopes (see Hampshire 1983, 80–100). But the ineradicability of evil is not simply bad because it proves to be unpleasant for the more optimistically minded among us. More importantly, it obscures the problems we face by marginalizing them: "The general trend during the eighteenth century, then, was to create a marginalized periphery in the social imagination that encompassed everything that rested outside of order and that by the force of association colored all the components with the same taint of unreason and threat" (Monleón 1990, 29). By placing all of the unspeakable outside the city (the materialization, if idealized [that is, rationalized], of civilization for Enlightenment thinkers) these thinkers attempted simultaneously to *marginalize* and *confine* all the "unspeakable" and non-cognizable elements of reality, such as madness, unreason, sickness, death, and "otherness" in general; and in this project evil too became marginalized.

The effect of this mindset is perhaps especially clear as regards the problem of pain. A great deal of pre-modern life was organized around the reality of suffering and pain, and how to live with it. But modernity has decided it does not want to live with it, so has undertaken to eliminate pain by a campaign of eradication. As David Morris has argued in his *The Culture of Pain*, this project has resulted not in the conquering of pain – the possibility of that, and only for a few kinds of pain, still lies some distance away – but in modern medicine's inability to handle pain's presence *as* a presence, not as something that can be removed but as a fact that must be acknowledged as present.[14] (As John Stuart Mill said: "One of the effects of civilization . . . is, that the spectacle, and even the very idea, of pain, is kept more and more out of the sight of those classes who enjoy in their fullness the benefits of civilization."[15]) But this, Morris points out, makes modern pain into "meaningless" pain, both in terms of material structures – for hospitals and the medical establishment have no place to acknowledge and endure it – and in terms of intellectual and imaginative structures – for it serves modern artists as a device to underscore "the absurd" in our lives (1991, 279). Hence chronic pain is "an immense, invisible crisis at the center of contemporary life," one which we cannot confront from within the modern approach to pain and suffering, and indeed one which our failures to acknowledge actually exacerbate (1991, 5; see 57–78, 244–69).[16]

[14] Morris 1991. N.b. Morris's discussion of doctors' use of an agonic language of "conquest" and warfare; doctors think of pain largely as a *puzzle* to be solved, an opponent to be defeated (22–3).
[15] Cited in Morris 1991, 271.
[16] I am not arguing that the medical advances of the past few centuries have not made great inroads on our physical ailments. I am simply saying that we will never be immortal, and that one of the unfortunate consequences of medicine's attempt to deny this has been medicine's denial of the signs of our mortality wherever they appear – of which pain is certainly an important one. (Thus Morris says, "The modern denial of pain is in the largest sense a denial of the claims pain implicitly makes upon us" [287].) I am not saying that medicine is bad; all I am saying is that it is not going to turn us into gods.

But there is a crucial difference between marginalizing evil and eliminating it, so evil, like pain, continues to haunt modernity, not as something directly addressable and confrontable, but rather as a form of sub-cognitive handling of the concept, through more primitive emotional responses like fear and horror. Evil comes back as the *monstrous*, what cannot be handled within the conceptual scheme we employ, but which "shadows the progress of modernity with counter-narratives displaying the underside of enlightenment and humanist values" (Botting 1996, 1–2). This is expressed best in the genre of imaginative writing (and, in our century, extending especially to film) that goes by the name of "Gothic" or "fantastic."[17] Much stimulating and suggestive work has been done on this genre of writing, and I will treat it as not simply a genre, but as part of our social imagination, supported not only by our own conscious (and sub-and semi-conscious) thoughts, concerns, anxieties, and fears, but also by a vast material structure which feeds it.

The name "Gothic" nicely captures the historical character of this implicit critique of modernity, for it "came into being as the result of the tensions produced by the inclusion of medieval beliefs within the reasonable framework of eighteenth-century bourgeois precepts" (Monleón 1990, 6). While the emerging Enlightenment consensus portrayed a world of reason and light, it ignored the dark passions of human existence. But this "repressed medieval epistemology" (Monleón 1990, 145) disappeared merely by going underground, appearing only on the margins and in the cracks of Enlightenment ideology. Hence, the Gothic is the secret mirror double of enlightened modern hope: the Gothic imagination expresses what cannot be articulated in the primary discourse of modernity – it is an expression (and recognition) of the failure of modern rationalism's claim to represent all human experience.[18]

The basic lesson that the Gothic imagination attempts to communicate is the sense of the profound limits on human improvement that the Enlightenment has forgotten or willfully repressed. As this epistemologi-

[17] Most scholars of these matters see "the Gothic" as only a stage in the development of the larger genre of the literature of the fantastic (see Monleón 1990, 51, 52, 62; Punter 1996). But these disagreements about the precise relation of these genres are immaterial for my purposes (see Thompson 1981). For my general approach to the processes of cultural imagination and formation, I am profoundly indebted to Raymond Williams 1978.

[18] Typically this is seen as *simply* the expression of modern rationalism's inadequacy, but in fact, what opposes modern rationalism is often depicted as a demonic counter-plan, or conspiracy, a secret mirror double of the modern. (On the importance of "doubles" see Botting 1996, 107.) Thus, in opposing modernity the Gothic finds itself in need of modernity's conceptual scheme, and shows how modern structures may be turned against themselves, à la deconstruction – but also, if inadvertently, reaffirming the structures' inescapability, at least for the Gothic.

cal unease, the Gothic is more like a mood than an ideology; and it operates as a mood, expressing its ideas not most basically through explicit articulate argument, but rather sub-rationally and imagistically. It does so most famously through the classic Gothic tropes of horror and the other. Horror is the mode in which the Gothic imagination is most at home; and it is the most homely mode (the most *uncanny* one) because it is evoked by the encounter with an alterity, an otherness, that is immanent or possibly even *more* than immanent: "Horror is thus ambivalently human, the feeling that preserves a sense of humanity at the very point that 'human nature' is most indefinite, most unbearable and most in danger of disintegration. Horror marks an encounter with the inhuman in its most *in*-human form" (Botting 1998, 131). The Gothic presents the reader with an "ontological challenge" (Varnado 1987, 131), merely by recalling "an otherness that lay next to the core of the bourgeois world, questioning by virtue of its tangential presence the nature of order" (Monleón 1990, 34). What this otherness represents is the idea that our selves are not wholly transparent to ourselves, that we are not totally in charge of our lives, that we are not our own, and that, in the words of Flannery O'Connor, among the greatest twentieth-century Gothic writers, "you're not who you think you are" (1971, 419). Yet, still deeper than its surface anxieties about horror and the other, the Gothic expresses an unease or discomfort, felt more than thought, about the picture of the self on which the Enlightenment founds itself and which allows it to marginalize and ultimately unthink the challenges of evil. The Gothic self is murky, opaque, dense and gnarled, imperfect, impure, significantly alien to our "best" self-images, and yet sufficiently recognizable as us to trouble our placid (and dull) Enlightenment consciences. And it is so because it makes us wonder whether we might not, after all, be implicated in the evil from which we reflexively dissociate ourselves.

Karen Halttunen argues this in her *Murder Most Foul*, in which she provides a genealogy of our present "Gothic" morality, which traces the root cause of our Gothic indigestion of the concept of evil back to a basic modernist "othering" of evil, the modern attempt to make evil totally foreign to our understanding of human nature:

Modern Gothic horror was the characteristic response to evil in a culture that provided no systematic intellectual explanation for the problem. The Gothic view of evil at work in the cult of horror was not an irrational reaction against an excess of Enlightenment rationalism, but an indispensable corollary to it, which ultimately served to protect the liberal view of human nature. The prevailing concept of human nature as basically good, free, and self-governed in the light of an innate moral sense, was protected from the potential threat of major transgressions by the imaginative creation of a monstrous moral alien, separated from the rest of humankind by an impassable gulf. (1998, 59)

This was not simply an ethereally intellectual problem; it was reflected institutionally, in the legal system and the mental-health establishment, through the procedures they developed, largely in the nineteenth century, to adjudicate their power.[19]

But the problem is that, because it was so sub-conscious and sub-rational, the Gothic "challenged the liberal narrative of criminal deviance as an alien phenomenon without ever fully destroying it" (Halttunen 1998, 170–1). Only an intentional, explicit, and articulate account of evil can come to understand what it was trying to say in a way adequate to the problems it expressed. Unfortunately, as we will see next, modernity's best attempt at such an account – theodicy – does not meet the need.

THEODICY AND ITS DISCONTENTS

When the problem of evil does rise to the level of intellectual concern for us moderns, it is typically handled, as are most other problems, by recourse to theory. We can see this reflected in the last several decades' debates around the idea of "theodicy." "Theodicies" are analyses of the problem which are meant to explain why evil can exist in a world governed by a wholly good God. ("Theodicy" may be too local an appellation, for this project can be generalized to include positions which are not theistic, such as Marxism; the key for these projects is that they attempt to show that the existence of evil does not disturb the equilibrium of our systematic theoretical account of the world as morally ordered.) While such accounts vary considerably in their shape, they share a common purpose in working to warrant our moral hopes, our faith in the ultimate goodness and justice of the world, by providing reasons for that faith.[20]

This typical response elicits an equally typical reaction, an expression of disaffection at the putative "solution" being offered. The putative solution, the disaffected proclaim, does not solve the problem at all, but instead avoids confronting the real difficulties that generated the attempt

---

[19] "The Gothic narrative of the crime of murder played a primary role in shaping the modern response to criminal transgression, both mandating the social quarantining of criminals in penitentiaries and mental hospitals, and reinforcing the radical otherness of the criminal deviant on which that quarantining rested" (Halttunen 1998, 240).

[20] The best theoretical theodicy I know of is Reichenbach 1982.

at a solution in the first place. Furthermore, the pseudo-solution works to quiet any feelings of real outrage we might have at the concrete evil, by explaining how its existence does not really challenge our moral worldview. Such critics of the purported solution are, to a significant degree, correct: the modern program in response to evil, even at its most reflective and articulate, is flawed on its own terms, and from its own perspective. But I do not want to trumpet the anti-theodicist cause, for supporters of theodicy grasp significant insights that its critics dismiss. In fact, the interminable debate raging around the propriety of "theoretical" theodicy reveals that we still cannot think about evil in its full complexity. Indeed the debate's interminability is due to the fact that each side apprehends different parts of a larger truth that escapes either's comprehension. Critics of theoretical theodicy condemn it as an inappropriate response to human suffering, providing an inert "consolation" which merely anesthetizes bystanders' immediate and appropriate desire to help sufferers; meanwhile, theodicy's defenders respond that the critics are the actual anesthetizers, because they dismissively label as "theoretical" real concerns that arise from our acknowledgment of apparently inexplicable suffering. And both have a point. This debate is sustained not by the contestants' disagreements but by their common assumption of a modernist dichotomy of "theory" and "practice," and more precisely their common assumption that theory is where things become settled – and if they do not, then practices are ways of coping with what are facts ineradicable from reality. But this whole debate expresses one of the central and interminable antinomies of modern thought; to get beyond it we need to transcend the premises from which both sides work.

Appeals to a theoretical solution to the problem of evil are not confined only to debates around philosophical theodicy. As Mark Edmundson has argued, they are visible even in the "modernist" movement in literature, "a relatively cerebral mode" of art, which intentionally rebelled against the Gothic sentiments of Romanticism, and understood itself as trying to get a better intellectual grip on the complex and destructive psychological forces that Romanticism celebrated rather than interrogated (1997, 110–13).[21] But modernists such as T. S. Eliot managed merely to destroy the psyche in order to save it, so modernism as a rebellion failed, because it "defeats the Gothic too completely . . .

---

[21] On the Romantic imagination of passions and evil, see Praz 1992, 53–94. I am using literary modernism as an example of something far broader (and present earlier) in modernity.

by utterly denying the Gothic, and especially messy Gothic passions, these intellectual forms have put themselves out of touch with large dimensions of human experience" (Edmundson 1997, 120).[22] The modernists merely elided the presence of the "Gothic passions," pretending that those passions were not there, and thereby avoiding the real problems those passions expressed. The worry here is that modernity uses theoretical sophistication as a means of avoidance.

Edmundson's critique of the modernists is intriguingly similar to the anti-theodicist critiques of "theoretical" theodicy. Such critiques argue that all attempts to formulate the difficulty as "the problem of evil" only partially comprehend what is in fact a very complex tangle of issues. By thinking of this difficulty as a problem, we are almost compelled by our grammar to seek a *solution*, a solution that resolves the problem: after this resolution, we think, the problem of evil disappears, or at least recedes into the distance as a "merely" practical problem (e.g., A. Plantinga 1974, 29; and Hick 1978, 9).[23] By abstracting from the concrete lived experiences of tragic suffering and evil, critics argue, theodicy accounts do not most basically create justifications for belief in God in a world suffused with evil and suffering, but rather justifications of our own continuing ignorance of and indifference to the actual realities of suffering and evil in the world. The theodicy tradition, that is, takes our anxieties and fears in the face of the real materiality of suffering and evil and distills from these anxieties and fears a purely theoretical puzzle, which it then attempts to "solve" – then argues that the solution provides an appropriate response to those anxieties and fears. But when we ourselves, or those close to us, come to grips with the actualities of evil, suffering, and tragedy in our own lives, we find that such practical issues are in fact fundamental to even the theoretical problems we thought we were addressing. Theoretical theodicies, that is, seem to leave unanswered the core issues which need to be addressed in the experiences of suffering that we encounter in our ordinary lives; they seem imperfect devices for meeting our needs.

Some critical scholars have gone so far as to suggest that theoretical theodicies are not only partial responses to the range of difficulties we face, but are in fact dangerously disingenuous and indeed immoral

---

[22] Compare Hilary Putnam's discussion of much modern analytic philosophy (in the tradition of Carnap) as analogous to modernism in architecture; see Putnam 1983.

[23] I have learned much from Plantinga's work, but I think that at times his claims that the theoretical issues surrounding the problem of evil can be isolated from the practical issues may be ill put.

responses to those difficulties. Such critics accuse theodicists of inhumane indifference before the real concerns of actual human beings. Michael Scott, for example, suggests that by attending to "a sanitized, abstract conception of evil," theoretical theodicy "facilitates reflection on human suffering that does not acknowledge (in anything other than an aside or preface) its particularity" (1996, 3). Such critics charge that the actual concrete concerns which provoke theodicist reflection are not expressed but suppressed by being formulated in abstract theoretical terms. This abstractive practice quarantines our larger ethical and religious convictions from any fundamental challenge by the realities of evil, and so anesthetizes our deepest moral and religious motivations from working against the presence of evil in our lives. These critics think that this "theoreticization" of our difficulties exemplifies theodicy's essentially *modern* roots, its commitment to a scientistic project which treats all difficulties by abstracting them from the concrete realities in which we meet them. Theodicists treat the problem of evil in the same way that engineers treat the problem of bridge building, as a problem soluble via technology: by means of abstracted theoretical algorithms, governed by disembodied, clinically dispassionate mathematical reason. Far from helping us understand and respond to evil and suffering, theodicies actually hinder our search for a genuine response.

According to these critics, theodicy merely interprets evils; the point, however, is to remove them. To do this we must shift our focus from what they see as an overly fastidious concern with the ethereal abstractions of theodicy to the concrete, messy, practical problems faced by actual people in their everyday lives. As Rowan Williams suggests, "perhaps it is time for philosophers of religion to look away from theodicy – not to appeal blandly to the mysterious purposes of God, not to appeal to any putative justification at all, but to put the question of how we remain faithful to human ways of seeing suffering, even and especially when we are thinking from a religious perspective" (1996, 147). The practices of "remaining faithful to human ways of seeing suffering" which Williams commends can involve listening to sufferers' experiences, and allowing ourselves – at times *forcing* ourselves – to accept their reality on their own terms, without concern for the theoretical frameworks we hold dear; to allow our abstract theoretical depiction of the world to trump their actual historical experiences is a sign of a fundamental mis-centering of our commitments. In response to these experiences, furthermore, we ought not immediately (or even primarily) to turn our attention to further securing our theoretical frameworks, to repair or seek better or more adequate frameworks to handle them; instead we ought to work at ways to reduce the suffering and evil actually being experienced at present – which, after all, is what our theories are *for* in the first place. For these critics, theodicist and theological "theory" must always and everywhere serve the needs of concrete historical *practice*, the practice of being with the sufferer, and working to remove the source of the suffering.

Such critical concerns have merit; there certainly has been a neglect of practical strategies for dealing with instances of concrete injustice and suffering, and it may be the case that the theoretical attention given to philosophical theodicies has in fact contributed to that neglect. But one wonders whether, in their altogether legitimate disparaging of the misuse of "theory," the critics have not gone too far in their renunciation of our theoretical reflexes.[24] The critics, that is, seem excessively resistant to admitting that *any* such theoretical questions are *ever* valid, and they suggest instead that those questions are wholly the product of "modernist" prejudice which favors distanciated Cartesian theorizing. Such claims seem not only historically inaccurate (for it is the case that many – indeed, almost all – pre-modern theologians were in fact concerned with such questions), but also simply unnecessarily prejudiced against theoretical issues: why cannot we engage in both theoretical and practical forms of inquiry? What does it mean to "resist" theory? What is rejected when theory is rejected?

Here the reply is made that the prioritization of practice is due to the peculiarities of the difficulties associated with evil and suffering. Simply put, our theories cannot offer us anything beyond inert "consolation," the inertia of which renders their purported assistance merely imaginary. A response to suffering and evil is necessary, but to think that such a response must be a theoretical one merely reveals the respondent's captivity to a modernist prioritizing of theory over practice. Theory is the religion – that is to say, the opium – of the intellectuals. Michael Scott, again, suggests that the problem lies in always seeking "verbal responses in the form of theoretical justification," when what one should recognize is that "no explanation, story or form of expression can be applied to this instance of suffering (without abrogating its terribleness)" (1996, 12). If, Scott continues, the victim himself or herself asks the sort of

---

[24] William Placher criticizes contemporary theodicists for undertaking projects that "would have seemed to many theologians before the seventeenth century to answer trivial questions and ignore the important ones" (see 1996, 206). But this is surely wrong; rather, those theologians saw the legitimacy of both aspects of the problem and treated both with respect, trivializing neither. Critics such as Placher err in thinking the theoretical concern "trivial." See Mohrmann 1995.

abstract questions a theodicist can answer, "this implies that the believer [note how our interlocutor is no longer a suffering victim but has been lexically transmogrified into a blank "believer"] is incapable of accepting that certain things are not appropriate objects of human understanding. But such a believer is surely fueled by an ambition to understand more suited to a philosopher than a person of faith" (1996, 12). (Note that now this position, curiously enough, *chastises* the sufferer for asking inappropriate questions.) Such a person requires the sort of anti-philosophical therapy practiced by philosophers like D. Z. Phillips. The problem is a *material* one: no response will be useful that does not address it on a directly practical level; to think otherwise is to be still in thrall to a modernist faith in theory.

If one responds that such an *a priori* (and indeed, to all appearances theory-driven) prohibition of theory seems to presume without proof that all language necessarily "abrogates" the "terribleness" of evil, anti-theodicists agree. For them, it is simply the case that such experiences as suffering and evil are not best met with the more theoretical capacities in our toolbox. This much is implied by the broader picture of the world that these thinkers employ: our situation in the world is such that our theoretical grasp of it – mediated as it always is through language – is never total; our linguistic representations and negotiations of the world are always only a part of our larger comportment in it.[25] Theory is not, as moderns dream it should be, a complete *representation* of the world, but rather just one tool among others for helping us navigate our way through material existence. Theory, that is, should serve practice.

At this point one may begin to wonder whether the critics are not themselves in the thrall of a different, though related, modernist presumption: namely, the presumption of an absolute divide between "theory" and "practice," and recoiling from the dubiousness of the former to the equally dubious latter. The classic "materialist" inversion of this dichotomy improperly anesthetizes our intellectual powers by affirming the modern schema and then simply flipping it upside down; here, as Raymond Williams points out, "the idealist separation of 'ideas' and 'material realities' has been repeated, but with its priorities reversed" (1978, 59). Better to jettison the dichotomy *tout court*: it is clearly the case that our theoretical proclivities are part and parcel of our practical life, and indeed develop from that life.[26] This insight is not

[25] See Surin 1989, x–xi; and Surin 1986 *passim*. I mean not to reject the commitments articulated there, so much as to *aufhebung* them. For a position more consonant with my own see Kerr 1997.
[26] I am grateful to Paul J. Griffiths for teaching me this.

exclusively the property of pragmatism; all ancient and medieval thought simply took their interrelation for granted.[27] In fact, it is the critics of traditional theodicy who seem here to take a theoretical escape route out of confronting the intellectual and theoretical problems associated with evil and suffering; they attempt to transform a difficulty into an impossibility, and so seek to make us turn a blind eye to the genuine theoretical problems. In refusing to address them directly, however, the critics only succeed in blinding themselves to the problems; furthermore, they are merely repeating (at the intellectual level) modernity's refusal to think evil, its implicit assumption being that evil is unthinkable and monstrous. The anti-theodicists, that is, by being committed to keeping evil's unintelligibility pure, unstained by theorists' fingerprints, ironically compel us back towards a Gothic account of evil, from which the theodicy project is an attempt, however imperfect, to free us.

Instead of a way to quarantine our theoretical questions, we need to connect them to our practical concerns in a manner beneficial to both. We need to provide, that is, a response to the problems of evil on both the theoretical and practical "plane," a response that does not dismiss or subjugate either theory or practice. It is just the case that what the critics call "theoretical" questions often *do* arise with experiences of suffering, and while they are surely often mere surface manifestations of deeper, more inchoate concerns, it is important to address them on the level at which they are raised. As James Wetzel says, "none of the caveats of practical theodicy . . . will displace the deepest motivation for the problem of evil: Our desire to determine the source and limits of a moral universe. For however long evil remains a part of our experience, we will be driven to find a meaning for it" (1992b, 363).[28] We experience the challenge of tragedy as a *total* challenge, one which challenges the entirety of our existence, including our reflective existence. As Edmundson says, we need to admit that we are "haunted" by these problems – which means, of course, that the problems do not go away as problems for thought, even while we address them as problems for thought.

The moral of this story is simple. Neither theoretical theodicy nor the opposed anti-theodicy is sufficient for our needs. Rather than a purely

---

[27] It is astonishing that this must still be said. For a helpful discussion of how our ignorance of this assumption in ancient thought continues to color our (mis)reading of that thought – especially in that most "theorizing" of ancients, Plato – see Reeve 1988, especially his discussion (115–17) of the difference between Plato's metaphysics – a metaphysics intended for "agents" – and our own – a metaphysics intended for "spectators." See also Struever 1992 and Hadot 1995.

[28] Cf. D. O'Connor 1988 and Hebblethwaite 1989.

theoretical theodicy or a sheerly practical one, we need a response to the challenge of tragedy which enlists the full range of our powers. As Wetzel puts it, we must "work through the countervailing sensibility" – namely, that sensibility that suggests that evil is somehow part of the truth of the universe – even as we admit that that process of "working through" can never stop, but only come to some provisional resting place (1992b, 361). We must find some way to talk in both forms simultaneously; our theoretical framework must not disable our practical response, but rather must enrich, enliven, and elicit it, and our practical response must find a way to express our theoretical statements in existence.[29]

But the problem of the theodicy debate is not the only problem. There is another concern, about the wisdom of using the discourse of evil at all.

OPERATIONALIZING EVIL

Many people will not even listen to proposals for a response to the challenge of evil, because they think that the concept of evil can never have a useful place in their moral lives. Their misgivings about the discourse of evil are better formulated than any articulate reasons they possess for wanting to keep that discourse alive. To a significant degree, our culture lacks an *operationalized* concept of evil, a concept with a real use in our society. The doubts that we can, let alone *ought* to, operationalize evil hold the field almost unopposed.

These doubts are all largely echoes of Nietzsche's challenge to get "beyond good and evil" by more fully inhabiting our natures. They see the language of evil as a fundamentally *moralistic* language, one fostering an essentially distanciated form of basically *condemnatory* judgment. I am not convinced by these criticisms, but I do think they reveal some broader cultural tensions that we should acknowledge and address if we want to continue to use the language of evil. The criticisms reflect, and are legitimated by, flawed assumptions about the nature of human moral agency, assumptions which we should refuse. By doing so, and by reinvigorating the concept of "evil," we can transcend some fundamental difficulties vexing moral psychology, and move towards both a more sober assessment of moral malformation, and a more hopeful vision of moral potentiality. But to see this, we must get at the criticisms.

---

[29] This position is similar to that found in Putt 1997. As he notes, "Ricoeur, himself, concedes that the failure of speculative theodicies in no way leads to 'a sheer capitulation of thought' but demands 'the continuation on another plane of thought's interminable work' " (467).

I shall first take up a set of concerns centering around too tight an association of evil and otherness. Some critics, looking at representations of evil in the cultural imagination, argue that we have too tightly tied together evil and otherness, so that we fear otherness and label it evil, and see in "the other" only things that we fear. Mark Edmundson, for example, argues that we have so totally identified evil and otherness that all externality, all that is strange, is evil to us. Edmundson's worry is that, because of this, our culture oscillates between a glib optimism of "facile transcendence" and a frightened, pessimistic "gothic" foreboding. In this situation, Edmundson thinks we should demystify our fear of others by defusing their connections with the idea of evil, and toss that idea into history's dustbin of discarded words. We are much better off with a vocabulary of social ills that does not imagine a demonic power or presence lurking behind them. Were we to do this, we would see our problems for what they are – not insurmountable, but simply requiring a lot of effort to overcome. We could, in the end, manage to *escape* the revenge tragedy that is history, the endless cycle of mourning and retribution, and be born fully into the present, unconstrained by our pasts (see Edmundson 1997, 150–60).

To do this, Edmundson recommends a vocabulary built around a picture of human life in which the basic problem is sado-masochism. On this account, we are all raised in fundamentally abusive cultures which habituate us to act out of a mindset of *fear*, the fear of being compelled to do things. The quasi-Freudian roots of this picture should be obvious: just as Freud saw civilization as a matter of the brutal and violent imposition of order, culminating in mechanisms of self-repression that are invariably imperfect, so Edmundson sees the roots of our social ills to lie in our presumption that our world is wholly governed by pure amoral *power*, and in our attempt to live by this creed.[30] But this expectation models our moral worldview on the mechanisms of repression to which we subjugate ourselves, mechanisms which are based on a dualism of "chaos" and "order," obedience and disobedience. We live in a perpetual dichotomy of "us" and "them," and that dichotomy translates into a dialectic of light and dark, night and day. Edmundson thinks that we can escape this sado-masochism by recognizing that we need to accept all the "dark and renovating energies" of human life and try not to expel any of them (1997, 163). We should follow in the footsteps of the great Romantics and Transcendentalists, such as Shelley and Emerson, who

---

[30] See Edmundson's "Introduction" to 1993, and his 1990.

sought to *step outside* the round of retribution that defines society, and refuse participation within it. This activity is, in effect, profoundly simple: you just stop playing the punishment game. Only by so wholly stopping the violence can we ever finally escape the patterns of brutality that presently entrap us.

It is worth pausing at this point to note the remarkable *simplicity* of the proposal offered here. There is no need for extended temporal endeavors; it is all a matter of spontaneous action. What we need is the truly, the radically *new*: "The only sin is Gothic bondage to the past" (Edmundson 1997, 161). Indeed the basic task is to awaken, like Joyce's Stephen Daedalus, from the nightmare of history; there can be no mourning, which Edmundson sees only as "a form of haunting" (1997, 160). But is it very realistic to think we could so simply stop our involvement in this violence? Is any violence *permitted* by Edmundson? What are we to do about inhabiting a world where many others remain trapped in the circuit of sado-masochism? This simple proposal is buttressed by an equally simple picture of agency. We all have it in us, Edmundson suggests, to step outside of the chains of ourselves and the fetters of our histories; we must simply do it. But whence comes this power? If we have all always possessed it, we are all the victims of a massive self-deception. Edmundson's promise is that by acting freely you will be able to enter into this freedom. But must not we have it *before* we attain it, precisely in order to be able to attain it? And anyway, what has happened to the power of *habit* in this account? Edmundson represents that modern position which cannot take evil seriously enough; his picture may be inspired by Freud, but it is far too optimistic for Freud.

Furthermore, the *purity* of the action is also worth noting. In offering this account of the individual free of the past and its Gothic horrors, Edmundson seems to forget his earlier desire for "a conjuncture of dark and renovating energies"; all the "dark" energies are gone – or at least he has not told us how to access or express them. There is an important gap between his profound aim of a conjoined harmony of our energies and the facile escapism he practically promotes. He offers an essentially Pelagian picture of agency, one committed to the idea of total voluntarism. He pictures us wholly as *ex nihilo* choosers, ontological shoppers, with no real past to our actions and no permanent effect on the future (because we are always different from what we buy, so our shopping is always a useless passion, a form of existentialist nihilistic consumerism, Jean-Paul Sartre at the Wal-Mart). He sees something of the goal we seek, but he does not see how to get there.

The problem at the heart of Edmundson's practical proposal is that his explicit picture of agency is just too simple. It is essentially a Pelagian picture of agency which ignores how our agency is habituated in certain patterns of action that we cannot simply "step out of" and change *tout court.* Agency is never as "pure" as his proposal assumes, and we will *never* wholly escape our captivity to sado-masochism (what Augustinians describe as our temptation towards the *libido dominandi*), and our proposals ought to take that into account. If Edmundson acknowledged this, I suspect his account would begin to have a place for *conversio,* and for the historical dimension of human life. He might then find a way to distinguish, as Freud did, *mourning* from *melancholia. Mourning* is the sorrowful attitude of those who know both that the world is cursed by suffering and evil, and that loss must be endured; it is a dynamic, ever-changing attitude sparked by historical events and living fully in history. *Melancholia,* on the other hand, is that experience of attempted *stasis,* the refusal to inhabit time, and accept loss, that is a sort of "bad faith" alternative to mourning. As Gillian Rose aptly puts it, mourning is "inaugurated," and looks forward in hope to its own end, while melancholia seeks to be really endless, a form of "interminable dying" (1996, 76, 103).

Edmundson errs in thinking that the problem is that we are still only partially free of evil's grip and that we must struggle to become completely free of it. On his account, the self can only look to itself for its salvation, and must engage in more and more elaborate political gymnastics, and psychological self-deceptions, to avoid recognizing this claim's absurdity. There is a pathetic air of desperation to the willfulness of the change Edmundson promotes, a desperation he does not recognize. Because of this, his position replicates in its own proposal the very activity it aims to condemn. It seeks to get over this "Gothic" fear of the outside by putting this fear outside; it intends to overcome our externalizing reaction by externalizing it. This does not seem a solution of the problem so much as a further symptom of it. Rather than indulging in the thing we are disparaging, it seems wiser to begin to resist it *right now*; and we can do that, I think, by not expelling the language of evil from our consciousness, but rather by more fully appropriating it, and *internalizing* it, seeing its presence in our lives, seeing ourselves as potentially – as likely as any others – doing evil.

Just because we should accept Edmundson's acute diagnosis of our problems, we must refuse his odd prescription. Evil is, in part, an experience of otherness; but that otherness can exist *inside* ourselves, and we should combine the alienness of evil with a recognition that that very alienness can exist, for us, within our own thoughts and deeds. Unless we are willing to move in this direction, I would argue, we will find that we will fall ever deeper into a "Gothic" attitude towards evil – just because the experience of evil, however (fortunately) rare it is for many of us, remains stubbornly irreducible, in its phenomenological quiddity, to anything but itself.

This need more adequately to digest and internalize the concept of evil might – and, as I argue in this book, *should* – lead us to recover something like the concept of sin, the idea that evil can be internalized. But this suggestion must face other critics, such as Richard Rorty, who think that such proposals actually end up crippling our ability to act. So if by arguing against Edmundson I have argued for internalizing evil, on Rorty's view I have jumped from the frying pan into the fire. For him, the problem with the language of evil and sin is not with its "external-ity" but with its internality: it is not primarily dangerous because it is superstitious, but because it is disabling and morally paralyzing. As he understands the language of sin, it indelibly stains the soul of the offender, implying "that the commission of certain acts . . . is incompat-ible with further self-respect" (R. Rorty 1998a, 32–3). This makes the lan-guage socially as well as psychologically inhibiting, and inhibiting of just the sort of open-ended experimental attitude to life that Rorty thinks we good pragmatists ought to have. To think that our experiments with life may appear unforgivably morally horrifying from their other end, so to speak, is already, for Rorty, to stifle the very sources of moral energy that might help us move beyond the crimes and injustices of the past and present. But that is what we condemn ourselves to do, he thinks, if we grant the language of evil any real purchase on our lives. We should instead think of evil as merely the failure of imagination, an inability to reach further than one thinks one can reach; tragedy is possible in this scheme, but it is hard to see just what tragedy means, apart from a pro-visional breakdown in the system (see R. Rorty 1998a, 33). We ought stu-diously to avoid giving anything like a dramatic significance to evil, for that can only cause us to fear and distract us from the important world- and self-building tasks at hand.

This makes Rorty's position more suspicious than Edmundson's – indeed, it makes it suspicious *of* Edmundson's. If Edmundson seeks some sort of willed world revolution, Rorty waits at the end of that effort, waiting to meet those who have tried it and failed, in order to offer them the consolation of ironic resignation. The important thing, for Rorty, is that we should not let the wildly ambitious and metaphysical language of sin make us expect more of ourselves than we can deliver. We need to offer a more *banal* language of political, social, and personal malfeasance, one better attuned to the contingent determining circumstances of time and place, that can narrate the history of evil and so offer us object lessons in where we have gone wrong. So, for example, Rorty proposes that the right way to see Stalinism is as part of a narrative "in which we leftists, often with the best intentions, tricked ourselves, fooled ourselves, outsmarted ourselves, yet gained a lot of useful experience" (1998b, 241). (What the "useful experience" might be remains [blessedly] undetailed [what could be worth this lesson?]; but no matter what it is, it is "experience" which some people – for example, anti-Stalinists such as Reinhold Niebuhr and Hannah Arendt – did not seem to need.) The right response to evil, whether local and petty or global and horrendous, is not glum brooding but renewed effort; reflection is to be reserved for problem-solving, where manageable problems are recognized.[31]

What Rorty is after, of course, is much larger game than the language of sin and evil; he is after the whole picture of the human within which such language has its place. He thinks this picture is vitiated by being radically *supernaturalistic*. Our excessive self-expectations in fact work to suppress what capacities for self- and world-transformation we actually have. The ways they do so are manifold. To take the example of evil, this language forces us into a deep anxious unknowing of ourselves. We can never know we are good, but we can be shown up as evil, as malicious in our true hearts, our *true* depths, with a stain which is forever inextirpable from our souls. So we are excessively cautious in acting, for fear of being "found out" to be (that is, indexed as) "evil."[32] But, Rorty says, this logic works only if we see the language of evil as revealing our *true* selves, our "deepest" selves. If we jettison the self-understanding that assumes a deep authentic self within us, we will find that we have no need for the language of evil, and no anxieties which such language can fuel. We should understand ourselves not as radically autonomous agents capable of such soul-staining evil, but instead as just parts of a broader cultural and natural web, just muddling along, making do with the attitudes and abilities granted us by our past and present, and seeking to meet the particular problems we face in succession as best we can.

This is essentially a deflationary proposal, one that shifts the burden from the agent's shoulders to the broader cultural (and natural) context within which they find themselves, and it is, of course, the outline of

---

[31] Which means, after the Holocaust, that we should just "pick ourselves up and try again" (R. Rorty 1998b, 175)!   [32] I am drawing here on Sedgwick 1990.

Rorty's famous argument for re-imagining ourselves in terms of contingency, the contingency of ourselves and our natures and our histories, of understanding ourselves as wholly, in scholastic terms, *accidental*. We come to accept that we have just happened to turn out this way. Rorty acknowledges that this is cold comfort, but it is still recognizably better than continuing to inhabit the guilt-centric "slave morality" of our past.

Rorty's vision of the human life moves along Manichean lines, towards a quietistic inhabitation of the world which effectively warrants a shrugging indifference to the kinds of political involvement that sustain human life. Central here is his deeply politically problematic, and philosophically dubious, insistence that the "private" can be wholly disjoined from the "public" (Herdt 1992). He offers a rationalization for a bifurcated life, combining a wholly privatized individualistic ethic of self-amusement with an insistence that the individual, secure within its ironic armor, can still feel solidarity with others (and be politically motivated by that feeling). Here again we see the offer of a "pure" space of selfhood promoted for our purchase, as a consolation for the turbulence and disappointments that attend to life in the public world. This subjectivistic picture cannot, however, finally offer us the consolations it aims to; it merely offers us a temporary means of avoiding the fact that we are implicated in the world. The privatized self Rorty promotes is actually a *deprived* self, a self with less existence.

More specifically, there are both conceptual and practical problems with Rorty's proposal. Conceptually, we may wonder at the mechanics of the change Rorty recommends: why and how would we do it? Or, to put it more precisely still, how does Rorty understand the appeal he is making to us, and what does he hope that we will do in response to it? The content of his proposal seems wildly at odds with its form *as* a proposal. Recall that for him we are better off changing our self-understanding from a picture of autonomous subjects with powers of reason and will into a picture of ourselves as ever-changing processes, governed in our changing by the conditions of our past and the constraints of our present. Hence central to his proposal is the claim that we would fare best if we jettisoned our belief in our capacity called "free will." But if we are to refuse this belief, how are we to come to understand how we have come to refuse this belief? The causality seems obscure. Rorty could not "persuade" us of it, because to persuade someone is to get them to change their views through persuasive argument (in the loosest sense of the term), and it is just this capacity for change, and just this capacity to *listen* (and not simply hear), that Rorty thinks we do not possess. But Rorty never makes clear just what this faculty is, or what role it can play in his overall deterministic picture of human beings. (When we ask our village liberal ironists for more information of this sort, typically we discover that they disappear, like squid, behind a cloud of black, ironic, ink.) So it is hard to see how the content of Rorty's message can be connected to the form of his argument.

Furthermore, apart from the appearance of internal incoherence, Rorty's proposal has problematic, indeed disastrous, consequences for our individual and corporate lives. It is true, and importantly so, that we have, at times, as a culture and as individuals, approached the moral life with the wrong sorts of moralistic questions, asking "How can I *avoid blame* in this situation?" rather than "What is the good or the right or even the best thing to do here?" And it is clear that the language of sin and evil is implicated in these failures. But the *misuse* of a language is not necessarily a devastating condemnation of its *proper* use. Words such as "guilt" and "sin" have received a lot of bad press recently, and this is not entirely fair. Patricia Greenspan's excellent book *Practical Guilt* (1995) shows very well, I think, the manifold and sophisticated ways in which something like a concept of guilt must operate to stabilize and pin down our moral framework, alongside other concepts like regret, remorse, and even sin. "Sin" helps us resist the sort of smug self-righteousness that Rorty does little to defuse (indeed, does much to reinforce) – self-righteousness which is in fact the idol we must keep free of moral stain, just because it suggests to us that we are, or ought directly to aim to be, morally pure.[33] Sin disputes this prescription vigorously: in its terms, no one is righteous. But sin is not cynicism: to *feel* sinful is precisely *not* to despair; it is only to know that one's hands are always dirty, and any water we have to wash them in is already muddy.

In fact, the language of sin can be profoundly empowering in both our private lives and our public ones. Publicly, it makes us understand and act in the world in a way more flexible, because more complex, than any more local discourse, such as the languages of biochemistry or of psycho-pharmacology, increasingly (and helpfully) used to diagnose "antisocial" behavior, could allow. Those languages are not really rivals to sin, but rather potential sub-discourses within it, because they are not flexible enough to capture all of our problems. For example, brain damage to the amygdala has been linked to violent behavior; but I do

---

[33] Indeed, perhaps the concept of sin can be *therapeutically* useful, to illuminate the passional dimensions of psychosis; on this, see Howespian 1997. See also A. O. Rorty 1997.

not think it would be wise to think one could generalize from some small studies of urban murderers in late twentieth-century America and somehow distill from them the essence of sin and evil. It may work for a good deal of evildoing, but not all; I suspect that Ratko Mladic and Robert McNamara have had relatively gentle lives, and probably show no neurological abnormalities. But I would want to say that they have done (and, in the case of the former, continue to do) a good deal of evil, and that in doing this evil they have sinned. And I think it is useful to associate them with brain-damaged murderers as a group of people eliciting a certain range of responses from us.

This language should not be used in a juridical or spectatorial manner – to stitch labels on the back collars of individuals' souls, as it were – but rather to find ways of making evil deeds, and patterns of behavior, somewhat more contiguous with our lives. I am doing this both to show us how we might be sinful – in order to chasten our own pretentions towards presuming our perfection – and to show us how the wicked are too much like us to be demonized, to expel them from our moral universe. This is the way that sin-language can become *practical* for us, guiding our actions in the world.

The moral of this story is simple. Modernity's attempts to escape evil only repress our acknowledgment of it; indeed, one suspects that that was the real point of such attempts at escape in the first place. We would do better to try to find ways to confront it, without pressuring that we can "defeat" it with our theoretical reflexes. Modernity's failure to do this is our basic problem as regards evil. But our problem is not finally one of finding the right method or technique; the problem is with the anthropological assumptions we pre-reflectively assume. What we need, then, in order to confront evil's challenges, is a more adequate anthropology, one which will allow us to accommodate the full complexity of evil's challenges to us. If we can do this, we will see why modernity is vexed by evil, and what we must do to escape it. The next and last section of this chapter attempts this task.

RETHINKING MODERNITY: EVIL AND SUBJECTIVISM

The persistence of these debates does not just demonstrate the perennial character of the challenge of evil, however, for recent discussions of the challenge have highlighted certain difficulties in understanding and responding to it which are peculiar to the modern context. In brief, these discussions show that typically modern accounts cannot handle the full complexity of the challenge evil sets before us, because they are crippled by untenable subjectivist assumptions. Insofar as our thought remains in thrall to subjectivism, we cannot adequately respond to evil's challenge to us, and any subjectivist response to evil's challenge will be vexed by the challenge's complexity: we either take it too seriously, and think of evil as a natural reality; or we do not take it seriously enough, and assume that, since it is due to us, we can straightforwardly change our actions and simply overcome it. That is, modern thought cannot handle evil because of its essentially subjectivist tenor. This last section of the chapter explains what this means, and why this is so.

"Subjectivism" here means an account of human existence which gives priority to the human intellect, and/or the brute fact of human action, over against some mute and inert reality, material or otherwise. The human agent has the capacity for self-determination (strictly speaking, *is* this capacity), and is an originating principle for events in the world, one uninfluenced by the world's causal patterns. This is, by and large, how we think about ourselves: we typically assume the subject's independence from outside influence or formation, and thus take human knowing to be a matter of matching subjective mental constructs with the outside world, and human freedom to be a matter of subjective "spontaneity," acting *ex nihilo* into an essentially exterior world, or intervening upon a world to which *we* are external.[34] On this picture, priority in human existence rests with the subject – our believing and desiring are ultimately due to what we do, not what the world does to and through us. For such accounts, in the beginning was the subject; subjectivism eschews the role of reflection or deliberation, assuming that wants and desires are, like taste, indisputable, basic (see Blumenberg 1983, Flathman 1992). Furthermore, these thinkers flesh out their accounts in subjectivist form; that is, they speak of the mysterious roots of action wholly in terms of the subject, the "depths" of the soul and the "darkness" of its motives, ignoring the reason-generating role of the world in which the subject finds its place. The self's status is

---

[34] It may be important to insist on the description as "us outside the world," and not "the world outside us," because (as I shall argue later) one experience that underlies this subjectivist picture is the experience of *estrangement*, most commonly from the world but also, in a way, from ourselves. Thomas Nagel makes the point well: "To be really free we would have to act from a standpoint outside ourselves, choosing everything about ourselves, including all our principles of choice – creating ourselves from nothing, so to speak" (1986, 118). This position is still often affirmed; apart from Blumenberg 1983, see Christman 1989.

determined in terms wholly internal to the self – the subject isolated
from the world "around" it.[35]

By "subjectivism" I do not mean simply relativism, though relativism
may be its progeny, nor more particularly emotivism or any such non-
cognitivist doctrine of human psychology. These are only local manifestations of a larger problem which "subjectivism" is meant to name:
namely, the problem that we far too easily assume the priority of subjective activity in intellection or action. This is not primarily a methodological concern, but an anthropological and ontological one. Furthermore,
the term "subjectivism" better captures the difficulties we face than
the typical alternative candidate, namely, "foundationalism."
"Foundationalism" only imperfectly captures the difficulties we face, for
there are times when we want "grounds" for believing.[36] The ultimate
problem we face, that is, is not a methodological one; it is rather the
material commitments underlying the methodology.[37]

The problem with this subjectivism, and indirectly the voluntarism on
which it relies, is that it fails to see *that*, let alone *how*, the world can matter
to the agent. That is, the usual accounts of agency leave no place for the
real importance of the world for our action. Susan Wolf has described
the problem well: "The idea of an autonomous agent appears to be the
idea of a prime mover unmoved whose self can endlessly account for
itself and for the behavior that it intentionally exhibits or allows. But this
idea seems incoherent or, at any rate, logically impossible" (1990, 14).
Friedrich Nietzsche's derision of it is more succinct; he calls it the
attempt "to pull oneself up into existence by the hair," and labeled it "the
best self-contradiction that has been conceived so far" (1966, 1 §21).[38] We
typically picture autonomy in terms of total self-determination, but ultimately this picture is totally alienating. Not only does it immunize
humans from any worldly influence; it also subverts our faith in our own
intelligibility. We think events in the world influence one another (that is,
in part, what the concept of "world" means); but subjectivism quarantines human agents from such influence. Furthermore, this picture ultimately subverts our faith in the intelligibility of human action: on what

[35] For an intriguingly similar discussion of the modern picture of the self, see Song 1997, 215–20.
Song notes the remarkable similarities between the modern subject and the God of Arius (216
n. 2). I have also been helped by Farrell 1994, though our readings of the pre-modern inheritance differ significantly.
[36] See Haack 1993, especially chapter one, "Foundationalism versus Coherentism: a Dichotomy
Disclaimed." See also Cavell 1989.
[37] I take myself to be disagreeing here with the many critics of modernity (prominently Hans-Georg
Gadamer, John McDowell, and Kathryn Tanner [especially Tanner 1988]) who identify the
central problem as a methodological one.   [38] See C. Taylor 1979, 154–66; and Pippin 1991, 153.

grounds can the self determine itself? If agents are so voluntaristically spontaneous, then their actions are finally not determined by even their *own* deliberations. The explanation of our actions then ends invariably in the raw existentialist claim "so I willed it." But that ends up rendering one's identity a riddle even to oneself; for why should I, a reflective, deliberative agent, identify myself with this willing "I"? Indeed, this "I" seems to be less *me* than an alien thing at the base of my agency. Thus subjectivist accounts do not really defend agency's worldly reality against extra-agential interference, but just the opposite: it transfers my agency to an unintelligible, hence practically external, voluntary power. The "reality" of subjectivity is secured only at the cost of cutting the subject off from direct contact with the world. Instead of rendering intelligible the self's existence in the world, this picture of autonomy goes too far, and leaves the self something of a gilded bird in an iron cage.[39] The intellectual history of the last two centuries is in large part the story of thinkers' growing recognition of this problem. From Kant, through Hegel and Nietzsche and beyond into the twentieth century, the attempt to combine something like genuine human freedom with an authentic acknowledgment of the human's being-in-the-world has exercised thinkers to no clear conclusion.

But subjectivism not only causes general problems for thinkers investigating the nature of human existence; more specifically as to our interests, it vexes our attempts to come to an adequate understanding of the challenge of evil. As the problem of the Gothic imagination suggests, evil subverts the central subjectivist assertion that the human is in full or even primary control of their life. Because subjectivism assumes that there is a clear distinction between what is and what is not "the subject," its attempts to comprehend and respond to the challenge of evil are inevitably confounded by the fundamental confusion of subjective and objective at the base of that challenge.

Indeed, our enthrallment to subjectivism seduces us into taking the challenge either too seriously or not seriously enough. Evil has both interior and exterior aspects; its challenge appears to arise simultaneously (and equally) both within and without our existence, both at our centers, as it is enacted through our free agency, and at our limits, as it impinges on our existence in *resisting* and/or *attacking* us.[40] That is, evil's challenge is internal to us, as it can appear (usually retrospectively) in our

---

[39] I borrow here from Mathewes 1999.
[40] The grammatical implication here, that the challenge of tragedy has some sort of independent agency, is neither intended nor helpful, but I know of no better way of saying this.

own actions, and so it is something we do; but it is also external to us, as it exists as evil, most properly speaking, as something that negates us.[41]

A subjectivist account may insist that evil's ultimate reality is located "within" the self, within subjectivity, as something that the subject enacts. Here, evil is describable wholly in terms of clear responsibility and voluntary fault, and resists any suggestion of victimization. Sin and evil then become elements in our psychological constitution, and there-fore rational options for action: evil is described as something that the self wills for itself, something that can be a genuine willing, that is, as an actualization of some real option for the self. This account insists on our responsibility for all that befalls us. But then this account cannot explain the real exteriority of evil, its foreignness to us and hence its non-neces-sity, indeed its absolute contingency, to our existence. This causes prob-lems when we try to hold someone responsible for something they do, if they are not responsible for becoming – in the sense of freely choosing to become – the sort of person who does that sort of thing. This is espe-cially pressing as regards evil because, as John Kekes notes, "the preva-lence of evil is largely the result of these nonautonomous patterns of action" (1998, 218). This account cannot, then, take evil's challenge to us seriously enough.

To avoid such problems, a subjectivist account may insist that evil's reality is ultimately located "outside" the self, in evil's ultimately *nihilat-ing* opposition to subjectivity. Here, evil's challenge is describable wholly in terms of resistance and externality, as that which threatens us from outside. Because the threat is one to our existence, it therefore cannot arise within our existence. This account seems built on the phenomenological acknowledgment of the external aspect of evil, and insists on the mutual resistance of (active and intelligent) subjectivity and (passive and mute or "dark") evil. But this account cannot acknowledge the genuinely *internal* character of evil, its real rootedness *in* our lives, that is as basic a mark of the challenge as is its externality. This position, that is, takes evil too seriously. Hence, if one is commit-ted to a subjectivist account of the human and reality, either one under-mines evil's *reality* by absolutizing its challenge as absolute otherness, or one subverts its *threat* by absolutizing its reality as a primordial part of our constitution. To do a better job, then, we should jettison our sub-jectivist assumptions and develop another, superior, account of the human's relation to the world.

---

[41] There are many problems with the "internal"/"external" language employed here; I use it here even while I admit its ultimate inadequacy. I have more to say about this in chapter five.

CONCLUSION: THE WAY TOWARDS HOPE

It would be a delicious, not to mention self-contradictory, irony if I appealed to our will to get us out of subjectivism. And I may be misread that way. But the particular nature of my diagnosis entails that a solution cannot come from more action on our part. The solution must come from a change not fundamentally due to our decisions. It must take the form of a redemption. I will argue, in this book, that the real change is a reinvigoration of our hope, which is sadly absent today.

What do I mean by saying that our deepest failure is that we disbelieve in hope? I mean that we do not believe we have any *right* to hope. The "hope" people appeal to today is usually nothing more than a promissory note that the future will be better than the present. This may seem like it stems from optimism – from a Promethean confidence that we can do what we want, that there are no limits on what we can do. Many people may think this way. But the deeper source of these failings lies in the common doubt that the world as it stands is fundamentally good – that, in other words, there is any reason to hope, any evidence for it. This sort of "hope" is based on an implicit recoil from our current condition. A worldview that justifies itself on this "hope" is not affirmative at all – it rather expresses a longing for a mythological future. Real hope, as Christopher Lasch argues, is quite distinct from an optimistic belief in progress:

Hope does not demand a belief in progress. It demands a belief in justice: a conviction that the wicked will suffer, that wrongs will be made right, that the underlying order of things is not flouted with impunity. Hope implies a deep-seated trust in life that appears absurd to those who lack it. It rests on confidence not so much in the future as in the past. It derives from early memories . . . in which the experience of order and contentment was so intense that subsequent disillusionments cannot dislodge it . . . Not that it prevents us from expecting the worst. The worst is always what the hopeful are prepared for. Their trust in life would not be worth much if it had not survived disappointments in the past, while the knowledge that the future holds further disappointments demonstrates the continuing need for hope. (1991, 80–1)

Our problem is that these words mean less and less to most of us as time goes on.

So it is not because we disbelieve in sin that we disbelieve in hope; rather, it is because we disbelieve in hope that we disbelieve in sin. It may seem odd to suggest that a deeper belief in sin is the route to a more vivid hope, but such is my claim. To imagine the acknowledgment of sin to be a negative emotion is fundamentally mistaken; just as people suffering from depression feel the worst as they are coming out of the depression – so that feelings of suffering are a sign of improvement, because they are feelings at all – the doctrine of sin is not ultimately a depressing doctrine; it is rather an expression of joy at salvation. Sin at least is somehow, in some way, finally *contingent*; it says that evil does not speak the final truth about the world. But many of us, at our best moments, fear that evil in fact does speak that truth, that our world is in the end not finally "not the way it's supposed to be," but that it is supposed to be this way (C. Plantinga 1995). Our disbelief in sin is borne out of our despair.

How have we arrived here? How has this deep despair come about? It gains its sheen of intellectual plausibility through the slow acceptance, so gradual as to be imperceptible across the past few centuries, of the belief in subjectivism. To accept hope is to accept a non-subjectivist picture of agency, because hope sees us as determined by forces outside ourselves (under sin, by our inheritance) and hence as not wholly self-determining. So, subjectivist commitments make us disbelieve in hope and sin because they make us claim that we can, ideally, determine ourselves *totally*, so are always in a "state of innocence" (though this is modeled increasingly on a state of pre-choice in a consumer setting). Therefore, our belief in subjectivism works to underpin our disbelief in sin and hope. Because of this, we picture evil as external and hence attempt to *fix* it; or we imagine it as internal, "natural" and hence something to be resignedly accepted. Either way, what happens is up to us. We feel abandoned. And that is another way of saying we are without hope, for hope is only superficially about the future; it is really about not being alone in one's struggles. The way out of despair, the way towards hope, is to help us see that we are not alone in the way subjectivism pictures us as being.

The Polish poet Zbigniew Herbert, in an interview, spoke for many as he ruminated on his grim century:

Teachers in our high schools pound it into us that "historia" is "magistra vitae." But when history crashed down upon us in all its brutal glory, I understood, in the very real glow of flames above my home city, that she was a strange teacher. She gave to the people who consciously survived her, and to all who followed her, more material for thought than all the old chronicles put together. A dense and dark material. It will require the work of many consciences to shed light on it. (in Weissbort 1991, 334)

In order for us consciously to survive, we must come to grips with this "dense and dark material." But we moderns have a hard time doing so.

When we are confronted with the need to think about evil, our choices seem to be either (a) to crouch in Gothic paroxysms of horror or (b) to wander off in peripatetic, head-in-the-clouds theodicies. We must find some way of keeping evil in focus, in order to think about both what it means for understanding ourselves and our world, and how we can best respond to its manifold challenges. But we can so think evil only by re-thinking the picture of the self that modernity often seduces us into accepting. So the real issue facing us, in rethinking evil, is rethinking our moral anthropology.

Are there *no* resources in modern thought to help us here? Of course there are. Some of the most important and influential thinkers of the modern age work in the direction I suggest, against the grain of most modern thought on these matters. One of the most important is Sigmund Freud, with whom we began; as Anne Williams suggests, "Freud writes in Gothic," and his work is best read *in toto* as a multivol-ume Gothic novel entitled "The Mysteries of Enlightenment."[42] More recently, a great number of philosophers, largely inspired by Nietzsche (or by the ancient Greek thinkers who inspired him) have also begun to address these issues. As Bernd Magnus says, "philosophers as diverse as Bernard Williams and Michel Foucault, Martha Nussbaum and Jean-François Lyotard, Walter Benjamin and Richard Rorty, are beginning to suspect that 'the moral point of view' *simpliciter* [where that point of view is understood as built out of a subjectivist assumption of the purity of the subject] may be an intrinsic part of the problem rather than a con-tribution to its solution" (1997, 18). There are a number of valuable resources, and a good many thinkers, who can help us here.

The Augustinian tradition seems another obvious source of insight on this issue. Just as those contemporary thinkers who have tried to think evil, and the implication of the human in it, have been forced to reach back behind modernity to the pre-modern past, and to recover ancient thinkers, so we might expect that Augustine, who so famously brooded over these problems for most of his career, would seem to be an almost ideal candidate for thought. And yet he is rarely cited, and often con-demned without a reading. Why? The next chapter attempts to answer this question.

[42] See A. Williams 1995, 239–48, 241; Edmundson 1997, 131; and Lear 1998.

CHAPTER TWO

The Augustinian tradition and its discontents

But all these grave objections cannot obscure the greatness of the perception that God works in us "to will and to accomplish," that we have nothing that we have not received, and that dependence on God is good, and is our possession. It is easy to show that in every single objectionable theory formulated by Augustine, there lurks a true phase of Christian self-criticism, which is only defective because it projects into history, or is made the foundation on which to construct a "history." Is not the doctrine of predestination an expression of the confession: "He who would boast, let him boast in the Lord"? Is not the doctrine of original sin based on the thought that behind all separate sins there resides sin as want of love, joy, and divine peace? Does it not express the just view that we feel ourselves guilty of all evil, even where we are shown that we have no guilt?

Adolph von Harnack 1899, v. 221

As chapter one argued that modernity has a hard time coming to grips with the challenge of evil, we should begin this chapter by acknowledging that, even before modernity, Christian thought has had its own difficulties with evil. Indeed evil is an especially pointed issue for Christian thought, because Christianity seems simultaneously to imply and to be defeated by it: *imply*, because the core or center of the Christian message is salvation, God's rescue of us from evil; *be defeated by*, because the very extremity of Christianity's answer seems all too desperate: The picture it offers of a perfectly good and omnipotent God not only seems wildly at odds with what evidence we can comprehend, as Hume points out; it also, as Nietzsche suggests, hints that there is something more than a merely "theoretical" interest in the problem – that "something more" being, for Nietzsche and those who follow him, the compound of desperate utopian hope and impacted and ingrown *ressentiment* which Nietzsche called "slave-morality." The world seems cruelly inappropriate for the sort of account Christianity proposes, and the protestations

59

of millennia of theologians, seemingly so blind to the blatant refutation of their theories by concrete cases, seem suspicious, motivated by interests other than surface theoretical concerns. In this situation, to say that "God is love" can seem like handing daisies to a psychopath. Christianity seems subverted by its own apparent *raison d'être*.[1]

In this context it is not surprising that Christianity, perhaps more than most other traditions, has spent considerable intellectual capital reflecting on these issues. And the Augustinian tradition is perhaps the greatest example of this. This tradition interprets the challenge of evil fundamentally in terms of the twin conceptual formulas of "evil as privation" and "sin as perversion"; it proposes a response to the challenge which acknowledges our complicity in injustice and suffering while still insisting that (a) this complicity can be constrained (and in some sense accommodated) within a larger affirmation of the fundamentally just purposes in which we are engaged, and that (b) such complicity is superior to refusing to participate in the transformation, and final redemption, of the world.

This chapter offers a rough outline of the proposed Augustinian interpretation of and response to those challenges, briefly formulates a series of worries about this proposal, and sketches how the work will respond to the worries. It sketches the Augustinian tradition's interpretation of evil as privation and sin as perversion. It next identifies several challenges to the Augustinian position. Finally, it offers a summary of its Augustinian response to those challenges. The elaboration of that argument, and through it the construction of the Augustinian proposal as regards evil's challenge, occupies the remainder of the book.

THE AUGUSTINIAN TRADITION: PRIVATION AND PERVERSION

The Augustinian tradition?

A word of caution is needed here. Even after my project is fully explained to them, some people will want more Augustine than I offer; others will want less. Both suffer from significant misunderstandings. The former fail to understand Augustine; the latter fail to understand themselves. Both fail to understand our hermeneutical situation, and my use of the phrase "the Augustinian tradition." To employ the concept of "tradition" as I do may strike some as an irresponsible and anachronis-

---

[1] In formulating the problem in this way, I am indebted to conversations with Charles Taliaferro.

tic attempt to extract proof-texts for what I want to say from figures of a very different historical world. Indeed this is always a danger; but to treat thinkers as purely historical artifacts is anachronistic in an even deeper sense.[2] Augustine was not interested in summarizing his historical era's *Weltanschauung*; he was interested in the truth, and in the service of that project his work remains as important to us today as it was in his own time. By talking about the "Augustinian tradition," then, I want to designate that whole constellation of themes, thinkers, concepts, and arguments which derive their essential insights from St. Augustine's thought, in order further to develop those insights.

The Augustinian *tradition?*

Of course my use of the phrase "the Augustinian tradition" may only make the project even more dubious. What do I mean by talking about "the *Augustinian* tradition"? I mean to refer to that tradition of moral and religious reflection inaugurated in the work of St. Augustine, and carried forward by other thinkers. There are two questions to raise here. First, how does Augustine *begin* it? Why not simply stick to the letter of Augustine's texts and avoid undertaking the dubious project of divining the presumptive spirit of his thought? Second, just *what* is it that he begins? Just what does he inaugurate, and other thinkers carry forward?

An adequate answer to the first question would require a book in itself, for the history of western thought since Augustine can be seen as a series of readings – or, better, *mis*readings – of his work.[3] Briefly, I do this

[2] As Richard Rorty says, "[s]uccessful historical reconstruction can be performed only by people who have some idea of what they themselves think about the issues under discussion. . . . Attempts at historical reconstruction that are selfless in this respect . . . are not so much reconstructions as assemblages of raw material for such reconstructions" (1998b, 251). It is an interesting fact that we still lack a term for the interpretive flaw that is the opposite of anachronism. "Historically reductionist" will not quite do; a better contrasting term would be something like "aphilosophical" or "atheological," or some phrase that would include all that they gesture at and more – a phrase, for example, like "intellectually inert." Perhaps however we should retain the term "anachronistic" and insist that it bear a larger reference than that with which it is typically credited. For a thoughtful exploration of these concerns by a contemporary Augustine scholar, see O'Donnell 1991. For a theological-ethicist, see Porter 1998, 107–9.

[3] See Menn 1998, Taylor 1989, Pryzwara 1957, Kent 1995, and Matthews 1992 and 1999. For a more complex and careful (albeit only partial) historical reading than any of these offer, see Saak 1997. (I am indebted to Michael Hanby for drawing my attention to Saak's essay.) On the complexities of the transmission of multiple Augustinianisms, see Kaufman 1982. Interestingly, Augustine himself seems to have thought in terms of traditions as well; his thought reflects his own appreciation of the significance of intellectual authorities for further inquiry. (See *DUC*, and of course *DDC*.) More intriguingly, in later years he seems to have realized that his own work would become a watershed for later thinkers, and he took great care (most apparently in *Retr.*) to delineate how he thought his own work should be developed. So Augustine turned his thought into a tradition, an ongoing mode of inquiry subject to development and change. The ironic

because I want less to *admire* Augustine than to *follow* him.[4] Some readers may expect a great deal of defensive exegesis, in the service of authenticating these ideas as genuinely Augustine's own. But I am not undertaking archaeology here; I do not worship what Mark Jordan calls "the old philologists' fetish of 'sources'" (1992, 28). Of course I do not dismiss Augustine's thought; I hope to capture its central dynamics here. Indeed one of the most important dynamics of his thought is expressed just by this non-fixation on capturing the letter of his position: as he said, contrasting himself to the writers of Scripture,

we who engage in public debates and write books . . . make progress as we write, we are learning every day, engaged in research as we dictate, knocking at the door as we speak . . . [So] do not even think of regarding as canonical scripture any debate, or written account of a debate by anyone . . . If I have said something reasonable, let him follow, not me, but reason itself; if I've proved it by the clearest divine testimonies, let him follow, not me, but the divine scripture . . . I get angrier with that kind of fan of mine who takes my book as being canonical, than with the man who finds fault in my book with things that are not in fact at fault. (*Sermo.* 162c, D.10, no. 15, based on 1997 translation, p. 176. See also *Conf.* XII.31.)

I am not directly interested in expositing Augustine's account of evil so much as developing an Augustinian one; I want to show how this thought system can become "operational" for our own time. Much of my elaboration of the Augustinian tradition's content occurs with only the slightest acknowledgment of wellsprings in Augustine's own writing.

Nonetheless, whatever my local failings of Augustine exegesis (and I have no doubt they are legion), this presentation of Augustine is relatively uncontroversial as regards historical research. Augustine's writings must always be read in their complex context, with its multiple audiences, in light of the many dynamic pressures and forces acting both to hinder and to enable (indeed, at times excessively amplify) his voice.[5] Furthermore, all of this was occurring while Augustine himself is – as his sermonic warning above makes clear – constantly developing his thought in new and unexpected ways. Augustine's mind was a restless

footnote 3 (*cont.*)
   perils of Augustine's transformation into a tradition are interestingly discussed in Rist 1995, 18–19, 290–313.
[4] See the discussion of "admirers" and "imitators" in Kierkegaard 1991, 239–43.
[5] For example, his magisterial *De civitate Dei* is commonly read as a "Charter of Christendom" for an era safely converted to the church and in which wise bishops counsel pious emperors; but recent historical research, and the recently rediscovered Divjak letters, depict a setting far more superficially, partially, and provisionally Christian than this, suggesting that Augustine's massive work was more an attempt to attain some small influence with an imperial administration largely indifferent to the squealing of bishops (see McLynn 1999).

one, working within dynamic and complex social and ecclesial constraints, speaking to quite diverse audiences (often simultaneously) and sensitive to the likelihood of his work's persistence beyond his lifetime. My obligation to the historical Augustine is real enough, though I do not want it to eclipse the crucially normative proposal I am making here. Essentially I must show only that those elements of Augustine's thought that I isolate are really his own, and operate for him as they do for me. I am not trying to summarize or systematize Augustine's thought on evil; indeed, to do so would, I fear, distort his position, for his mind developed quite a bit, and the different presentations of his thought on evil were shaped for the particular audience he was addressing. (Thus, for example, he sounds more philosophical in *De civitate Dei*, more Pauline in *Confessions*, and more Christological in *De Trinitate*.)

Where I might be more historically controversial is in the effect I claim for Augustine's overall development on evil. While the detailed historical work of scholars such as G. R. Evans (1982) is indispensable, I suggest that they do not attend to the basic effect that Augustine's thought on evil has for later thinkers. This is his constant attempt to *demythologize* evil, to work to more fully secularize it. In all his work, he struggled against the temptation to grant malice any theological, or indeed supernatural purchase – a temptation of which Manicheanism was only a symptom. Augustine's world was one in which real spiritual presences filled the air, and some of them were malicious. As Neil Forsyth argues in his magnificent *The Old Enemy: Satan and the Combat Myth* (1987), despite the Platonic elite, the weight of popular historical tradition in his world lay heavily on the side of seeing the cosmos as essentially a battlefield on which the forces of good and evil were locked in an eternal struggle.

Augustine did not (of course) wholly escape this worldview; he still affirmed the reality of immaterial demons who tempt humans to sin. But his thought bore the seeds of a profound challenge to this worldview; for after all, even the immaterial demons were only immaterial because of the nature of their good created being; insofar as they were demonic, they were actually struggling (though they would not admit it) to become not finally ever more *material*, but ever more *secular*, ever more fully part of a world apart from God. Of course, in his final years he recoiled against the Pelagians' too facile extrapolation from his anti-Manicheanism that human evil was easily overcome, so much so that his final works against them perhaps come dangerously close to identifying human nature with human sinfulness in order to combat their optimism. But his debates with the Pelagians are not simply nor even centrally about the nature of human sinfulness and the scope of proper human optimism; rather they are better seen as about the nature of God's presence in the world – about whether God is best seen as a wise counsellor and lawgiver, or as an actual agent, a medical doctor intervening in our souls to heal us. Here again, Augustine's theology turned out to underpin a far more profound optimism than the Pelagians' thin-lipped elitist moralism could muster.

This last part is crucial. Augustine's demythologizing of evil was of a piece with his radical metaphysics of God. God's absolute goodness so exhausted the conceptual space of transcendence for Augustine, that evil had to be solely a consequence of the created order's swerve away from God. Furthermore, it was not just (or even centrally) a philosophical conviction that led Augustine to this view; it had exegetical foundations for Augustine in the idea that a wholly good God created a wholly good creation. Because creation is a monarchy, Augustine was, in a sense, "boxed into" a long-term project of demythologizing evil. (This argument is made more thoroughly in chapter five below.[6]) It is this dynamic that is at the center of the Augustinian tradition's response to evil.

The second question – about the *content* of the Augustinian tradition as regards our concerns – is more manageably answered. I take as central the famous (or notorious) Augustinian account of evil as privation, and sin as perversion. But, as the above implies, the Augustinian tradition is not primarily fixated on evil and sin, for those concepts are an integral part of, and disastrously distorted apart from, an essentially positive, indeed ecstatic cosmology. Furthermore, that cosmology is essentially practical, underpinning, informing, and motivating a certain kind of practical response: it frankly admits the provisionally irresolvable character of evil's challenge, yet insists that we must respond to it. That is, we must understand that evil is not the way things are supposed to be; but we must equally understand that we can do nothing now to remove this problem, but must inhabit the world at present in what is essentially an attitude of *waiting*, waiting to be saved by God from evil's domination. And in order best to understand oneself as waiting, one ought to under-

---

[6] Such a position may seem obviously the right one for Christian theology to take; but the seeming obviousness of that claim is itself an index of the triumph of Augustine's position. As we will see in this chapter, many Christian thinkers still suspect that demythologizing evil is inappropriate, because it avoids confronting evil's real power. (Nor are all such thinkers putatively "liberal" theologians; Gordon Graham's recent *Evil and Christian Ethics* argues from a self-proclaimed Christian position that "our experience of evil is the outcome of a fundamental struggle between forces of light and forces of darkness, a struggle in which the death of Jesus of Nazareth proved to be a decisive victory" [2001, 181–2; see 192, 220].)

stand evil through the conceptual frame of privation and perversion: we admit the priority of the challenge of evil to human responses to it, by understanding sin anthropologically as an original *perversion*; yet we also refuse to grant evil any normative acceptability in our worldview, by understanding evil ontologically as primordial *privation*. So this framework enables for Augustinians a powerful and fruitful response to evil.

Nonetheless this framework is, to say the least, controversial today; indeed, Augustine's overall proposal has become deeply problematic to many contemporary thinkers precisely because of its account of evil. As I noted above, many even suggest that his proposal is in fact partly responsible for our current perplexities, and that it is practically danger-ous: they typically charge either that Augustine's ontological account of evil as privation elides the reality of evil in a glibly triumphalist (and escapist) manner, or that Augustine's psychological analysis of original sin associates evil so closely with human nature as to be indistinguishable from a general pessimism about our "natural" condition *simpliciter*. Centrally these charges are accusations that the tradition is irremediably *moralistic*: such critics charge that when we come face to face with the ravages of evil, the tradition offers us only an inert *consolation* (through its talk of evil as mere "privation"), while, when we confront the tragic necessities of action, it works to internalize in us a paralyzing *guilt* (through its talk of sin as an original "perversion"). This charge of moralism is formulated in terms either of an inadequate theology or an inadequate moral psychology; theologically minded critics suggest that the tradition's framework inhibits our acknowledgment of the sove-reignty and transcendence of God, while more secularly minded critics suggest that it distorts our understanding of natural human life. Hence, conceptually, critics suspect that its analysis of evil fundamentally mis-apprehends the real nature of the challenge; perhaps evil is not best described as ultimately merely the absence of good, and perhaps sin is not best understood as ultimately always the perversion of our originally good natures. Furthermore, practically, the critics complain that, even bracketing its accuracy, the conceptual scheme so elaborated offers no useful practical guidance to people faced with apparently inexplicable suffering and apparently inescapable moral perplexities. Far from pro-viding any insight into or useful response to evil, the critics charge, the Augustinian tradition works to cripple our response to it, by making us passive sufferers before it and by making us internalize an enormous inertial guilt whenever we seek actively to respond to it. How can this account meet and defuse these concerns?

Most basically, what we have here is a failure to communicate: the critics misunderstand the Augustinian account, and they do so for precisely the same reason that we are perplexed by the problems of evil – namely, our commitment to subjectivism, and the Augustinian proposal's resistance to it. Given that the basic Augustinian proposal is that we can do nothing to *solve* this problem (we being the crucial part of it), but can only *respond* to our implication in it, it is no wonder that we moderns, corrupted by subjectivism, think the Augustinian proposal far too passive. Yet the Augustinian proposal's innocence of subjectivism is just what makes it so powerful an alternative to subjectivist accounts, particularly as regards evil: exorcising our subjectivist assumptions brings into high relief both the full complexity and coherence of the Augustinian proposal, and that proposal's genuine fruitfulness for responding to evil's challenges. Thus, the Augustinian proposal offers so profound an interpretation of and response to evil precisely because it so thoroughly resists subjectivism.

To help do this, I want to explore the work of two twentieth-century thinkers who address evil's challenge to us in deeply Augustinian ways, Reinhold Niebuhr and Hannah Arendt. They are participants in "the Augustinian tradition" – not in the sense of apostolically descending through some discrete set of disciples over the fifteen centuries since his death (though it would be harder, for most of that time, to find thinkers who would want to *dis*sociate themselves from Augustine), but rather in the sense of appropriating a complex deposit of insights, strategies and attitudes which have offered a viable and operative option for moral and religious reflection.[7] The proposals of Niebuhr and Arendt reveal how the Augustinian account's conceptual scheme is both theoretically viable and practically applicable in understanding and responding to evil. Niebuhr's program of "Christian realism" helps to demonstrate that an Augustinian account of sin as perversion is both conceptually defensible and practically useful; Arendt's account of "the banality of evil" helps to show how an Augustinian account of evil as privation is intelligible,

---

[7] See Menn 1998, 69: "The history of Augustinianism is a history of plural Augustinianisms, of individual revivals of Augustine by individuals who had been attracted to the texts of Augustine by his fame and "authority," and who had discovered there some new aspect of Augustine's thought which seemed to offer a way out of the impasses of their contemporaries, and to suggest a new philosophical or theological project. This is by sharp contrast with the history of Aristotelianism, which was above all a teaching and commentary tradition, in which each master perceived Aristotle through the framework of questions disputed by the schools, and it was all but impossible to return to the text for a fresh discovery of what Aristotle's own agenda had been." See also Rist 1995, 6–7.

illuminating, and practically action-informing. While neither Niebuhr nor Arendt offers entirely adequate accounts, they take us a good distance towards such an account.

The Augustinian tradition*?* *From archaeology to ethnography*

My proposal faces not only the material challenges sketched above; it also faces a methodological challenge to which we must attend, a question revolving around the idea of "tradition." Here the challenge comes not from prototypically modern positions, but from supposedly *anti-*modern ones, from thinkers, following Alasdair MacIntyre, who argue that we exist "after virtue" in a state of profound moral chaos, and that we are best served by returning to more particular traditions of moral inquiry (see, most succinctly, MacIntyre 1990). My basic claim – that the Augustinian tradition helps us resolve problems which are irresolvable from within the common contemporary (and crucially subjectivist) mindset – might be read rhetorically as a sort of MacIntyrean diagnosis of, or jeremiad against, the self-images of the age, and a MacIntyrean prescription for our survival. But my actual argument for this claim seems oddly antithetical to MacIntyre's project – because I argue that this tradition has been operative in modernity, and operative in figures who seem so prototypically "modern" as Niebuhr and Arendt. So the rhetoric and the actual argument seem to be at odds. Does this fact reflect a loss of nerve when faced with the extremities of critique that MacIntyre's thought demands – does my appeal to Niebuhr and Arendt finally signal a retreat to the cozy insularities of modern thought, in lieu of a serious attempt to recover the tradition from modernity's indifference to it? I do not think so; instead I think MacIntyre's work needs the sort of refinements mine offers. Understanding why helps to illuminate the sense I give to the concept of "tradition."

MacIntyre's apocalyptic depiction of the state of our moral language and moral understanding is essentially archaeological: we inhabit the wreckage of an earlier time, and we sit, musing amidst the ruins of a once vibrant moral order, with only the slightest hint of our incomprehension of its fractured magnificence.[8] It is a powerful image, and one which, if not fully plausible, nonetheless possesses great insight – greater insight than many of his more locally accurate critics will allow. And yet it is not fully acceptable, for, as Jeffrey Stout has pointed out, it is difficult to understand how we can appreciate MacIntyre's point – namely,

---

[8] It is worth noting that one of MacIntyre's most important influences, R. G. Collingwood, was an archaeologist and historian as well as a philosopher.

that we have lost the ability for reasoned moral discourse and deliberation – without ourselves embodying its contradiction (see Stout 1988).
Furthermore, morality is more tenacious in human life than MacIntyre
allows; it outlasts the decay of one culturally specific moral framework,
although such a decay can bring with it a concomitant loss of moral
articulateness and suppleness.

It may be useful to contrast MacIntyre's archaeological image with an
ethnographical one (see Moody-Adams 1997 and Tanner 1997). Often
ethnographers gain insight into ancient cultures through anthropolo-
gists' observations of the current occupants of those long-gone cultures'
territory. Artifacts remain in active, though doubtless very different, use;
cultural activities remain significant, though with a different spin; patterns of physical habitation cast an oblique, but still illuminating, beam
on the ways the ancients lived. This is not, of course, in any simple way
a matter of straightforwardly reading off current patterns and applying
them to the past; a good deal of cultural acuity and methodological tact
must go into such work. But such work can yield insights into how long-
lost cultures ordered themselves. This method can operate the other way
round as well; sometimes our apprehension of ancient realities can cast
light on present practices, and can allow us to understand why and how
we do things today – indeed, can even refine or transform how we do
things today.

Mine is more an ethnographical project than an archaeological one.
I want to grasp the "deep structure," so to speak, of the Augustinian
attempt to understand and respond to the problems of evil, suffering,
and tragedy. While we have forgotten a good deal of its logic, we have
never fully forgone its practices.[9] The modern world, for all the vast and
drastic changes that have taken place in it, is still employing resources
that are continuous with ancient thought.[10] Certainly we need to critique
the self-images of the age; but these self-images are our own, and we
cannot act as if they were a foreign intrusion on our minds. We have met
modernity, and it is us.

[9] The difference between this position and MacIntyre's own (if there is a genuine difference) may
not be merely formal, but may have something to do with our differing material commitments.
MacIntyre's work identifies itself as developing the Thomist tradition, while this work understands itself as fundamentally Augustinian. I will not enter into this here, but suffice to say that
I think that significant differences separate these two positions (perhaps especially around the
concept of nature), and that their dispute may be the most continuously interesting and fruitful
intermural dispute in western Christian thought.

[10] In these matters I am somewhat closer to Charles Taylor than to MacIntyre (though *Sources of the
Self* could not have been written, as Taylor recognizes, without *After Virtue*). But MacIntyre himself
seems to have moved in this direction in recent years; see MacIntyre 1998, 136–52.

This picture may seem less attractively grim than MacIntyre taken straight; but in fact it entails a different, and perhaps more difficult, task than his rather breathless call for a new St. Benedict. (Indeed, while he seems materially so critical of modernity, formally there is a significant connection between the structure of his work and the structure of much modern thought, found in his longing to jettison the past and start all over again.[11]) In this context we must undertake not the almost *ex nihilo* "revaluation of values" of those who have sternly turned away from their cultures to make a new world, but rather the difficult work of accepting our inheritance as it comes to us, with all the marks of its previous handlers. We need not make any great exertions to "recover" our Augustinian inheritance; it has been present in us all the time. We must bring that inheritance more fully into reflective apprehension, more fully to inhabit its vision, and concomitantly to resist other, less helpful, visions we might also inherit.[12] We find ourselves forced to take our inheritance and make something of it.

This is the real work we face, the work of tradition. And our real problem lies in an understanding of "tradition" that depicts it as simply a deposit of faith. For it is better understood as an activity, an ongoing act of forgiveness. We inherit our ability to reflect from our elders, and we come to see that their tools only imperfectly fit the problems we face. Hence, unless we wish totally to jettison our minds, we find ourselves compelled to work through that inheritance, accepting its imperfections (and, furthermore, accepting that our own solutions will cause our descendants similar problems), and this acceptance involves, indeed just *is*, in part, forgiveness. This is not a false piety; it is simply the condition of being responsible in one's thought to one's predecessors, a fact ingredient in thought *simpliciter*. Nor is this a distinctly modern problem; Plato's *Republic* is so centrally concerned with the difficulties inherent in inheritance that an alternative title for that dialogue might be "fathers and sons."

All of this may strike some readers as bringing sand to the beach; after all, is it not simply uncontroversial that the Augustinian vision is still part of our cultural atmosphere? Indeed, is it not simply the case that "modernity" as a whole, through the work of Descartes (in epistemology) and Duns Scotus (in thinking about the will), profoundly

---

[11] I do not need to suggest that this is MacIntyre's intention; rather, his work speaks into a rhetorical setting suffused with longings for "total revolution." See Yack 1986.

[12] I make little effort to detail a demonology of such other accounts; beyond discussing our common predilections towards subjectivism, I leave each reader to their own exorcisms.

"Augustinian"? Even if this is so, it does not release us from undertaking an interpretation of this inheritance for meeting the challenges we face today.

Intuitive origins

The tradition's essentially practical character can be seen in the fact that its conceptual framework can appeal not only to dogmatic propositions but also to two intuitions phenomenologically available to reflection. First it claims that, phenomenologically speaking, evil is in itself strictly *evil* – always bad, always to be avoided if possible, never to be affirmed for its own sake or for some nebulous titillating tickle we receive from it in our bourgeois comfort. Its second intuition concerns goodness. The second intuition observes how, in the face of the massive and persistent presence of evil in the world, we continue to insist that the basic truth about the world is its goodness – if not its justice, at least its basalt worthiness and inherent value.

The first intuition is admirably (if obliquely) expressed by the poet and writer Wendell Berry, in disputing another poet (William Matthews) on the desirability of experimenting with lack of form and chaos in poetry. Berry is deeply critical of those, like Matthews, who suggest that we are excessively afraid of chaos:

> The fear of chaos, Mr. Matthews maintains, originates with "people who get up every morning at eight o'clock, teach an Aesthetic Theory class at 10, get the department mail at twelve o'clock, give a graduate student exam in the afternoon, go home and have two drinks before dinner." Maybe so. But it seems to me more likely that the *praise* of chaos must come from people whose lives are so safely organized. Mr. Matthews does concede that "There's a kind of chaos which is awful – the moment before civilizations collapse, or when three members of your immediate family or friends are killed." But I do not believe that people who have experienced chaos are apt to praise or advocate any degree or variety of it. (1983, 12)

This seems absolutely right, and indeed applicable well beyond its direct context: those who have most tasted evil and chaos, or most closely approached to tasting it and have managed to escape, seem most immune to temptations to welcome it. There may be need for disturbance, but such disturbance is never good in itself; as Berry further says, "the reason we need to have our *false* certainties shaken is so that we may see the possibility of better orders than we have" (1983, 12). Evil in its purity appears here as what is *purely bad* – as that which is not good in *any* respect; while a leaven or alloy of good is often found with evil, it does not arise in any way *from* evil.

The second intuition, about goodness, was well formulated by C. S. Lewis:

> The very strength and facility of the pessimists' case at once poses us a problem. If the universe is so bad, or even half so bad, how on earth did human beings ever come to attribute it to the activity of a wise and good Creator? Men are fools, perhaps; but hardly so foolish as that. The direct inference from black to white, from evil flower to virtuous root, from senseless work to a workman infinitely wise, staggers belief. The spectacle of the universe as revealed by experience can never have been the ground of religion: it must always have been something in spite of which religion, acquired from a different source, was held. (1996, 13)

"In spite of which" – in this phrase we perceive something remarkable, namely, the fact of our stubbornness in insisting that the basic truth about the world is its goodness. But we should not be self-congratulatory about this stubbornness; it is not something we seem to will consciously to affirm – it is not, that is, most basically a form of moral courage, but rather a form of what we might call moral acknowledgment.[13] Paul Ricoeur calls this affirmative stubbornness "attestation," which he sees as the human's most fundamental mode of apprehending moral reality (1992, 21; see Anderson 1994). Ricoeur argues that such attestation is not purely positive merely in the content of its attestation, but also in its form, in the fact that it is always purely a *yes* to existence. It is in experiences of affirming justice and moral goodness in the face of evil that we meet attestation's fundamentally ethical face: "On the level of the ethical aim . . . solicitude, as the mutual exchange of self-esteems, is affirmative through and through. This affirmation, which can well be termed original, is the hidden soul of the prohibition. It is what, ultimately, arms our indignation, our rejection of *indignities* inflicted on others" (Ricoeur 1992, 221). Thus this stubbornness that attests to the fundamental goodness of the world operates through us, but is not something that has its origins "in" us, *qua* conscious intentional agents; rather, it points to a fundamental reality in the background of our existence, which we do not control, but can at best acknowledge.

From these two intuitions we can construct the following picture: humans naturally resist evil – they even, in part, resist their own evil, sinful deeds – and should do so, for evil is inherently evil; and in their very resistance they manifest some sense of goodness and justice, a sense

---

[13] See the discussion of the difference between "knowing" and "acknowledging" in Cavell 1976.

which seems a provisional witness of some basic goodness present in[14] the world. The Augustinian tradition seeks to articulate and render systematically coherent these two intuitions.

The fact that both of these claims are fundamentally practical insights is significant. Our reflection on evil does not begin from distanciated theoretical presuppositions, but by attending to and reflecting on our "pre-theoretical" responses to conflict, suffering, and evil. This is another way in which the Augustinian proposal entails a moral practice as well as a moral theory: understanding is placed in the service of action, and the final criterion of our account's adequacy must be how the account allows us to move forward in our lives.[15] Furthermore, while these insights are formally of the practical sort, an Augustinian account argues that they also share a common material root in love, our various loves and the stubbornness with which we hold them. If evil is formally a fundamentally practical problem, it is a problem best described materially as one of informing, ordering, and ultimately reconciling the various modes of love which always guide our actions.[16] By addressing it as a fundamentally *practical* problem, and by rooting it in love, the Augustinian tradition most basically offers not in essence a *theory*, but a *therapy*. It does not, that is, most fundamentally provide a heretofore absent answer to a persistent problem; rather, it takes up and develops (or refines) an already present, though more or less inchoate, response, helping more fully to reintegrate us as whole, loving beings. How it helps us do this is the subject of this book.

The polemical development of the Augustinian proposal

Augustine's account developed by a complex dialectic of inheritance, polemic, and confession. The inheritance aspect of this is often over-

[14] There is some trouble in understanding the sense of "present in" in this sentence. At least this sense of justice or rightness is in consciousness, but does this reflect some order or justice present in – or how is this consciousness otherwise related to – the "external" world? And to what is this world "external"? Are we not *in* it and so part *of* it?

[15] By saying this I do not mean to discount the cognitivity or referentiality of religious or moral claims; this is not an ontological point but an epistemological one: the kind of cognitivity and understanding manifest here is fundamentally practical. The language of theoretical versus practical is too bulky for their equally primordial presence here.

[16] Augustine had fixed on the rudiments of this love-centered account as early as the early 390s, before he became a bishop (see *DeMor.*, especially xv and xxv, on all the virtues as forms of love). But the contours of the account became ever more refined as he progressed through his career; eventually he came to understand how the practices in which we engage help us to move towards a certain form of gracious integrity and responsive wholeness by helping us to respond to God's call to loving relationship with the Trinity, through participating in the mystery of Christ, as manifest in the ecclesial practices and institutions that incarnate Christ's present presence on earth. See Burnaby 1938 and Rowan Williams 1990.

looked; but it is worth noting that Augustine did not, contrary to popular rumor, invent the doctrine of original sin: it had powerful precedents in the North African Christian thought he inherited, especially in Cyprian and Tertullian (see Harrison 2000, 89 n. 18). But he investigated it far more searchingly, and developed it far more thoroughly, than anyone before him had done. He had to do this because issues surrounding the challenge of evil were quite alive in his setting. Augustine faced a number of concerns about the felt reality of evil, the general feeling that malevolence has some sort of positive power in the world. Manicheanism, with its claim that materiality *itself* is evil, is only one extreme version of that anxiety; equally present in the cultural imagination of the day (and probably much more prevalent among the *rudes* who comprised the majority of Bishop Augustine's flock) were concerns that evil had more localized manifestations in the world (airy demons, or devils, or what have you) and operated, as it were, outside God's jurisdiction – theological highwaymen waiting in ambush to pounce upon the pilgrims traveling the route to the City of God.

In light of this, one can begin to appreciate some of the pastoral value of an account of evil which sees it as wholly privative and parasitic. Evil, on this account, cannot defeat God's will; recognition of this helps to quiet some of the anxieties about life that Augustine's parishioners surely felt, so the privation account works to subvert these popular anxieties by striking at their most common metaphysical and conceptual expression (see Brown 1995, 16–24; also Brown 1972). Against those who argue that evil is essentially outside us, that there are specific objects that are evil, Augustine insisted that no particular things are *in se* evil, but rather that it is our inordinate love of those things that is evil; thus we reassert human responsibility for tragic conflict. Against those who argue that evil is inside us but in a contingent way, and that the evil we do is a disease we can finally eliminate, or an error we can readily rectify (pick your metaphor), he affirmed that moral perfection is, as Reinhold Niebuhr put it, no "simple possibility" for us, because our wills – the only instruments we could use for our perfection – are themselves deeply corrupted by sin and actively enjoy sinning; thus we reassert the limits on our freedom in the face of such conflict. In sum, Augustine affirmed both the present reality of evil, and its ultimate futility and nothingness.

His essential complaint against all opponents is that each tries to depict the roots of the challenge of evil too simplistically, as either wholly other, entirely external to our "true" selves, or wholly ourselves, and so something that we fundamentally are. Sheerly "external" accounts may depict these roots in terms of evil – as a mass of deathly matter nearly smothering our essentially good and godly core, which remains an "oasis of purity"; or it may appear as mere "rust" on the surface of our real selves, which we can with some moral effort remove. In contrast, sheerly "internal" accounts may suggest that the human is simply trapped with an at least partially vicious nature, so must find a way of containing or at least accommodating that natural wickedness. Both cases suffer from essentially the same problem: neither account can comprehend how evil infects our very essence, dividing *us* at our core, making us its principle agents, but also, and thereby, crippling our own capacity to overcome it – all of this while still remaining, in itself, not a reality at all but radically external to existence and hence simply the malfunctioning of good beings. In one sense, then, neither account takes evil seriously enough, for they do not see how evil can be so crippling of our capacities to fight it; but in another sense they both take evil *too* seriously, for by investing evil with separable existence, they grant evil the compliment of being a genuine option in a way it is not.

Augustine tried to avoid the extremes of his opponents by arguing that evil is, in its essence (or in whatever it has that is close to an "essence"), in us, in the form of sin; but it is not primordially in us, it is there in a sort of secondary way, in some sense as a violation of our natural order and goodness, a sort of "second nature."[17] Hence Augustine affirmed sin's "naturalness," the presence of the roots of evil, tragedy, and moral conflict in our natures and our wills, and not just in our sporadic wicked choices (or intentions); but he also suggests that this "naturalness" is a *false* naturalness, parasitic upon a deeper, true, good, and loving nature. This is indicated in what is perhaps Augustine's most famous line, from the first chapter of the first book of his *Confessions*: "You have made us for yourself, and our hearts are restless till they rest in you." On this account, then, evil is really in us, in the sinful misdisposition of our will, articulated in our habits (both individual and social) and bad judgments; but it is in us as being a contraction, a destruction or corruption of ourselves, a self-harm we inflict on our natural integrity.[18]

Augustine, and those who followed him, summarized this account under the rubric of "original sin," and argue that evil is not an object able to be studied in itself or responded to directly, but must rather be

---

[17] See Rist 1995, 175–85, for a helpful discussion of Augustine's account of "second nature." In Augustine's late polemic with the Pelagians this is a dominant theme; but references to second nature as our carnal habituation also appear in Augustine's early writings; see *DeMus.* 6.19; *DLA* III.18.52.   [18] See James Gustafson's discussion of sin as "contraction" in 1981, 304–6.

understood in terms of what it destroys or corrupts. The tradition's aggressiveness is preemptive resistance; by attacking the conceptual premises which could undergird any claims about evil's primordiality, it seeks conceptually to defuse those interpretive temptations which might lead one to make such claims. In doing this, the tradition is not merely attempting to deflate evil, to trivialize it; it insists that, just because evil has no real power of its own, it is all the more dangerous. By denying evil any roots in the metaphysical framework, or as some demonic counter-deity, the tradition entails that evil's real roots lie in ourselves. The Augustinian tradition goes on the offensive against evil simultaneously conceptually, metaphysically, and psychologically: it takes our excuses away from us, one by one, until we see that the problem is *us*, and not some external reality that victimizes us.

A conceptual summary: privation and perversion

The Augustinian proposal derives from these intuitive beginnings a sophisticated conceptual framework centering around the Christian concept of sin, as our self-inflicted evil which also affects the rest of God's creation.[19] Augustine understood evil's challenge in terms of two distinct conceptual mechanisms, one ontological and the other anthropological. Ontologically he defines the concept of evil as simply the *privation* of being and goodness. Anthropologically he defines human wickedness in terms of original sin, and sin as fundamentally the *perversion* of the human's good nature – created in the *imago Dei* – into a distorted and false imitation of what it should be. *Privation* and *perversion*: together these summarize the Augustinian tradition's interpretation of the problem of evil, and delineate the conceptual contours within which the tradition proposes its practical response to it.

This conceptual framework arises from extended reflection on several different sources. One source is a series of (fairly uncontroversial) ontological commitments which seem to be implied by the Christian faith (themselves shaped by some broadly Platonic philosophical intuitions), commitments about the perfect goodness, omnipotence, and transcendence of God; another source is found in certain psychological convictions about the nature of the (ideal) rationality of action, a conviction that action is "rational" insofar as one can give explanations for it, and such explanations are satisfactory only insofar as they (at least ultimately)

---

[19] As Dalferth 1984, 178 notes, we must not oversimplify the conceptual richness of "sin." My talk here about sin as a "concept" need not entail that it has a single clear meaning.

connect to the way the world is. The tradition's final considered position arises out of its ongoing attempt to hold those commitments in some sort of reflective equilibrium (see Kamitsuka 1996). In this way, the proposed interpretation of evil is connected to both metaphysical and theological commitments as to the absolutely good nature of God, and psychological convictions about the character of what an impartial but morally aware observer would call "evil action" (see MacDonald 1999).[20]

Ontologically, the tradition affirms what we call a "monarchic" and "asymmetrical" ontology and axiology.[21] This metaphysical account derives from the commitment, typical to most orthodox Christian theologies, to the absolute sovereignty of God. Deriving these claims in large part from scriptural warrant (especially Genesis, Psalms, and the Johannine writings), Augustinians insist that God creates all things and sustains them in creation through the Divine's constant affirming will for creation, and that God's will is absolute. Thus the Augustinian proposal starts down a road which leads towards the account of divine providence for which it is most well known (for some, indeed, most notorious).

By giving God so absolute an authority over creation, the tradition can seem vulnerable to worries about the Divine's responsibility for evil.[22] But in fact Augustine's proposal defends itself against such worries by means of the concept of evil as privation. If evil is the *lack* of being, then God cannot have *willed* evil, because God's will is precisely what is not evil, and evil is precisely the lack of accordance with God's will. The idea that evil is simply a lack of being is in fact not a direct conclusion of an argument, but rather an indirect implication, a corollary of the broader argument investing God with perfect goodness and absolute sovereignty over creation, resulting in the identification of being with goodness.[23] Given that God is the absolutely sovereign creator of all things, and given that God is supremely good, love itself, and that God deems all creation to be good, it is a natural move to claim that every-

---

[20] The impartial observer in this hypothetical situation observes the action under the actor's description, or at least attends to that description in coming to her or his considered judgment.
[21] This very schematic account derives from recent work in philosophical theology, especially Morris 1987 and MacDonald 1991. (Suggestions of my strategy are found in Hebblethwaite 1989, 135, 142–3; and MacDonald 1999.) The roots of this in Augustine go very deep, and can be found in clear and succinct expression in one of his early anti-Manichean polemics, *DNB*, especially 1, 4, 12, 17, and 27-30. See Cress 1989 and Torchia 1999.
[22] Precisely what Augustine's own final response to these concerns was, and especially the nature and plausibility of his own late account of grace, remains debated. See Burns 1980 and Wetzel 1992a.
[23] See MacDonald 1991. The formulations of this in Augustine are innumerable; see, for example, *Conf.* VII.12.18; *DNB* 4, 6.

thing that is, insofar as it exists, is good. We can call this (following Scott MacDonald's proposal) the "universality thesis": all things, insofar as they exist, are good, and they exist insofar as they realize their natures in participation in God's beneficent plan for all creation (MacDonald 1991, 6–7).[24]

Because the Augustinian tradition affirms a monarchic (and hence asymmetrical) ontology and axiology, one that affirms that all creation is good, the tradition is led to conclude that evil is, strictly speaking, non-being, precisely because it is *privatio boni*, the privation of goodness. For the Augustinian tradition, all existence flows naturally from God, so that evil, rebellion against that creation, is simply the refusal of existence. As John Rist notes, this means that, beneath our distinction of "moral" versus "natural" evil, Augustine sees all evil as primarily *ontological*, an experience of lack, and therefore suffering, on the part of creation (see 1995, 262). This account has often been accused of being "merely meta-physical," and there are genuine concerns about its potential for being essentially escapist, concerns which I will lay out below (and against which I argue in chapter four). But there is a more superficial under-standing of this worry which is best dealt with here, namely, the worry that the *privatio* argument essentially seduces its adherents into denying that there is a problem of evil at all – that the account is essentially a theodicy in the sense discussed in chapter one. Whether or not this was the case when Augustine wrote *De libero arbitrio*, it was certainly not the case by the time he wrote *De civitate Dei*. As Donald Cress argues, Augustine's privationist account is not so much a theodicy as it is an attempt to prevent theodicy questions from arising in the first place (1989, 116). The argument is not about solving, and hence dissolving, the problem of evil, but rather about bringing into focus the real problem, the absurdity and inexplicability of evil's reality, in order better to face it, to have courage when one confronts evil.[25]

This ontological framework has considerable psychological support, through reflection on the inner structure of "bad choices" (a term which

---

[24] I realize that, in using the words "nature" and "participation," I am here running together two ideas that MacDonald distinguishes as differing accounts of the character of goodness (1991, 4–6). But no necessary distinction exists between them.

[25] MacDonald 1999 argues that there is no undue inexplicability here, but that the failure of atten-tion on which the primal sin relies is sufficiently intelligible to us, because inaction (which is the root of sin, glossed as "inattention") need not meet the same demands of explicability as action (131). But this is wrong insofar as the "inattentiveness" builds as it must upon the agent's willful ignorance of what God created to be obvious – namely, God's providential governance of crea-tion. We are left, *pace* MacDonald, with the reality of apparently absurd action.

includes both mistakes and malicious actions). By reflecting on such bad choices, we can, so to speak, "back into" an account of the privative negativity of evil. Here the privation thesis helps to explain the curious aphasia which arises from our failed attempts to understand an agent's rationale for bad actions. To understand this one must recognize a basic truth about our moral psychology: things in the world factor into our action explanations as "that for which" we do things, and our actions are normally elicited by our apprehension of some good which we seek to achieve (Anscombe 1963, 75–6). With evil action, however, this is not the case. Instead, when we seek to understand why we act maliciously, we find we cannot give an answer beyond our malice – we find we cannot hook our actions up to the world in any intelligible manner. (Recall Augustine's mystified analysis, in *Confessions* II, of the theft of pears from a neighbor's orchard.) Evil cannot be chosen for itself, for there is no "itself" there to be chosen. Evil action is a kind of action which fails, in an important way, to be action at all: it is ultimately folly – irrational, inexplicable, as much a causal hiccup as a willed, intentional act. Evil action so understood is, ontologically speaking, a refusal to act, not a failed attempt to respond in loving affirmation of God's creative will, but rather an attempt to deny it.[26] Thus evil action is not an act in the sense of "actualization" at all, but rather a nihilation, an ontological defection:

> One should not try to find an efficient cause for a wrong choice. It is not a matter of efficiency, but of deficiency; the evil will is not effective but defective. For to begin to have an evil will, is to defect from him who is the Supreme Existence, to something of less reality. To try to discover the causes of such defections – deficient, not efficient causes – is like trying to see darkness, or hear silence.[27]

The effect of such action, on the actor as well as that or those who are acted upon, is disastrously destructive, as "the evil of mutable spirits arises from the evil choice itself, and that evil diminishes and corrupts the goodness of nature. And this evil choice consists solely in falling away from God and deserting him, a defection whose cause is deficient, in the sense of being wanting – for there is no cause" (*DCD* XII.9, based on 1972 transla-

---

[26] This capacity for refusal, for a radical denial of relation, suggests the enormous power, for good and ill, which this account gives human free will.

[27] Augustine, *DCD* XII.7, based on 1972 translation, pp. 479–80. I have been much educated on this issue by Stanley Fish's discussion of Milton's manipulation, in *Paradise Lost*, of this (putatively universal) human phenomenon – of seeking a cause where none exists – to implicate the reader in original sin – or, rather, reveal the reader's prior implication in it. See Fish 1967, 256: "The Fall is no more an object of understanding than the prohibition it violates" (though I would contest the voluntarism implicit in the second half of this passage); and 259: "The reader who finds a cause for the Fall denies it by denying its freedom, and succumbs to still another form of Milton's 'good temptation.' "

tions, p. 481).[28] "Vice in the soul arises from its own doing; and the moral difficulty that ensues from vice is the penalty which it suffers. That is the sum total of evil" (*DVR* xx.39, based on 1953 translation, p. 243). Thus the ontological argument for the privationist account relies on an account of human action, both in the world, and before God. In the light of these broader commitments, and in the absence of a compelling explanation for evil actions, the tradition discerns a crucial clue for the ontological truth about evil, namely, that evil action is in itself not action at all.

But is it possible absolutely to refuse being? Could there be a creature which could purely and consistently will itself out of existence? Not for Augustine; "no creature's perversion is so contrary to nature as to destroy the very last vestiges of its nature" (*DCD* xix.12, based on 1972 translation, p. 869).[29] Humans surely cannot: we need something beyond ourselves (a rope, a gun, gravity and a flat surface far below us, a river) by which we can "kill ourselves." For Augustinians, this empirical fact about humans reflects a profound truth – that existing creatures have as part of their nature the will always to stay in existence. As Augustine says, "no one, when he commits suicide or attempts somehow to put himself to death, really feels that he will not exist after he is dead . . . The whole object of wanting to die is not non-existence but rest. So while a man erroneously believes that he will no longer exist, his nature longs to be at rest, that is, to have fuller being" (*DLA* iii.8.23, based on 1953 translation, pp. 184–5).[30] Revolt against existence – which is what sin most basically is – can never succeed; the human is always attempting, and failing, to escape the condition of our existence, so the revolt inevitably takes the form of flight. But where can one go where God is not? The flight is always simultaneously a flight from God and from oneself, from one's own recognition that that flight is impossible.[31]

---

[28] For a later restatement of this theme, see Anselm 1998. See also Ricoeur 1974, 371: "punishment is nothing more than sin itself . . . it is not what a punitive will makes someone undergo as the price of a rebel will . . . punishment for sin is sin itself as punishment, namely, the separation itself."   [29] For a modern restatement, see H. R. Niebuhr 1963, 114–15.

[30] It is not that suicides do not happen; the will to exist may be overmastered by another part of the self – best described *not* as the will not to exist, but as the will to escape one's present condition – without being wholly destroyed. (One might say that Augustinians believe that there are only two ways to be killed: by oneself, or by the hand of God.) For an Eastern Orthodox correlate to this, see Zizioulas 1975, 444–5, where he discusses the light this idea throws upon the claim that Hell is eternal torment: "personhood as demonic will be eternally 'tortured' by the very ontological fact that the choice of annihilation, of the rejection that is of the given world, will be unrealisable." I thank Aristotle Papanikolaou for calling my attention to this essay. Cf. Walls 1992 and Kvanvig 1993.

[31] See Picard 1951. See also *Conf.* viii.ix–xi. This is why "spatialized" depictions of sin, which present the self at a distance from God, can mislead; sin must be presented as a dynamic *attempt*

Not only can they never succeed, however; such attempts at revolt inevitably end up mimicking, in a parodic, perverted way, the proper purpose of the creature. Sin is an index of our creaturely power, a manifestation of our ability to act even against God's will for us. But it is as much a manifestation of our creatureliness as our power, because, in the monarchical ontological framework of the universe, our exercise of freedom against God's will is most fundamentally an attempt at resisting existence, an attempt whose failure manifests God's glory in creating us. Hence, instead of total revolt, we get partial parody, and the depraved perversion and "contraction" of the creature's true nature.

So the second anthropological (or psychological) step of the Augustinian tradition's argument is that the sinner is merely a perverted *imago Dei*, one who has chosen the wrong object of love. The argument about evil action's essentially privationist nature and effects is complemented by an argument that sinful acts are basically the freely willed perversion of an originally good nature. Evil action is thus not action done for simply "evil" ends, but is rather action which, while it tries to be wholly independent from God, ends up being a perverted parody of God; as Augustine says, "sin for man is a disorder and perversion: that is, an aversion from the most worthy Creator and a conversion toward the inferior things that He has created" (*QAS* 1.2.18, based on 1953 translation, p. 400).[32] In falling away, in sinning, evil is always most basically the choice of a lesser good over a greater one, "the perversion of a will that has turned away from the highest substance, you, God, toward the lowest things, forsaking its most inward parts and rushing after things that are outside it" (*Conf.* VII,16).

If sinful action can be materially described as the perversion of the soul's natural affections away from the ultimate good of God toward some lesser good, it can be formally described in terms of *idolatry*. Again, Augustine puts this well: he describes "the primal vice of the rational soul" as

the will to do what the highest and inmost truth forbids. Thus was man driven from paradise into the present world, i.e., from eternal things to temporal, from abundance to poverty, from strength to weakness. Not, however, from substantial good to substantial evil, for there is no substantial evil; but from eternal good

---

footnote 31 (*cont.*)

   at alienation. See O'Daly 1987, 2: "It is distinctive of Augustine's thought that he approaches psychological questions through an elucidation of man's perceptive and cognitive activities." See also Principe 1982 and Milbank 1997, 206–7.

[32] On the nature of human sinfulness as corruption and not intrinsic badness, and on the ennobling effects of this position, see H. R. Niebuhr 1996, 181.

to temporal good, from spiritual to carnal good, from intelligible to sensible good, from the highest to the lowest good. There is therefore a good which it is sin for the rational soul to love because it belongs to a lower order of being. The sin is evil, not the substance that is sinfully loved. (*DVR* xx.38, based on 1953 translation, pp. 242–3)

We see here what we saw earlier with the other, ontological aspect, namely, that the Augustinian account of wrong moral action entails some fairly heavy metaphysical, as well as anthropological, freight: specifically, it implies a picture of humans as essentially "hard-wired" towards the good, and of the world as essentially harmoniously ordered in the good which is God. The account thus insists on affirming both an intractable human nature within a normatively ordered moral universe, and a certain flexibility or elasticity to human character which permits humans to exercise their free will, in part to dissent from that order. Thus the perversion is "secondary" to the primal good nature. Again, the surface pessimism of this view entails a deeper hopefulness about human nature's essential goodness; as Neil Forsyth says, "Augustine's theory of sin was, paradoxically, the way in which he learned to understand [his] wholeness" (1987, 396).

But in what sense does sin become our second *nature*? While evil acts are in themselves the absence of action, and because they are also "enacted" wholly by us, it might seem that evil is in fact a fairly simple problem for us to solve: simply stop acting sinfully, and all will be well. But this appeal to simple action (or, rather, to *resisting* simple action, or temptation) founders at once, because it ignores the depth of our corruption by sin. Our perversion goes deeper than our explicit choices: it is not most basically that we produce sinful acts from a fundamentally good character, but rather, we ourselves are corrupted. We can see this to be so, and yet we remain powerless to do anything about it, for we are "held captive" by our wills.[33]

This, then, is the shape of the Augustinian tradition's interpretation of evil, on which it founds its manifold responses. It sees the challenge to be rooted in creatures' attempts at ontological annihilation, and in creatures' concomitant psychological (or essential) distortion. It sees this both in terms of evil-as-*privation* and sin-as-*perversion*. *Privation* and *perversion*: together these two terms capture, without significant remainder, the Augustinian tradition's interpretive response to evil.

---

[33] The classic description of this is found in *Conf.* viii. 9–12, where he describes the sinful will as divided, torn between two loves. Typically Augustine uses the language of "habit" to talk about this. See Prendville 1972.

Both facets of the Augustinian account elicit criticism, and both do so from two directions, from those more pessimistic, and from those more optimistic, than the account permits. Some focus their criticism on the tradition's anthropological depiction of original sin as our "second nature," particularly as original sin is depicted as the willful perversion of an originally wholly good human nature. On this issue, more optimistic thinkers suggest the account offers a far too rigid and cripplingly limited picture of human possibilities; other, more pessimistic thinkers suggest it reveals a delusionary denial of the reality of our essential implication in tragic conflict, suffering, and evil. Another set of criticisms are directed at the tradition's ontological depiction of evil as privation, particularly at the insistence that evil is "outside" the Divine's ordained plan for creation. On this issue, more optimistic thinkers suggest the account illegitimately forbids a certain set of experiences or events as "evil" and hence blinds its adherence to their potential fruitfulness; other, more pessimistic thinkers suggest that, by labeling some things as privatively evil, the account protects its merely "theoretical" dogmas from fundamental challenge by our experiences of evil and suffering – experiences which, such thinkers suggest, were they considered soberly, could compel us to re-evaluate our belief in God's comprehensible goodness. We will address these criticisms in turn.

Anthropological worries: is wickedness really perversion?

We will first talk about broadly "anthropological" worries surrounding the account of human fault as fundamentally describable as the condition of "original sin," which itself means the perversion of our fundamentally good natures and the creation of a practically inescapable "second nature" willfully perverted towards loving the wrong ends. Two different sorts of worries can be distinguished here. First, there are broadly optimist worries, worries that the concept of original sin is too restrictive on human freedom, and does not see how what it calls "perverted" human acts are not perverted at all, because there is no significant and rigid human nature to be perverted. On this account, humans are more mutable, more free, than our proposal will allow; the original sin account works to suppress the human's true creative freedom. Second, there are broadly pessimist worries, worries that the "perversion" account is flawed not because it affirms an oppressive and static

naturalism to human existence, but because it refuses to see that so-
called "wicked" actions are *equally* natural. On this account, humans are
less free than any Augustinian proposal can admit; the "perversion"
account is simply an attempt to hide from ourselves the chilling fact of
our own natural complexity and brutality.

It is a commonplace to say that the deep problem with Augustine's
whole theology lies in his understanding of original sin, and it has been
criticized for being most basically an excessively theoretical and aesthetic
formulation of the anthropological problem, one designed not essentially to aid in illuminating and guiding practical life, but rather to fit into
the conceptual prejudices which Augustine accepted from Platonism. As
James Wetzel suggests, the concept of original sin represents for many
"the traditional Christian evasion of tragedy," the attempt to justify all
suffering as punishment merited by our inherited fault – an account
Wetzel labels an example of "*ad hoc* cynicism" (1992b, 359). Others agree
with Wetzel on this, suggesting that the concept serves simply to silence
debate about suffering by saying that all suffering is simply deserved.
Most critics especially lambaste Augustine's attempt at explaining the
transmission of original sin via biological inheritance, arguing with
Philip Quinn that "moral guilt cannot be transmitted from one person
to another by biological or other kinds of causal mechanisms" (Quinn
1997, 544–5, 48). Some see even more cynical reasons behind
Augustine's account of original sin than simply an excessive concern
with theoretical fastidiousness; Elaine Pagels, for example, argues that
Augustine's account suppressed sexuality and worked fundamentally to
legitimate the political power of the ecclesiastical hierarchy, and that he
is not the "doctor of grace" so much as the author of sin.[34]

One common contemporary formulation of this worry can be quickly
dismissed. This worry fixates on the fact that it is *inherited* sin – that it is
somehow biologically at odds with what we know about human existence. But in fact this is simultaneously an anachronistic worry about
Augustine and conceptually incoherent today. It is anachronistic,

---

[34] See Pagels 1988, xix, 125–6. Augustine "argued for a view of nature utterly antithetical to
scientific naturalism," and persuaded "the majority of Christians that sexual desire and death
are essentially 'unnatural' experiences, the result of human sin" (1988, 130). See also Nussbaum
1990, 370; and 1994, 18–19, 460. (Given the importance of thick accounts of morality for
Nussbaum's work, it is noteworthy that she has not deigned to engage Christian formulations in
any responsible manner, but only caricatures them; see Jones 1992.) For more general formulations of such worries see Mahoney 1987, 44–48, 58–68 and; Delumeau 1990, 191. Helpful general
responses to such works, which bring out the anachronism saturating their indictments of
Augustine as responsible for all later sexual repression, are Markus 1990, Russell 1990,
Lamberigts 2000, and Lawless 2000.

because it imposes upon Augustine a concept of "biological nature" absent of value, a concept of nature which he did not (and indeed could not) hold, because it builds on the "fact/value" dualism marking modern scientism. It is conceptually incoherent today, because the best contemporary accounts of human beings do not hold to this shibboleth either; the best work in biology and psychology underscore the deep implication of our "personalities" in the physical facts about us.

But the deeper root of the criticisms remains, in the critics' common aversion to the proposal's attempt to affirm both nature and freedom as primordial to human existence. This is fundamentally, as the critics say, a *moral* concern, a concern about the character of moral responsibility. The Augustinian account insists that humans are accountable *for* themselves, *to* something outside themselves. As Pagels puts it, Augustine's account satisfies our "peculiar preference for guilt," which allows us "the illusion of control over nature" (1988, 147). It is this rather promiscuous (and paralyzing) distribution of responsibility against which the critics rail.

All of them, furthermore, derive from that most profound critic of modern thought, Friedrich Nietzsche. No matter how many epithets the Augustinian (and like-minded) accounts collect – labels such as "moralism," "dualism," scientistic inhumanism, or whatever – these critiques are variants or developments of Nietzsche's famous charge of "slave-morality." Nietzsche's account of the philosophical and cultural importance of tragedy, and what passes under the name of "evil", and his development of that account into something like a general critique of existing ethics, is the most profound and fruitful investigation of that phenomenon yet available. His basic insight is that the challenge of tragic conflict and suffering is far more basic than modernity had acknowledged. It suggested to him that the self-understanding of humans in modernity was wildly incompatible with the possibilities opening up for human existence, and that our self-understanding had been imposed on us by a twisted minority of "ascetic priests" (of whom Augustine was perhaps the greatest) who thought of nature as something we should rise above, and of our animal passions as opportunities for repression. Nietzsche thought that we inherited a largely juridical moral language – a language of judgment – which is disconnected from the real wellsprings of our being. He worried both that we needed to free ourselves of this picture of agency and responsibility – we needed to get "beyond good and evil" by uncovering their origins through a genealogy of morals – and that, in so doing, we would come to see that human nature was both more and less important for our lives than we had thought it was.[35]

Later thinkers developed this last "more and less important" in two different directions, leading to two distinct critiques of proposals such as the Augustinian tradition, critiques which are usefully categorizable as either "optimist" or "pessimist" readings. An optimist reading of Nietzsche emphasizes his quasi-voluntarist insistence on the importance of human freedom for self-creation, suggesting that there are no moral norms of natural significance, and what appear as immutable laws of human nature are really contingent historical accidents, accidents which have their day and then pass away. The key is to continually create new ways of manifesting our freedom and creativity; our only task is to keep things interesting for ourselves. A pessimist reading emphasizes Nietzsche's reductively naturalist "monadology of the Will to Power," insists on the plurality of (and conflict among) drives motivating our activity, and suggests that we have simply been illegitimately ignoring a good many of them. On this account, our present appreciation of the import of nature for morality is far more partial and one-sided than we recognize, and we are alienated from some important wellsprings of our existence.[36] These two developments of Nietzsche's critique represent two distinct anthropological worries about the Augustinian proposal here espoused. The first critiques the Augustinian proposal for fixing as "immutable" what is in fact sheerly contingent. Such optimists understand evil and tragic conflict as simply contingent realities, perplexities which can be overcome by changing the terms of the debate; they concomitantly see humans as plastic enough to change decisively for the good. The second critiques the Augustinian proposal for being unwilling

---

[35] See Nietzsche 1967, 116–18 on "ascetic priests," and 1966, 64, 112 on Augustine as such a priest. Note also the letter to Franz Overbeck of March 31, 1885, in which Nietzsche suggests that Augustine offered a vulgarized "Platonism for the masses" (Nietzsche 1982, 34–5). For interesting accounts of Nietzsche's psychology, see Parkes 1994, Roberts 1996, and Pippin 1997, 351–71. For a contemporary Nietzschean argument against Christian commitment, see B. Williams 1993b; for a Christian riposte, see Jackson 1993.

[36] In attempting to distinguish distinct forms of the Nietzschean critique, I do not want to suggest that they take only one side of Nietzsche's broader picture, but rather that they take one facet as central and others as subsidiary to it. Thus the optimist can acknowledge the role of the drives in the Nietzschean account, and the pessimist can accept the place of creativity in Nietzsche's ethics. This is in large part due to the fecund confusion of Nietzsche's own work. The worries that these two formulations express are, when fully formulated, quite distinct and apparently incompatible, so on both accounts the import and power of these alternate strands is muted somewhat, in order to be placed within the larger framework of the optimist's "creative anti-realism" or the pessimist's "realistic naturalism." Here I am employing Alvin Plantinga's schematization of the alternatives to an Augustinian Christian philosophy. Again, see A. Plantinga 1992.

to admit the natural necessity of tragic conflict between human ideals and the world's realities. Such pessimists think that our experiences of tragic conflict and evil reveal the limits of human control; they demand the modification of human hopes and, in turn, the shape of human moral life. We will discuss the optimist concerns first.

Optimist concerns

Is this Augustinian proposal's account of human nature too stiff, too unyielding as an account of our lives? Are tragic events telling us something about our natures or something about our contingent intellectual confusions? Are they really *perversions* of our natural goodness? Indeed, have we any "nature," in a philosophically interesting sense, at all? Such worries about an Augustinian anthropology may be framed in a number of ways, and may be attached to a variety of positive proposals, all of which suggest that "evil" is contingent upon some particular self-understanding, and hence a challenge we can surmount by altering that self-understanding. At its most extreme, this position rejects the traditional (both philosophical and popular) image of the human as possessed of a relatively fixed "nature," in favor of a picture of the human as more or less wholly contingent, and hence thoroughly transformable. The idea of an immutable human nature, and the framework of inflexible moral rules inevitably (or so the critics charge) attendant upon it, work to "asphyxiate" human ingenuity; we should change our understanding of humans to give us greater freedom in replying to the challenges we face (Connolly 1993, 68–9). If the Augustinian proposal suggests that our nature is "hard-wired" in such a way that it resists our attempts at total overhaul, so much the worse for the Augustinian proposal: just do it.

An adequate defense of the Augustinian tradition against these concerns must wait for the next chapter, which will detail the practical implications of its account of sin as developed by Reinhold Niebuhr. But even without that we can note some problems with this proposal as a positive alternative. Most significantly, it leads ineluctably towards voluntarism, a voluntarism of rather extreme "self-refashioning" which sees the human character as plastic. A good example of this, and an inspiration of many such optimist proposals made today, is Emerson. For him, the key is not remaining trapped by any fixed public persona, but always keeping one's private self secure from capture by one's office. This "Emersonian individualism" moves towards transforming the entirety of the world into an arena for the continual remaking of the self. It is both

unwarranted and unhelpful to say that experiences of tragic incommensurability are in any way revelatory of "the way the world really is;"
human beings can jettison those accounts which give the appearance of
the possibility of incommensurability, "reinterpreting" themselves – by
their bootstraps, presumably – out of all vulnerability to such dangers.

This remaking is often premised upon a deep and abiding division
between public and private. Some versions of this (such as Richard
Rorty's), impressed with naturalistic accounts of human existence, move
towards framing such refashioning in a language of naturalist causation
which renders the whole program "ironic" (though what this means is
never clear); others (such as Stanley Cavell) hold onto a traditional view
of agency. In either case, however, there is an absolute division between
the self and the outside world, the public and the private. Optimists must
impose on the *cognoscenti* a sort of consensual schizophrenia, a schizophrenia which affirms the "quarantine" of the private, "real" self from
the public. This elitist conceit is tempted towards a post-modern gnosticism. Charles Guignon puts it well: this proposal depicts "a culture split
into two groups: the suckers who keep trying, and an elite band of his-
toricist intellectuals, hooting and jeering from the sidelines, who see it all
as a transient game" (1991, 95; see Herdt 1992). To avoid suffering and
evil, all we must do is simply reject overidentification with anything in
the world, and we can do this merely by *becoming ironic* about things – do
not take yourself seriously, do not believe in the things you say, do not
think you are anything but an organism responding to stimuli with noises
as well as raw physical actions.[37] Hence the problem is that the account
cannot formulate resistance to the will to change as anything other than
a hindrance, and so face the problem of what to do about existence in a
world. In Augustinian terms, they ignore the reality of the self's loves in
favor of an excessive (and subjectivist) emphasis on the self's freedom.
This is revealed when one asks how they can be *committed* to anything
outside themselves.

The optimist worries about the Augustinian tradition are genuine
concerns, but those who formulate them must be careful that they
address the full complexity of the problem and not simply dismiss one
side in favor of the other. The optimists' failure to do this and the consequent problems with their positive proposals leave open the possibility
that humans *do* in fact have a nature which *is* in fact philosophically

---

[37] Note the connection with Alvin Plantinga's argument about the implausibility of a truth-
directed epistemology in an evolutionary schema (1993, 216–37).

significant, not least in resisting the human's will to change. We are, as optimists recognize, able to change ourselves, to re-imagine our lives in important new ways; but that must be coupled with the awareness that we suffer a strange inertia in that changing (see Rahner 1961, 347–82). Optimists err in ignoring that inertia; but their challenge to the Augustinian proposal remains profound: can Augustinians do full justice to the human's capacity to change?

Pessimist concerns

The Augustinian proposal is targeted not only by more optimistic anthropological critiques, but also by more pessimistic ones. Against the optimists, such criticisms accept the proposal's belief that suffering and evil are not simply eliminable by some self-willed reconstruction; but they dispute the Augustinian account by suggesting that those aspects of our agency which engender wickedness and make us vulnerable to tragic conflict are, in fact, as basic to our natural constitution as are the "good" aspects of our character. The reality of suffering and tragic conflict, realities which optimists think are finally contingent, are, for this pessimist vision, crucial (and often ignored) clues to the real character of human existence. As William Connolly says, not to acknowledge them is to indulge in wishful thinking: "To treat an evil human will to be the source of an otherwise unnecessary rift in being, and to plead for redemption from the effects of this primordial fault for which you are primordially at fault, is to express resentment against the human condition" (1993, 119).[38] The original-sin/perversion account is wrong, pessimists suggest, not because it is too stiff-necked, but because it is too weak-kneed, not because it denies that we can transcend our problems, but because it fantasizes that our "true" selves – or some ultimate yet interior template of what our true selves will turn out to be – are wholly, naturally, pure and good, whereas in fact our tendencies towards wickedness are no more alien to our character than our tendencies towards kindness. The language of "nature" is acceptable, but there is simply no useful distinction to be made between our "first" and "second" natures, and our characters' implication in tragic conflict must be accorded the respect (though not the endorsement) which we give to the rest of our "nature." Such pessimists reject not only Augustine but the grand tradition of philosophical ethics as a whole. As Bernard Williams suggests, "Plato, Aristotle, Kant, Hegel, are all on the same side, all believing . . . that the

---

[38] For a response to Connolly, see Dodaro 2000.

universe or history or the structure of human reason can . . . yield a pattern that makes sense of human life and human aspirations" (1993a, 163). We have constructed our anthropology around the fantasy that we are God-like; as Williams says, "atheists say that in forming ideas of divine judgment we have taken human notions of justice and projected them onto a mythical figure. But also, and worse, we have allowed the image of a mythical figure to shape our understanding of human justice" (1993c, 254). For pessimists, this faith is woefully unrealistic; to exorcise such false and insidious beliefs, we must revise our understanding of human nature in order to "de-deify" it.

The challenge is not most fundamentally to the presumptive goodness ascribed by the theological and philosophical traditions to human agency, but rather to the idea of agency or character as an autonomous sphere of purely agential control itself. Central to this alternative vision is a vision of the self as having at best a ramshackle coherence, both within itself and with the world. We are not, as the "morality" tradition argues, "pure" agents, isolated engines of autonomous will, moral selves who are without ethical character in any relevant sense and fundamentally uninfluenced by the world; rather, we are "impure" agents, beings whose reality is not fully under our control (Walker 1993). For Williams, human agency is like "a web," some of whose connections connect our agency with non-agential realities. "Responsible agency . . . is not a superficial concept, but . . . it cannot ultimately be purified" of such non-agential connections; "[i]f one attaches importance to the sense of what one is in terms of what one has done and what in the world one is responsible for, one must accept much that makes its claim on that sense solely in virtue of its being actual" (B. Williams 1981, 29–30). These pessimists think we need to jettison the Augustinian tradition's insistence that human wickedness is a perversion of our wholly good natures. On the contrary, the idea of "natures" must be significantly expanded.

Given this picture, pessimists suggest a rather bleak response to evil; if it is due to the incommensurability and plurality of genuine human goods, and the ineradicability and indeed equiprimordial "naturalness" of conflictual (even destructive) human drives, we should recast our ethical conceptions so as to handle these facts. For them, one can, in the end, only report – tell the facts of suffering and of horror – and thereby acknowledge that even our own actions, intended though they may be to avoid just such a fate, can lead us into the crucible of the tragic. There is nothing more to tell than this report, and in particular there is no *moral* to be drawn from it, nothing edifying in the manner that thinkers such as Plato or Kant (or even Rorty) wish there to be. Indeed the point of our reporting the tragic facts is precisely to demonstrate that the fact that there can be no moral drawn from the story just *is* the story's only moral – that all moralizing about such events is deeply flawed. There is no consolation of any sort for extreme suffering and destitution – no consolation which does not, by being offered, turn at once into a mawkish sentimentality, or "monkish" world-hating which serves only to obscure what in the instant of suffering is blindingly – because bewilderingly – because terrifyingly – clear.[39]

But if there is nothing more to say about individual action in the face of evil, might there be something to say about political or social action? The problem of "dirty hands" cannot be resolved, nor the fact that we must accept the necessity (and perhaps, indeed, the routinization) of brutality and violence. We are morally justified in wanting politicians whose character allows them to ignore genuine moral claims which arise in political activity (see B. Williams 1981, 60–70). This is not to license Thrasymachian wickedness, nor pseudo-Hobbesian social Darwinism. It simply acknowledges that human beings' corruption, and the world's bewildering complexity and tragic vexations of our plans, can at times *necessitate* the use of violence and brutality, and legitimate our transgression of morality's presumed borders for the sake of securing some relative justice.

This is a powerful and not entirely unattractive view. But it entails that we become players in tragic brutality, and implicate ourselves in brutalizations, in order to attempt to limit, and hopefully (though only partially) control, tragic events. We resist total tragedy, that is, by becoming tragic ourselves. But is this vision absolutely incommensurate with an Augustinian emphasis on the brokenness of our moral agency? – not really, as we will see in chapter five. But what constructive proposal is offered by this alternative? While, as Dr. Johnson said, he who makes a beast of himself gets rid of the pain of being a man, one wonders whether the sort of brutalizing pessimists propose, *à propos* the reality of evil, has really adequately acknowledged the capacities of humans for self-transcendence, or whether such pessimists have simply denied their reality and labeled them too quickly as fantasy. Perhaps the pessimists, that is, are not realistic enough: whereas the vice of the optimists is to create too distant a view of human nature as regards the world, perhaps the pessimists offer too accepting a view of the world as it stands, an essentially submissive view of the world (see Mendus 1996, 199–200).

---

[39] On "monkish" virtues, see Hume 1975, 270; and Baier 1994.

We need not pursue such thoughts here. All we need to do is note that both of these optimistic and pessimistic concerns exploit a truth that the Augustinian tradition also exploits, namely the fact of the potential incommensurability of human projects with the world and themselves. The Augustinian tradition's response to evil attempts to accommodate the possibility of genuine though proximate conflict and incommensurability, while holding out the hope for some ultimate commensurability of agents with themselves, one another, the world, and God. Its depiction of sin as perversion is partly meant to capture just this vision of our situation. We are natural beings, and we are made for this world; but at the same time we have revolted against our nature and have so violated it that we can no longer be considered as living wholly as we were intended to. We are able to do this because we are in significant ways free beings, able to transcend our local situation and able to violate our proper purposes and mode of existence. The exercise of freedom is not itself some sort of violation of our nature, for part of our nature just *is* to be free beings in loving relationship to one another; we are the children not of Prometheus but of Eve and Adam (see Ricoeur 1966 and McDowell 1994). But nonetheless our freedom does operate in our lives as a window open to sin, violating our nature at the same time as it employs it; and because it does, the Augustinian tradition finds the best description of this state to be perversion. In contrast, as we have seen, optimists and pessimists criticize this position as flawed and unstable.

However, we have also seen that the optimists' putative "naturalism" is not really a naturalism at all, but an indulged-in temptation to naive voluntarism, with no genuine concept of "nature" to which humans are confined. And we have also seen that the pessimists' "realism" is not fully realistic, but instead an indulged-in temptation to brutalizing despair. In sum, then, it seems that we must acknowledge both optimist and pessimist concerns as genuine concerns, while also keeping in mind their positive character as *temptations*, temptations we should resist. In this resistance we are attempting to affirm both that humans are free enough to become incommensurate with their nature, and that we are genuinely natural in such a way that that incommensurability is always felt as a violation of some more primordial harmony of life with life, a "perversion" of our true nature. Here, the question remains – and we must keep it in mind – whether our proposal can do any better at comprehending and responding to evil than these other proposals.

Ontological worries: is evil really privation?

The broadly anthropological worries discussed in the last section are complemented by a set of ontological worries, worries about the place and status of evil in the Augustinian proposal's ontology. In brief, these are worries about the adequacy of the proposal's depiction of evil as essentially privative. Here also, there are optimistic and pessimistic challenges. The optimist worries that the proposal's ontological exclusion of evil is simply too hasty, and limits God's omnipotence; on this account, evil is really just another, albeit more obscure, aspect of goodness, and both good and evil alike work for the providential purposes of God. On the other hand, the pessimist worries that the ontological exclusion of evil simply does not work – that the idea that evil is simply *privatio boni* cannot be sustained, and that the reality of evil returns to haunt us in ways that *no* ontology can accommodate – and thus signals a sort of absolute limit on humans' comprehension. Both of these worries are versions of a resistance to the claim that evil is quite literally *not good* – the first suggests that evil is in fact part of the good, while the second suggests that evil always escapes placement as sheer absence.[40]

These concerns begin from recognition that there are limits to the amount of work that sheer thinking can do to help to resolve the problems with which evil confronts us. In his study, *Tragic Method and Tragic Theology*, Larry Bouchard summarizes the three "fundamental limits to thinking about evil" disclosed in reflection on tragic experience. First, evil is "always already" there: in reflection on our experience, we discover the persistence of evil, no matter how far "back" we go. Second, evil is profoundly internal to human experience – we are ourselves torn, as manifest in experiences of defilement, sin, and guilt, and the struggles between good and evil which take place in our own souls. Third, evil is ultimately irreducible to any other, or prior, reality: neither finitude nor natural necessity nor any other reality is the sufficient cause of evil. Evil is, in some sense, *sui generis* (Bouchard 1988, 222). There are two ways in which to take this last summary claim. First, one can assume a substantiality to evil, and give evil an ontological primordiality. Second, one can assume a non-reality to evil – indeed identify evil with non-reality, with the absence of existence. Recent theological reflections on tragedy, sin, and evil typically wish to avoid choosing between these two options; while acknowledging

---

[40] See Simon 1989, 138: "Random events which create disorder belong also to the eternal order," while Augustine's "curious form of positive optimism in *The City of God*" (56) "accords ill with the experience of individuals and nations" (79).

that their accounts have ontological implications, they remain in the realm of thought, of human reflection about evil. However, those recent accounts of evil that do make claims on this ontological level overwhelmingly affirm the first sense of this claim (e.g., E. Farley 1990, W. Farley 1990, Sands 1994, Suchocki 1994, and [from an entirely different perspective] Graham 2001). For them, evil simply *is* – it is a natural part of the world as it has always existed. Such thinkers typically take Augustine's account to exemplify all flawed attempts to deny the persistence of evil, through the use of a theoretical theodicy. Augustine's account, they say, essentially denies the reality of evil – it is a denial carried through only by reasoning captivated within a dubious theological ideology. Such critics charge that Augustinian theory renders evil invisible, and Augustinians insensible to the tragic realities of injustice and suffering.

Unlike the anthropological worries' common anchor in Nietzsche, there is no central figure behind these ontological anxieties. This suggests the commonness of such worries across different historical, ecclesiological, theological, and philosophical contexts.[41] Indeed one may with some justice see these concerns first formulated as concerns in relation to Augustine's own work – in the Pelagian controversies of Augustine's own time, when certain followers of Pelagius, notably Julian of Eclanum, accused Augustine of returning to a Manichean affirmation of the primordial reality of evil.[42] In so doing, Julian pointed to just those tensions in the Augustinian position which generate the theo-ontological worries discussed in what follows. How can evil's metaphysical non-existence, its "presence" as pure absence, warrant the (what Julian saw as) extreme pessimism of Augustine's doctrine of grace? How, in short, can one affirm evil as a mere privation of God's good order and still affirm evil as so prevalent, and so profound?

This question can be taken in two directions. Here we actually have exemplary representatives of these positions whose accounts we can employ. The optimist, represented here by John Hick, answers that evil's prevalence can be accounted for by placing it within the providential will of God, thus making evil work wholly for the good. The pessimist, represented here by Paul Ricoeur, answers our question by suggesting that

---

[41] Irenaeus and Schleiermacher stand here as exemplary ancestors; see Robert R. Williams 1984, Wyman 1994. Of course Schleiermacher is in many ways very much an Augustinian; see Schleiermacher 1928, §68 on the consciousness of sin as a "derangement" of our originally good nature, though this is coupled with his claim that our consciousness of sin is a consciousness of its reality both within and without or beyond us.

[42] See Augustine's discussion of Julian of Eclanum in his *OpImp*. iii.67, 136–7, and i.97 for his denial that he holds Manichean beliefs.

evil's reality is inexpungeable from our understanding, so we should accept evil as basic to our world. I begin first with the optimistic worries.[43]

Optimist concerns

John Hick's book *Evil and the God of Love* well represents this optimist position. He explicitly contrasts his ("Irenaean") position with an "Augustinian" one, and thereby identifies some of the main concerns quite sharply. In brief, his main claim is that "a Christian theodicy must be centred upon moral personality rather than upon nature as a whole, and its governing principle must be ethical rather than aesthetic" (Hick 1978, 198).[44] His whole argument is implied in that passage; to understand it, we must first see why he calls the Augustinian position "aesthetic" and focused on "nature as a whole," and then, second, investigate the sense of his contrasting "ethical" approach, focused on "moral personality." His real concern here is not fundamentally about human freedom, but about the providence of God – whether evil is, speaking in strict metaphysical terms, an accident, or whether it is not, in the end, a necessary aspect of God's providential order.

Hick's fundamental criticism of the Augustinian proposal is that it depicts original sin, and hence evil, as existing outside God's plan; Hick argues that this entails a flawed conception of freedom, one which makes freedom indistinguishable from randomness. This is essentially a metaphysical critique, an attack on the intelligibility of the Augustinian claim that humans are finally responsible for the "self-creation of evil *ex nihilo*" (66). The basic problem lies in the Augustinian picture of the original perfection of creation and the concomitant belief that the Fall is against God's will and plan. Hick's challenge here is that this picture offers "no alleviation of the dark mystery of evil" (173–4), but offers instead the "wanton paradox" of a picture of (finitely) perfect agents in a perfect environment "falling" out of that perfection into sin.[45] In brief, the Augustinian free-will account of original sin makes evil "either impossible, or else so very possible as to be excusable" (280). For the Augustinian position, Hick argues, the burden for the origin of evil must be shifted from the shoulders of humans to the will of God; that is, that evil serves the purposes of God. For Hick, "there must have been some moral flaw in the creature or in his situation to set up the tension of

[43] For a different account of Ricoeur and Hick on evil, one which emphasizes their similarities, see Anderson 1992.   [44] All references in the next two paragraphs are to this text.
[45] Hick likes this phrase so much he uses it (at least) twice (174, 251).

temptation" (250), and if this is the case then evil is, in effect, destined to happen, and evil is part of the will of God. Hick's position – that evil is the will of God – has two aspects: first, that evil is a necessary element in our maturation, and second, that it is finally converted into goodness by the grace of God. In other words, Hick makes sin necessary and Hell impossible.

Hick's position is not without its problems, however.[46] Two in particular stand out. First, he claims that his position better accounts for the reality of evil within a Christian framework than other positions – notably the Augustinian tradition – and yet it admits that its claim is still largely a promissory note. While his analysis rests on the claim that evil is entirely for our own good, he admits the present obscurity of the justice of suffering and pain, and appeals to mystery and to the necessity of faith, especially faith in the redemptive moment of the eschaton. But it is hard to see any relevant difference between this appeal to mystery and faith, and similar appeals within the Augustinian tradition. Indeed, Augustinians might be in a better position, as they attribute only one mystery to God – namely, God's will to create beings of the sort who *could* fall – while they insist that wickedness is due entirely to contingent human activity; in contrast, Hick's position commits him to a rather more extravagant claim, namely, that *every* instance of evil shall, in the end, be shown to have been for the best. Secondly, Hick must face the thorny question of the coherence of finite human freedom and divine determinism, and yet he seems to want to have it both ways. Humans are free enough to reject God in sin – naturally, even necessarily to do so – but that freedom will in the end be overwhelmed by God's grace. But this overwhelming seems retrospectively to undo all human freedom, to make humans not free at all. Indeed, it is still a question as to whether, if they "inevitably" sinned, they were significantly free even in the beginning. In brief, in extending creation over history – to include the maturation in history of humans as created – Hick suggests that God's action requires time to work itself out. But why must this be so? Further, if humans had to be independent enough to reject God once, why so certain they will return to God at the end? And if they must enter into love of God in the end, why must they be independent in the beginning? Furthermore, Hick is committed to the idea that there *are* in fact limits on God's omnipotence, limits on what God can do, or at least on how God can do it; most centrally, God gives us this limited "finite" freedom

---

[46] See Stump 1985, especially 396–7, for a solid summary and critique of Hick's proposal.

precisely because without it we can never freely come to love God. But if this is the case, then it seems no less formally plausible that God created humans *radically* free from the start – that is, in perfect love with God, but able to *break* that love – as a condition of *genuine* (i.e., truly free) love. (For what sort of love *necessarily* manifests itself in the end?[47]) Hick's basic argument is to claim greater honesty: it is better to conceive of God as *directly* responsible for evil, than to insinuate, as the Augustinian proposal does, that God is either *limited* or in part *malicious*. But Augustinians can claim that Hick's account has serious liabilities in itself, especially with its added mysteries, and that the Augustinian proposal has more to commend it than Hick allows.

Pessimist concerns

The optimists' fundamental worry about Augustinian proposals is that they fail as theodicies, as attempts to explain evil; by claiming that evil is not part of the will of God, Augustinian accounts obscure God's loving providential control over all aspects of existence. There is, however, another, more pessimistic set of worries elicited by Augustinian proposals, worries that such proposals are flawed, not because they *fail* as theodicies, but rather because they are *too much* theodicies – too much attempts to gain theoretical mastery over the reality of evil in a sheerly intellectual manner. For such concerns, evil is so profoundly, troublingly vexing that it inevitably frustrates our intellectual attempts at control. For such pessimists, the problem with our Augustinian account of evil-as-privation is not that it offers too pessimistic an account of the place of evil and suffering in a world governed by God, as optimists like Hick claim, but rather that it offers too *optimistic* an account, one which errs in thinking it can expel evil from the world, one which fails to see how the challenge of evil invariably returns to haunt it. Such pessimists claim that evil opens a perpetual fissure in all thought; evil's character as this aporia must not only be theoretically acknowledged but practically accommodated, by seeing it as implying claims about the right way to live. These "pessimist" worries are brilliantly articulated in the work of Paul Ricoeur.

Ricoeur's basic argument is that evil and tragic conflict resist complete capture and domestication in any theoretical framework, and that it is the task of thought repeatedly to rediscover and express this

---

[47] Hick seems to assume an essential symmetry between divine and human love. But this need not be so; see McCullogh 1992.

truth (1974, 285).[48] In the case of theodicy the truth is glimpsed in the vexation of the very attempt to think consistently about evil; that is, it is not only the fact of unjust suffering in the world which vexes thought, but thought's own contradictory testimony about such suffering. The evil with which thought grapples is revealed to be there before the thought itself; in fact, phenomenologically speaking, evil is "always already" there, before we act, and it seems to have a quasi-existence as a power in itself (1974, 283–4).[49] We of course never experience this evil outside its manifestations, as some sort of autonomous Satanic power, so we cannot speak of it apart from ourselves; but it seems to have such an independence. Augustinian accounts of evil as privation fail because they too simplistically deny the phenomenologically real, if theoretically mute, witness of evil as a force which exists outside us in the world.

What, then, are we to do? Thought's failure to comprehend evil calls neither for more rigorous attempts at theodicy nor for sheer passivity and resignation in the face of such evil; rather, our resistance to evil continues – for such resistance is an integral aspect of our being – but shifts from resistance in theory to resistance in practice. We must resist the great miasmic temptation of thought, for thought may not only distract us from action, but may also become evil itself; in the face of suffering it may seduce us into resignation, complacency, or even participation, seeing such sufferings as somehow "merited." We resist it by seeking to reduce suffering. This does not directly meet evil's challenge to thought, but rather redirects our attention: "The response, not the solution, of action is to act against evil. Our vision is thus turned toward the future, by the idea of a *task* to be accomplished," in lieu of thought's recurring fascination with the origin of evil in the past (1985, 645). But Ricoeur recognizes that deeds alone are insufficient; our encounter with evil and suffering requires not simply discrete disparate acts, but some fundamental dispositional change; here we undertake the slow *conversio* from self-centered thought and action to the renunciation of such self-centeredness. We must come to this renunciation (which Ricoeur infelicitously calls a "renouncement") by passing through stages of unknowing, complaint, belief "in spite of," and a (provisionally) final acknowledgment of the value of suffering as in

---

[48] Ricoeur thinks that evil limits all systems of thought, and he critiques Augustine's thought, insofar as he critiques it, *qua* theodicy; see 1985, 635.

[49] See 1985, 636, where Ricoeur speaks of the "strange experience of passivity," of "having been seduced by overwhelming powers."

some sense divinized, because undergone by Christ on the Cross.[50] This leads towards a form of self-understanding for which our lamentations are transformed, or rather left behind, as we come "to love God for nought" and thus "to escape completely the cycle of retribution to which the lamentation still remains captive" (1985, 647). While such renunciation and understanding of suffering is reserved for only a few, it can serve as something of an ideal goal for our response to the mystery of evil, inseparably connected, as it is, to the mysteries of the history of salvation.

Ricoeur's proposed turn to *praxis* moves in the right direction. We must find a way to affirm both our realization of the disparity, perhaps even incommensurability, between our experience of inexplicable suffering and tragic conflict in the world, and our tradition's insistence (and indeed the attestation of our lives) that God is supremely good and supremely powerful; a necessary and fundamental step will be to pry apart our presumption of God's comprehensibility and our faith in God's justice and love, and to affirm the latter but not the former. However, there are difficulties with the details of the practical response Ricoeur proposes. He does not explain how to distinguish his "renunciation" from *resignation*, and, at its most extreme, from nihilism. If we love God for nought, what are we doing? Does not that aim gain plausibility only by covertly importing an illicit value in the term "God" itself? It seems plausible for someone to respond to Ricoeur by arguing that his position does not explain why the proposed relationship of faith "in spite of," on the far side of lamentation, remains a relationship with anything we can recognize as a personal, loving God. The environmental philosopher Jim Cheney suggests this:

> Why, exactly, is all this packaged and labeled *God?* Look for the moment at the baggage that is still carried by this word . . . God is still a transcendent creator God . . . The fundamental personal relationship for Job is with a transcendent creator (or architect) God stripped of his goodness and justice but not of his power and personal relationship with Job . . . Job's conception of God is transformed, certainly, but only to the extent that is logically required by the existence of innocent suffering and a God who responds to a demand for an explanation or justification by a show of power. (1997, 307)

Furthermore, does Ricoeur's proposal have the practical or moral consequences he claims for it? One wonders whether Ricoeur's chastened

---

[50] Here Ricoeur suggests that some may "find a consolation without any parallel in the idea that God too suffers and that the covenant . . . culminates in a partnership in the suffering of Christ" (1985, 647). Cf. Weil 1951, 117–36.

sense of the dangers of thought leads not to thought's proper chasten-
ing, but rather to thought's renunciation, to the denial of the propriety
of thought's resistance to evil as an important truth. In part this dispute
concerns the relative power of thought in helping us cope with such
challenges (a power to which I suspect Ricoeur gives too little credence);
but it also concerns whether Ricoeur's account can really sustain hope
in the face of evil. Are appeals to an "unverifiable faith" really very
helpful here (Ricoeur 1967, 315–21)? Can we not supplement such
appeals with further arguments? If evil is a quasi-natural force, why
should we trust in its eventual defeat? This is finally a properly theological question, or, more precisely, a properly Christological one: how does
Ricoeur's position deal with Christian claims about Christ's victory over
evil and death, however provisional, that is now proclaimed in the
Resurrection?

These are not conclusive arguments against Ricoeur's position, but
rather openings for further dialogue with it. For Ricoeur is right:
Augustinian thinkers have often not fully plumbed the deep reality of
evil, but have rather wavered between an optimistic denial of its reality
and a pessimistic naturalization of its power. Ricoeur simply points out
that such a resolution leaves much about evil unthought. In one sense,
Ricoeur's voice is the voice of Job, refusing all the consolations of philosophy and theology, demanding that the apparently unmerited character of evil be taken with absolute seriousness. Our response to these
worries must not fall into the role of Job's comforters, we must insist on
the propriety of the complaint, even if we insist – as, again, we must –
on that complaint's provisional status, its non-finality.

Evil raises disturbing questions about the moral nature of our universe,
questions which can work to subvert our hope in future action. The
Augustinian tradition's proposal – that evil be interpreted ontologically
in terms of a privationist account of evil – is meant fundamentally to
affirm our faith in and hope for the final justice and harmony of all creation under a just and loving God. Thus the account is built fundamentally on the religious vision of a harmonious and loving world, governed
by a wholly good God. But Augustinian proposals elicit concern from
both those more optimistic and those more pessimistic, who challenge it
as fundamentally impious, because it attempts to constrain the Divine
within our vision of goodness. Evil seems a more intractable problem
than the Augustinian framework lets us admit – indeed, it seems sometimes to be God's will. And there are alternate resources in the Christian

tradition, these critics suggest, that the Augustinian proposal simply elides. Can an Augustinian proposal meet such concerns? Can it affirm that sin is not part of God's positive purposes while yet acknowledging the real presence of sin in the world today? Moreover, can it do this without getting caught in the crossfire between such optimistic and pessimistic proposals? Further engagement with these detailed positions will profit the Augustinian tradition.

THE AUGUSTINIAN ACCOUNT: SUMMARY AND OVERVIEW OF THE ARGUMENT

This book addresses the worries detailed above by demonstrating how two thinkers, Reinhold Niebuhr and Hannah Arendt, appropriated and developed themes culled from Augustine's thought in ways that help us not only to quiet these concerns, but also to exhibit the real power and attractiveness of the Augustinian account. This appropriation uncovers some difficulties in the work of Niebuhr and Arendt, so it must at times criticize them for not fully developing, and at times indeed inadvertently contradicting, their most significant insights. The programs of Niebuhr and Arendt contain certain insights, and employ certain argumentative methods, that (a) offer us the foundations of a useful and productive proposal about evil, and (b) are, in significant ways, rooted in the work of Augustine; this is the book's main *exegetical* argument. However, their constructive programs contain problems which vex any simple reiteration of their thought; this is the book's main *critical* argument. Nonetheless, the insights and methods they identified and employed remain viable, so to harvest this assistance we must develop their insights beyond their own formulations; this is the book's main *constructive* argument. Niebuhr's and Arendt's most powerful insights are best understood (indeed, better understood than they themselves could understand them) within a more thoroughly Augustinian framework than either of them inhabits; when their insights are deployed within that framework, they help us understand the Augustinian response to evil in a way which meets the common worries that attach to that response.

As the word "worries" suggests, the concerns that motivate the above critiques of the Augustinian proposal are based on misunderstandings of the proposal; as such, they are best met not by defensive counterattacks but by further investigation of the grounds for concern. These worries are not simply *mistakes*, frivolous complaints tossed off with hardly a moment's thought; these are genuine concerns formulated by profound minds engaged in searching inquiry. We cannot simply dismiss them wholesale, but must find a way of understanding their plausibility, their grip on our minds. And our proposal will be more satisfying to the extent that it enables us to appreciate, as insight, the driving thoughts of those who take the worries to pose insuperable problems for the tradition, even after we have shown how they may be met.[51] We must attempt to understand *both* the significance of these insights, *and* the worries that seem naturally to arise from them.

Both formally, as a matter of method, and materially, as a matter of the specific challenges raised, this essay seeks to turn these problems into opportunities – opportunities to articulate, for our context, the persuasive "deep structure" of the Augustinian proposal.[52] The anthropological worries about this account of sin as perversion, most basically challenge the affirmation that humans are both free (or transcendent) and natural beings. Similarly, the ontological worries about this account of evil as privation most basically challenge the affirmation that the world is fundamentally intelligible and good – I use the worries as invitations into a more basic analysis of the Augustinian account of humans as naturally free, and yet importantly constrained in their freedom.

In responding to these concerns, the work deploys and develops the thought of Reinhold Niebuhr and Hannah Arendt as usefully Augustinian thinkers. The claim that Niebuhr and Arendt are Augustinian may seem perverse. Not only do both seem quite securely "modern," both explicitly critiqued and rejected some of Augustine's most cherished affirmations. However, their criticisms of Augustine do not reflect fundamental rejections of their Augustinian inheritance, but only complicating extensions of it. Each was profoundly influenced by Augustine's thought early in their education (indeed, Arendt wrote her dissertation on his concept of love), and throughout their careers each continued to engage Augustine, both as ancestor and adversary.

Seeing Niebuhr and Arendt as Augustinians helps us develop insights into their thought. Niebuhr's anthropology allows us to affirm the very compound of freedom and nature which underlies the Augustinian account of sin as perversion. Similarly, Arendt's political ontology illuminates the tradition's claim that evil is simply the privation of goodness,

[51] Here I repeat, almost verbatim, John McDowell's description of his own method (1994, xxii).
[52] It is for this reason important to notice that Arendt and Niebuhr both advance an important claim about the Augustinian tradition – that evil can *never* be the explicit/primary subject of inquiry. We can begin from questions about evil (as Augustine did) but they cannot be primary to a systematic exposition of our situation.

and that goodness is fundamentally describable in terms of its world-constitutive character. Together, they offer us the "raw materials" required for an adequate Augustinian account of evil, one which acknowledges our responsibility for and complicity in situations of moral conflict, and yet which also helps us resist it by not becoming guilt-ily obsessed with evil but affirming goodness instead; that is, this proposal offers us a way of responding which admits evil's *interior* presence within us and yet its *exteriority* to us as well.

While their work is helpful, we cannot simply repristinate them; their works were addressed to the needs of their day, not of our own. But they can still help us respond both to the problem of evil as it confronts us, and to the particular concerns about the Augustinian proposal detailed above. This project is fundamentally a *hermeneutical* one, offering not repristination, but interpretive development.[53] And interpretation involves criticism. Both projects suffer from severe problems, manifest in problems with their proposals concerning sin and evil, to which we must attend. Niebuhr's account of sin as "inevitable yet not necessary" turns out to be a distinction without a difference; and his account cannot help but invest evil with an ontological reality which vexes his larger theological framework. Arendt's account of human action as absolutely sponta-neous renders her account dangerously voluntaristic and irrationalist, and undercuts the grounds of the hopefulness she wants to promote. Furthermore, neither thinker was sufficiently shaped by Augustine's thought. Both of them combine important Augustinian insights with anthropological assumptions which subtly subvert them. Furthermore, in a way analogous to their material positions, the methods they propose are importantly *partial*; neither one is independently adequate to evil's full complexity. Arendt's phenomenological and ontological analysis plumbs the depths of evil and reveals its fundamental ontological "superficiality," but her method is too narrow, and refuses to see the con-nections between these ontological truths and broadly religious concerns which arise within them. Niebuhr's existential analysis, surveying the complexity of human existence, accommodates the full breadth of facts about the human's complex and conflictual attachments to itself, the world, and God, but his method is too shallow, and cannot properly

---

[53] Here I am drawing on my reading of Hans-Georg Gadamer on tradition and historical thought; see Gadamer 1989, 397: "*To think historically* means, in fact, *to perform the transposition that the concepts of the past undergo* when we try to think in them." It is this "performing the transposition" of Augustine's concepts (as mediated for us by Niebuhr and Arendt) in order to meet the challenges that evil sets before us today, that is this book's central purpose.

adjudicate between human perception that "sin presupposes itself," entailing a demonic element in evil, and the theological insistence on the ultimate unreality of evil. Hence, while the Augustinian tradition is aided by their attempts to develop strands of the tradition's thought, in the end both positions are flawed materially and methodologically, and require reconstruction if we are to advance beyond them.

In resolving the problems faced by both accounts, we are helped by a more thorough *ressourcement* of the work of St. Augustine. It is precisely those aspects of Niebuhr's and Arendt's thought in which Augustine's influence does not penetrate their modernist shells that were most vulnerable to subjectivist temptations, while those aspects of their thought that were most Augustinian were most secure from such temptations – and indeed served them as the launching pads for powerful critiques of each other's subjectivist commitments. Thus our interest in offering a less subjectivist account than they admit may be materially advanced by offering a more thoroughly Augustinian proposal than they do. Augustine's theological anthropology resists our subjectivist temptations, and offers a well-worked-out alternative to them: against subjectivism, a properly Augustinian anthropology understands human agency as always already related to both God and the world, and so chastens modern predilections for absolute autonomy while still affirming the subject's importance. To be less subjectivist, then, we must be more Augustinian. That is what part II attempts to show.

Genealogy: remembering the Augustinian tradition

CHAPTER THREE

Sin as perversion: Reinhold Niebuhr's Augustinian psychology

How cold the vacancy
When the phantoms are gone and the shaken realist
First sees reality. The mortal no
Has its emptiness and tragic expirations.
The tragedy, however, may have begun,
Again, in the imagination's new beginning,
In the yes of the realist spoken because he must
Say yes, spoken because under every no
Lay a passion for yes that had never been broken.

Wallace Stevens, "Esthétique du Mal," VIII

How plausible is the Augustinian proposal to interpret human wickedness in terms of perversion? For some, the emphasis on perversion does
not take the human's capacities for change seriously enough; it represents a conservative and pessimistic obeisance to obsolete and absolutist
beliefs about human nature, beliefs which restrain social experimenta-
tion and, therefore, progress. For others, it does not take the human's
"naturalness" seriously enough; it reflects a fantastically optimistic delu-
sion about our rectitude, and irresponsibly ignores the fact that we
inhabit a world, and possess a nature, that is only partly aligned with our
ethical aspirations. For both optimists and pessimists, then, the
Augustinian tradition's insistence on sin as "second nature" is not a
source of real hope but an expression of despair laced with self-hatred.
Can the Augustinian proposal be developed in a way that meets these
worries? Indeed it can, and the very evidence which these critics think
the most problematic aspect of the Augustinian proposal – namely, its
complex anthropology – turns out instead to support it. There is something right about the Augustinian defense of the human as free enough
to violate its nature, and yet natural enough never to escape the consequences of that violation.

This was shown in the twentieth century by Reinhold Niebuhr, who developed and deployed an Augustinian psychology to support his "Christian realism." His work is most valuable for his insistence on accommodating all the "facts" about our nature and destiny. From this insistence we can harvest both methodological and material insights. Methodologically, Niebuhr always opposed all "simple" and "one-sided" accounts of human existence – accounts which depicted humans either as wholly "natural" and so subject to scientific manipulation and reconstruction, or as so overwhelmingly "free" as to be able by sheer action to escape all tragic conflict. In contrast to both simple naturalisms and voluntarisms, Niebuhr's "Christian realism" depicted the human as both natural and free – a creature of "finite freedom" – thereby providing a more plausible picture of the human's predicament than simplistic reductionisms could allow. Niebuhr's critical and constructive project advances in large part by developing, in this manner, the Augustinian account of the human as *imago Dei*, in order to explain the tragic *complexity* of action – how action inevitably entails some positive vision of the good, but how action's character as "partial" (in several senses) leads invariably to tragic conflict, conditions Niebuhr describes under the rubric of "sin." As we will see, Niebuhr develops the Augustinian insight that all action seeks some good, and that sinful action is most basically describable as the choice of some lesser (typically selfish) good over the proper good of God. As such, Niebuhr is the greatest twentieth-century Augustinian psychologist of sin, and in order further to develop such an Augustinian psychology, we must begin with him.

The choice of Niebuhr to fulfill this task may seem perverse, for today he is more typically condemned than commended. Most especially he is criticized for gifting us with an unremittingly bleak pessimism about the human condition, a pessimism which warrants a terribly cynical approach to social life.[1] And it is certainly the case that, historically, such criticisms have a point. Perhaps the grandest example of this is the *Time Magazine* cover of March 8, 1948, which portrays Niebuhr's brooding visage emerging from a dark and sinister background of black clouds, illuminated only by a tiny, glowing white cross at the base of the picture. As if to spell it out for more textually minded folk, the caption reads: "Theologian Reinhold Niebuhr: man's story is not a success story" (see Fox 1985, 233). This picture of Niebuhr as a dour pessimist underlies charges that he was the theologian of containment and the Cold War,

---

[1] While I think that concerns about Niebuhr's "liberalism" are in fact contingent upon this more profound concern with his "pessimism," I do discuss the concerns about his "liberalism" below.

the eloquent defender of the *status quo*, the "apologist of power" (see Kellerman 1987). "The irony of Reinhold Niebuhr," as Stanley Hauerwas and Michael Broadway argue in a powerful essay with that title, is that his prophetic cultural critique ended up supporting the very liberalism it aimed to undo (Hauerwas, with Broadway, 1997).

The point of this chapter is not to contest these critiques directly – indeed as will be seen I largely agree with them – but to contest their use as justifying a rejection of Niebuhr's thought *tout court*. For we should forgive him, to reclaim both his diagnostic intelligence about politics and society and the deep theological roots of that intelligence. Even his present-day critics admit that his diagnostic insights were remarkable; John Milbank allows that "the substantive analyses of political and social processes in *Moral Man and Immoral Society* are impressive," and others such as Kathryn Tanner concur (Tanner 1992, viii; Milbank 1997, 234). These and similar admissions may warrant treating Niebuhr as a particularly acute political commentator camouflaged as a classically liberal theologian – that is, with very little camouflage at all.[2] But his work is deeply theological; George Lindbeck, whom few would identify as Niebuhrian, has written that Niebuhr was "perhaps the last American theologian who in practice (and to some extent in theory) made extended and effective attempts to re-describe major aspects of the contemporary scene in distinctively Christian terms" (1984, 124). Niebuhr's genius resided not just in prophetic critique, for alongside those statements commonly read as supporting pessimism in Niebuhr's work stands an insistence on hope, love, and the possibilities of human freedom as *real*, if not "simple," possibilities. Robert McAfee Brown speaks for many who were inspired by Niebuhr when he describes Niebuhr as a "pessimistic optimist," and after all, the last word of Niebuhr's *magnum opus*, *The Nature and Destiny of Man*, is "hope."[3]

The typical picture of Niebuhr as essentially a pessimistic conservative renders incomprehensible his almost maniacal activism, his impassioned championing of causes, and his consistent rejection of

---

[2] Here I dispute Ronald Stone's claim that Niebuhr's basic commitments were fundamentally and typically theologically "liberal" (see Stone 1980, 133–5, carried forward by Dorrien 1995, 141–9). It helps here to make a distinction between theological liberalism and political progressivism; while Niebuhr's political commitments were thoroughly progressive, his basic commitment to the illuminative power of the Christian doctrine of sin, no matter how described, would trouble many classical religious liberals.

[3] "Our most reliable understanding is the fruit of 'grace' in which faith completes our ignorance without pretending to possess its certainties as knowledge; and in which contrition mitigates our pride without destroying our hope" (1943, 321). See R. Brown 1986, xi. Compare Niebuhr 1986, 3–17.

authoritarianism in favor of democracy. Indeed, Niebuhr is best seen as a sober judge of both the problems and the possibilities of human community, who prefaced his famous (or notorious) saying, "man's capacity for injustice makes democracy necessary," with the claim that "man's capacity for justice makes democracy possible" (1944, xiii). It is Niebuhr's preaching of the complexity of all human endeavors that is the most distinctive note of his thought. His insistence on human complexity was the consequence of his attempt to see all the recalcitrant "facts" of human existence (Niebuhr 1955). Niebuhr was most basically neither a radical critic of the social order, hurling jeremiads down from the Gothic magnificences of Union Theological Seminary, nor some sort of court theologian, ministering to the best and brightest of Babylon. The very variousness of the criticisms of Niebuhr should warn us against too ready an assent to the charges.

This is not to say that his theology is flawless. On the contrary, it is deeply flawed, as critics such as his brother H. Richard perceived long ago. But such criticisms do not entail jettisoning his thought entirely. Those who think this typically take him to offer an explicit systematic theological position which we ought to refuse.[4] But we should heed H. Richard's typically prescient perception that "Reinie's thought appears to me to be like a great iceberg of which three-fourths or more is beneath the surface and in which what is explicitly said depends on something that is not made explicit" (H. R. Niebuhr 1996, 97). The genius of "Reinie's" thought lies not in its explicit theology, but in its theological anthropology.[5] As he himself said, "I cannot and do not claim to be a theologian. I have taught Christian Social Ethics for a quarter of a century and have also dealt in the ancillary field of 'apologetics'" (Niebuhr in Kegley and Bretall 1961, 3). While I do not want to get caught up in the Quest for the Historical Reinie, I think we should take Niebuhr at his word – that we should take him more literally than he has been taken by many readers. Of course to take him literally here does not mean *not* to take him seriously as a theologian. But I think we should take him seriously as a theological anthropologist, and especially in his

---

[4] John Howard Yoder speaks for many when he says: "For Reinhold Niebuhr his parting of the ways with the pacifism of his earlier years was the hinge on which turned his entire social ethic, and thereby his entire theological anthropology, and thereby his entire reconstruction of theology. His majestic *Nature and Destiny of Man* is the *a posteriori* exposition of the foundations of his *Moral Man and Immoral Society* and his *Interpretation of Christian Ethics*" (Stassen, Yeager, and Yoder 1996, 276, n. 55).

[5] See Gustafson 1986, 40: "The deepest justification for Niebuhr's Christian view of man . . . is the unmasking of illusion and deceptions, and the unveiling of what humanity 'really' is."

analysis of the theological motives at the base of the self – an analysis, we will see, that is essentially Augustinian.

The charges against Niebuhr – charges from thinkers as diverse as James Gustafson, Hans Frei, John Howard Yoder, and John Milbank – are accurate enough about his work not to be dismissed, but they miss something important latent within it. We can read Niebuhr against himself, using his theological anthropology to diagnose and critique his explicit theology. Doing so also allows us to retain valuable aspects of his thought that his critics forbid themselves to appropriate.

Most basically, Niebuhr's thought fails because of its subjectivistic epistemology; it gives priority to the subject as knower, a priority expressed in the distinction between "general" and "special" revelation. We need an epistemology which insists that, from the very beginning, the knowing subject is "always already" related to the larger reality within which she or he finds themselves. Augustine's concept of sin implies such an epistemology, one which both affirms an ineliminable (even if only residual) positive knowledge of God, and limits all knowledge of God. And this concept seems to be also called for by Niebuhr's own, highly Augustinian, account of sin as "self-deception," and the positive picture of fundamental human integrity that that account requires. This kind of epistemology may be called "confessional," in the sense that one confesses both that one cannot demonstrate the truth of one's first principles, and that one begins all inquiry from those first principles. The failure of Niebuhr's explicit Cartesian epistemology, then, can be repaired by replacing it with the Augustinian epistemology implicit in other areas of his thought.

Such is the task of this chapter. The first section outlines the overall movement of his thought and the second details the many criticisms of Niebuhr's work, diagnoses their root in Niebuhr's partial entrapment to a modern subjectivist epistemology, and goes on to argue that Niebuhr offers us, in his Augustinian theological anthropology, the very resources we need to transcend that subjectivism. The third section argues that the insights Niebuhr provides are significant, and ought to be retained, by understanding his practical proposal as centering around the ethical recommendation of *acknowledging responsibility* for our situation, as an outflowing of his essentially incarnational vision of the Christian moral life.

REINHOLD NIEBUHR'S TRAGIC CHRISTIAN REALISM

Niebuhr's position can be briefly summarized. It begins in his criticism of modernity, which is that modernity possesses a flawed anthropology, which flowers in an *optimism* that is as incredible in itself as modernity is pathetic for having no alternative to it in its intellectual options.[6] As he said, late in his career: "The faith of modern man contains two related articles: the idea of progress and the idea of the perfectibility of man. The latter is frequently the basis of the former article. Man is regarded as indeterminately perfectible because it is not understood that every growth of human freedom may have evil as well as virtuous consequences" (Niebuhr in Kegley and Bretall 1961, 15). Niebuhr's life-work can be understood as an attempt to subvert this picture, and to offer an alternative in its stead. He argued that it is an inescapable fact of our lives that, as we are free, we live in history and participate in sin. Yet this need not lead us to despair because we can have faith in Christ as the final revelation of God, and this faith allows us to "front life" in hope, always chastened by the knowledge of our own impurity but also chastened by the knowledge that that impurity cannot excuse our efforts to inhabit the world as we are meant to do. This section explains this proposal in (somewhat) less sketchy form.

The keys to understanding: history, freedom, sin

Niebuhr is more famous for what he *dis*believed than for what he believed; he is remembered less as a powerful expositor of the Christian faith than as a critic of the overly simple or naive formulations that he opposed. While there is something right in his reputation, his famous skepticism has its positive uses: it allows him to explicate his account not so much in terms of positive affirmations as negative suspicions, his *dis*-belief in the alternatives, which he calls the "classical" and "modern" accounts, and thereby to offer what he calls a "negative proof" (1941, 131) for the Christian faith, and particularly his anthropological affirmation that the human is a subject with "finite freedom," a compound of freedom and nature.[7] The classical account fails because it seeks redemption from history through nature by denying that our predicament is due to us, and insisting instead that human fault is necessary for our existence. In Christian terms, it denies our responsibility for sin. In contrast, the modern account fails because it seeks redemption from nature through history; while it affirms our responsibility for sin, it

---

[6] See Niebuhr 1941, 121–2; Stone 1980, 38–9, 105.

[7] While Niebuhr's interpretations of particular thinkers and traditions are notoriously sketchy, to say the least, they are not meant to serve in the first place as detailed representations of alternative positions, but rather as heuristic devices to illuminate his own proposal.

ignores the fact that we cannot ourselves overcome our own wickedness, or our vulnerability to the malice of others. In Christian terms, it denies our enslavement to sin. Both accounts "can not do full justice, either to the multifarious vitalities and configurations of history or to the tragic antinomies of life which are the consequence of the corruption of freedom" (1949, 58). For Niebuhr, the Christian tradition offers a humbling alternative to these two; while it does not pretend to resolve all the perplexities, and "confesses the darkness of human sight and the perplexities of faith," it suggests that we see the "ultrarational pinnacles of Christian truth" as "keys which make the drama of human life and history comprehensible" (1986, 247; see 224).

For Niebuhr, the most important facets and figures of the Christian account and human existence can be conceptualized as such "keys," symbols that we must employ but never fully comprehend.[8] Central here are the three concepts of *history, freedom,* and *sin.* For Niebuhr the great errors of most accounts of human nature and destiny lie in large part in their insufficient appreciation of these three symbols' power to illuminate and guide human action. Niebuhr's work can be seen as a lifelong attempt to critique false understandings of these concepts, and to propose a more appropriate account of them. Classical accounts could not understand the importance of history, nor therefore fully realize the character of human freedom from nature; modern accounts could neither comprehend the corruptions of history nor truly admit the fragility and finitude of freedom; so neither rightly understood the character of human fault, namely, sin. Niebuhr's own constructive proposal used the resources of the Christian tradition to critique both accounts, and to build on this critique a positive exegesis of the symbols. He thought these concepts entailed one another; as he said, "where there is history at all there is freedom; and where there is freedom there is sin" (1943, 80). To understand that aphorism is to apprehend the core of Niebuhr's thought.

History
By "history" Niebuhr means the ongoing series of events which humans both shape and are shaped by; thus, for Niebuhr history is the inescapable and partly self-created environment of human existence. The failure of alternative accounts to understand the real character of human existence in the world are in large part failures to see the human's

---

[8] In this Niebuhr stands firmly in the line of Christian theologians from Paul through Augustine, Aquinas, and the Reformers. See "Deceivers yet True" in Niebuhr 1935.

full implication in history. For them history is, in some sense, disposable; classical thinkers suggest we can escape it, while modern thinkers believe that it will have an end, a point at which all our problems are resolved.[9] Against the former, Niebuhr always affirmed that history is the realm of real human creativity and genuine human freedom; against the latter, Niebuhr always affirmed that history is not "self-explanatory," that it does not bear its own meaning immanently in itself or eschatologically, in the final achievement of "the end of history." He thought both accounts fail and that their failures are illuminating.

Classical thought failed due to its anthropology; it thought that the necessities of nature and the necessities of mind exhausted the possibilities for humans to make sense of themselves, and it could not see a distinct and genuine historical realm beyond those two. But classical thought's false anthropology rests upon a flawed theology, its ignorance of our need for a "god" intimately involved with our lives. Classical thought imagined that the human had to achieve its good on its own. It had no way to conceive of humans as needing something which must be given, nor of any concept of grace; in short, it had no way to conceive of us as internally related to something beyond ourselves.

Modern thought, on the other hand, overestimates the character and extent of human freedom; it sees all problems as puzzles, soluble by the simple exercise of human will, warranted by modernity's "illusion of budding omnipotence" over non-human nature and presumed to cover human nature as well (1949, 88). But power cannot be exercised reflexively on the self in the same way it is exercised instrumentally on the external world. "There are certain bounds of human finiteness which no historical development can overcome" (1949, 70). But moderns were driven to such wild affirmations of human power by modernity's second anthropological assumption, namely, the identification of freedom with goodness. This is really a theological claim, the expression of modernity's belief that humanity is on its own, in a morally vacant universe, and must save itself by itself. On this view, what is evil is what obstructs the expansion of human control. The human will cannot be bad; only what limits it is wicked (see Blumenberg 1983 and Flathman 1992).

In Niebuhr's opinion, this picture is built on a false understanding of the human predicament, a misconstrual which avoids recognizing our responsibility for this predicament, our sin:

---

[9] Compare Fukuyama 1992 with Niebuhr 1943, 328: "The belief of an age that it has reached the end of history is pathetic."

The modern man is . . . so certain about his essential virtue because he is so mistaken about his stature . . . He is consequently unable to understand the real pathos of his defiance of nature's and reason's laws. He always imagines himself betrayed into this defiance either by some accidental corruption in his past history or by some sloth of reason. Hence he hopes for redemption, either through a program of social reorganization or by some scheme of education. (1941, 98)

Hence, Niebuhr's diagnosis of the flaws inherent in modern accounts does not leave us merely with a negative lesson about the limits of human power, but also with a sharpened sensitivity to the fact that the human is implicated essentially in the very realities of nature and history which it seeks to transform. The human is partially self-transcendent or, in Niebuhr's phrase, a subject of "finite freedom." Human wickedness is "a fixed datum of historical science," but it is not simply natural (1949, 94). The ultimate failure of the modern solution is that it cannot understand how both freedom and nature are part of the human's conundrum – how, in Christian terms, the human really does suffer from the free perversion of their true nature. Modernity, in short, is ignorant of "the mystery of original sin" (1949, 101). To understand this, we must understand how it misconstrues human freedom.

Freedom

As history is adequately understood only through the concept of sin, so sin is adequately understood only through an analysis of freedom. By "freedom" Niebuhr means to emphasize *our* existence in the world, our presence in the world as agents, our capacity to effect the course of history in ways unforseeable by the simple analysis of the past. Niebuhr sees freedom as basic to human existence, manifest in different ways in different aspects of our existence. We are not rigidly determined by our natures, for our experience of freedom is something more than the conflict between the various heterogeneous energies which conflict with our natures; yet we cannot simply remake ourselves *de novo*, for our freedom is constrained by our nature, and particularly our finitude, in ineliminable ways. Freedom is not any simple exercise of human will which can overcome all constraints, for our freedom bears within itself vexations and limitations which make it always dangerously "partial." We are only partly free and hence remain partly governed by forces outside its own intentional control; and even our limited exercises of freedom always favor some faction or fraction of the relevant truth to the detriment of other, equally valid, perspectives. Given this, we become most free by realizing our freedom's limits and our sinfuless – in the paradoxical idea, extending at least as far back as St. Paul, that our freedom is found under the form of bondage. Indeed, for Niebuhr, "man is most free in the discovery that he is not free" (1941, 260); our freedom is manifest most clearly, and apprehended most completely, at those moments when we understand the real limits on our existence.[10]

Even if freedom is finite, it is still real; so Niebuhr disputed not only modern voluntarists, but also classical naturalists, who interpreted history not as a succession of novel and unpredictable events, but rather as the reiteration of basic circular energies in nature; they see the human's moral problematic as structural conflicts within human nature, or nature as a whole.[11] In a sense Niebuhr offers a transcendental argument: if one wishes fully to understand history *as* history, one must understand it in terms of a series of novel events, each related to and yet estranged from those that came before – and only humans have the freedom of action required to initiate such novel events.[12] To understand history as history, one must understand it as a realm of human freedom; if humans exist in history, then humans are free beings. To reduce humans to patterns of law misunderstands both human nature and history.

While the human is partly subject to law, any formula of "natural-law" reasoning is inadequate to human agency, for not only can we revolt against any law, we are also dynamically related to the structures ordering our being in a way that natural-law reasoning, which Niebuhr saw as essentially conservative, inevitably obscures; we are never just what our putative "natures" want to restrict us to being. As Christian faith symbolizes it, we are created in the image of God.[13] Nevertheless, even though Niebuhr insists that human freedom is real, and therefore that our moral vocabulary is an essential part of our worldview, he does not relax into an easy Pelagian moralism. History is not simply "made" by humans for human freedom, because human transcendence is not total. So "history does not solve the enigma of history" (1949, 233). The exercise of freedom is complicated and corrupted in its essential structure. The challenge of evil is due, in part, to the fact that humans are

---

[10] See E. Farley 1990, 109–18, and especially. 172: "elemental passions are tragically structured but not evil."

[11] For one example of this position in contemporary thought, see Kuhns 1991, who reduces all tragedy to sexual conflict (see, e.g., 76).   [12] See 1955, 44–52; 1949, 20–1.

[13] See 1942. Ironically, though, Niebuhr thinks that this problem was at least genuinely identified in classical thought, especially by the tragedians, in contrast to the moderns' typical ignorance of it (see 1940).

partially contingent, historical beings. But if the contingency of history itself is not exactly the solution, neither is it, *pace* the modern account, completely the problem. What is? Niebuhr's answer is straightforward: sin.

Sin

Niebuhr means by "sin" the vexations which invariably attend the exercise of human freedom in history, and argues that it best captures our complex situation, the *grandeur et misère* which is one of our distinguishing features: "the Christian view of human nature is involved in the paradox of claiming a higher stature for man and of taking a more serious view of his evil than any other anthropology" (1941, 18). Modern and classical thinkers cannot understand the basic character of the human's problem because they do not understand the basic character of the human; their failure is rooted in "the lack of a principle of interpretation which can do justice to both the height of human self-transcendence and the organic unity between the spirit of man and his physical life" (1941, 123). Because the moral problem that humans face is not finally something external to themselves, but is rather lodged in their being, humans cannot, within history, expect to be free of sin; the best we can hope for in history is some provisional and partial realization of our ideals. Niebuhr thinks that basic to the human's situation is the fact that we are driven by our anxieties to create radically flawed self-understandings which we use to attempt to anchor ourselves *on* ourselves, to ground our lives on self-justifications which are invariably false and self-deceptive. History and freedom are perennially ambiguous because *we* are perennially ambiguous: the symbol of original sin shows us that good action is no "simple" possibility (1942, 57–8); Christianity's truth lies in its honesty about the complexity of our sinfulness.

The classical and modern accounts cannot understand the real character of evil because they both deny this. They locate evil in "the natural or the primitive" and suggest that humans seek to escape such evil through their own actions (1949, 68). But because it is the *whole* human, and not just some aspect, which is at fault, there is no aspect of the human to which we may look for salvation; as we are our own problem, we cannot be our own solution. We cannot rescue ourselves from ourselves. Our tragic situation involves our whole beings in a strangely compound manner: we cannot adequately understand our situation, or ourselves, from our standpoint alone; yet our implication in tragic conflict is due in significant degree to our necessary but inevitably partial attempts at self-comprehension. We cannot comprehend ourselves by ourselves, but our situation affords us no other choice but to try to do so, and in attempting to do so we end up entangling ourselves ever deeper in tragedy. "In its yearning toward the infinite lies the source of both human creativity and human sin" (1941, 122). To modify Pascal, all the wretchedness of mankind is due to the fact that we cannot sit quietly and listen for the word which tells us who we are.

Niebuhr's analysis of how sin is "original," how it is "inevitable" yet "not necessary," is justly famous. As humans are meaning-seeking beings – creatures who ask questions about themselves, their world, and their ends – we seek some ground, some standpoint from which to ask such questions. As "man has always been his own most vexing problem"(1941, 1), we must seek answers to the enigmas we find ourselves to be, and what answers we discover bear the unconditional character of religious claims. In asking such questions, the human is asking about what, in effect, it takes to be its "god": "Since Man transcends both nature and himself he is bound to seek for a principle of meaning which will give coherence to his world, beyond nature and himself" (1942, 48). The problem with this project, for Niebuhr, is that the human's self-transcendence forbids any secure grounding at the same time that that same self-transcendence insists on it. The human asks questions to which it cannot find the answers – at least, not by itself. That is, "man is . . . in the position of being unable to comprehend himself in his full stature of freedom without a principle of comprehension which is beyond his comprehension"(1941, 125). In this situation we inevitably begin to suffer anxiety; and rather than wait patiently, we fall.

What is central to this vision of sin is the idea of idolatry. Forced to choose some "principle of comprehension," we suffer angst, arising from fear of error and, indeed, fear and resentment at being forced to make such a choice at all. Such angst inevitably tempts the human to self-deception, in order to avoid facing this anxiety. But this self-deception obscures not only our anxious condition, but also the result of this condition: our inevitable fall into idolatry. In the absence of the word of God, and suffering anxiety in the face of necessary action, humans will "inevitably" turn towards some finite center for their grounding, and take some provisional principle of coherence for an absolute anchor. Humans typically turn to an idolatry founded on excessive self-love: they "conceive God in their own image" (1942, 47). This sin is, for Niebuhr, a matter of "partialness" in two senses: first, it exhibits our partial apprehension, our grasp of what is finally only a portion of the full good;

second, it reveals our partialness to, our favoring of, our partial goods over the (equally) partial goods chosen by others. In Niebuhr's view, sin is this "partiality," the selection of some partial and provisional "center of meaning" as our ultimate, center and thereby we plunge into an egotism induced by our own freedom. We will always "refuse to admit the particularity of his viewpoints and the contingent character of his existence" (1942, 58). We fall into a false self-understanding and thus a life of self-deception and lies.

In all this, Niebuhr's thought is centrally theological; the human has been made in such a way that its true happiness can be found only in the Divine both beyond and within all the proximate ends which it seeks. The completion of human desires and the accomplishment of human projects wait upon the divine's self-giving. But this theology, when seen from the human perspective, is only negative: for Niebuhr, the true God is *Deus absconditus*, the hidden God of whose existence fallen humans are reminded most definitively at those moments when they violate that God's laws. But this negative theology merely aggravates the human's condition, for all it ever does is shatter our idols, one by one. The human is "homeless" in the world, and "cannot find the meaning of life in itself or the world" (1941, 14). Niebuhr's negative theology entails a negative anthropology; insofar as one is ignorant of the true character of God, one is ignorant of oneself. There is no determinate framework within which we can understand ourselves; to comprehend ourselves is to comprehend ourselves as comprehended from *beyond* ourselves: "The self . . . cannot understand itself except as it is understood from beyond itself and the world" (1941, 14). We find ourselves to be mysteries, and we investigate our mysteriousness in and through our relationship both to God and our fellow humans.

Furthermore, Niebuhr's theology is not just bare theology but is explicitly Christocentric, in a way that often goes unnoticed. The mystery is none other than the mystery of love at the base of ourselves, and that love is the presence of the divine *logos* in our hearts. "The Christian faith affirms that the same Christ who discloses the sovereignty of God over history is also the perfect norm of human nature," so what appears first to be a hermeneutical problem, a problem of self-understanding, is revealed to be a moral problem (1943, 68).[14] The hermeneutic blossoms into the erotic, and beyond the erotic, into the agapic, the vision of self-giving in community embodied in the figure of Jesus Christ.[15] What

---

[14] I agree with Ward 1986, 66, that Niebuhr has a "high view" of revelation.
[15] For a fascinating analysis of how inquiry bears within itself the seeds of community, and thus is a form of love, see Lear 1990, 183–222.

seemed to be a question of interiority is seen, when pressed to its conclusion, to flower in the relations among humans, and among humans
and God, which are given their sense in the person and life of Christ.

In raising the question of Christology, we reach the heart of Niebuhr's
theology. Given his critique of the alternatives as he sees them, what is
his response to our conundrum? What positive resources lie latent in the
Christian account of sin? Niebuhr tries to answer this question through
his account of the human as *simul iustus et peccator*, and his analysis of
Christ as the crucial clue to what it means to live "beyond tragedy."

Beyond tragedy

How does Niebuhr's diagnosis of our tragic situation, as powerful and
sobering as it is, help us with the fundamentally *practical* task of seeking
to sustain realistic hope for our lives in the world? How can we trans-
late this vision of history and the self – the nature and destiny of
humanity – into an ethical proposal for guiding our lives? Can we
warrant and elucidate the hope we feel for our lives in the world? Here
Niebuhr's vision is surprisingly positive. He saw that the Christian
message is not simply *critical*, preaching the wisdom of "all is vanity"; as
he says, Christian faith "does not involve self-negation but self-realiza-
tion" (1941, 251). The positive apprehension of our proper center of
meaning is accessible through our apprehension of the special revelation of God in Christ (1941, 15).

Revelation and atonement
For Niebuhr, Christ responds to the problem of the destructiveness of
human beings, formulated by the Hebrew prophets in terms of the relation of God's justice to God's mercy: as "all history is involved in a perennial defiance of the law of God," the question is whether God is
merciful enough to "redeem as well as to judge all men" (1943, 29–30).
While the prophets never resolved this problem, for Christians it
received an answer in the person of Jesus of Nazareth.[16] Jesus is the
Christ because it is in his life, death, and Resurrection that humans
glimpse the nature of God's love. It is through Christ on the Cross, the

---

[16] Of course the revelation of Christ has more than merely epistemological effects in both its
content and form; it does more than simply inform and therefore clarify our intellect. The
broader, extra-cognitive effect of Christ on human existence is simply taken for granted here,
and discussed more fully in the third main section of this chapter. In a sense, it is the suspicion
that Christ's epistemic effects have an at best tangential relation to the shape of human existence
that Niebuhr's work challenges – but more on that later.

suffering of God, that we discern that "vicarious suffering [is] the final revelation of meaning in history" (1943, 45). Christ is the promise of God to the world that God will not let the world fully void itself of meaning and significance. God would rather suffer and die than abandon the world; total nihilism is ruled out.[17]

Still, this revelation does not yet completely reveal how this will be accomplished. The Crucifixion and Resurrection of Christ gives this promise a strange status, the mystery of "now" and "not yet," in which "sin is overcome in principle but not in fact" (1943, 47, 49). Christ's vicarious suffering for the world means neither that tragedy is gradually overcome, nor that tragedy is simply the sorrowful fact we should look straight in the face; rather, it means that God so loves the world that God's mercy will ultimately transcend God's judgment. "God's sovereignty over history is established and his triumph over evil is effected not by the destruction of the evil-doers but by his own bearing of the evil" (1943, 46). The tensions inherent in history will not be resolved in history, but are still not the last word about human existence. As Niebuhr puts it, Christ reveals that time will not be annulled, but somehow "taken up," in all its brokenness, into eternity. While "the final consummation of history lies beyond the conditions of the temporal process," nonetheless this consummation "fulfills rather than negates, the historical process" (1943, 291). Christ thus teaches us that there can be no simple harmonies in history; but it also teaches us that at the end of history the world will not be erased or transcended, but transformed and transfigured.[18] History remains an "interim" (1943, 51), but one whose weight can now be borne in the knowledge that God will redeem the time, and that nothing can separate us from the love of Christ.

God's revelation in Christ gains determinate shape through the doctrine of the Atonement. In that doctrine, God is understood "as both the propitiator and the propitiated" (1943, 56). The mystery of the Atonement can be stated (though not explained!) in the following terms: God's just wrath and God's freely given love intersect in God's relation to the human; where they intersect they form a cross, and on that cross the Christ is hung.

---

[17] This does not mean that Niebuhr thinks the human race will necessarily not destroy itself in some sort of technological-environmental holocaust, but that such a holocaust would not retrospectively invalidate history. Niebuhr's understanding of the eternal's relationship to temporal history ensured that history is not significant only (or especially) because of its outcome; it is significant also in itself. See Gilkey 1975, 43.

[18] But Christ does not merely or most basically have an *epistemological* impact on us; Christ provides sources of *power* which we may access. I discuss this below.

The wrath of God is the world in its essential structure reacting against the sinful corruptions of that structure; it is the law of life as love, which the egotism of man defies, a defiance which leads to the destruction of that life. The mercy of God represents the ultimate freedom of God above his own law; but not the freedom to abrogate the law. (1943, 56)

God will not abrogate the law, because the law is good; humans cannot follow the law, because they are in sin; so God freely accepts suffering rather than abandon the world to sin. The Christ-event is thus the crucial hermeneutical key to the proper understanding of the self and history. The Word of God is not simply spoken against the world; "a truth of faith is not something which stands perpetually in contradiction to experience. On the contrary, it illumines experience and is in turn validated by experience" (1943, 63).[19] By analogy with our knowledge of other persons, our understanding of the significance of the life, death, and resurrection of Jesus Christ completes, clarifies, and corrects our knowledge of God (1943, 64–5).

This issue is important for Niebuhr because it distinguishes him decisively from other neo-orthodox theologians (most notably Barth) who seem to veer towards fideism. Whatever may be the case with Barth, Niebuhr is definitely not a fideist; the dynamics of our historical existence point beyond themselves, however ambiguously and ambivalently, toward some sort of completion or perfection which is beyond all plausible expectation. In this Niebuhr affirms a continuity between Christian faith and "worldly" reason that is anathema to fideists. Furthermore, his anthropology allows him to invest such religious insights with cognitive content; as Pascal said, the heart has reasons which the reason does not know. What must be accepted – without apparent reason – is the good news of God's sovereignty over, and God's love given freely to, the world. To gain access to these reasons requires not more or stronger rational cogitation, but rather a subjective act of faith, the supra-rational realization that the truth about us is not in us, but rather beyond us.

While the Word of God acts upon us to convert us to the truth, but only by and through our subjective act of faith, Niebuhr still affirms our need for revelation. Christ resolves not only our confusions about our relationship to God and our own self-understanding, but also our con-

---

[19] Niebuhr's account here seems to me so commensurate with recent anglophone philosophical accounts on the nature of human understanding (particularly that of Davidson 1984) that I was initially surprised at the prescience of his thought. Then I realized that the same had been said by previous thinkers – such as Augustine and Aquinas – and only with Luther (I cannot speak about Calvin here) do we come upon the notion of *total* depravity.

fusions about our motivations in the wholly "worldly" historical realm. This is especially so in the fact that we care for one another. From an imagined perspective wholly within the flux of history, humans cannot see the value of genuine other-regard or *agape*; it is a "violation of natural standards of morals, as limited by historical existence" (1943, 69). But this wholly historical perspective can only be imagined, not inhabited, for we can and do experience these moments of *agape* in our ordinary lives. Such an *agape* thus "represents a tangent towards 'eternity' in the field of historical ethics" (1943, 69). Nonetheless, such moments are in fact "the support of all historical ethics," for "natural" human life is infused with such moments, and thus natural life is never purely "natural," in the sense of being closed off from divine transcendence; it invariably contains moments which "disclose the tangents towards the eternal" within history (1943, 76).[20]

Christ, the form of love

But Christ did not come to inform but to transform, to empower human agents with love.[21] For Niebuhr, the concept of love, especially in its for-mulation as *agape*, is in some sense the key concept of both Christian faith and human existence. This principle underlies his interpretive framework, both positively – as elucidating the proper shape of our lives – and negatively – as allowing him to diagnose and critique the flaws in our lives and in the lives of others. Love is the root principle by which we understand reality, for human existence is governed – oriented and motivated – by what we care about, what we love (see Frankfurt 1988 and Lear 1990). But God's love, as revealed in Christ, can only appear in history as a tragic love, a love that suffers because it refuses to take sides and instead seeks to love all, a love that is tragic "because it refuses to participate in the claims and counter-claims of historical existence" (1943, 72) while yet remaining in that existence. All of Niebuhr's thought is bathed in the light of the Incarnation; but that light is eclipsed by the Cross, so we live in an eerie theological half-light, with illumination enough to know only that our vision is distorted and dim, and that what light there is is only a foretaste of the true illumination God intends. Christ gives humans the ability to understand themselves as *simul iustus*

---

[20] The parallel with Karl Rahner's notion that "pure nature" is a "remainder concept" should be clear.

[21] Of course, Niebuhr's account is not non-cognitive, and does not dismiss questions of the rela-tion between reason and the heart; rather, for him, these two fundamental aspects of human existence are too intertwined to be treated in isolation from one another. For a helpful analysis of how cognitive and affective development may be correlated, see Wainwright 1995.

et peccator, by doing so, however, Christ takes away from humans any pretension to *self*-justification. Even after Christ, there is no perfection in history. This gets at the heart of the "now" and "not yet" of the Gospel, what Niebuhr calls "the paradox of grace."

The "paradox of grace" is at the center of Niebuhr's anthropology: how is it that, even as "saved," as willing adherents to the Christian faith, we remain subject to sin? While he is interested in describing the moral turpitude and ineptitude of those outside the Christian faith, his real genius comes in his critique, and analytical diagnosis, of the complexities of human life within the church. In this, Niebuhr is again a descendent of Augustine, admitting the possibility of "Christian mediocrity" against all (pseudo-)Christian perfectionisms, while yet condemning such mediocre Christians *as Christians*, as faulty, though typical, participants in the reception of and response to the grace of Christ.[22]

Niebuhr takes it as axiomatic that the righteousness we receive in Christ's death and Resurrection is not "proper" to us. Justification is the event by which the self, "so created in freedom that it cannot realize itself within itself," is given its completion from beyond itself by the graceful love of God (1943, 108). This new life requires, or is constituted by, the human's freely given response to God's freely given initiatory activity. In some sense, this is the location of the human's power before which God is powerless, in the sense that God's action to help the human in this life (but not to *save* the human) relies upon a response by the human which God cannot compel. God's grace can be *resisted*; without the acknowledgment of this fact, the concept of responsibility, in both its moral and spiritual dimensions, becomes meaningless (cf. 1943, 116–18). Because the grace of God is always *offering* itself to us, our perfection depends upon our own "appropriation" of that grace, our decision to live under its yoke. Because of this, however, we always discover that "the new life is not an achieved reality" (1943, 119). It is with this fact that a fissure appears in grace, and within the graced human, one patterned after the human's immediate participation in both time and eternity.

The failure of grace to perfect the human immediately and absolutely is not a failure of the quality of God's grace – as if God were

---

[22] See Markus 1990. Markus's essay is excellent, as far as it goes; but it leaves unthought the value of the enormous critical leverage that Augustine's admission that weak-willed Christians are still Christians gives him, for it allows him to chastise them as bad Christians. The more impatient Pelagians forbade themselves this leverage, by simply rejecting such persons' claims to be Christian.

"holding back the *really* good stuff"[23] – but rather a failure of the human will, a failure rooted in the nature of its sin. For Niebuhr, the fact of our estranged condition – even in grace – from this world and from God in this world, the human's status as *viator*, suggests that "in the development of the new life some contradiction between human self-will and the divine purpose remains" (1943, 121). Because our freedom is not abolished but perfected in grace, we can still deny our true relation to God. We are *simul iustus et peccator*, simultaneously justified and sinners. As always with Niebuhr, we must affirm both the insights of those who appreciate the corruption of human agency, even after receiving grace, and the insights of those who appreciate the illimitable capacities of human agency, even before the reception of grace.[24]

Now we have before us a brief summary of Niebuhr's position. It is an inescapable fact of our lives that, as we are free, we live in history and participate in sin. Yet this need not lead us to despair, because faith in Christ allows us to live in hope, though this hope is chastened both by the knowledge of our own impurity, and by the knowledge that that impurity cannot excuse our efforts to live righteously.

NIEBUHR'S PARTIAL AUGUSTINIANISM

As Niebuhr is so insistent that we cannot be without flaws, it should come as no surprise that his work possesses them as well. Most basically, the problem is that the properly Augustinian elements of Niebuhr's proposal are combined with elements that corrupt it, so we must use the former to critique the latter. By doing so we move "beyond" Niebuhr's formulations in a way that incorporates his insights at the most basic level, thus further carrying forward the Augustinian tradition.

---

[23] There is an important point about eschatology here. As the medieval doctrine of Purgatory (which I am not interested, at the moment at least, in trying to repristinate) implies, the Divine is doing *all things possible*, to the point of *death*, to save humans *now*. The need of an eschaton in the Christian tradition is an index of the weakness of our will; its promise is an index of the greatness of God's power and love. (Again, see Gilkey 1975.) This fact has interesting implications for the long-running (purported) dispute between Eastern and Western Christianity about the "economic" or "immanent" nature of God as Trinity, at which I only gesture.

[24] This is in essence the "synthesis of Reformation and Renaissance" that Niebuhr speaks about in 1943, 204–12: an acknowledgment of the Reformation's insight into human corruption, coupled with an affirmation of the Renaissance's insights about the creative potentialities of human freedom.

Realism as pessimism: epistemology and sin

The criticisms of Niebuhr's Christian realism are typically twofold, concerning his account's Christian-ness and its "realism." To its critics, Niebuhr's theology seems to refuse the first-order Christian language any real purchase on reality, preferring instead to fend it off with a symbolic interpretation of the language, and a "realistic" interpretation of its moral grip on us which makes the Great Commandment of love an "impossible possibility." This makes Niebuhr's "realism" not realistic at all but depressingly pessimistic, in a way that warrants a cynical Constantinianism. These criticisms are right to note that his account is tempted towards both a moral and an epistemological pessimism.[25] These problems are rooted in his subjectivist epistemology.

In essence, Niebuhr's metaphysical pessimism is rooted proximately in the fact that he has "naturalized" sin. His analysis of sin as "inevitable yet not necessary" is meant to explain why we cannot help but sin, yet retain responsibility for so doing (1941, 251). But as several commentators argue, this is a distinction without a difference in Niebuhr's thought (see Gamwell 1975). His argument is that humans exist, as John Hick says, at some "epistemic distance" (Hick 1978, 281) from God – a distance of which we are made anxiously aware by our sense of emptiness, the knowledge of an absence which is the negative knowledge given in "general revelation" – and that, given the anxiety that situation naturally elicits, they inevitably fabricate some comforting idol for themselves as a consolation prize.

The problem is best expressed in terms of the language of "general" and "special" revelation which Niebuhr assumes. For Niebuhr, "general" revelation is "an overtone implied in all experience," the perpetual "testimony in the conscience of every person that his life touches a reality beyond himself, a reality deeper and higher than the system of nature in which he stands" (1941, 127). "Special" revelation, on the other hand, is the "positive" revelation of God to us, the content of which was slowly revealed in the salvation-history of the Israelites and was consummated in Christ. In short, "special" revelation clarifies the general senses apprehended in subjective existence with a special "word" made manifest in public history (see 1941, 130).[26] So "special"

---

[25] Nonetheless, Niebuhr was far more a progressive than a conservative. See McCann 1981, chapter four.

[26] This account allows Niebuhr to develop positive support for his argument while not insisting or expecting it to be convincing to all his interlocutors. He is very certain that his system cannot be

revelation quiets the anxiety the human feels by being created with "general" revelation.

But whence this anxiety? Is it not itself a sign of a prior sinful mistrust? Indeed, this sinful mistrust seems elicited (at least reasonable, and possibly even required) by the condition in which we are created by God – at least on Niebuhr's picture of that creation. All Niebuhr says in defense of his account is that the doctrine of original sin expresses how human experience teaches us that sin "presupposes itself":

> No matter how far back it is traced in the individual or the race, or even preceding the history of the race, a profound scrutiny of the nature of evil reveals that there is an element of sin in the temptation which leads to sin; and that, without this presupposed evil, the consequent sin would not necessarily arise from this situation in which man finds himself. (1986, 245–6)

Sin cannot be explained without temptation, but the inner logic of temptation reveals an evil lurking therein, which hides a further temptation, which reveals a further evil, and so on *ad infinitum* – so that, in evil, we find a (quite literally) vicious circle.[27] The recognition of this reality requires a "provisional defiance of logic" in order to capture the "dialectical truth" of the doctrine of original sin (see 1941, 262–4). In this situation Niebuhr can appeal to paradox and demand the "provisional defiance of logic" for as long as he wishes, but the account he offers of sin "presupposing itself" still avoids the issue. Niebuhr invests evil with causal power; he reproduces Adam and Eve's sinful attempt to describe a causality with its first cause beyond them (i.e., in the serpent – see Gen. 3:12–13). In doing this, he rejects his putative Augustinian roots, because evil for Augustine (as we saw in chapter two) has no genuine reality, and

---

proven, but requires a subjective assent – faith – which may be *warranted*, or supported, by arguments and evidence from history, personal experience, etc. I am using the word "warranted" in a way in which Niebuhr himself never does; but I do not think this does much violence to his argument. See 1941, 141: "while the course of historical events does not inevitably yield the prophetic interpretation of events, it is significant that history does justify such an interpretation, *once faith in the God of the prophets is assumed.*" (Emphasis mine.) For Niebuhr, reason and faith are not exclusive forms of enquiry; rather they complement one another. Reason is not wrong, it is simply insufficient (see 1986, 235). As should become clear, this essay disputes precisely this epistemological claim, suggesting on the contrary that there is no clear distinction between particular faith and universal reason, and that all inquiry proceeds from first principles (which complement and render adequate the minimal first principles of logic, etc.) which, while open to a kind of evaluation, are (in this world) never indisputable.

27 See 1941, 250–1: "The actual sin is the consequence of the temptation of anxiety in which all life stands. But anxiety alone is neither actual nor original sin. Sin does not flow necessarily from it. Consequently the bias toward sin from which actual sin flows is anxiety plus sin. Or, in the words of Kierkegaard, sin presupposes itself. Man could not be tempted if he had not already sinned" (see 254, 262–4).

hence no causality. His account of the God–world relationship stacks the deck in favor of the Fall. But this makes it difficult for us to see the Fall's real and essential absurdity. In effect, he explains the Fall too well.[28]

Niebuhr's account not only explains sin too well; it also makes faith and hope seem absurd, miraculous, contrary to all available evidence. Niebuhr's work depicts the human as inevitably sinful and the human world as inevitably conflictual, a vale of tears which we can never escape. The fact that sin seems reasonable, and hope and faith unreasonable, are for Niebuhr's critics merely symptomatic of his deep metaphysical pessimism. The problem is not that this metaphysics is explanatorily asymmetrical, but that the asymmetry is the wrong way round: Niebuhr's asymmetry is that of the Manichees', one which pictures our world as a world of corpses, a world in which God is not simply epistemically hidden but actually absent.[29] This pessimism about existence in the world, and its emphasis upon limits, serves to quarantine the "really important" issues of our lives from contamination by historical and material existence, and tempts us to a more conservative stance than necessary, a demoralized and demoralizing worldview in which worldly involvement, however necessary, is inevitably disappointing. Niebuhr's account still insists that our real goods are not themselves really *worldly*, that our existence in the world remains merely a necessary evil. For all his animadversions, Niebuhr's thought remained perpetually tempted to become a "theology of containment," and to affirm a politics of deflated expectations and inevitable disappointments.

Niebuhr's account is not only metaphysically pessimistic; it is equally so epistemologically.[30] This epistemic pessimism underlies his account of sin as "inevitable yet not necessary," for it entails that human attempts to think God are invariably projections. The human mind is nothing but a factory of idols, fabricating anthropomorphic Gods as comforters of our anxieties. What truth we can know about God is wholly *negative*: God is not here, God is a *Deus absconditus*, a hidden God. We know only God's

---

[28] See Bonhoeffer 1997.

[29] On Niebuhr's vision of the world as "two-worldly" and implying a "pre-Christian" eschatology see H. R. Niebuhr 1996, 94, 98.

[30] At least with regard to our knowledge of God. While I argue only that Niebuhr's thought is epistemologically pessimistic as regards knowledge of God, this is because Niebuhr's epistemology was only developed in sufficient detail as regards knowledge of God. So I suspect this restriction is only due to Niebuhr's never having elaborated a general epistemology. (But who would do that without a gun to their head?)

My criticism here is nicely paralleled by Robert Song's worry that Niebuhr's epistemology "can resemble Averroist scepticism (based on epistemological finitude) more than Augustinian humility (based on original sin)." Song 1997, 77 n. 118. See also Kroeker 1995, 134–9.

absence; it haunts us, because we know vaguely that we need just such a presence to be whole creatures.[31] Religious language is thus fundamentally a *negative* language, revealing to us the inadequacy of any of our conceptualizations and our lack of any positive knowledge. We know God most fundamentally as what we fail to comprehend, as limit.[32] This is argumentatively useful; his symbolic or mythic account of Christian discourse works to fend off any challenge that his metaphysics is underdeveloped. Furthermore, it is coherent with his metaphysics: Just as his metaphysics is built upon a picture of God as *Deus absconditus*, so his epistemology ends up entailing a *theologica absconditus*. In all this he is in part justly iconoclastic. With the early Barth, and with much recent so-called "postmodern" discussion of the difficulty of naming God, he is wary of any anthropomorphizing, any Babylonian captivity of the Divinity. But one may say, as one can to the early Barth (and many "postmoderns"), that while it is good to protest that one cannot say "God" merely by saying "man" in a loud voice, neither can one say "God" just by saying "no" in a loud voice. Iconoclasm can be idolatrous.[33]

These criticisms are not new. They extend back to H. Richard Niebuhr, and have received their most incisive recent formulation in John Milbank's critique of Kantian "theologies of right."[34] Such criticisms suggest that the root problem lies in Niebuhr's excessively "transcendent" theology, his picture of God as not immanent in us and hence not immediately present to us – a picture which gives too much validity to our essentially sinful perspective which (of course) pictures God as somewhere else, not here. But the deep problem is not Niebuhr's anthropocentric theology but his theomorphic anthropology, his assumption that humans must come to construct their understanding of the world on their own – his assumption that they are gifted with an epistemological analog of God's *ex nihilo* power. This may seem to be a simple problem with Niebuhr's epistemology and his refusal to give up claims of "faith" versus reason, and has been read as such by some critics.[35] But the issue seems more basically anthropological than episte-

---

[31] Here we see some of the worries that blossom in "postmodernist" critiques of the idea of God (see M. Taylor 1984), and of "presence" in general (see Steiner 1989). Deconstructionist "atheologies" have been recently accused of a fideism similar to Niebuhr's own; see Wennemyr 1998.

[32] This is the issue over which Reinhold Niebuhr and his brother H. Richard Niebuhr part ways. For H. Richard, Reinhold misses the way that his account of the *Deus absconditus* loosens the world from God's providential control, which is too high a price to pay for making such sense of sin. (This reminds us again that God's providence was meant to be a doctrine of comfort.) See H. R. Niebuhr 1996, 95–6, 100.   [33] See Damascene 1980 and Schweiker 1990.

[34] See Milbank 1997, 7–35.   [35] See for example Gamwell 1975.

mological. As Rebekah Miles has perceptively noted, the basic problem lies in "a weakness in his model of the self," which is his separation of "boundedness and freedom within the self."[36]

Miles describes what I call Niebuhr's subjectivism. The term "subjectivism" refers to that set of understandings of human existence that assume that human subjects have priority over against what is "outside" them – that human subjects make the first move in acting in the "outside" world, coming to understand the world, and in general in all their "relations" to that outside. Subjectivist worldviews picture the self's relations to the world as essentially technological. Furthermore, the world itself becomes a "wilderness of mirrors," for such worldviews create the basic anxiety that, in seeking some way to relate to the world, to get to the "outside," we will never get there – that, as Emerson said, "use what language we will, we can never say anything but what we are" (Emerson 1957, 271).[37] "Subjectivism" so described encompasses a wide variety of views; voluntarism, projectivism, and solipsism are all species of subjectivism.[38]

Niebuhr's subjectivism manifests itself in his epistemology, his picture of the human inquirer. *Contra* Tillich, who famously claimed that Niebuhr had no epistemology,[39] Niebuhr in fact built his account of sin upon one. This account assumes that the human is primordially independent of the world, and must achieve an understanding of the world by itself, through constructing an intellectual bridge to it. This is so for theology as well as ontology; as we are necessarily, though tragically only partially, self-transcendent creatures, we know we must trust in some external power, but we cannot know anything about it. All we know is our lack; we are "in the position of being unable to comprehend [ourselves] in [our] full stature of freedom without a principle of comprehension . . . beyond [our] comprehension" (1941, 125). The deep root of sin thus lies not in disobedience but in our misinterpretation of our relation to God. What is crucial here is that *the human* must do the interpret-

---

[36] See Miles 1996, 140. Miles's essay locates the crucial disagreement between feminist theologians and Niebuhr as rooted in confusions on both sides about the character of human agency. Part of this chapter's task is to exploit the conflicting resources in Niebuhr about agency that Miles's essay identifies.

[37] The phrase "a wilderness of mirrors" is from "Gerontion," in Eliot 1970.

[38] I have nothing invested in restricting this understanding of human existence to "modern" thought; it seems more of a perennial temptation.

[39] Though of course Tillich also wrote an essay about this epistemology (and used this quip, disarmingly, at the beginning of that essay); see Tillich 1961, 36: "The difficulty of writing about Niebuhr's epistemology lies in the fact that there is no such epistemology. Niebuhr does not ask, 'How can I know?'; he starts knowing."

ing, the human is the actor: for Niebuhr, the self constructs its own self-understanding *ex nihilo*, without access to any set of givens to which it may appeal.

Nor is this subjectivism effectively countered by Niebuhr's insistence on the importance of the "special revelation" of the Divine, for "special revelation" is only superficially a moment of God's activity: God's "special revelation" is still realized or grasped by human faith, and must be "constantly apprehended inwardly by faith" (1943, 57). "Special" revelation is "special" not because of the epistemic mode by which it is apprehended, but by the particular content of what is apprehended.[40] Niebuhr's account of "special" revelation really refers only to the *historical* specificity of the revelation; it is "special" in the sense of being "particular," but it is only metaphorically "revelation." Niebuhr's tradition insists that God's action is essential for human salvation, so seems to necessitate some positive revelation of God, but Niebuhr's subjectivist commitments entail that humans must be themselves wholly responsible for their self-understanding, and his epistemology opts for the latter against the former. To gain knowledge of God, human subjects must act first, that is, must ask questions and thereby enter into any kind of relation with God; it is human agents who must both realize its status as a question, and then grasp the special revelation which answers that question. Thus Niebuhr makes God's "special revelation" essentially a passive sort of "action" on God's part, an offering which neither breaks into the human's consciousness, nor is always already within it, but rather waits upon the human to apprehend it.[41] No wonder, on this picture, that sin is "inevitable": if the revelation of the authentic source of human meaning waits upon God's revelation, and if we humans are anxiously impatient for such comprehension, we invariably settle on some partial vision as grounding ourselves. (This also explains his account of the [at best] negativity of religious language and myth.) Niebuhr's picture of the God–world relation is too metaphysically dualistic, and his realism is concomitantly too ethically pessimistic, because his anthropology is partially subjectivist. I am not alone in condemning such subjectivism in theology; echoing Bonhoeffer, I am saying that "epistemology" is sin – or rather a consequence of sin – and that our recognition of that fact should make us wary of giving epistemology an

---

[40] Note Niebuhr's location of action in his analyses of these moments; "faith *discerns*" (1941, 136; my emphasis).

[41] This is where the implicit criticism (in Gustafson 1986) of Niebuhr as offering a "theology in the service of ethics" has some purchase on Niebuhr's thought.

overly systematic, or overly central, role in our theology or anthropology (see Griffiths 1999b). But I am alone in suggesting that Niebuhr himself offers us a standpoint from which this criticism becomes possible. For the above is not the whole Niebuhr; and as J. L. Austin said, there is the part where you say it and the part where you take it back. Niebuhr's Manichean elements (or tendencies) are paralleled by a fundamentally Augustinian account of the perversion of human nature, an insight built upon Augustine's love-psychology. That is, while his explicit theology is written from the perspective of sin, his theological anthropology is written from the perspective of grace, and in fact is built upon the thought of the Doctor of Grace, St. Augustine.

Niebuhr's Augustinian anthropology: sin without cynicism

Niebuhr's realism can be construed, not as a pre-given set of claims about the world, but rather as an attitude of humility before it, an attempt to develop a "Christian realism" which is not pessimistic but rather empowering, as Robin Lovin has convincingly demonstrated (see Lovin 1995). This realism is not governed by the subjectivistic epistemology detailed above, but is instead rooted in the altogether different and more fertile soil of an Augustinian anthropology of love. I want to detail this love-anthropology and show how it offers a (quite literally) radically different form of realism, one immune to the problems that cripple the other.

Lovin's account suggests that Niebuhr is most basically a *reflexive* realist, a realist about the value and perils of "realism" itself. Niebuhr is aware of the fact that our root motive for reflection, for theory – the need to find our way through a complex and bewildering world – is best served by resisting theory's hegemony, refusing to crown theory the master of our consciousness and our conscience.[42] Niebuhr's realism hence entails a fundamentally humble approach to both understanding and undertaking action, a humility which serves as one of the keystones of his thought. In terms of understanding, if we want to transcend partial

---

[42] "By becoming explicitly aware of the often implicit role and influence of theoretical considerations in our lives, we may be better able to demystify our own theoretical positions, recognize their proper limitations, and check their imperialistic ambitions. Theories are finally responsible to us, not we to them. Awareness of how deeply theories reflect us and the conflicts we face should, I hope, help us to put an end to the dangerous tendency to treat theories as religions . . . Practical theorizing should take the form of thoughtful, workmanlike design and tinkering, and should accept as its starting point a generous conception of the conflicting values that are its subject matter. Theoretical reflexes . . . are ultimately a sad category mistake" (Hurley 1989, 383).

accounts, we might want to develop an account which acknowledges both the imperfections of our own position, and all its real insights, rather than jettison some of them in a fit of excessive epistemological pique. That is, we might want to place supreme value on having the most *comprehensive* account possible, even if that account is at present not fully *comprehensible*.[43] Breadth of vision is more important than any fastidious fixation on seamless theoretical coherence; it is better to violate our canons of consistency than allow our (most likely narcissistic) concerns about the elegance of our epistemic framework to trump our appreciation of ontological realities. When seen in this light, "realism," as Niebuhr offers it, is most basically the claim that content surpasses form: *what is true* is more important than *how we know* that it is true. Our practical concerns must not be subordinated to our methodological ones. Indeed, "realism" is a method most basically by being an *anti*-method.[44]

Understood in this way, Niebuhr's famous skepticism about claims to innocence or purity is not a disabling, paralyzing hermeneutics of suspicion, but rather an "enabling humility," an empowering recognition that perfect knowledge and total purity are not only impossible but unnecessary, and that our desire for such perfection is pernicious.[45] Far from trapping us in despair, this skepticism liberates us by equipping us to resist two opposing temptations for partial resolutions of our quandary – a presumptuously optimistic "rationalism," which presumes it can attain (or rather always already *has* attained) some ideal of total knowingness and thus can perfectly control existence; and a despairingly cynical and iconoclastic "skepticism" which is the condition into which disillusioned rationalists inevitably recoil.[46] We know in part and in a mirror dimly; this realization compels us both to act and to beware the partiality (in several senses) of our understanding. This form of Niebuhr's realism allows us to recognize sin without lapsing into cynicism.

---

[43] Niebuhr's pragmatism makes this the basis of his critiques of others as much as it is for his positive articulation of his own work. Indeed, he is a dialectical thinker precisely in presenting his positive position through a detailed critique of others' failings: he advances his own position by demonstrating other accounts' failure to accommodate "all the facts," and defends his own position as more comprehensive, if possibly less logically tight, than their own.

[44] See Smith 1995. Niebuhr's work here fits in well with recent developments in anti-foundationalism in epistemology and theories of inquiry generally. For good examples of this, see Murphy 1990 and Foley 1993. For a manifestation of this in ethical theory proper, see Hursthouse 1996, 31–2.

[45] I borrow the phrase "an enabling humility," and much of the thought behind it, from Merrin 1990.

[46] See Niebuhr 1986, 218–36, 248: while the world and God will never be fully transparent to us, nonetheless "our faith cannot be identified with poetic forms of religion which worship mystery without any conception of meaning."

This realism is built upon a positive picture of the human, a "transcendental anthropology"[47] whose intelligibility and hermeneutic adequacy is detailed "realistically," via Niebuhr's existential analyses of humans as self-interpreting beings existing in the world, an analysis of both the inner dynamics of human agents and their relations to what is "outside" them.[48] But this anthropology in turn is not constructed *de novo* by Niebuhr; it is premised upon a psychology of human sinfulness in terms of dishonesty and perversion, a psychology that relies on an Augustinian account of the human as "always already" positively related to God and the world.[49] (Niebuhr himself recognized this debt; as he himself said, "I was first influenced not so much by the Reformers as by the study of St. Augustine" [Niebuhr in Kegley and Bretall 1961, 437; see 1953].) On this Augustinian account, the Fall is never total, because every explicit rejection of God by the human implicitly affirms the human's true dependence upon God. As Niebuhr says, "the dishonesty of man is thus an interesting refutation of the doctrine of man's total depravity" (1941, 203). Sin's character as dishonesty reveals that a genuine anthropology is ineliminably a *theological* anthropology. Human sin is never the simple revolt of the whole human against God, and the consequent complete alienation of the self from God; sin is best described as the disruption and division of humans as we try to live explicitly without God while implicitly, in our very revolt, relying upon God. This rebellion of the self against itself is seen in the human's own conscience: *"The 'I,' which from the perspective of self-transcendence, regards the sinful self not as self but as 'sin,' is the same I which from the perspective of sinful action regards the transcendent possibilities of the self as not the self but as 'law.' It is the same self"* (1941, 278–9). Just as its conscience directly reveals the self's ineliminable self-transcendence, so it indirectly reveals the self's ineliminable rootedness in a divine other. For it is only because the human relies upon God, even in abandoning God, that the human's act is sin and not simple self-annihilation. But humans avoid recognizing this, so our sinful lives are extended attempts to live out a lie we tell to ourselves.

This account of human agency ensures human responsibility by locating the origin of sin not in God's absence from the self, but in the self's attempt to absent itself from God, in its preemptive seizure of

---

[47] See Lear 1998, 247–81. For a good analysis of anthropology as distinct from ethnography in this sense, see Sperber 1985, especially Essay 1, "Interpretive ethnography and theoretical anthropology."

[48] Donald Meyer calls *The Nature and Destiny of Man* not so much a technical theology as "an exercise in philosophical psychology" (1988, xviii).

[49] I have learned much from discussions on this with Franklin I. Gamwell.

priority from God, and its attempt to be *sicut Deus*, like God.[50] Thus what my first section detailed as subjectivism turns out to be not simply a common (and debilitating) problem in modern thought, but also the proper description of sin. The priority of human activity over against the Divine, and the consequential infinite distance separating God and the world, is what we sinners *want* to be the case, what we would like to be true. The self's lack of faith in God causes it to lose its coherence and become a "lesser self"; however, it is not exactly appropriate to describe the "less"-ness of that self as a lost thing, but rather the continually tormented *attempt* to lose something – namely, to lose one's dependence on God.[51] But the soul cannot lose that ground, for to do so would be not to exist. So it wrestles with itself, perpetually struggling to escape God, and hence itself. The inescapably present possibility of salvation is due not to their own explicit or conscious self-will, but rather to their implicit or unconscious dependence upon God – or, rather, God's continued support of them, support which, despite the human's best efforts, refuses to permit the human to annihilate itself. This phenomenon is often called the "divided self"; but perhaps it is better, to describe this phenomenon not so much in terms of division as revolt, the *whole* self revolting against both God *and* itself; most basically, the self is not *divided*, but *self-deceiving* (see 1941, 278).

This psychology of duplicity offers an account different from, and superior to, the epistemological one between "general" and "special" revelation. Rather than identifying God's positive revelation with special revelation, the self is always already related in some positive manner to God, and implicitly acknowledges that relationship. The human's ontological dependence translates into an epistemological dependence; thus, humans are able to know only insofar as they know God. Thus, even fallen humans have some vestigial knowledge of God, the loss of which would render them incapable of any thought at all.

Confessing sin: beyond Niebuhr

The revised account offered here is properly what H. Richard Niebuhr called a "confessionalist" account, because it begins from premises which it does not initially attempt to demonstrate, but rather which it assumes and builds upon, in the hope that the account it constructs from

---

[50] See Bonhoeffer 1997 on "*Sicut Deus.*"
[51] See Bonhoeffer 1997 on having life "not as a gift but as a command," and how this is the essence of death, in *Creation and Fall*.

these premises will be able subsequently to quiet its interlocutors' concerns (see H. R. Niebuhr 1963, 42–5). But the other valence of the term "confessional" is also significant, for the term admits in its connotative aura both the speaker's fallibility and their responsibility for that fallibility. This is not a "fideism" in the sense that the convictions being confessed are beyond critical investigation; rather, they are ineliminably indexed to the situation of the agent, and represent that agent's best attempt to understand the convictions they hold. Still, such epistemic humility differs from humiliation, and confessionalism shares with fideism an indifference to, and indeed a dismissal of, impatient demands that the claims must be immediately justifiable in a way that quiets every skeptical concern. As Newman said, it is as easy to torture, as to argue, a man to belief; confessionalism is thus the epistemological manifestation of an attitude of repentance, continual conversion, and a humble recognition of the improbability of convincing all interlocutors.[52]

This "confessionalist" method begins by recognizing the sinful self's self-recognition as sinful, but only from the perspective of grace. The human's status as sinner always already implies the attempt of God to redeem them, and their own at least implicit assent to such redemption; hence the first step humans take is to acknowledge the situation of futile rebellion in which the self finds itself. There is not an initiatory moment of self-introspection in which one recognizes the absence of God; rather, one's introspection reveals a struggle which itself predates all possible introspection. This is the proper sense of Niebuhr's claim that "sin posits itself" – the originality of sin is not ontological, but epistemological; sin is not present as a temptation, as sheer possibility; rather, sin is always already present as the situation into which the self has fallen, and behind which it cannot see.

The key affirmation for this confessionalist account is its affirmation of the priority of some reality to thought about it. God is not *thought to*, but *thought from*; the first principles are prior to, and ground, cognition.[53] And the reality of God is grasped, for this account, by the human's

---

[52] One might understand this contrast in terms of different understandings of justification: subjectivist accounts suggest that one must be epistemically self-justifying, while a confessionalist account suggests that one is ultimately not self-justifying at all, but is justified only by God. I am not at all sure that the distinction between the kinds of justification here elaborated – the one epistemological, the other soteriological – in the end invalidates the contrast.

[53] This is in some ways an account analogous to "externalist" epistemologies, in that this account takes human beliefs to be formed not by introspectionalist mechanisms, but by reality (in some sense) "impinging" upon the self. It differs, however, in its ability to account for error; that is, it acknowledges that reality has a limited capacity to influence human thought, and that human thought can deeply misconstrue the character of reality. See Foley 1993.

ability to realize the real character of their own state as *fallen* beings. Fear of the Lord is the beginning of wisdom, says the Psalmist, and that may be true; but the origins of all wisdom are in God's self-giving to all creation. As its name implies, a "confessional" account begins with this recognition, and cannot step behind it. In dialogue with opponents who do not acknowledge its basic insights, it can only, positively, refute their accusations of incoherence, and, negatively, demonstrate the incoherence of those other accounts. But it cannot prove to them its own truth, for such "proof" is unavailable to the account; assenting to its truth is a matter of recognition, and recognition can never be compelled. To borrow from the philosopher Erazim Kohák, "here philosophy needs not to speculate but to see" (1984, 60); the origins of belief are not in argument but, in some metaphorical sense, in vision.

A confessionalist epistemology is implied by Niebuhr's account of sin, and can helpfully replace the troublesome subjectivist epistemology which Niebuhr himself employs. Such a confessionalist account avoids the confusions between epistemology and ontology that Niebuhr's account otherwise entails, and can accommodate the full power of his account of sin as a basic perversion of our true natures, which remain distorted but still present, in our sinful existence. In its deepest roots, then, Niebuhr's account of sin is premised on a theological anthropology which locates human sin within an overarching horizon of divine love. This is a profoundly Augustinian vision; central to it is Niebuhr's development of Augustine's insight that humans always act for some love, that sin is the consequence of our flawed pursuit of genuine goods, and that the world is composed of two "cities," two distinct principles or orientations of human love or forms of existence, one of which tries to live solely in and through itself, the other of which lives in and through God.[54] In this sinful world, neither of these is ever present without the other, although our sense of the proper form of love reveals the final futility of self-centered love, and the need of our transcendent comprehension.

This Augustinian theological anthropology not only sets the terms for Niebuhr's critiques of other accounts, typically as projects of *recurvatus in se est*; it also operates constructively, both to motivate and chasten our involvement in the world. That is, the proposal is finally practically valuable, and in a way that many of its critics have not yet managed to be, because it promotes a fundamental attitude of *acknowledging responsibility* in inhabiting the world. We will see what this means next.

---

[54] The classic account of this is found in *DCD* XVIII.28.

NIEBUHR'S AUGUSTINIAN REALISM: ACKNOWLEDGING
RESPONSIBILITY

One might respond to the above: so what? At best it lets us extract from
Niebuhr's work a theological anthropology innocent of the accusations
leveled against him. But one might think that I have merely exonerated
Niebuhr on technicalities. That misses the point, however, for what is
really valuable is Niebuhr's use of this account to develop a program of
"acknowledging responsibility" which encourages a certain kind of participation in "the world" that he thinks Christianity promotes. His proposal motivates us not to escape the world, but rather more fully to enter
into it; it works to make our lives, as Robin Lovin suggests, "fully political" (1995, 189).

The practical program: Niebuhr and democracy

But ought a theology to be "fully political"? What does this suggest about
Niebuhr's proposal? Niebuhr's thought is often understood as "political"
in a problematic sense, as just a theological *apologia* for "democracy."
And there is much in Niebuhr to support this interpretation. Niebuhr
himself can be read as arguing that this proposal culminates in a religious legitimation for democracy, and he famously claimed, "Man's
capacity for justice makes democracy possible; but man's inclination to
injustice makes democracy necessary" (1944, xiii; cf. 1943, 268, 282).
Niebuhr's thought does seem vulnerable to accusations that he offered a
"theology of America."[55] While I do not think this is what he meant to
do, Niebuhr's intentions are of no ultimate concern for me here; in
developing his thought we need not take on whatever ideological tint it
took.[56] For the account's practical conclusion does not in any straightforward manner simply recommend democracy. Rather, it forces us into
the continual turbulence of dynamic disagreement which serves both to
uncover new insights (about the nature and destiny of mankind) and in

---

[55] See, for example, Hauerwas and Broadway 1997.
[56] This would be a good place to talk about Niebuhr's understanding of the church. I avoid this
discussion only because there is too much to say. There is something in the worry that Niebuhr's
church was America. But Niebuhr does not think that churches are ontologically different from
any other human association; Christ is as present, and as governing, outside the church as within
it. Niebuhr, as I am reading him, has a high Christology and what we may call a low ecclesio-
logy. This does not entail that we need to assume that Niebuhr thought – let alone that Niebuhr's
thought (in the form in which I have commended it here) compels *us* to think – that the churches
are irrelevant to salvation; it is just that they may not be as different from the world as we might
like to think. Eschatology does include a "not yet" alongside the "now."

turn to relativize those insights, to insist on their provisionality, by subjecting them to further criticism. Certainly such a practical vision has the potential to flower in democracy. But such is not the project's ultimate aim.

Niebuhr's practical proposal is as complex as the anthropology that sustains it. For Niebuhr, in order to resist our perennial tendencies towards sin, we must limit our own power. Niebuhr distinguishes two distinct facets of human existence which we need to govern with an awareness of our own impurity. Niebuhr calls these two facets "the quest for truth" and "the achievement of just and brotherly relations," or "the struggle for justice," which together "comprise the cultural and the socio-moral problems of history" (1943, 213). He proposes a dialectical affirmation of both the need of toleration in order for all to seek and more fully apprehend the truth, and the importance of that truth for human existence. He also proposes a dialectical affirmation of the necessity of justice within an acknowledgment of our fundamental love of and care for one another, a love that knows its own fallibility and hence willingly constrains itself for its own more ultimate goals.

Justice and love

Niebuhr's famous account of the relation between justice and love is not simply a "two-tier" account of how one kind of private (theoretical) motive can warrant a general, lowest common denominator form of public (practical) consensus about justice; it instead works to subvert such simplistic accounts.[57] Niebuhr recognizes that the sober appreciation of our self-centered and mutually uncomprehending motivations leads us to chasten our will to community, even as a sensitive appreciation of the genuineness of our love still leads us forward: "Even if perfect love were presupposed, complex relations, involving more than two persons, require the calculation of rights" (1943, 252). As Langdon Gilkey says, "there is, granted the continuation of sin, an ineradicable tension between the possibilities of communal justice and the requirements of perfect love" (1975, 48). Nonetheless, while his account resists the simple application of "love" on the world, it remains in its deep structure a

---

[57] See Ward 1986, 85. Lovin himself, whose argument about Niebuhr's concept of love and justice has decisively shaped my own, can seem at times to verge on something like this – see 1995, 231 where he argues that, despite "theoretical differences" between Niebuhr's position and "contemporary liberal theories" such as those of John Rawls, the "practical effect" is almost the same. Lovin's argument here may be read as assuming a division between theory and praxis that we have good reason to doubt and that, on my account, Niebuhr need not affirm (see Pinches 1987).

"love-ethic," promoting a project of "building up" from our local attachments to a proper moral comportment in all our dealings. As he says, "justice is an application of the law of love. The rules are not absolute but relative. They are applications of the law of love and do not have independence apart from it. They would be independent only if they were founded in an "essential" social structure . . . [but] it is not possible to define an essential structure of community except the law of love" (Niebuhr in Kegley and Bretall 1961, 435–6). Justice is not an external constraint on love, it is the critical corrective love imposes upon itself in order to ensure that it does not overwhelm its object.

This has two crucial implications. First, Niebuhr's account insists that restrictive appeals to purely prudential considerations, so dear to most contemporary political theorists, will not suffice to legitimate any account of justice (at least an account of justice that we would recognize as "justice"); we are moral beings, in part naturally other-regarding, and an adequate theory of justice must acknowledge this fact. In proper Augustinian fashion, this means that justice cannot be anchored on our fears, but must be based on our loves; however risky that seems to some people, it is the only way it can be done. (Appeals to prudence only superficially support an ethic of respect in any event, while they more deeply corrode such ethics by reinforcing a consumerist attitude towards reality as a whole.) This opposes all contemporary versions of the ethics of inarticulacy, those ethical programs which refuse to acknowledge our positive motives towards justice, and seek to quarantine those motives to the private realm. His rejection of such ethics is as crucial for moral epistemology as it is for moral psychology, for it entails that we need not jettison our particular reasons when we act in public, nor conform our actions to some putatively universal (or at least supposedly non-local) canon of rationality. Form and content cannot come apart that way; the public and the private are neither ontologically primordial orders of creation nor historically immutable; they were based upon what Sabina Lovibond calls "the metaphysics of commuter-land," the dichotomy of (implicitly feminine) emotional motivation with (implicitly masculine) neutral and dispassionate reason (1983, 96).

Second, as Niebuhr's critique of natural law should make clear, the account makes justice a *dynamic* reality rather than a static achievement, and insists that we cannot rest complacent with any minimal conception of justice.[58] This is not simply (or even often) a request for more passion in political struggles for justice; it is more centrally a request for greater

---

[58] See 1943, 244: "No fixed limits can be placed upon either the purity or the breadth of the brotherhood for which men strive in history."

attention to how passion is always already operative in politics, both in motivating and in hindering justice. At some historical moment, the limits to the degree of justice we can reasonably expect are in all likelihood not because we do not love enough, but rather because we love other things too much; and while a wise Niebuhrian would resist desires for state control over our pursuits of happiness, she or he would equally demand a more serious and sustained public discussion of how the (tragically partial) forms of happiness that we overwhelmingly pursue became preeminent, and what we can do to escape their thrall.[59]

Truth and tolerance

In trying to understand how best to accommodate human claims to truth, Niebuhr's account has both negative and positive facets. Negatively, Niebuhr seeks to steer a middle course between "sanctificationalist" and "progressivist" ideologies, positions which claim either that epistemological certainty is located in a particular (and "sanctified") human institution, or that by a process of putatively free inquiry we will be led ever closer to a perfect grasp of the truth.[60] Sanctificationist views are "structurally intolerant," for they do not "understand that the one everlasting truth of the gospel contains the insight that mere men cannot have this truth 'remote from all fluctuations due to individuality and existence'" (1943, 222); on the other hand, the "tolerance" of modern rationalism is actually an indifference which either expresses an "irresponsible" total skepticism (and "suspension of judgment"), or camouflages a dogmatic absolutism which it refuses to defend (1943, 238).

For Niebuhr, our existence in history is ineliminably ambiguous. Our apprehension of the truth is incomplete, and always corrupted by both an "ideological taint" and an "ignorance of our ignorance" (1943, 213–15); any attempt to deny this is a sinful attempt to escape the condition of the human as *simul iustus et peccator*, and results in either skeptical despair or a perilous fanaticism. Our fate (and our duty) is to participate in, but not master, our world; this participation takes the epistemological form of tolerance, and the acceptance of a critical hermeneutic of suspicion, a provisional skepticism which recognizes our historical contingency and relativity, and thus the always-provisional quality of our

---

[59] All of this only begins to gesture at how the vectors of Niebuhr's thought intersect with the recent interest in "deliberation," and hence participation, as crucial democratic energies in political theory. See Sandel 1996 and Cavanaugh 1998.

[60] See 1943, 216. Whether or not Niebuhr's representation of either of these accounts is correct, both of them appear to be typical forms of dealing with the problems here described. See Carr 1992.

knowledge, yet which recognizes that ossified skepticism, the absolute refusal to judge, is impossible (see 1943, 235–9). Any and all claims made by human beings must be made provisionally, and remain open to dispute (including this one);[61] thus, it claims that all humans are fallible, and require the correction and check of others in order to improve. The wise love a rebuke for the same reason that God loves a contrite heart. To refuse to listen to others in dialogue is to claim an unwarranted completion in history; to be open to a completion from beyond the self, and to be open to the voices of others, is precisely to acknowledge and accept the grace of God working within history to overcome the evil present in history. This humility leads to the provisional tolerance of difference: "Loyalty to the truth requires confidence in the possibility of its attainment; toleration of others requires broken confidence in the finality of our own truth" (1943, 243). While all human claims aspire to finality, no human can ever claim to have achieved it.[62]

A politics of Incarnation: supernaturalizing the natural

All this means that, insofar as Niebuhr's program pushes us towards a "fully political" stance, we must understand "politics" here in a different sense from that allowed by our typical degenerate depictions. It is not simply, nor even centrally, political lobbying about legislation, but is instead the open pursuit of meaning and flourishing in our lives. It is the kind of visible activity whereby the early Christians distinguished themselves from the various esoteric heresies and mystery cults that populated their world. We respond to the grace of Christ most basically by fully embracing our existence in the world as a fragile gift. Of course, Niebuhr's proposal is not for a *theocracy*; we act with knowledge of our sin, so we act with an eye to justice, even as we recognize that, because of our sin, we cannot perfectly realize justice. Our action, that is, must acknowledge its implication in the kinds of things it resists – an acknowledgment related to what Bernard Williams has called "agent-regret" (see 1981, 27–8). This is not, for Niebuhr, a consequentialist abolition of moral scruples (or more accurately, an absolution of moral cruelty); we act "in the contrite knowledge of the guilt of our action," in a way

---

[61] This is not to say that all statements are on the same epistemic level, and subject to the same adjudicability; for precisely *that* statement remains, it seems, irrefutable. What it means, rather, is that human beings are susceptible to (and often tempted by) statements, claims, or beliefs which contain (at the least) an element of falsehood within them. For a valuable discussion of this issue, see Gamwell 1990, especially chapter 1.

[62] For support for Niebuhr's position here, see Graeme 1996, Tanner 1996, and Mathewes 1998.

"which refuses to make sin normative but which also refuses to withdraw from history because all history is sinful" (1942, 64, 63). This differs from Williams' more pagan proposal by being an incipiently incarnational vision. In this sense, Niebuhr's account, while famously emphasizing the importance of the Atonement, more deeply reveals the import of the Incarnation for a properly Christian account of politics.

The Incarnation's centrality for Niebuhr is seen clearly in the centrality of love in his Augustinian psychology. Our lives are organized around "forms of love," which are both affective orientations and cognitive estimations and valuations. This love, or *agape*, is neither wholly "transcendental" nor wholly "material"; while it is fundamentally at home in the world, it stands also beyond the world as both incomprehensible and (now) sinfully vexed within it. This position is more controversial than it may at first appear: against "sentimental" rejections of talk about justice in favor of insisting on the straightforward governance of all relationships by love, *agape* is not a "simple historical possibility"; against "absolutist" interpretations of *agape* as strictly non-worldly, totally inoperative in the world, he insists it is not simply *outside* history, but rather both suffuses and transcends the historical world.[63] We have no direct "worldly" comprehension of *agape*, so we must seek "beyond" the material world to understand them; as Niebuhr says, "the harmonies which are actually achieved in history always are partly borrowed from the Eternal" (1943, 84). But we are meant, naturally, to be agapic: "The 'essential,' the normative man, is thus a 'God-man' whose sacrificial love seeks conformity with, and finds justification in, the divine and eternal *agape*, the ultimate and final harmony of life with life" (1943, 81). Niebuhr's claims about the self-transcendence of human ideals derive from his reflections on the implications of our drive to self-giving love.[64] For Niebuhr, we want these experiences of love; the consummation of our lives is found in such engagements with others. But these desires are, strictly speaking, not worldly warranted, but are "tangents toward the eternal" which find no home in the closed-circuit calculus of the *saeculum*. Hence, insofar as we rightly understand these experiences of self-giving love to be *genuinely* self-giving, we are compelled to seek for a

---

[63] See 1943, 84, 247, 251. Niebuhr's position here is interestingly similar to Oliver O'Donovan's critique of "Jesuology" (1996, 120–2), though O'Donovan (like others) associates Niebuhr simply with the criticism of idealism and misses the positive picture of *agape* underpinning that critique.

[64] Obviously Niebuhr's work here is not very developed, relative to the enormous amount of debate in recent decades on the topic of "the gift." But I think his account is deeply interesting and has much support in contemporary discussions.

"supernatural" source, which we find in the primordial divine *agape* that creates, sustains, and redeems us.

But the term "supernatural" is deeply misleading here; Niebuhr's project, like Augustine's, in fact subverts the whole language of natural versus supernatural. All is interpreted in terms of the theological motivations of human agency. As nothing is properly ours, there is no "natural" ethical reason to be quarantined from "local" truths of revelation. This explains his critique of natural-law doctrines: not only do such accounts fail to see how local and contingent is the putatively "universal" and "natural" law they promote, so that their "general principles are . . . too inflexible on the one hand and their definition too historically conditioned on the other hand"; they also tend "to make the law of love an addendum to the natural law," and thereby make Christianity a particular motivation to the order of nature, rather than insisting that "the order of nature" is not a self-contained order at all, but instead ineliminably and pervasively related to God (Niebuhr in Kegley and Bretall 1961, 435; see 1941, 281). There are no natural virtues quarantined from theological ones; all the virtues are rooted finally in *caritas*, the self-giving love which is God.

This does not forbid us from appealing on extra-theological grounds to non-Christians; it merely forbids such appeals from setting the theological agenda, for they are *provisional* accommodations, to be replaced where possible by first-order theological discourse.[65] In realizing that such an adequate (albeit transcendent) ground does exist, our temptations towards resigned indifference are shown to be mere temptations, and the realization that our motives are genuine motives, real longings for some higher harmony, can motivate us to struggle toward more such harmony. With John Milbank, Niebuhr's work presses towards "supernaturalizing the natural" rather than "naturalizing the supernatural"; as Robin Lovin says, Niebuhr's work would suggest that "the problem with the contemporary affirmation of human finitude is not that it expects too much, but that it demands too little. Freedom . . . depends on a critical self-awareness of the limitations of our perspective on events *and* on a creative effort to go beyond those limits, to imagine, and then to realize, new forms of social life that open new possibilities for freedom" (Milbank 1990, 207; Lovin 1995, 139). This theological *ressourcement* of our love does not make us zealots, but rather mitigates our own anxieties about and pretensions to having firm foundations: in apprehending

---

[65] For Niebuhr's own use of this strategy, see his 1991.

God's love for us as our salvation, we acknowledge that our desires for final synthesis are not rooted only in the realities of this world, so we become less "grasping," less anxious about finding them some "concrete" home.[66] "The fulfillments of meaning in history will be the more untainted in fact, if purity is not prematurely claimed for them" (1943, 213); because there are no determinate limits to our capacities, we must check ourselves lest our "ardor" lead us to destroy the world in order to save it, and it is wise for us to incorporate some such check into our practices.

Acknowledging responsibility: the meaning of hope

With this picture in place, we can now see how Niebuhr's work helps us meet the basic criticisms leveled against Augustine's *perversio* doctrine. Against optimist claims that evil is wholly internal to human agency and thus that humans can overcome evil by a simple act of will, Augustinians insist that while evil does in fact spring from human beings, it is not simply superficial or episodic; it arises from a perversion not of particular actions but of the root of all our actions. We cannot transcend evil simply by sloughing off those aspects of ourselves from which such evils spring, because the only way to do so would be to destroy our wills entirely – which, were it accomplished (an impossibility in any case), would destroy ourselves. Evil is deeper in us than any program of reformation or reconstruction can reach, because it infects the instrument by which any such reconstruction would proceed. Such a response to the optimist might seem to surrender the field to the pessimists' call for Augustinians to admit that is natural to human existence. But Augustinians respond by insisting that, even as we acknowledge the practical historical ineliminability of evil from our lives, we yet remain solely and sheerly responsible for our own participation in evil, and we can neither (1) collapse under the weight of the burden of guilt into a despairing quietism about the necessary brutalities of power, nor (2) use the fact of our perennial wickedness to excuse our own further evildoing. This insistence on moral courage makes Augustinians more open than pessimists are to the possibilities for moral transformation and improvement. We can affirm that evil is *not* part of the way the world is, nor an inevitable consequence of our existence in the world. (Indeed, to say that

[66] This is an important point at which the "use"/"enjoyment" distinction gains relevance; I mention it only in passing here.

would be to challenge the conceptual coherence of the concept of evil, for that concept seems to imply that what it designates as "evil" is not part of the world's proper structure.)

In contrast to both optimists and pessimists, contemporary Augustinians can follow Niebuhr in insisting both that the human is responsible for evil and so must never think of it as a fundamentally natural reality (as pessimists suggest), and that there is no "simple" resolution to the challenge (as optimists imply), for it is our "second nature" which is perverted by sin. The Augustinian proposal defends its perversion account not directly but indirectly, by affirming its greater hermeneutical adequacy to the complexity of the problems than the alternatives to it: the challenges do not undermine the Augustinian account, then, because they cannot comprehend the problems' full complexity, while our account can.

While this is not an optimistic picture, it is a hopeful one. And understanding it explains the centrality of the virtue of hope to Niebuhr's thought. Not only is hope the last word in Niebuhr's *The Nature and Destiny of Man*; it is also the virtue he wanted most to teach. And, as chapter one suggested, we need his lesson. Niebuhr's account assumes that we feel something like an inchoate sense of hope, and aims to deepen and sharpen it, to show us more clearly what our hope is *of*, and what it is *for*, and how better we can cultivate it. We cannot equate hope with any simple expectation of things improving, as if we could expect some sort of moral correlation to the perpetual advance of some sort of quantified measure of "the quality of life" (as if sheer quantification would quiet anxieties about the permanence of progress). Nor is hope some sort of psychological *superadditum*, an optional appendix and/or extra to a properly formed set of (essentially "sober" – that is, pessimistic) Christian realist motivations, rather like frosting on a block of ice. Nor is it a blind faith in some Piercian ideal-historical teleology, nor any sort of ultimate consequentialist avoidance the preferential option for the eschaton in settling our problems with the unfairnesses of the world. Hope is none of these; it is about the future because it is an appreciation of the present, and particularly of the present presence of love, the appreciation of the fact that almost everyone is trying to do good, and that that initially disconcerting and yet deeply hopeful fact also and simultaneously marks the depth of the problem. The real problem we face is not simple maliciousness, but our self-deceived self-righteousness in pressing our own parochial and partial causes. Niebuhr places hope not primarily in the future, but rather *in people* – that they are unable totally to deceive themselves, that they are finally not wholly lost. This kind of hope is not sentimental; indeed, its flip side is irony. By "irony" I do not mean Richard Rorty's gnostic knowingness (which is actually only an awkward amalgam of consolation and self-congratulation), but rather the kind of irony elicited by the recognition that our actions are never entirely our own, and that we nonetheless must act – that our responsibility not only exceeds the horizon of our foreknowledge, but that that foreknowledge is itself not fully our own.[67]

The basic ethical program that Niebuhr recommends is a program of *acknowledging responsibility*.[68] This phrase has two components. First, we must acknowledge our *responsibilities*, "own up" to our actions and be accountable for them. But this is not a sheerly voluntarist or existentialist claim of taking possession of what was not one's own before one claimed responsibility for it; one does not create but *acknowledges* what is already true. Indeed, "acknowledging responsibility" is not simply an ethical principle; it undergirds Niebuhr's project as a whole, for "Christian realism" is essentially nothing more than the insistence that we must acknowledge responsibility for our understanding of our world as well as for our actions. Niebuhr's thought remains a touchstone of moral sanity, precisely because he insists that we have no intellectual resources for "handling" evil, if "handling" it means *managing* it. Our thought is always torn open at its side, as it were, and bleeds from the knowledge that we sinners, we evildoers, are at fault, and are yet the vehicles whereby God's salvation is made manifest. Niebuhr's gloss on the Cross is his proposal for acknowledging responsibility, which is always a cruciformed acknowledgment, always one that says there is no way to resurrection but through death.

But this account does not focus exclusively on the Crucifixion; as was argued above, it offers a profoundly incarnational and participatory vision of Christian existence. We ought not to understand the Christian life as a matter of extricating ourselves from some demonized and God-abandoned "world," but rather as a matter of accepting that God has chosen to redeem *this* world, and coming to participate in that redemption, most basically by being its primary site, just as we are the primary

---

[67] See, of course, Niebuhr 1962. There is a deep connection between the doctrine of Providence and the concept of irony here, which I mention only to note it merits further reflection.

[68] See Lear 1990. Kathryn Tanner argues that the idea of definite limits on human action as such is inherently anti-progressive (1993). In contrast, Mark Platts argues that we need not mark our moral beliefs for special attention in terms of our "responsibility" for them, for they are in all relevant ways structurally similar to all beliefs we have that putatively make realist claims about the way the world is (1997, 253).

loci of creation's initial fall. We are not "resident aliens" so much as simply alienated – from ourselves, from our world, and from God – and we do not need further practices of estrangement (which are just another form of cheap grace), but ways of becoming less estranged. The dynamic at the heart of the Gospel is towards ever fuller, ever more complete Incarnation: it is not that we need to escape the world; rather, we need to be fully in it, in the way that God is fully in it. So Niebuhr is also an Augustinian in affirming this incarnational dynamic, and the final unity of all the virtues, and their origin in love:

Nothing that is worth doing can be achieved in our lifetime; therefore we must be saved by hope. Nothing which is true or beautiful or good makes complete sense in any immediate context of history; therefore we must be saved by faith. Nothing we do, however virtuous, can be accomplished alone; therefore we are saved by love. No virtuous act is quite as virtuous from the standpoint of our friend or foe as it is from our standpoint. Therefore we must be saved by the final form of love which is forgiveness. (1962, 63)

This project is in deep communion with the thought of his brother H. Richard, of course; but behind both the Niebuhrs stands Augustine's adage "love and do what you will" (*IoEp.* vii.8).

Niebuhr is not the only Augustinian among twentieth-century thinkers. We turn next to Hannah Arendt, who developed Augustine's work to construct another, equally though differently compelling, interpretation of and response to our tragic condition. Arendt's account develops the Augustinian ontology of evil as privation to meet the worries of her own day; the next chapter discusses her proposal.

CHAPTER FOUR

Evil as privation: Hannah Arendt's Augustinian ontology

Take but degree away, untune that string,
And hark what discord follows. Each thing meets
In mere oppugnancy. The bounded waters
Should lift their bosoms higher than the shores
And make a sop of all this solid globe;
Strength should be lord of imbecility,
And the rude son should strike his father dead;
Force should be right; or rather, right and wrong,
Between whose endless jar justice resides,
Should lose their names, and so should justice too.
Then everything includes itself in power,
Power into will, will into appetite:
And appetite, an universal wolf,
So doubly seconded with will and power,
Must make perforce an universal prey
And last eat up himself.

William Shakespeare, Troilus and Cressida, I.3, 109–24

Suppose evil were a vacuum-oil salesman – what then? Such was the actual occupation of Adolf Eichmann, before he became famous as the senior bureaucrat of the Holocaust (Arendt 1965, 29–31). The gap between his pre-war life and his actions in the war is not unique to him; it is a general fact about the Nazis that few of their biographies seemed to predict, in any way, that they would eventually perpetrate crimes of such magnitude; many of them were "ordinary men" (Browning 1992). What does "ordinary" mean here? To the victims, of course, these men were anything but "ordinary." Was their "ordinariness" therefore mere appearance – were they really always essentially evil? Or did the evil they perpetrated infect them, like a disease, of which they were merely the "unfortunate" victims? Or are such evils closer to the "ordinary" than we care to admit? Or is character not in fact relatively fixed after all, but instead radically malleable; will we do whatever we are ordered to do, as some psychologists suggest? Most basically: can we acknowledge the immensity of the perpetrators' monstrous evil yet still see them as continuous with the rest of humanity? Ought we to undertake this project at all?

Sometimes such questions lead to others about the particularity of the Holocaust, questions concerning its distinct character. Those are very important questions, but they are not mine here. Instead I pursue another line of inquiry: can the character of events and persons in the Holocaust cast any light on the nature of evil in general? This is not to dismiss the particularity of the Holocaust; but it is to locate that particularity in the narrative history of evil, as Berel Lang has put it (Lang 2000). Does the experience of the Holocaust – of evil emanating out of the putative heart of civilization, not from the space beyond civilization, where the "heart of darkness" can be safely revealed – represent the ultimate explosion, and exhibition, of a "monstrous" evil, one unable to be captured by accounts of evil as privation? Is there a way of talking about the perpetrators' evil which does not turn them into demons, something sub-(or super-)human?

Hannah Arendt tried to do this. In her work as a whole, and not just in *Eichmann in Jerusalem*, she diagnosed the inner character of the perils facing our attempts to live flourishing lives today, and to show how those perils are best met. In the service of this project she deployed a "political ontology" which is, I will argue, recognizably Augustinian in its emphasis on intelligibility and participation (more commonly called "agonism"). And her account of the "banality of evil" is the consequence of this ontology – its implications for evil. Thus the criticisms she received for her account of totalitarian evil as essentially "banal" can be usefully understood to express concerns about any Augustinian account of evil as privation. Such worries are reducible to the suspicion, or the accusation, that the "banality" thesis is essentially "metaphysical," not dealing with reality but rather fundamentally escapist and consolatory. The worry is that the privation thesis is nothing more than a *sneer* at evil – a description of evil that is not directly about evil, but rather indirect, spoken to one's peers, and evaluating the phenomenon *aesthetically*, on entirely the wrong register, the foppish categories of elite effete taste. Does Arendt help us here? She does, particularly through her analysis of the reality and implications of human freedom in the public world. But again, as with Niebuhr, her work only helps us part of the way; it must be purged of a subjectivist leaven which undercuts its insights. Explaining these claims is the project of this chapter.

Arendt's insights are both methodological and material. Methodologically, she employed an approach which can broadly be called a phenomenology of the human condition, and especially of the *vita activa*, or "active life," which begins from her insight that our basic mode of being-in-the-world is what she called *amor mundi*, "love of the world," the mode of existence most appropriate to our condition as "worldly" beings; from this premise, Arendt analyzes the shape and nature of human life as a manifestation of that fundamental *amor*, seeking to discern the political and ontological implications of that fact for our existence. Like Augustine, she begins with the affirmation that we are love-oriented beings, whose loves are a primary clue to the real character of our existence and to the existence of the world we inhabit, and which seeks most fully to exegete and articulate the significance of those loves in a full and systematic manner. Materially, Arendt's political theory developed around her understanding of Augustine's "discovery" of the human will, captured for her in his phrase *Initium ergo ut esset, creatus est homo, ante quem nullus fuit* – "that there would be a beginning, man was created, before whom no beginning existed" – a passage she (mis-)cites in a number of her works.[1] She labeled "the power of beginning," the fact of "natality," the reality of humans' capacity for novelty, for a "second birth," into the public world. The crucial fact about natality is its self- and world-constitutive power: action creates both a "who" and a "what." But it also relies for its birth and sustenance on conditions "outside" itself, and hence action has an essentially *participatory* character, as it participates in the humanly created- and sustained-"public world" in and from which it gains its character as action. Only by understanding the Augustinian facets of Arendt's phenomenology will we rightly understand her controversial analyses of totalitarian alienation, "worldlessness," and "the banality of evil." For Arendt, evil is nothing precisely because it is *wholly negative*, a self-annihilating vacuum properly understood only when seen in the light of the broader "political ontology" she details. From this interpretive framework she developed a practical response quite unlike that offered by Niebuhr, a response best described as one of "enacting resistance."

---

[1] This, Arendt's central referential appeal to Augustine, is (accidentally and unimportantly, but still) always referenced as coming from *DCD* xii.20, while it is in fact found in chapter 21; the only time in Arendt's corpus that this was corrected was in the posthumously published (and edited) *The Life of the Mind*. Furthermore, whether Augustine means by it what Arendt wants him to mean by it is also disputable; but, keeping a firm (and firmly Augustinian) grasp on the distinction between the spirit and the letter, I pass over that debate for now.

Before we begin, a caveat is in order. To read Arendt as this chapter does is to court misunderstandings that will excite two sorts of critics. Both more "orthodox" (in a broad sense) Christian theologians, and typically agnostic political theorists, may find such appreciative theological attention given to so explicitly an anti-Christian thinker to be *prima facie* dubious, if not willfully perverse. But I am not trying to convert Arendt; her disputes with religious thinkers are well known. However, we misunderstand her fundamental anti-religiousness if we do not appreciate her long-running engagement with Augustine and the tradition of "otherworldliness" she took him to represent.[2] Furthermore, this disagreement is not simply an opposition to Augustinian thought; her work builds on insights shared with Augustine. And we, in turn, can build on her development of those insights; in Augustinian terms, we can *use* Arendt's work, even as we do not attempt to *delight* in her personally.

Of course, this does not mean that we disrespect the integrity of her thought. But there are plausible charges against it, charges that force us to think beyond it. Ironically the charges revolve around suspicions that her work is nostalgic, elitist, and consolingly "metaphysical," that it does not support but subverts our commitment to political existence. (The criticisms of her famous [or infamous] "banality of evil" thesis are formulated essentially in these terms.) Elements of her thought, the critics charge, work against both a clear vision of our situation, and our full participation therein. A good portion of the chapter will be spent telling the story of how Arendt's work fell prey to the same problems she found in others. For Arendt's work *does* so fall prey to these problems; and the second half of the chapter will attempt to find out which parts of her work must be jettisoned in order to retain her genuine insights. But in doing so we will see that her proposal is flawed not because it is too metaphysical or still residually Augustinian, but because it is not metaphysical and Augustinian enough: her inarticulateness about the ontological grounds of human agency makes her account of action indistinguishable from anarchism. We will see that we need a theory of moral agency more adequate, because less voluntaristic, than Arendt's, which fails because it refuses to place any metaphysical limits on the human will, and thus invests agents with a radical originality in their actions. We

---

[2] In the current (and welcome) renaissance of Arendt scholarship, Arendt's relation to Augustine has not engaged the attention of many interpreters. They seem more interested in clarifying her thought's capacity to interpret the contemporary political situation than in investigating how her broadly philosophical interpretation of the human condition undergirds her political thought. I say more about this on pp. 178–82 below.

need instead an account of action which affirms that, from the beginning, humans are "always already" responding to the more primary action of the larger reality within which they find themselves.

However, as with Niebuhr, there is hope, for such an analysis is entailed by Arendt's highly Augustinian analysis of the "banality of evil" and the positive asymmetrical ontology it requires. This asymmetrical ontology entails an ontological concept of human agency (a "grammar of assent"), which affirms both the reality of human freedom and the reality of limits upon that freedom, in order to identify the true character of sinful behavior. This understanding of agency depicts all action as occurring within an ontological framework which gives to acts their normative valence. The failure of Arendt's explicit voluntarist theory of action, then, can be repaired by replacing it with the Augustinian agency implicit in other aspects of her thought. Arendt herself offers us some clues as to how to transcend her own formulations, particularly in her guiding idea of *amor mundi* as the basic "attunement" humans should take.

We see her "Augustinian-ness" in her participatory ontology; her exposition and development of this ontology, and her exploration of its implications for the character of evil in our century, will be our central focus. After offering a brief précis of Arendt's overall account of the human condition and the modern situation, I will detail several criticisms of Arendt's proposal, and trace the flaws in her account back to her partial appropriation of Augustinian themes. I will then attempt to exploit the resources Arendt's work offers while avoiding its weaknesses, in order more fully to exploit the Augustinian themes present in it.

THE VITA ACTIVA AND THE MODERN THREAT OF
"WORLDLESSNESS"

The past decade has seen a revival in Arendt scholarship, though much of it seems more to mention Arendt than actually to engage her. No longer is her position taken to be a straightforward form of "existentialism politicized."[3] Nor are those interpretations plausible of Arendt's work as negative and nostalgic, a form of "polis envy"[4] driven by a horror-filled hysterical recoil from the mass politics of the twentieth century, pining for the intellectual securities and elitist provincialism of the German philosophical tradition embodied for her by Heidegger (see

---

[3] The phrase "existentialism politicized" is from the title of an essay by Hinchman and Hinchman 1994.   [4] I borrow this phrase from Jean Bethke Elshtain.

Holmes 1979, 117). Recent scholarship has moved beyond such caricatures, and it has begun to grasp the importance of Arendt's account of
totalitarianism for her work. George Kateb, for example, argues that
Arendt's work is fundamentally concerned with understanding the
extreme phenomena of the twentieth century: "Totalitarianism, in its
most vivid form, obsessed her" (1992, 199; see Kateb 1983). Such
accounts depict Arendt as a pessimistic modernist, whose basic concern
was fighting for the future in the "dark times" of the present, agreeing
with René Char that "our inheritance was left to us by no testament"
(Arendt 1961, 3). Margaret Canovan agrees that Arendt's analysis of
totalitarianism is more central to her thought than was previously
recognized, though she argues that it is not the negative reality *of*
totalitarianism, so much as her proposed positive remedy *to* totalitarianism – namely, the fact of human plurality – which is fundamental to her
work. For Canovan, Arendt's basic contribution to her intellectual
descendants was neither a terminal nostalgia for the Greeks nor a dour
awareness of the death camps, but rather a sober but hopeful appreciation of *plurality* as a basic fact of human existence.[5] In all her work
Arendt resisted both a sullen and wistful nostalgia for the traditions and
authorities of the past, and the idea of some perfect future consummation or *telos* towards which history is ineluctably moving.[6] In this she is a
prototypically modernist writer and thinker.

But focusing on her modernism elides her more classical reflexes –
reflexes as much a part of her work as were her ("reluctant") modernist
sensibilities. Most basically, hers was a classically tragic vision; as her
Doktorvater Karl Jaspers saw, she was struggling for "a vision of tragedy
that does not leave you despairing" (Arendt 1992, 506).[7] Central to this
quest was her life-long concern with that capacity of human beings
which fostered the horrors of totalitarianism – namely, our capacity for
evil. "The problem of evil," she wrote in 1946, "will be the fundamental question of postwar intellectual life in Europe" (1994, 134). The
"vision of tragedy" on which Arendt's work is grounded takes as its
central concern the terrible, and yet ultimately self-nihilating, character
of the totalitarian destructiveness of the twentieth century. Her tragic
vision rests on the account she offers of the evil threatening us, an evil

---

[5] In Canovan 1992, 281; see 110, 197, 199, 205, 279. See Benhabib 1996 for a similar argument.
[6] See Arendt's comparison of the method of "collection" which destroys tradition, and the tradition it putatively feeds off of, in 1968, 198–200.
[7] Jaspers made this comment after reading *On Revolution*, but it applies to her entire corpus. See
Canovan's useful discussion of Arendt's tragic vision, in 1992, 249–52.

which she ultimately characterized, famously (or infamously) as "banal," "superficial," wholly a matter of emptiness. Nonetheless, this negative vision is unintelligible apart from her profoundly positive phenomenology of the *vita activa*, the active public or political life.[8] The *vita activa* has its consummation and justification in what she calls "action." "Action" holds all the promise of human life for genuine meaning-making activities, and yet is in itself perhaps humans' most fragile achievement, the one most prone to self-destruction. The "world-constitutive" power of the *vita activa*, and its realization in "politics," properly understood, is what gives human life its distinct splendor; and yet, as Alan Keenan puts it, "the loss of 'the political' . . . is . . . a loss that cannot fail to happen" (1994, 316). This is especially so in modernity, with its fixation on technological solutions and its forgetfulness of the distinct good of human action, a good incomprehensible in technological terms. Hence, to understand Arendt, we must understand her account of the *vita activa* and the perils attending it in modernity.

Labor, work, action

Arendt thought that previous philosophical treatments of the *vita activa* have understood it in largely negative terms, as what is *not* the *vita contemplativa*, and this has obscured the "inner distinctions" within the *vita activa*. Arendt identifies three different elements with the terms "labor," "work," and "action," and argues that these are three distinct activities both because of what they do and because of their phenomenological distinctiveness as experienced activities. All three contribute to the creation and perpetuation of the world in distinct ways.

"Labor" is the most natural of all three faculties, that activity "which corresponds to the biological processes of the body," and is "the metabolism between man and nature or the human mode of this metabolism which we share with all living creatures" (1987, 32). It embodies the human's necessary rootedness in the natural processes of growth and decay, processes which are endless and serve only to reproduce themselves. As such, labor is rooted in, and especially experienced as, fertility, our ability to reproduce ourselves – both in nourishing ourselves and in our offspring – to no end beyond our own reproduction.[9] Its distinct

---

[8] It is interesting to note that the title *The Human Condition* was not her choice; she wanted to call the book *Vita Activa*, but the publishers insisted she change it (see 1977, 6).

[9] This is one point at which Arendt's concerns begin to take on some of their complexity in relation to contemporary feminist scholarship. For more on this, see Yeager 1988, and Honig 1995a.

good is the direct "blessing" which it bestows on the human in the form of satiety, a blessing which is no less a blessing for being one which we have in common with all other animals, for after all it teaches us (or reassures us, once again) that we are of the earth. Labor is good not merely for its rooting us to the earth; it also, albeit indirectly, anchors us in the present and so serves the first precondition of our worldliness.

"Work" is the human faculty of fabrication, of making "the sheer unending variety of things whose sum total constitutes the human artifice, the world we live in" (1987, 34). It is rooted in those experiences of *techne*, of instrumentalized making, which mark the production of use-goods. Thus work is essentially an instrumentalizing activity, one which determines both the process and the product by means-end calculation. The realm of work, then, is equally the realm of instrumental or purposive thinking, which Arendt calls "computation." Accompanying those experiences is always a sense of violence against nature: as maker, the human assumes the role of "lord and master of the whole earth," and conducts a "Promethean revolt" against the earth (1958, 139). Work is the realm within which we experience human strength as a power separate from, and indeed opposed to, natural necessity. Work also contributes to the reality of the human world. The objects work produces do not only secure the world's objectivity as distinct from our subjectivity; they also secure the world's continued stability, its *durability*. The relatively objective fabrications of work "give the world the stability and solidity without which it could not be relied upon to house the unstable and mortal creature that is man" (1987, 34). Like labor, work is a prerequisite for politics though not a direct part of it; work secures the stability of the world and thus gives the world a stable "past" on which people can rely.[10]

Not only are labor and work not distinctly political activities; they are not even distinctly human activities. Action alone is unique to human beings. "Action" is neither cyclical (as is labor) nor terminal (as is work), but is fundamentally an open-ended activity. Phenomenologically speaking, it is rooted in the human's experience of beginning, the wholly novel act, in our capacity for a "second birth," the power of "natality." If labor establishes the present and work secures the past, action provides us with a future, the chance for novelty and unpredictability; as labor's intellectual form is logical necessity and work's is means-ends calculation, action's is *thought*, properly speaking, the capacity imaginatively to reflect

---

[10] The similarities with George Orwell's work, especially *1984*, should be here apparent.

upon the particularities of the human world. Action reveals who we are in our personhood and agency. Action is not a precondition for the public sphere; in a sense, it just *is* that sphere. As the human world is perpetually confronted with the fact of our mortality, the fact of decay and the threat of our natural and necessary ending, action overcomes and transcends that mortality with natality, and so is "the miracle that saves the world" (1958, 247).

But can this miracle save itself? Action is also profoundly vulnerable to obstruction and, indeed, destruction; it is the greatest of human achievements, but it is an irremediably *fragile* achievement.[11] Why is that?

"The miracle that saves the world": action

Action has both positive and negative aspects. Positively, action is important for it creates an agent, a "self" with a history and an indeterminate future, to inhabit the new world which every action inaugurates. Negatively, action is important because it serves as the sole bulwark against the annihilation of the human's distinct form of existence, an annihilation threatened both by the fact of the human's natural mortality and by our capacity for *self*-destruction, our temptation to deny or destroy the space necessary for human individuality to appear. As the absolutely spontaneous creation of novelty in the world, it disrupts and defies all predictability, so defeats attempts at imposing determinism on human agents.

Action not only creates genuine persons; it also creates genuine community. For Arendt, no one can "act" in isolation from others, nor are communities real without allowing space for genuine individuals to exist. Furthermore, the mutual dependence and interaction of individual and community creates the "world," the human world of the public realm. Action's most basic good is found neither in the creation of selves, nor in the creation of political community; action's most basic value lies in its creation of the world, a "public" realm in which both self and community can arise.[12] It is not some sort of romantic individualistic revolt against community, but rather community's realization. Here, Arendt's work touches on one of the most complex issues in modern philosophy

---

[11] For an interestingly similar account see Nussbaum 1986.
[12] It is interesting to note the similarities between this position and something like a political elaboration of Wittgenstein's famous "private language argument;" for a similar account along Wittgensteinian lines, see Lovibond 1983.

– the relationship between individual and community – and her solution is to affirm the equal primordiality of both.

Furthermore, action is not mere mute "deeds"; it is inextricably intertwined with language, that distinctly human ontological capacity to bring things into "the space of appearances" and infuse them with meaning. Here the influence of Heidegger is decisive: just as language is the "house of being" for Heidegger, the medium of intelligibility through which we have a world at all, so for Arendt language is the manifestation of political (and hence "worldly") existence's intelligibility; thus "speechless action . . . does not exist, or if it exists is irrelevant" (1987, 40). But she diverges from Heidegger by refusing to root language directly in "Being," in *Sprache*'s preexistence of (and "speaking" of) humans; she thinks language is rooted not straightforwardly in nonhuman nature, but in the summit of the human condition, namely, action. She argues that "action and speech are so closely related" because individuals act into an always already existing human world, a world in which others will always seek to understand the agent: "the primordial and specifically human act must always also answer the question asked of every newcomer: 'Who are you?'" (1987, 39–40). Action is essentially our capacity for significant spontaneity, our ability to create new meanings for ourselves before (and for) others, so it cannot be finally controlled or constrained.

However, action's virtue also contains its vice; for while we can be transformed by it in hopeful and fruitful ways, its salvation is capricious, often vexing our best intentions. Part of action's vulnerability is due to the enormous complexity of the public realm in which it appears; it involves itself irreversibly in the "web of relationship," and must negotiate its place within that web (Yeager 1988). But there is another, and deeper, cause of action's unpredictability, namely, its character as wholly "spontaneous," a font of novelty in an otherwise determinate world. Strictly speaking, for action to be free it needs to be more than merely complex:

Action, to be free, must be free from motive on one side, from its intended goal as a predictable effect on the other. This is not to say that motives and aims are not important factors in every single act, but they are its determining factors, and action is free to the extent that it is able to transcend them. (1961, 152; cf. 151, 165–9, and 1963, 214)

This is a radical claim: action must be ultimately undetermined. As Dana Villa argues, "*Arendt's theory of political action should be read on the sus-*

tained attempt to think of praxis outside the teleological framework" (1996, 47). If we know what we are always going to do, we will never transcend our narrow and captivating self-understanding, we can never really become something new.

Of course, Arendt's account equally entails that action's basic danger is its spontaneity, the fact that, even in its origins, it is under no one's control. While action's enemies have no absolute power over it, it still remains vulnerable to vexation by itself. It suffers from what she calls "the twofold darkness of human affairs," namely, the unpredictability of its consequences and the genuine liberty of action itself (1958, 244). Action is both the engine of human creativity and individuality, the principle cause of the human's "worldliness," and the source of the deepest threats to the human world; it is, in short, a highly ambiguous power.

What saves us from action's caprices can only be action itself; as such, the fragility of life must be met not by theoretical or philosophical solutions, but by ongoing *political* engagements. Arendt particularly notes the abilities action gives us to promise and to forgive. The capacity to promise holds that aspect of action which best ensures the continued stability of agents in the world; it creates commitments, those "islands of security," on which we can rely as we navigate the public realm's "ocean of uncertainty" (1958, 237). While promise-making secures some stability for our future, forgiving frees us from the fetters of the past. In forgiving, we acknowledge that an agent's responsibility for the consequences of their actions does not extend (as those consequences themselves do) *ad infinitum*, but rather have a limit. Without forgiveness history would be little more than a "chain reaction," a blood-feud of endless retaliations for past misdeeds.[13] Action is thus the only guard against itself we can have. (*Quis custodiet ipsos custodes?*) No matter what we do, no matter where we seek for guarantees, we are, in Margaret Canovan's apt phrase, "driven back to politics," back to the messy and contingent frailties of the public realm, whose only savior is itself (1992, 162).

Despite its hazards, action remains our one consolation against mortality, against the natural decay and final doom of all things. It is finally the only real game in town, the greatest glory that humans can individually attain; but it is also and equally a form of communion, an (at times agonistic) participation in a public space and society. At the end of *On*

---

[13] Note how this definition of forgiveness seems to elide the possibility of (what one might call) *genuine* forgiveness, forgiveness for deeds *intended* by their agents; I discuss this more in the next chapter.

Revolution – the work that Jaspers described as "a tragedy which does not
leave you despairing" – Arendt argues that political action, grounded
upon the fact of natality, "enabled ordinary men, young and old, to bear
life's burden: it was the *polis*, the space of men's free deeds and living
words, which could endow life with splendor" (1963, 285). For humans,
truly to live on the earth is to live in the "public" and "political" world
of human actors, and to share in the creation and sustenance of that
world; to do less is to be less than fully human.

But in the modern world, the *vita activa* faces threats unimagined by
earlier thinkers, threats arising from the character of modernity itself.
Arendt was one of the pioneer explorers of these threats.

Modernity and totalitarianism

The claim that "modernity" is the first age which finds itself to be a
problem sounds platitudinous, but like many platitudes it conceals a profound philosophical truth. The challenge of "becoming modern" gives
our age a Sisyphean task, for it promotes an impossible ideal: the ideal of
total autonomy, of complete self-creation. Rooted in the political ideals
of the more radical thinkers of the seventeenth and eighteenth centuries,
moderns' desire for total autonomy has led not only to remarkable political and social achievements, but to possibly unmanageable challenges.
On the political level, this philosophical drive for absolute autonomy,
combined with the heretofore unimagined technological power of
human beings to effect (though not control) their environment, renders
all human hopes for the future deeply problematic. Just as moderns begin
from the assumption that the present is initially estranged from the past,
they have also rendered problematic the future's continuity with the
present (see Kemp 1991). This is not merely a matter of brute ecological
holocaust; even if we survive our own environmental follies, we have
reached a stage at which we can alter our own nature in such a way, and
to such a degree, that those who come after us may no longer be *like* us.[14]
The problem of modernity is not simply the problem of whether we will
ever be "modern"; it is, in fact, whether "we" will continue to *be* at all.[15]

Arendt defines modernity in terms of three interrelated facts: the
experience of mass loneliness, the rise of "the social," and most basically,

[14] See Ramsey 1970, 25–6. I am grateful for William Schweiker for this thought.
[15] Thus the prescient comment by Michel Foucault: "For millenia man remained what he was for
Aristotle: a living animal with the additional capacity for a political existence. Modern man is
an animal whose politics places his existence as a living being in question" (1978, 143).

a situation of general "world-alienation." We moderns have turned away from the common public world into the pure subjectivity of the self or the pure objectivity of its scientific *doppelgänger*, the universe. Our "worldlessness" destroys the genuine communality once shared among individuals and casts all into "loneliness," which in turn annihilates all possibilities for self-understanding. Instead of true human (agonistic) community, we have the horde-like existence of rootless refugees, who are the most characteristic political reality of our age. A terrible aphasia settles over all things human; what most needs to be discussed, our separateness from one another, our inability genuinely to be agents with and for one another, is rendered unspeakable; even our acknowledgment of our muteness is made impossible.

The loss of the "world" drives both the public activities of politics and the private necessities of bare human nature into the "social realm," an "exchange market" and negotiation space for our solitary and atomistic selves, in which can exist only the "society of jobholders" (1958, 322).[16] The eclipse of the private and public realms by this bloated social realm obscures the distinct features of both, and allows the human world to be understood in terms of an objectified nature, on the model of the natural sciences. The social world becomes simply one more version of the "natural" world, and thus "the momentum of history and the momentum of nature" become "one and the same" (1973, 464). The effect of this "unnatural growth of the natural" (1958, 47) on the human world is disastrous. It obliterates the distinctions that make the world intelligible. As the subjective and objective are pressed together into this false unity, both genuine community and genuine selfhood become impossible. The three distinct spheres of labor, work, and action all collapse into labor, that aspect of human activity necessary for our simple survival; life is divided schizophrenically between the mechanistic and alienated tedium of labor, and the whimsical and (strictly speaking) "useless" frivolity of a degenerate concept of leisure.[17] *Anomie* sets in, and the human condition comes to resemble mere animal existence on the one hand and robotic repetition on the other. In being alienated from the public world, we are alienated from ourselves; we lose a context for conversations about those things we care about, and we suffer from moral aphasia which cripples all attempts at self-understanding. Hence the rise of the social both embodies and signals the reduction of human

---

[16] For an example of what Arendt might mean here see Mike Davis 1990, 223–63, on the destruction of public space in Los Angeles.

[17] For interestingly similar accounts, see Pieper 1952 and Postman 1985.

life into the mute "natural" cycles of birth and death (see Arendt 1961, 197–226).[18]

Totalitarianism is most basically a *response* to these conditions, not their cause. It is an attempt to respond to the realities of the destruction of the public world, and the rise of mass loneliness and the creation of the social realm. Indeed, ironically enough, totalitarianism is the *most* genuinely "modern" political structure for Arendt, because it best understands and represents the modern world. Faced with the frightful unpredictability of the human world, totalitarianism is the ultimate modern "scientific" solution to the problem of politics, a retreat into the "tyranny of logicality" which struggles to change the world to fit itself – to "make the world consistent" with its ideology – rather than change itself to fit the world (1973, 458). It embodies the triumph of computational scientistic "method" over all other forms of human thought (cf. 1958, 171–2). It takes our worldlessness and loneliness as normative, and seeks to normalize and "naturalize" it (see Kideckel 1993; see also Riesman, Denney, and Glazer 1950). Without genuine forums for political action, humans will seek whatever pseudo-political opportunities that arise; in the modern rise of the homogenized social, those opportunities inevitably take the form of the natural sciences' regular, "natural," objectivist necessity. Totalitarianism expresses the modern desire to live only according to rational syllogisms; its dogmatic rationalism perfectly complements the experiences of loneliness and worldlessness, for it is the ultimate denial of other people, of the variable and complex human self as such. It represents the triumph of a perverse idealism which is fixated on rendering itself coherent by ignoring or destroying all that could possibly contradict it (see Oakeshott 1991). Totalitarianism is an *anti*-politics; if it is not the logical conclusion of modernity, it is at least the conclusion of modernity's logic.[19]

But totalitarianism not only opposes the "external" world and the "other"; to be perfectly secure against the vagaries of human existence, it must also deny the reality of time. Totalitarianism denies the "unknowability" of the future by claiming an absolute (and scientistic) power of prediction; and it escapes the hard realities of the past by consuming it and controlling what people know about the past (thus entailing the perpetual rewriting of history). Totalitarianism lives wholly in the singular and in the present, and thereby aims to live "outside" both

---

[18] Arendt's discussion of the dominating power of technology is interestingly similar to Augustine's distinction between "use" and "enjoyment." See Pitkin 1998.

[19] See Ortega y Gassett 1932 and Bauman 1989 for interestingly similar accounts.

human plurality and time; but it can do so only because we moderns do in fact live, at least partially, outside plurality and time.

Ultimately, the totalitarian state seeks to render the human super-fluous. The systematic imposition onto human action of the "iron band" of necessity, principally through all the mechanisms of terror possessed by the regime, seeks to prevent the human's unpredictabil-ity, natural to humans as free agents, from obstructing the regime's quest for absolute stability, or disturbing its achievement. As freedom exists by definition outside law, totalitarianism must outlaw freedom; and, as free agency is essential to our understanding of human exis-tence, the totalitarian regime's project invariably entails the destruc-tion of human agency. In so doing, totalitarianism seeks to change the human's very nature, creating "a kind of human species resembling other animal species whose only 'freedom' would consist in 'preserv-ing the species' " (1973, 438). Thus, "what totalitarian ideologies there-fore aim at is not the transformation of the outside world . . . but the transformation of human nature itself" (1973, 458; see 468). The total-itarian state knows that the fundamental obstacle to the realization of its aims is not the discrete acts of resistance in which particular agents engage, but the human capacity enabling such resistance. Hence, in the battle against totalitarianism, "human nature as such is at stake" (1973, 459).

Even more catastrophically, for Arendt our intellectual heritage actu-ally hinders our appreciation of these truths, and is partly to blame for the rise of totalitarianism itself. This is so because of the alliance, char-acteristic of modernity, of philosophical and scientific attempts to escape the human world. (This is why she was so suspicious of space exploration.) For Arendt, philosophy essentially is a basic mood of dis-ease about the world, a desire to escape it; philosophers have merely for-malized and rationalized their suspicion of politics, seeking to avoid it by turning away from *nec-otium* – the contingent turbulence of the *vita activa* – towards *otium* – the peace brought on by contemplating the eternal ver-ities of the *vita contemplativa*, the only fit home for philosophical contem-plation (see 1957).[20] Philosophy suggests that politics is simply another form of philosophy, albeit one which is poorly understood; this simply

[20] As with Niebuhr's "classical" and "modern" worldviews, Arendt's concepts of "modernity" and "philosophy" are painfully general and vague; she paints her picture with an extraordinarily large brush. But we should give her the hermeneutic charity she does not allow her victims, and work with the concepts she employed. For analyses of contemporary political theory very much along Arendt's lines here, see Barber 1988 and Isaac 1998.

confuses the unique activity of politics with the entirely different activity of philosophy, and seeks to graft criteria and methods from one onto the other.[21] But philosophy is not solely responsible for modernity's crisis; it needed the objectivism of modern natural sciences, which confirmed philosophy's deepest belief, that the human is "not of this [public, political] world" (1958, 278). The sciences did so by transforming our sense of the world itself, through the construction of a world picture that relies on technologies – especially the telescope and the microscope – that seem to extend, but actually subvert, the human senses. With its discovery of realities hitherto undreamed of – not, properly speaking, "above" that of common sense (as philosophy sought), but rather "below" or, more literally, *beneath* it – science caused (or, better, constituted) an epistemological revolution, one both in how and in what we know (see Galison 1995). When science's explanatory power and technological success confronted the messy and shambling natural human senses, thinkers rejected those senses, abandoning both the "common sense" of human community and the five physiological senses as trustworthy sources of knowledge in their own right. The new "worlds" discovered by these instruments demanded the construction of new interpretive frameworks with no reference to the human world of common sense, and thus ultimately subverted it. Thus the philosophers' hostility towards politics, and the scientists' reliance upon methods and assumptions requiring nothing more than an isolated, observing "I," eventually created what they had all along assumed: a world within which appeals to "common knowledge" or intersubjective consensus could not be voiced, a world within which even the appeals of others not to be harmed by the self require the validation of that self to be legitimate moral claims.

By turning away from the common world, philosophy and science ensured that world's irrelevance for thought – but not, tragically enough, their thought's irrelevance for that world. The ultimate nature of philosophy's turning away from the political is revealed to be a turning *upon* the political, like metaphysical guardians run amok and turned traitorous. Politics becomes mechanics, and humans are transformed from

---

[21] This criticism reveals Arendt's indebtedness to, and also her distance from, Aristotle's political thought. For Aristotle did contrast politics and philosophy in precisely the way she criticizes, elevating (in Book x of the *Nicomachean Ethics*) the contemplative life of *theoria* above the life of *praxis*. On the other hand, she finds in Aristotle a predecessor to her second criticism of the tradition – namely, that the meanings of political terms are discovered empirically, in the public realm of political *praxis*, and all attempts to derive them from philosophical considerations should be rejected. For an alternative reading of Aristotle, see Reeve 1992.

potentially autonomous agents into automatons. This understanding of politics is essentially Hobbesian; to turn Clausewitz upside down, politics becomes war by other means, and action is simply a species of violence (1958, 228).

The banality of radical evil

Arendt paints quite a bleak picture. But it is not a hopeless one; for while totalitarianism may be the inevitable peril of modernity, it is not modernity's inevitable fate. Totalitarianism holds in itself the clues to its own overcoming; in its bumbling disastrousness, it reveals what has gone wrong in the modern world, and how to correct it. Arendt meant to express this in her phrase "the banality of evil."[22]

Arendt's description of Eichmann as "banal" seems a significant change from her account, in *The Origins of Totalitarianism*, of evil as "radical," but the change is less important than it seems.[23] The difference between the two formulations may be partly explained by the two books' differing rhetorical purposes. In *Origins* she wanted to "mythologize" a peril – to construct an image of a threat only inchoately apprehended by her audience, and thus alert them to its danger and provoke a determined response to it; in *Eichmann* she wanted to "demythologize" a certain *too* clear, falsely monstrous image of evil that attached too easily, too smoothly to the Holocaust, in order to block received clichés about evil and provoke thinking, in order to resist despair and instill hope in her audience (see Young-Bruehl 1982, 211). But these rhetorical changes mask a deeper continuity. In her earlier work, Arendt related totalitarian evil to Kant's discussion of "radical evil" in Book I of *Religion within the Limits of Reason Alone* (Kant 1960, 16). Arendt agreed with Kant that evil is "radical" when it corrupts the root of human agency; but she disagreed with him by insisting that radical evil need not take a Miltonic-demonic form. Arendt argued that the problem is not the agent's internalization of a "wrong maxim" (either of mixed self-interest or sheer perverse love of evil), but rather, the lack of any maxim at all. This

---

[22] I say "employed" instead of "coined" because Karl Jaspers used a similar phrase in a letter to her in 1946: "We have to see these things in their total banality, in their prosaic triviality, because that's what truly characterizes them" (Arendt 1992, 62). This remark, in turn, seems to have been inspired by some of Arendt's remarks about the Nazis' acts being incomprehensible as crimes, which may place the bouncing ball of originality back in Arendt's court.

[23] As Berel Lang says, "Arendt's ambiguous judgment of Eichmann is itself part of a larger view of the politics of evil that Arendt had begun to develop long before the Eichmann trial" (1991, 149; see Kateb 1983, 73–4). In his more recent work Kateb argues that Arendt's account of banality is a "corrective" to her earlier emphasis on evil's radicality (Kateb 1992, 199).

sort of evil is not a matter of "perverted ill-will" (1973, 459) at all, but is untraceable to individuals' motives, and "puts an end to the notion of developments and transformation of qualities" (1973, 443); hence it is invisible to Kant's account of individual wickedness.[24] Arendt's "radical evil" is rooted in totalitarianism's desire to avoid human agents' unpredictability by replacing them with a rigorously systematized "method" of political decision-making. Radical evil is thus *radical* because of its annihilating effects on political community and individuals: "the psyche *can* be destroyed," the psyches of the victimizers along with their victims (1973, 441, 446). But how then can we understand human existence within radical evil? Arendt's answer is simple: we cannot. We cannot understand "what it's like" to participate in totalitarianism, not because such understanding is somehow beyond us, but rather simply because there is nothing to understand.[25] So her two accounts of evil can be seen as not only compatible, but even mutually supporting: on this view, only if we understand what Arendt means by "radical evil" can we see what she means in calling it "banal," and vice versa.

She made her case in *Eichmann in Jerusalem*, through her analysis of Adolf Eichmann, the Nazi bureaucrat responsible for many of the murderous minutiae of the Holocaust. The controversy surrounding this book has always obscured Arendt's main point about the precise character of totalitarian evil, and the character of our response to such evil. Certainly Arendt's account of the Holocaust is too simplistic, perhaps especially on the matter of the history of Jewish resistance to slaughter (Wolin 1996, 12–14). But to focus on this is to misunderstand what she was doing, which was to draw her audience's attention to the fact that the Holocaust was not a conspiracy of Satanic *Übermenschen*, but rather an essentially bureaucratic phenomenon, and had to be addressed as such. And she thought that this was not acknowledged in Jerusalem: while the prosecution sought to portray Eichmann as a devil, he himself displayed none of the maliciousness attributed to him – he talked only in clichés, borrowed words and phrases, and exhibited no ability to think, nor any capacity for imagination. The disparity between the prosecution's portrayal of Eichmann and the uncomprehending, cliché-

---

[24] For a reading of Kant which argues that his account is closer to Arendt's than she allows, see Allison 1996. As I am not at this point interested in Kant's thought, but in what Arendt took to be Kant's position, I will not discuss this helpful essay here. For a position disputing that of Allison, see Murdoch 1985, 79–80, who argues that Kant merely provided theoretical praise of Milton's Lucifer.

[25] Arendt 1971. For an interesting argument on the centrality of this idea of "what it's like" for our understanding of the world, see Nagel 1979.

spouting, automatically mendacious idiot in the prisoner's dock was so great at times as to threaten to turn the trial into a farce. He was not an assembly-line Lucifer, but rather a bumbling bureaucrat; his root fault was simply his absolute thoughtlessness, his total lack of sympathy for, or empathy with, anyone else. Indeed, Arendt thought, the idea of attributing intention or motives to such a creature was almost out of place: "Except for an extraordinary diligence in looking out for his personal advancement, he had no motives at all . . . He *merely*, to put the matter colloquially, *never realized what he was doing*" (1965, 287). To call Eichmann wicked is to miss the point of his example, to err in thinking that he had a wicked character that contributed something especially vicious to his crimes, whereas in fact he was a nobody, a nebbish, whose most distinguishing characteristic was the sheer passive resistance he put up to comprehending the reality of any situation, whether (as it seemed from his testimony) in the war or (as Arendt herself ascertained) in his trial.[26] Arendt saw in him, quite literally, "sheer thoughtlessness" (1965, 287). The problem with Eichmann, as she said a decade later, was "entirely negative: it was not stupidity but a curious quite authentic inability to think" (1971, 3). Eichmann is thus not a sort of superbeing, a *mysterium tremendum* from which we recoil in horror; he is a sort of unreal "nonentity" whose most basic characteristic is its "grotesque silliness" (1965, 252). As Jean Bethke Elshtain puts it, Eichmann exemplifies "the unbearable lightness of non-being," the strange stupor-inducing effect that participation in a totalitarian regime can have on people (Elshtain 1995a, 81). Eichmann's crimes were not rooted in a wicked character: he had no character to be wicked.

That totalitarian evil is "banal" does not make it trivial;[27] for Arendt, it is banal because it banalizes the most horrific realities conceivable, and disconnects evildoers from their evil deeds. Arendt's point in calling Eichmann banal was not to affirm his existence as an ordinary man, as if "anyone would have done" what he did in his situation; rather, she simply claimed that Eichmann's evil did not require superhuman capacities on the one hand, or a certain kind of cultural background on the

---

[26] The whole section (47–52) makes disquietingly fascinating reading.

[27] This is a common misunderstanding of Arendt's proposal; for one recent example, see Hollander 1997, which reduces Arendt's argument to "the belief that mass murderers were ordinary, 'normal' people, undistinguished by any moral stigma or deformity, who found themselves in situations which led to their brutal behavior, and that virtually anyone could become one under the appropriate circumstances" (55). Contrast Hollander's argument here with Zillner, Harrower, Ritzler, and Archer 1995, 8–12, 194. See also Lang 1991, 146–7, on Arendt's use of "banality."

other (1965, 278). As she said, "evil is never 'radical'," in the sense of being demonic, but "is only extreme, and that it possesses neither depth nor any demonic dimension" (Arendt 1978b, 251). Her claim that Eichmann's evil is banal implied simply that Eichmann's shallowness was as deep as evil *could* go. The "profundity" of evil is not something which inheres in evil in itself; rather, evil gets its pseudo-profundity, and indeed its pseudo-reality, by being the absence of good. As she argued, evil's reality is its very *un*reality: evil

can overgrow and lay waste the whole world precisely because it spreads like a fungus on the surface. It is "thought-defying," as I said, because thought tries to reach some depth, to go to the roots, and the moment it concerns itself with evil, it is frustrated because there is nothing. That is its "banality." Only the good has depth and can be radical. (1978b, 251)

Evil is empty, destructive of the possibility of real human community, community manifest through action in speech and creative of a common world in terms of which we find our meaning and our flourishing. For Arendt evil is ontologically describable only negatively, in terms of what it destroys, and what it lacks.

Evil is essentially a matter of absence – not simply a metaphorical and subjective "absence," such as the absence of conscience in the individual actor; rather, it is the literal absence of a lively and responsive presence with which we can engage in mutually creating and sustaining a human and public world. As such an absence, evil is essentially a threat *external to* our real "worldly" existence, a threat whose "reality" exists only beyond the boundaries of our world. Of course, its exteriority and absence does not make it fundamentally *passive*; rather, it can be an *active* exteriority, the "presence" of a nihilating absence which attacks us. But for Arendt the fact of evil's aggressiveness must always be coupled with an awareness of evil's "worldlessness," its essential exteriority to our public world.[28]

Still, Eichmann's banality does not excuse him from responsibility for his crimes, and Arendt tried to identify his real criminality with some degree of precision, while still holding on to the perception of his essential personal nothingness. Essentially, she thought, Eichmann merits

---

[28] This sense of the exteriority of evil is part of her larger political ontology which connects publicity, speech, power, and action, and opposes them with "violence," which is mute and non-communal. See her comments in *On Revolution*: "violence itself is incapable of speech, and not merely that speech is helpless when confronted with violence," for "where violence rules absolutely . . . not only the laws . . . but everything and everybody must fall silent . . . It is because of this silence that violence is a marginal phenomenon in the political realm; for man, to the extent that he is a political being, is endowed with the power of speech" (1963, 9; see also Arendt 1972).

condemnation for participation in a totalitarian regime whose effect on
him was not to reveal some basic bestiality latent in him (or his culture)
before the Nazis, but rather to turn him into a kind of non-self, an unreal
creature whose essential reality was his "remoteness from reality" (1965,
287–8). Eichmann deserves condemnation for what he *did*, not who he
"was" – simply because who he essentially was is totally irrelevant to the
trial, and appeals to it can seduce us into thinking that Eichmann's evil
actions reflect some sort of ontological reality of demonic evil in the
world. He was complicit in mass murder, while at the same time being
in no way the sort of personality one would expect to have the malice
capable of carrying out such acts. Eichmann's self-deception, and his
remoteness from reality, just reflect the universal remoteness from reality
of nearly the entire Nazi German society. As Arendt said, evil in the
regime had become the norm, had lost its sense of temptation for people
like Eichmann. She used the phrase "the banality of evil" neither to
shock, nor to excuse, but quite simply to get at the truth of Eichmann
and what he represents – and what he represents, in the end, is the utter-
most extreme of modern "politics."

With this picture of Arendt's account of modernity and totalitarianism in place, we can see that Canovan is right: Arendt is not purely reacting against totalitarianism, she uses that threat to investigate the positive
character of politics. But Canovan also misses something: for while the
positive picture within which she understands evil is clearly modern,
it has distinctly Augustinian valences, for it sees evil as the negation of
genuine human goods, and as the contraction of the human agent to
something ultimately sub-human. For Arendt, despite her attraction
to Kant's account of "radical evil" and Nietzsche's idea of a near-
demonic power "behind" or "beneath" the human will, such evil is fundamentally a *negative* reality, a nihilating power whose own reality is
wholly parasitic on the genuine goods of human action and existence
(see Villa 1992 and Allison 1996).

The insights this account offers us today are considerable. In a world
increasingly captivated by private pleasures and increasingly vexed by
national and international anomie, she shows us how and why we must
care for our public world. In an apathetic and apolitical age, Arendt
demonstrates that our hope lies in "politics," of a very peculiar kind.
This account has generated enormous critical enthusiasm, building
upon the basic truth that Arendt apprehended and her intellectual
inheritors have developed: genuine human political activity is a constit-
uent of both a healthy *polis* and a full human life (Elster 1983, Habermas

1983, Lyotard 1984, and Havel 1985). Arendt's account of politics is essentially asymmetrical: in fighting for the goods of politics we are literally fighting against nothingness, against an opponent whose sole reality is our own failure. Hers is no Manichean struggle of good against evil, but rather a struggle of good against the void. We cannot despair, because there is nothing to despair about; our opponents are not demonic agents of an antihuman conspiracy, but rather the banal bureaucrats of some potentially subhuman world empire. This account of evil gives us hope, for it suggests that our only opponents are ourselves made less real, "banal."

But is this narrative merely a *consolation?* Many worry that this is so. Critics accuse Arendt of being essentially an elitist, and of offering a consoling myth for other members of the elite, expressive of a nostalgic longing for another age, when she and her mandarin-literati friends mattered, and when the world seemed to cohere with the education they had received. For such critics, Arendt's account of the banality of evil is more an impotent sneer than a useful response to the challenges evil puts to us. And despite their biliousness, their complaints have some force. So this is the topic we must next address.

THE BANALITY OF MORALITY

The critics' charges are simple: calling evil "banal" can seem little more than swatting at a dragon with a quill. Indeed it seems so underwhelming in its effects, and so vociferously mocking in its tone, as to suggest that it knows its powerlessness and is attempting to avoid confronting it. (It is worth noting that these charges are versions of the charges made against Augustine's *privatio* thesis.) This criticism splits into two basic complaints about her work. First of all, ontologically, critics charge that the "banality" thesis does not really get at the heart of evil at all; can we really believe that the Holocaust is a matter of nothingness? Second, practically, critics charge that, whatever its ontological validity, the thesis simply does not help us respond to evil at all. Does not Arendt offer us an *apologia* for an elitism that is merely a this-worldly form of the philosophical longing for the *vita contemplativa* which she so effectively disparaged? Is not this really a political theory built around snobbishness, an essentially consolatory defense against evil built upon a sneer?

The problems are real, but not rooted in elitism, nostalgia, or a flaw symptomatic of all "metaphysical" language. They are caused by Arendt's implausible picture of human agency, which leads to an anthropological anarchism subversive of all politics. The proposal rests fundamentally on the human's reality as a "principle of natality," a force of beginning which can disrupt the rationalist mechanizations of totalitarianism. But her analysis of action invests agency with an autonomy so extreme that it cannot be understood as determined by anything outside itself, including our own agential control (indeed and on the contrary, this agency seems to control *us*). This anarchism is not only bad in itself; it also subverts her proposed response to evil. Most basically, her effectively Pelagian concept of human freedom distorts her development of Augustine's privationist account of "the banality of evil."

The question of judgment

We can begin with a question: on what grounds does Arendt condemn Eichmann? It seems that she judges him for his crimes; but if Eichmann is truly "banal," can he be responsible? If he is really thoughtless, if he really "had no idea" of what he was doing, if he really is without a self, is it an appropriate response for us to put him to death? As Berel Lang puts it, "if Eichmann acted as he did because of the expression of totalitarianism as a political form, in what sense was he – or anyone else – responsible for what was done?" (1991, 151).[29] Indeed, as Jacob Rogozinski suggests, Arendt here seems to be accepting totalitarianism's self-understanding as an inevitable historical force: "In denying that [totalitarianism] could be the result of an act of freedom, she tends, paradoxically, to accept the representation of itself which the totalitarian movement puts forward" (1993, 261). The worry here is simple: if Arendt is right about Eichmann's banality, then is not totalitarianism right in part of its claim? And if this is so, does this not make it impossible to justify punishing Eichmann?

It is important to be clear on what I am suggesting here. I am not attempting to insinuate that Arendt was a self-hating Jew, and so secretly, perhaps unconsciously, sympathized with the Nazis in general, or Eichmann in particular (as Dan Diner is only the latest to remarkably suggest).[30] The problem is quite the opposite: she seems hard pressed to attribute *any* humanity to him. But dehumanizing him, in this way, does not actually help her work at all. It may make him pathetic to us; but it

---

[29] See also Brunner (1996, 83), on the need to talk about motives to be able to talk about responsibility.
[30] Diner 1997, 185: "Arendt's line of argumentation has more in common with justifying the perspective of the perpetrators than it does with the viewpoint, marked by suffering, of the victims."

does not explain why we should hold him accountable for what he did. If anything, it subverts ascriptions of blame to him (see Nino 1996, 135, 141–2). Theoretically and ontologically, it makes genuine action seem just as incomprehensible as totalitarian evil. Arendt's account renders good and evil formally indistinguishable. If this is so, why is the "banality" of one more troubling to us than the anarchy of the other? Arendt's inability to distinguish formally between world-constituting action and world-denying totalitarian evil means that her account, which begins from and relies upon our intuitive resistance to evil and worldlessness, cannot finally make sense of just those intuitive wellsprings. Most pointedly, Arendt's account cannot make sense of *hope*: it can neither give an account of action which puts it within our power, nor find a way finally to distinguish evaluatively between action so construed and the world-destroying banalities it supposedly counters.

Because Arendt depicts evil as a momentary opponent, her proposed response to it is only partial, a sort of "heroic" agonal politics (Keenan 1994). Politics is the realm of appearance, that space within which we actualize or realize ourselves; in this space, evil appears here essentially in an oppositional form, as somehow "outside" us, an enemy with whom we can struggle in order to be more fully ourselves. This is because of the inevitable agonal quality of politics: for Arendt, politics is an essentially conflictual and agonal activity, an activity in which struggle is seen as a good, because it creates for us appearances by which we truly (because publicly) appear. But this is surely an inadequate account of what politics is, and inadequate for essentially the same reasons as is Arendt's account of evil. Without acknowledging the real persistence of evil, and its insinuation into our own lives, politics degenerates into oppositional theater; it concerns not so much what we care about as whom we fight against. Politics is thus a sort of total or permanent revolution, a perpetual upheaval, anarchy without end (Yack 1986).

This is clearly a significant part of any account of evil; there are times when we need simply to resist threats, when opponents do exist and must be fought. But sometimes we meet the enemy and he is us, and "agonal" understandings of politics are less adequate to such situations. A more adequate account of politics would acknowledge our implication on both sides of any struggle; it would acknowledge that "the political" cannot finally be contained within the definite limits of some restricted "political" space, and that our putatively "private" interests play a critical role in all "public" political activity.

Arendt's attempt to quarantine the political from the rest of human

life is the most typically attacked part of her work (Pitkin 1981). But such
critics do not usually notice how this issue reflects her account of action.
The crucial fact is that Arendt so overemphasizes political freedom that
she cannot but see as "totalitarian" *any* attempt to connect up our cares
with politics, and so absolutely divides our "public" and "private" lives.[31]
So desirous is she to use freedom to resist totalitarianism's encroachment
on our lives, so insistent is her appeal to our "capacity to begin," that
Arendt does not recognize that, by valorizing freedom as she does, she
finally expels it from the world.[32]

Arendt's offer of the anarchy of permanent revolution is not very
attractive. Her account leaves us not only beyond good and evil; it tempts
us towards just that nihilism that getting beyond good and evil was
meant to help us avoid. Both totalitarianism and Arendt's "politics"
seem equally banal. So while her account illuminates for us the ontological underpinnings of "evil," her positive proposal offers us no explanation for why we should think that her alternative is ultimately more
attractive than the totalitarianism she so rightly disparages. Her genuine
insights – about the essential and constitutive character of human action
for genuine human existence, and her unflinching acknowledgment of
the tragic fragility of all such human achievements – are inadvertently
subverted by the subjectivist voluntarism that she employs to support
those insights. Evil becomes *sporadic*, wholly episodic, so Arendt cannot
account for evil's historicity, its persistence across time as a real and
genuine problem, part of our past and so part of our present. Arendt's
account is too psychologically simple. It is an account of evil as an episodic adversary, not an ongoing problem. While it is ontologically reas-
suring, it is not very helpful for us in dealing with the evil we find around
us, and *in* us, every day.

Arendt's work seems to exemplify what Charles Taylor has labeled
"the ethics of inarticulacy," an ethics which cannot explain why it values
what it values.[33] Recall that Arendt ascribes shallowness and banality to

---

[31] It is important to note that, in order to do this, we need not utterly *annihilate* the distinctions
between public and private; we need merely keep them non-ultimate.

[32] This is in fact an allegory of any attempt to absolutize the individual's political autonomy, though
I cannot argue that here. There are also interesting connections here to more "canonical" existentialists (though the idea of "canonical existentialists" is an odd one), especially Albert Camus;
see Isaac 1992. Because it is precisely this part of Arendt that I find most dubious, my criticisms
of Arendt can be expanded into a critique of any such existentialist politics *simpliciter*. Another
thinker to whom Arendt is clearly indebted for this vision is Max Weber; the same criticisms
apply in this case too.

[33] See Taylor 1989, especially chapter 3, "The Ethics of Inarticulacy." Margaret Canovan acknowledges this problem in Arendt's thought (1992, 198–9), but suggests that Arendt thought that

totalitarian evil because for her it has no depth, and offers no access to comprehension in itself. Evil's absolute exteriority to our human world, for Arendt, renders it essentially "speechless." But how is this argument any different in form from Arendt's account of "action"? For action too is wholly autonomous, wholly other than what came before. Action's unpredictability and absolute spontaneity make futile all attempts to connect action to the remainder of our lives; all we can say is that it happened.

An Arendtian might counter that we do have a form of understanding appropriate to action, namely the form of retrospective story-telling (Disch 1994, Benhabib 1996). But one may say two things in response to this: first, it is not clear to what degree such "story-telling" differs from the sort of stories Arendt tells in *The Origins of Totalitarianism* and *Eichmann in Jerusalem*, so appealing to "story-telling" does not help us differentiate the stories she tells about genuine political action from those she tells about totalitarian evil. Second, insofar as these two types of story do differ, it may be because Arendt relies on unthematized elements of action that make it intelligible to us, because of the way it connects up to the way the world is – just those sorts of connections, in fact, that Arendt's account of action's autonomy is meant to forbid. So Arendt's concept of action may implicitly rely on ontological resources it explicitly repudiates.

The problem is that Arendt remains captive to a subjectivist account of the human's agency in the world, so she affirms the spontaneity of the will in a way that is finally impossible to distinguish from irrationalist voluntarism. Her work remains committed to the absolute autonomy of the will's choice, the totally *ex nihilo* spontaneity of the acting agent unconditioned by any external factors at all – including intention or desire. Unfortunately, this subjectivist commitment eventually subverts her constructive insights: by claiming for the will so extreme a political freedom, her account of freedom renders the human, as an intentional agent, a passive victim or sufferer of the will's actions, rather than the agent who acts. Furthermore, this makes it hard to see how we could *employ* action, our one putative weapon against worldlessness, to combat that evil.

This looks like a simply political problem, about the *sui generis* character of political action, or its isolation (as "public" and "political") from

footnote 33 (*cont.*)
  explanations (and perhaps even investigations) of such convictions are otiose in politics. In contrast, see Lovin 1995, 240: "We cannot settle our disagreements about what we ought to do without reference to our understandings of a fully human life."

issues of the "personal" and "private," and many of Arendt's interlocutors have interpreted it as such (e.g., Habermas 1983). But in fact the problem here is not most fundamentally about how to avoid rationalist or totalitarian reductions of human agency to pseudo-"natural" causality; while that is one of Arendt's most constant worries, the deep root of her argument lies in her subjectivist presumption about the subject's priority, her implicit belief that freedom is not real unless the action is uninfluenced by any determining forces.[34] It is this form of subjectivism that Niebuhr sees as the deep problem of modern thought, the problem of voluntarism. Arendt fails to see that there are significant determinants of our actions, determinants that we must recognize and explicitly acknowledge, if we are responsibly to address them.

To see what I mean, we must briefly exegete her account of agency. Arendt's analysis of spontaneity suggests that the human agent is identified with this willing force; but this willing force is more fundamental than the agent's powers of understanding, capacity to reason. If the will is wholly spontaneous, it cannot be within the control of the agent. Human agents, as conscious participants in their actions, are therefore estranged from their actions. In the service of affirming the genuine reality of human action, Arendt goes to an untenable extreme; her emphasis on action ignores the other aspects of human existence, and her emphasis on humans' capacity for natality, "the principle of beginning," ends in a dubious voluntarism which cripples both her appreciation of the full complexity of politics and limits the usefulness of her proposed response to evil's challenges. Her proposal suffers from her unwillingness to place this insight within a rich picture of human life as an integrated whole. For Arendt, "action insofar as it is free is neither under the guidance of the intellect nor under the dictate of the will" (1961, 152); action, insofar as it is free, is free of *us*.

But if this is so – if the nature of action is absolutely unpredictable – human agents must be surprised not only at the effects of what they will, but at the very character of their willing, the form and direction it takes. At this level, Arendt's voluntarism, while clearly defending action's autonomy against all deterministic reductionisms, ends up so isolating action that it leads to just what the initial move was intended to avoid: namely,

---

[34] I will avoid, for the moment, the question of whether Arendt's account is either "compatibilist" or "libertarian." Whatever her stance on this metaphysical issue, on the phenomenological level at least she insists that to be free is to be undetermined. Naturally I think this entails metaphysical claims, and particularly the claim that this commitment to phenomenological libertarianism entails a fissure between (putative) agent and action. But this discussion can be carried on at this point without reference to the "compatibilist"/"libertarian" arguments.

removing action from an agent's control, and hence her or his responsibility. Her concept of willing, then, seems fundamentally incoherent: if an action is, properly speaking, spontaneous, it can have no connection with what came before, and this undermines the basic framework of the self's continuity, a continuity necessary for the self's actions – and indeed the self itself – to be intelligible. Action is thus rendered irrational, and the capacity for deliberation is rendered otiose. Furthermore, ironically enough, this irrationality makes the concept of free will incoherent – for if there is no way to explain a human's action, then surely the acting human agent cannot explain it either. The agent is simply a rider on a runaway train – or, rather, on a train that was never under its control in the first place. Hence Arendt's account, paradoxically enough, makes the human basically passive before the action of the will. She could appeal to the phenomenological evidence that we seem consciously to choose to act, and that therefore it is not our action but *we* who are unpredictable, not something outside ourselves but our very selves. But this move merely pushes our passiveness back one step further, deep into Humean territory – for if our acts are identifiable with us, then our motivations which generate our acts – our desires – must be beyond us, and hence not us. In the end, Arendt's account entails that there is a fountain of novelty, a source which is foreign to our conscious selves, an unintelligible wellspring of action.

Arendt recognized this problem, which she described as the "impasse" brought about by the fact that "we are *doomed* to be free by virtue of being born, no matter whether we like freedom or abhor its arbitrariness" (1978a, 217). She attempted to solve it, but could not. Her early claim that "principles" can guide action foundered on the fact that such "principles" can only be a *redescription* of action (1961, 152–3; see Kateb 1983, 12–13). In her later work she turned to the idea of explicitly political "judgment," but this turned out to be only a device for resignation, what Ronald Beiner calls the activity "by which [agents] can come to terms with what irrevocably happened and be reconciled with what unavoidably exists" (Beiner 1982, 96; see Dostal 1984). But this "judging" is itself a kind of action, and thus again falls within the realm of human actions which are outside the agent's conscious control; so, as with her appeal to principles, the appeal to judgment seems more like a *deus ex machina*, brought in at the end to save the day. Nor have her descendants helped much. Either they attempt to combine her account of action as pure spontaneity with the phenomenological experience of the person's stability, or they affirm that the account entails rejecting the apparent experience of continuity, and the attendant conceptual framework of character and intentionality.[35] But against the first, spontaneity does not admit of degrees: if the self is free in the sense of being truly spontaneous, the self can perpetually recreate its character, can simply transform itself into a wholly new thing at any moment.[36] And against the second, the disruptiveness of action (and indeed for all experience's ruptures, about which post-Nietzschean philosophers have spilled so much ink) presumes a felt framework of stability within which such disturbances gain their "disturbing" character.[37] That is, for difference to be recognized *as* difference, it must be framed by a basalt sameness or identity. Furthermore, Arendt herself admitted her need of some stability to make sense of agency, and to ensure the reliability of promising and the intelligibility of forgiving. Whom is one to forgive for the past, when the only continuity in persons is a matter of mere flesh? Something like Nietzsche's "active forgetting" seems more appropriate here than any notion of forgiveness, or perhaps what Dietrich Bonhoeffer called "cheap grace."[38] And how can one rely on one another's promises if we cannot rely on one another to remain the same? Promises are not ontological butterflies fluttering about the void; they derive from agents who can be held to their word.[39] Both capacities we have for reaffirming our commitment to the political realm – and hence to the world itself – turn out to be undermined by the very capacity they were meant to protect. Freedom seems, quite literally, both self- and world-destructive.

This is what I meant when I called Arendt's anthropology essentially *Pelagian*. It depicts us as acting from a position of no prior commitments, and like the Pelagians her absolute faith in the *ex nihilo* spontaneity of human agency offers too narrow a picture of human agency, and leaves uninvestigated both agency's interesting interrelations with the world outside it, and its internal complexities as well. Of course, this is not unique to her; indeed, her popularity in political thought suggests something of the depth with which such voluntaristic convictions are held by many contemporary thinkers. She exemplifies moderns' typical reliance on the power of human freedom as the self's salvation.

---

[35] The best representative of the first position is Suzanne Jacobitti; see Jacobitti 1988 and 1996. The best representative of the second is Bonnie Honig; see Honig 1988.

[36] To attempt to replace the ontological category of spontaneity with the epistemological one of unpredictability, and then to insist that nothing important is lost in translation, is manifestly false.

[37] Here I am developing Donald Davidson's point, made in Davidson 1984. Honig's attempt to transform Arendt into a Nietzschean political theorist ignores, for example, the differences between Arendt's account of "forgiving" and Nietzsche's "active forgetting," whose difference I gestured at earlier.

[38] On the connections between cheap grace and forgiveness I am indebted to Jones 1995.

[39] I dissent from Honig's hypostatization of promises in Honig 1988, 84–5.

In a way interestingly analogous to Niebuhr, then, the most compelling part of Arendt's account – her analysis of evil's challenges in terms of the world-destructive "banality of evil," and her concomitant positive account of *amor mundi* – is undermined by the account of agency in which she couched it. This is unfortunate, for she was fundamentally right in her affirmation of both our freedom and our worldliness. To do better, we must acknowledge the role of our ongoing motives and interests in political life, an acknowledgment which implicates agency in history and the world. We must transcend her subjectivist voluntarism, yet still affirm her insistence that human action matters in the world – that is, by making humans more fully worldly creatures than her account allows, and by making politics continuous with, because in part arising out of, our everyday lives. But we can do this only if we become articulate about ontology. And here, her essentially Augustinian ontology can help us.

Amor mundi: *Hannah Arendt's inverted Augustinianism*

The great advances in the last decade of Arendt scholarship have largely ignored her work's persistent engagement with Augustine, whom she called "the first philosopher of the will and freedom" (1978a, 84).[40] If, as Canovan suggests, we focus on "plurality" as Arendt's major contribution to political thought, we risk obscuring her work's deep movement by pandering too much to the interests of our time. Arendt is not a nostalgic reactionary, nor is she a "pessimistic modernist," nor a harbinger of some post-modernist critique. We should be wary of making Arendt *too* much our contemporary.

Most basically, she offers us a profoundly positive vision of the human good, and an account of how to resist the threats that imperil that good. To understand Arendt best we must understand her work through her concept of *world*, and her concomitant proposal of *amor mundi*, or "love

---

[40] Margaret Canovan's recent book (1992) exemplifies the renaissance in Arendt scholarship, in its careful exegesis of Arendt, its thoughtful application of her work to contemporary political issues, and its curious yet resolute indifference to her relationship with her predecessors, especially Augustine. Exceptions to this are (a) Elshtain 1995a, who dedicates an entire chapter to investigating the relation between "Augustine's Evil, Arendt's Eichmann," (b) the editors' (Joanna Vecchiarelli Scott and Judith Chelius Stark) essays in the recent English translation of Arendt's doctoral dissertation (Arendt 1996), and (c) Beiner 1996, which rightly highlights how her account of worldliness developed out of her engagement with Augustine. Furthermore, as I noted in the introduction to this chapter, this is exegetically damaging, for in several important passages in her work, she appealed to a passage of Augustine on action as "beginning," signaling a crucial indebtedness to his work.

of the world," as the central virtue of politically active life or *vita activa*.[41] This concept helps us understand Arendt both philosophically and genealogically, for from her perspective, the concept of *amor mundi* is precisely what the philosophical tradition as a whole ignores or willfully rejects; and only *amor mundi* can provide us with the genuine goods of human existence.[42]

Arendt's concept of *mundus*, or "world" is basic to her positive vision as a whole, which is unapologetically constructive: her method of "phenomenological essentialism" does not attempt to defend its account of the *vita activa* against skeptical challenges, but rather details a comprehensive account which gains its validity through its illuminative power for our situation (Benhabib 1996, 123–4). It is also thoroughly ontological: as Dana Villa says, Arendt's proposal "stakes its hopes entirely on the rethematization of certain ontological dimensions of human experience (action, the public world, and self) which [modernity's] blurring obscures, denatures, and makes increasingly difficult to articulate" (1992, 302). However, this ontology derives not from theoretical speculation, but from reflection on lived experiences: we understand "world" only by reference to Arendt's concept of "action," and "action" by reference to the role she thinks *speech* plays in action, all of which is broadly encompassed under her concept of the *vita activa*. By coming to understand this, we better understand her worry that modernity fundamentally threatens us with "worldlessness," and her understanding of evil as ultimately and essentially world-negating. Furthermore, understanding her concept of the "world" is crucial to understanding her engagement with Augustine, for, as Ronald Beiner has suggested, "the entirety of Arendt's philosophical work merely elaborates the question she had posed directly to Augustine: 'Why should we make a desert out of this world?'" (Beiner 1996, 281). An investigation of Arendt's concept of world is thus crucial in order to understand her whole project.

By "world" Arendt meant not simply the physical environment, the earth that sustains us (although she saw our "earth-alienation" as a sign of the last stages of our world-alienation), but more complexly the world

---

[41] Her first title choice for the book that eventually became named *The Human Condition* was *Amor Mundi* (see Young-Bruehl 1982, 324). Also see Bernauer 1987 and Pitkin 1998, 106–7, 265. Pitkin does not see the connections with Augustine's *amor Dei*, however; she suggests it "was clearly meant to contrast with the philosophers' traditional rejection of earthly concerns, *contemptus mundi*" (106). For Arendt's general "repression" of religious thought, see Brunkhorst 1999.

[42] In this Arendt revises Heidegger's account of Being-in-the-World to talk about how the world is *fragile*. For an interestingly similar development of this point, see Sabina Lovibond on ethics as a "physiognomy" (1983, §50). On Arendt's general intellectual indebtedness and implicit critique of Heidegger, see Bernstein 1992 124–8; and Villa 1996. Cf. Benhabib 1996, 104, 110–12, 117.

that comes into existence *in* and *through* the creative power of human action, and serves as the stage on which such action occurs. The "world" is for Arendt essentially a human achievement, an artificial "space" created between humans in which we appear as "worldly" beings. The world depends upon our material fabrications, on the "things" we make, things which create a habitation for ourselves in the essential wilderness of nature; these things include both use-objects, such as tools, with clearly utilitarian purposes, and objects without any utilitarian point at all (see 1958, 93–6). But the "fabricated" character of the world does not subvert its reality; on the contrary, as so durable and "objective," it is more objective even than nature, which is pre-objective (1987, 35). Still, while material objects play an essential role in the constitution of the world, it is essentially a creation, as Margaret Canovan puts it, "more cultural than technological" (1992, 112).[43]

Arendt's concept of world is intimately related to her understanding of human existence; for her the world and the self are co-founding concepts. The self must have a world in which it is involved, in order to be a real self. This is the basis of her critique of modern political theory, especially modern "liberal" atomistic political theory. The world does not build up out of atoms of selfhood, in some sort of ontological variant of Hobbesian contract theory. The public realm is not simply the aggregate of all of our private realms, nor is it merely the space between them. The public is *prior to* the private; this is why the self must be involved with the world in order to be fully itself. To live finally in ironic distanciation from the public world is symptomatic of the malaise of "worldlessness" with which Arendt is so concerned, precisely because that mode of existence is parasitic on the "worlding capital," the "surplus" of commitment to sustaining the public world that has been built up over generations, and in which some people still invest today, but which, because of large-scale anomie and indifference to politics, seems increasingly to be draining away.

Recent debates about "the social construction of reality" and the role

---

[43] Arendt here employs a contrast between "world" and "environment" (in German, *Welt* and *Umwelt*) common to post-Heideggerian thinkers; for a helpful discussion of the contrasting terms, see Gadamer 1989, 438–56. (For the best account of Heidegger's concept of "world" in English, see Dreyfus 1991, 88–107, 128–33; for an interestingly similar analytic account, see Searle 1995.) Intriguingly, Arendt's concept of "world" touches on issues that have in recent decades become pressing questions for philosophers on both sides of the "analytic"/"Continental" divide. These questions center on issues related to relativism and the nature of the human's responsibility or "answerability" to the world as something significantly resistant to (not merely, though centrally, intentional) human control (see McDowell 1994, 114–19).

of humans in creating their world apprehend, and attempt to express, a crucial truth, namely, that any attempt to understand human existence without taking into consideration human self-interpretations will both (a) at best capture only a part of human existence, and (b) fundamentally misconstrue even that part of the human world. All attempts at atomic analysis, à la Cartesian (or any contemporary) reductionistic naturalists, are bound to fail, because they attempt to grasp one half of the dialectic as basic, so throw the whole system out of balance.[44] Nonetheless, the world is not for Arendt in any simple way a human "fabrication," which we can change or alter at our whim; our ability to act stands beyond simple utilitarian end-oriented "production." The language of social "construction" is deeply misleading; it attempts to explicate the notion of the human-relatedness and human-groundedness of our "world" to something like economic metaphors, which are finally grounded on false anthropological understanding of the human's relation to this "world" as essentially a matter of *choice*. But this is fundamentally misconceived; the world is not basically *alien* to us, something with which our most basic relations are what are called in philosophy "external relations," relations which are not internal to our own self-constitution (for example, relations most basically of *indifference, alliance,* or *conflict*). "The world" is not most basically what is "outside" the solipsistic Cartesian *cogito*, either as what we meet (and attempt to represent) in the world or as what we make; rather, it is the entirety of existence which sustains and "enframes" the subject, who comes-to-be by emerging through a complex dialectic engagement with the "world." The world does not have a merely contingent relation to our existence; it is partly determinative of that existence. The ontological interchange flows in both directions; the "world" and the "human agent" emerge together.

The connections to Heidegger's thought should be apparent. Yet whereas Heidegger thinks our problem is a basic "forgetfulness" of Being as such, Arendt thinks the basic problem is not our forgetfulness of Being, but rather our forgetfulness of freedom. Heidegger's interest in "thinking Being" becomes for Arendt "thinking freedom," and her work is in some ways an attempt to ask about "the meaning of freedom." By placing the human's center in birth, in a spontaneous capacity to begin, she placed her own work in implicit opposition to Heidegger's famed prescription of an authentic "being-towards-death," and she located the source of her own positive position in Augustine's account of

[44] See Taylor 1985, and Heidegger's critique of Descartes in Heidegger 1962, 130–4.

the free will as part of the human's *imago Dei*. In this context what is especially interesting about this project is that she, like Heidegger (whom
Robert Pippin has called "the greatest modern Augustinian" [1997, 277])
before her, refers to Augustine as a crucial figure for a more appropriate
conceptualization of human existence. Indeed she goes further than
Heidegger by arguing that Augustine was the first thinker to glimpse the
real significance of human freedom for understanding our condition.
According to Arendt, Augustine saw that "if we have a nature or essence,
then surely only a god could know and define it, and the first prerequisite would be that he be able to speak about a 'who' as though it were a
'what' " (1958, 10). She argued that Augustine was right to suggest that
the fundamental human question is (as we have seen Niebuhr say) a
theological question: "The question about the nature of man is no less
a theological question than the question about the nature of God; both
can be settled only within the framework of a divinely revealed answer"
(1958, 11 n. 2). Augustine, she thought, saw that the analysis of the
human condition was the ontological prelude to a discussion of the ultimate determining factor of that condition, namely, human nature as
revealed in our relatedness to God. Arendt agrees with this, but alters it
slightly, though decisively: as there is no God, we need ask only about
the shape of the human condition, as we find it in the world. Thus, in a
sense, Arendt's restriction of her own inquiry to "the human condition"
is meant simultaneously to acknowledge Augustine's insight and to distance herself from it.[45]

By understanding and underscoring the way humans participate in
the creation of the world – indeed, in a certain way just *are* the creators
of the world – Arendt's work offers the pieces of a profoundly ontological interpretation of the import of human action. Can we assemble
them into a plausible picture?

Overcoming anarchy: a grammar of agential assent

To save Arendt's insights, we must construct an account of action
immune to the problems vexing her formulations. We must deny the
human will's primordiality, its *ex nihilo* power; rather, the will acts always
in response to some prior act upon it, so action is best understood in

---

[45] Whether or not Augustine found himself committed to the idea of human "nature," he certainly
did not buy into the static account of nature which Arendt tries to foist upon him here; see Rist
1995, 145–7, for a depiction of Augustine's agnosticism about human nature before the eschaton.

terms of assent to and dissent from the reality of those prior acts. One finds the rudiments of such an understanding in Arendt's account of politics as "world-constitutive." Because that account depicts evil as a momentary opponent, it offers only a partial response, an agonal politics exemplified in permanent revolution. But a lot of politics is boring, ordinary stuff, ill handled by the blades of the *sans-culottes*. Arendt cannot recognize this because she sees *all* attempts to connect up our cares with politics as improperly confusing "nature" with the (supremely unnatural) political life, because she cannot understand how genuine action could be conceptualized as "determined" in any way at all.

To offer a realistic account of human interaction, political theory must acknowledge the interrelations between agency and ends, and in particular the end-oriented character of action (Wolf 1980, Mathewes 1999). Politics, that is, must see itself as continuous with, and indeed at times even identical to, hermeneutical and metaphysical inquiry, about the "being" of the people, and the community, and the world that the community makes. This thought is available to Arendt, because for her politics is precisely the realm of being, properly speaking – that region of human existence in which humanity comes most fully into its own, becomes most fully itself. An ontological interpretation of politics supports both Arendt's positive proposal of *amor mundi*, and her negative analysis of political evil's essentially "world-denying" reality. We evaluate action's "political" pretensions by determining whether it affirms or subverts the public world. When action is good, it is ontologically good, "worlding" in its effects. In contrast, action which dissents from the world harms it, and is not properly speaking "action" at all, but rather a form of non-actualizing, of denying or destroying reality. As Jacob Rogozinski notes, "banality" and "abandon" share a common lexical root: "banality is the condition of man who has been forsaken, banished" (1993, 271). World-nihilating, anti-political action is bad for Arendt, not centrally because of any autonomous *in se* maleficence it possesses, but rather because of its destructive effect on our common world. This framework for understanding political action may explicitly shun a moral vocabulary, but it ultimately adverts to a set of ethical criteria for its elucidation – namely, the health of the public world.

The ontological structures of her work are not only readily available to a re-theologized Augustinian framework, they actually illuminate that framework, especially its account of evil as ontologically privative. This account recognizes both that humans are free from necessity, while also placing that freedom within a framework of commitments which render it deliberatively unintelligible. Thus an Augustinian account of agency grounded on a "grammar of assent" can support both Arendt's political ontology and her account of totalitarian evil, where the troublesome subjectivist theory of agency which Arendt herself employed cannot.

ENACTING RESISTANCE: HANNAH ARENDT'S JOYOUS CRITIQUE

By placing Arendt's insights within a more thoroughly Augustinian account of agency, then, we can root her account of the banality of evil – and through it our Augustinian argument about evil as privation – in her political ontology, resulting in a thoroughly ontological politics. But would not such a profoundly "metaphysical" theory have deeply anti-worldly effects? Not at all; as we saw, Arendt's basic project was one of promoting the *amor mundi* or "love of the world," that she thought was under attack in (and by) modernity. As we will see here, the "ethics" that derives from her political ontology is anything but escapist. We can begin to see this by grasping how the central point she makes in *Eichmann in Jerusalem* is neither an historical nor a merely spectatorial argument, but rather an essentially *practical* critique.

The critique of the judgment

The reception of *Eichmann in Jerusalem* has always been colored by the notoriety of Arendt's broadly historical argument about the uniqueness of the Holocaust, the causal relationship between historical antisemitism and the death camps, and the conduct of various groups, especially including the Jewish town councils, in the Holocaust. But these arguments are not Arendt's main focus, and these controversies have obscured the book's more sustained and fruitful arguments. One is the political and legal argument about the flawed character of the trial as a trial, investigating "how well our present system of justice is capable of dealing with this special type of crime and criminal it has had repeatedly to cope with since the Second World War" (1965, 286).[46] Another is the larger argument, obliquely advanced, about the character of our response to such evil. In this subsection I will discuss the former argument; in the next, the latter.

The basic story of *Eichmann in Jerusalem* is the mutual incomprehension of the parties involved in the trial. Not only did Eichmann not

---

[46] Throughout this final section of the chapter, all references to this text will be included in parenthesis in the body of the essay.

understand what was happening to and around him, but also the judges, the prosecution and indeed the audience did not grasp what Eichmann really represented. At his trial, Eichmann displayed none of the demonic character attributed to him; the chasm between the fumbling fool in the docket and the satanic anti-hero conjured up by the prosecution's rhetoric seemed unbridgeable (1965, 276). Furthermore, and alongside Eichmann's blatant incomprehension of the trial, no one else involved with the trial recognized the real nature of the crimes: "None of the participants ever arrived at a clear understanding of the actual terror of Auschwitz, which is of a different nature from all the atrocities of the past, because it appeared to prosecution and judges alike as not much more than the most horrible pogrom in Jewish history . . . politically and legally, however, these were 'crimes' different not only in degree of seriousness but in essence" (1965, 267). The traditional forms of juridical-legal understanding failed to comprehend Eichmann's crimes, and thus the trial revealed the "inadequacy of the prevailing legal system and of current juridical concepts to deal with the facts of administrative massacres organized by the state apparatus" (1965, 294). So Arendt's claim that "the present report deals with nothing but the extent to which the court in Jerusalem succeeded in fulfilling the demands of justice" (1965, 298), is not false humility but an accurate description of her purpose.

Quite literally, the work is a "critique of (a) judgment," the judgment of the court in Jerusalem, on two levels. First, Arendt thought the actual judgment on Eichmann was flawed, because it tried to judge not Eichmann but the Holocaust and totalitarianism *simpliciter*.[47] Second, she argues that this judgment gained its plausibility because of the faulty, overly interiorized concept of practical judgment that the court assumed. That concept compelled its adherents, almost by logical necessity, to insist that Eichmann's crime lurked at the base of his character: he *had* to be wicked, on this view, simply because no one could do what he did and not have their soul stained red, their conscience turned to ashes.[48] But Eichmann himself seemed not at all "wicked" – he was just

[47] The prosecution essentially tried to depict Eichmann as the consequence of a long history of antisemitic prejudice in Germany (and Europe more broadly), and also as a singularly wicked and vicious facilitator and enactor of the Holocaust. Notwithstanding that the two aspects of this argument have nothing to do with one another (and indeed the former may seem to undermine the latter [1965, 19–20]), there were many other actors who played roles in the Holocaust (indeed, not only Nazis and citizens of the occupied countries, but even some Jewish town councils [see especially 117–19]); to suggest that Eichmann was personally responsible for so many crimes seemed to be an attempt to erase the guilt of all other Nazis.

[48] Thus we often make claims about some evildoers being wicked "deep down inside."

a nobody, who talked only in clichés, borrowed words and phrases, and suggested no ability to think, nor any capacity for imagination (1965, 47–9, 51–5). Indeed, in their judgment the trial judges effectively rewrote the prosecution's case in order to focus on Eichmann's direct responsibilities and not on his general culpability for the Holocaust *tout court* (1965, 211–19). The problem was not that people were wrong to prosecute Eichmann; the problem was simply that Eichmann himself was, in terms of the traditional legal and philosophical concepts of "malice aforethought" and the like, well-nigh unprosecutable, because he was hardly an agent.

For Arendt, the problem with the trial stemmed centrally from the application of a (fairly Kantian) concept of agency, a concept which was extremely inappropriate to Eichmann's case (1965, 49). This legal system assumed a morally normal society, in which evil was typically discernible as deviance from the norm. The difficulty in Eichmann's case, however, was that certain forms of evil had become so systemic that the typical systems of self-correction and moral guidance did not function. The appeal to conscience is exemplary here; to ground our moral resistance on an inner conscience would be, Arendt thinks, naive to the point of willful stupidity, for language of "conscience" can serve to deflate or misdirect resistance to evil into effective paralysis through the language of "inward opposition." This language, common in postwar Germany, fundamentally misconstrues the nature of morality, for it suggests that the morality of the agents professing it is in fact nothing but a moralism, in which the value of interior moral stances (meant to manifest themselves in actual moral behavior) could become an end in themselves, and ethics be a matter of moral fastidiousness. "No secret in the secret-ridden atmosphere of the Hitler regime was better kept than such 'inward opposition' " (1965, 126–7). The problem with the idea of conscience as an "inner voice," for Arendt, is that the voice can remain *too* inner.

Furthermore, because conscience is influenced by societal norms, appeals to an interior conscience can be positively harmful: by ignoring the ways that the moral rhetoric of conscience and duty can reinforce an individual's obedience to socially "legitimated" immoral duties by moving them to go beyond the call of duty, can actually promote totalitarian evil. Eichmann's case is paradigmatic for this: "It was not his fanaticism but his very conscience that prompted Eichmann to adopt his uncompromising attitude during the last year of the war" (1965, 146).[49]

---

[49] See 95: "Yes, he had a conscience, and his conscience functioned in the expected way for about four weeks, whereupon it began to function the other way around."

In the Nazi era this happened across the whole society: Germany, and large parts of occupied Europe, suffered not a moral collapse, but a moral inversion. In this context, Eichmann "did not need to 'close his ears to the voice of conscience,' as the judgment has it, not because he had none, but because his conscience spoke with a 'respectable voice,' with the voice of respectable society around him" (1965, 126). In that inversion, "conscience" – understood as at least partially socially established – did not cease to function:

> Just as the law in civilized countries assumes that the voice of conscience tells everybody "Thou shalt not kill," even though man's natural desires and inclinations may at times be murderous, so the law of Hitler's land demanded that the voice of conscience tell everybody: "Thou shalt kill," although the organizers of the massacres knew full well that murder is against the normal desires and inclinations of most people. *Evil in the Third Reich had lost the quality by which most people recognize it – the quality of temptation.* Many Germans and many Nazis, probably an overwhelming majority of them, must have been tempted *not* to murder, *not* to rob, *not* to let their neighbors go off to their doom (for that the Jews were transported to their doom they knew, of course, even though many of them may not have known the gruesome details), and not to become accomplices in all these crimes by benefiting from them. But, God knows, they had learned how to resist temptation. (1965, 150; first emphasis mine)

When evil loses the "quality of temptation," when it begins to become the norm, "inward senses" of right and wrong do not lose their force as directives; they are perverted to immoral ends.

Arendt's critique of the judgment in Jerusalem, then, was focused on the concept of judgment itself, the picture of human moral and political deliberation that the court assumed. Arendt saw in this question "one fundamental problem, which was implicitly present in all these postwar trials," namely, the problem of "the nature and function of human judgment:"

> What we have demanded in these trials, where the defendants had committed "legal" crimes, is that human beings be capable of telling right from wrong even when all they have to guide them is their own judgment, which, moreover, happens to be completely at odds with what they must regard as the unanimous opinion of all those around them. (1965, 294–5)

The deep problem that cases such as Eichmann's pointed to is that we have no understanding of what sort of judgment could avoid the traps which ensnare our traditional, and over-internalized, concept of judgment. If the trial was to lead to such an improved concept of judgment, Arendt felt that it fell to her to sketch it.

Arendt, who once studied with Rudolf Bultmann, aims to *demytholo-gize* evil – to have rendered its reality as clearly as she could, but also to demystify the idea so that we see it for what it is – ourselves, writ small. She meant her argument about the "banality" of evil "to destroy the legend of the greatness of evil, of the demonic force, to take away from people the admiration they have for the great evildoers like Richard III" (quoted in Kateb 1983, 79). She wanted to instill courage in her listeners, to help them realize that evil did not happen on its own, did not swoop down upon an unsuspecting populace in Central Europe and usurp their agency. We cannot despair, because there is nothing to despair about; our opponents are not the demonic forces of an antihuman conspiracy, but rather the banal bureaucrats of an automated bureaucracy. Evil is not an independent power; there is no Satan here. Human evil lies most basically in attempting to escape the essential conditions of humanity – the danger is that we can, at least in part, escape them, while remaining something even in that escape.

From the perspective of this asymmetrical political ontology, one can see that depicting Eichmann as a demon, or suggesting that there are historical rationales for what he did, would not only affirm naturally contradictory claims; in itself, each claim is problematic and harmful to our political life. To counter both of them, we should appreciate the absolute inexplicability of these crimes – the absence of any deterministic connection between the act and either the character of the agent or the nexus of historical forces at work behind the agent – and affirm the absolute responsibility of the person, *qua* free agent, for their actions, *precisely* because there is no explanation for them other than the agent's inexplicable "decision." If we succeed in "explaining away the responsibility of the doer for his deed in terms of this or that kind of determinism," Arendt insists that

no judicial procedure would be possible on the basis of them, and that the administration of justice, measured by such theories, is an extremely unmodern, not to say outmoded, institution. When Hitler said that a day would come in Germany when it would be considered a "disgrace" to be a jurist, he was speaking with utter consistency of his dream of a perfect bureaucracy. (1965, 290)

In our day, when many people judge judgment itself to be the only absolutely wrong thing (see Midgley 1992), Arendt's words carry even more significance than they did in her own.

Eichmann was not a demon, and we should admit that the most horrific crimes can be committed by people who have never fully become real agents; to insist that great evil deeds must come from great evildoers only cripples our understanding of the dangers we face from totalitarian evil. It would be better were we to accept that our typical understanding of moral judgment and moral agency is confused, and work towards a more adequate understanding, than continue to hold onto it as it drags us further down into confusion. Nor should we seek historical explanations for horrific crimes of Eichmann's type, explanations which would remove responsibility from the agent for their deeds. To look for such a rationale would not only implicitly attempt to reintegrate evil into our world; it would also further obscure, and perhaps ultimately elide, the idea of responsibility, and hence the fundament of agency, which it is totalitarian evil's purpose to destroy. Hence to attempt to "judge" Eichmann's inner wickedness, or to see him as a manifestation of supra-individual socio-cultural processes, is to do the wrong thing; it is fundamentally to seek understanding, where one should simply judge him for his deeds.[50]

Enacting resistance, or "partisanship for the world"

Here we have the centerpiece of our response to worries about the "banality" thesis, or the "privation" thesis on which it relies, being essentially escapist because it is essentially indirect. The indirectness turns out to be precisely the way this is *not* escapist: for Arendt sees all attempts to explain or understand evil as fundamentally wrong-headed, and proposes an altogether different program, one responding to evil by *resisting* it, *indirectly*.[51] Its attempts to respond to evil are responses which are not reactions to evil at all, but rather reaffirmations of the goodness of the world, demonstrating that evil is harmful to the world and incomprehensible from the standpoint of that world, and insisting that even in these experiences we can see the possibility of good manifest in those who resist evil. This is as far from an ironic or cynical sneer as one can get. Such a response is centrally and exhaustively *world-affirming*, a form of what Arendt called "partisanship for the world," a perpetual attempt to better inhabit the world and more fully contribute to its sustenance

---

[50] This is why the "Epilogue" to the book – which was the concluding section of the book's first edition, before Arendt added a "Postscript" to respond to the controversy which surrounded the book's first publication – ends with her alternative articulation of a judgment upon Eichmann.

[51] See 1963, especially chapter six. See Isaac 1992 and Honig 1995b, 137–8 on "resistibility" as the crucial component of Arendt's response. For more on the prominence of metaphors of "resistance" in postwar European intellectual life, see Wilkinson 1981, 261–79.

(1968, 7–8). She is interested most deeply in inspiring us towards a participatory politics, a way of being which is fundamentally interested in participation with others in the world. Arendt's method of "enacting resistance" builds upon her vision of the character of evil not most basically as *cruelty*, the harming of private individuals *qua* private individuals, but rather as the radical (and by necessity banal) act of *unworlding* that threatens our private realms precisely by threatening our public ones. By understanding the character of evil in terms of its privative effects on the public world and hence on our selfhood, then, Arendt offers a powerful way to resist the evils we do encounter. Political engagement is a better cure for what ails us than irony.

Given Arendt's sense of the essential exteriority of evil's challenge to our worldly existence, it is not surprising that her proposed response differs dramatically from Niebuhr's proposal for "accepting responsibility." Recall that Niebuhr, impressed with the deep and complex psychological roots of evil's challenge as essentially *interior* to our selves, proposed accepting responsibility as a way to better comprehend that complexity, and to restrain its dangers through limiting (though not fleeing) our own power. For Arendt, on the other hand, any such internalizing process would be disastrous; because she sees the challenges as coming from outside our worldly existence, to internalize it would be the equivalent of opening the gates to the invaders. She proposes instead that we more fully externalize our political world, and hence also more fully implant it – and, through it, ourselves – in the everyday world. We may call this "enacting resistance," engaging in forms of political activity which do not incorporate the challenge into our lives, but instead more extremely estrange it from us, make us more aware of its essential alienness to the realities of our worldly existence. Formally speaking, such a project cannot intend to combat evil's threat directly; it must rather counter it indirectly, by reaffirming the good. Hence Arendt proposes an indirect resistance, which is actually more basically just a redoubled commitment to the political world, though now with the ominous knowledge of the fragility of that world. Insofar as it attempts to respond to evil directly, it will do two things: first, it will emphasize the way evil is harmful to the world and incomprehensible from the standpoint of that world; second, it will insist that even in these experiences we can see the possibility of good manifest in those who resist evil. That is, Arendt's proposed mode of "enacting resistance" talks about evil's negativity, its *banality*, and affirms goodness's real possibilities. Arendt's response to evil is essentially to reaffirm the good.

If the form of this response is essentially affirmative, active, and externalizing, its content is essentially participatory. Arendt's type of politics is often described by her interpreters as an "agonal" form of activity, an activity which essentially involves struggle and conflict among participants (see Honig 1995b). But this description may mislead. While "agonal" entails an understanding of politics which is fundamentally conflictual, it need not be non-collaborative: alliances can form, friendships can be made, and people can join together in a common cause. Much less must such an agonal politics be violent or essentially Hobbesian: in competition, properly speaking, one need not despise one's opponents; rather, one must simply see the competition as essential to one's own sense of self; one must judge oneself by one's neighbors.[52] To engage in such agonistic activities, one need not see one's interlocutors as enemies whom one must harm; rather, the essence of such activity lies in individual distinction. It is a competition to see who can shine the brightest; as Bonnie Honig argues, "the agonal passion for distinction, which so moved Arendt's theoretical account, may . . . be read to be a struggle for individualism, for emergence as a distinct self" (1995b, 159; see also Honig 1993). (Again, politics is not only community-constitutive, but also self-constitutive.)

Rather than describing it as sheerly "agonal," shorn of Arendt's hyper-voluntarism this form of politics is better described as *participatory*. There is no doubt that it is individualistic: it does not primarily seek changes in the political structures of our lives – though Arendt insists on the value and perhaps necessity of certain forms of political existence over against some others (see 1963, 268–78) – but rather seeks changes in individuals' action. The proposal is not fundamentally interested in structural responses to the challenge of evil, in programs for reordering society or politics, as Niebuhr proposes; rather, it aims most basically to inspire us towards a participatory politics, a way of being which is essentially interested in participation with others in the world. Certain political structures can better support and foster such increased activity, but they cannot compel them; hence Arendt appeals for a more participatory politics directly to individuals themselves.[53]

<hr/>

[52] For a position that argues otherwise, see Keenan 1994, 316: Arendt places "conflict and violence *within* the heart of the political itself." As will be clear, it is the quick association of "conflict and violence" that I dispute.

[53] Thus Lisa Jane Disch's argument (1994, 215–21) that Arendt best helps us revise our political structures seems fundamentally misplaced. See Honig 1995b, 137–8, and Villa 1996, 269, where he is critical of appeals "to platitudes concerning . . . the institutions of representative democracy."

But this emphasis on individual action must not obscure the importance of political community for Arendt; for her, political freedom is not a matter of securing rights to privacy: "Political freedom, generally speaking, means the right to be a participator in government, or it means nothing" (1963, 221). Politics is not simply an external or "merely" superficial activity, nor can our individuality be reached without reaching out to others in communality; for Arendt, the results of the Germans' "inner migration" during the Holocaust demonstrate that the "inner ocean" of subjectivity and the *vita contemplativa* is essentially a trap. "External" political action creates *selves* as well as community. In arguing this, furthermore, Arendt's proposal for "externalization" responds to the external threat of a world-nihilating evil in a way that also supports her distrust of interiority and her emphasis on appearance as the essential reality of the self; as Dana Villa says, "only by living 'superficially' – as artists, as political actors, as glorifiers of appearance – do we escape the tragic wisdom of Silenus invoked by Nietzsche at the start of *The Birth of Tragedy* and by Arendt at the close of *On Revolution*" (1992, 287).

It should be clear that it is not what typically goes by the name of "politics" in our politically vacuous culture; that activity is largely the bureaucratic management of the hegemony of the social over our lives. But it can happen; alongside her oft-mentioned fascination with the workers' councils of the Hungarian uprising of 1956, Arendt was very interested in groups in the United States practicing civil disobedience (1972, 98–102). She thought that this movement, in some ways historically unique to "the American experience," offered an important exemplar for those trying to re-imagine a richly political human life in the dark times of the twentieth century. And it was available, she thought, wherever humans imagine it. Such a "politics" need not be centrally interested in issues of policy (though it ought not to dismiss those as unimportant), nor need it be centrally a project of *lobbying* politicians to promote more effectively some group's interests. Most basically, such a politics must be affirmative, inhabiting the "public sphere" (and thereby creative of that sphere), insisting that things of this world are what should matter to us and manifesting in one's own life just that care for these things. Such a "politics" can take the shape of art or poetry – or of writing convoluted and dense political treatises, such as *Eichmann in Jerusalem*. But first and last it must be *participatory*, involving us in the activity of creating a "world" which is fit for human habitation.

The reality of (political) goodness: Arendt's Augustinian realism

In this return to the primacy and priority of politics Arendt's project comes full circle. Her inquiry into the character of totalitarian evil ultimately reveals that the only possible legitimate response to it is a redoubled commitment to the very realities that it seeks to destroy. Indeed, as was the case with Niebuhr's "Christian realist" proposal for "accepting responsibility," for Arendt theory and practice are revealed to be two sides of the same coin. In *Eichmann in Jerusalem* both aspects of this are manifest, as the text not only explores the character of Eichmann's crimes, but also goes into the possibilities of goodness in the face of such situations. Thus the work also tells the story of what we might call the reality of goodness as well as the banality of evil, a reality found most powerfully in the story of Sergeant Anton Schmidt of the *Wehrmacht*. This account of goodness is meant to stand as an exemplum of a proper response to evil, both in practice – in the historical context in which the events took place – and in theory – in Arendt's retelling of the story. It is found in the chapter in which she also emphasizes the almost universal corruption of Europeans under the Nazis, and it details Schmidt's attempts to subvert the slaughter of the Jews by helping them to escape and giving food to hidden Jews. Schmidt was caught and executed for his attempted subversion, but his story shone out "like a light" in the trial (see 1965, 230–3).[54] For Arendt, stories such as that of Schmidt demonstrate that evil's goal is, in the end, an impossible project; totalitarianism cannot erase all remembrance, nor therefore the possible re-emergence, of human agency: "It is true that totalitarian domination tried to establish these holes of oblivion, into which all deeds, good and evil, would disappear, but . . . the holes of oblivion do not exist" (1965, 232).[55] The lesson of Schmidt's deeds is, for Arendt, a crucial clue to the true nature of totalitarian evil:

. . . the lesson of such stories is simple and within everybody's grasp. Politically speaking, it is that under conditions of terror most people will comply but *some*

---

[54] See the similar account of the effect of one man's resistance in a Nazi concentration camp, in Jones 1995, 91–8.
[55] Arendt's position here contrasts with George Orwell's in his "Reflections on Gandhi": "It is difficult to see how Gandhi's methods could be applied in a country where opponents of the régime disappear in the middle of the night and are never heard of again. Without a free press and the right of assembly, it is impossible not merely to appeal to outside opinion, but to bring a mass movement into being, or even to make your intentions known to your adversary. Is there a Gandhi in Russia at this moment [1949]? And if there is, what is he accomplishing? The Russian masses could only practice civil disobedience if the same idea happened to occur to all of them simultaneously, and even then, to judge by the history of the Ukraine famine, it would make no difference" (Orwell 1981, 178).

people will not, just as the lesson of the countries to which the Final Solution was proposed is that "it could happen" in most places but *it did not happen everywhere.* Humanly speaking, no more is required, and no more can reasonably be asked, for this planet to remain a place fit for human habitation. (1965, 233)

"No more can reasonably be asked": *this* is the final insight of Arendt's inquiry into the character of evil and the shape of our proper response to it. We seek more in the way of reassurances that our action will be guaranteed success, that our hopes are certain to be satisfied. But no such guarantees are forthcoming, nor can they be reasonably required. Action can never guarantee its own results – that would traduce its claim to be truly free. To be free is to be free of all such guarantees, for good or evil alike.

Arendt is aware that this insight can seem unsatisfying and indeed deeply disturbing, that "it seems to tell us no more than that we are *doomed* to be free by virtue of being born, no matter whether we like freedom or abhor its arbitrariness, are 'pleased' with it or prefer to escape its awesome responsibility by electing some form of fatalism" (1978a, 217). But this need not lead us to despair. In fact, it is the only sound foundation for our hope: for good, in the end, is "greater," because more real, than evil – indeed it is real in a way that evil can never be. The reality of goodness and the reality of human agency are, for her, identifiable; the ultimate good of humans is found in the creative action in the world of human existence. Such a vision, even if it does not totally satisfy our longings for security, still gives us a great gift, an awareness of the incredible power that human beings working together can have, a power not only to change things in the world but even to *create* a world. With this power humans can stand up to evil, and in standing up to it they win the only sort of short-term victory they can have – but it is a victory which can, if fortune is with the actors, create a world.[56]

What is perhaps most surprising about Arendt's attempt to create a new political vocabulary for our new situation is how very Augustinian (albeit, only partially so) her resulting position turns out to be. Evil is radical in its effect on community and individuality, corrupting all aspects of human social existence; but the nature of this corruption, and its effects on individual humans, is wholly nihilating: evil makes us shallow, "banal." The connections to Augustine's argument that evil is

---

[56] This may be, in the light of the revolutions of 1989, the one part of Arendt's work which has, in a real sense, been "validated" by historical experience. It is certainly the part of Arendt's work which has drawn much attention from scholars of political engagement; beyond the works of Jürgen Habermas, Jon Elster, and Vaclav Havel mentioned in this chapter, see Isaac 1998.

merely the *privatio boni* are important and deep: it is Augustine's basic ontological framework, a framework Arendt employs in her admittedly very original manner, which allows her to affirm totalitarian evil's ultimate banality.[57] Just as, for Augustine, goodness is a matter of participation in God's creation through the (intelligible) Word, and evil is a measure of non-participation in the Word – a lack of reality and a mute unintelligibility – so for Arendt evil is ontologically describable only negatively, in terms of what it destroys, what it lacks. Evil is empty, shallow, banal; it destroys the possibility of real human community, community manifest through action in speech and creative of a common world in terms of which we find our meaning and our flourishing. Furthermore, the two projects share a similar critical purpose. Just as Augustine used this ontology critically, to deconstruct the Manicheans' claims about the metaphysical reality of evil, Arendt similarly employs it to undermine modern anxieties about the possibility of evil being some sort of heroicdemonic, Satanic wickedness within the world. Even after she has politicized it, Arendt's use of this asymmetrical ontology, following Augustine's own use of it, deflates and indeed demythologizes such worries. As both constructive and critical, then, Arendt's account of evil, and the ontology of which it is an outflowing, is thoroughly Augustinian; indeed it is an Augustinian *realist* account.[58]

Furthermore, while the form of moral realism which has received most attention lately is that of Aristotle's work, and the historical thinker most associated with Arendt has been Aristotle, Arendt's is a distinctly *Augustinian* realism.[59] She saw Augustine's advantage over Aristotle to be the former's appreciation of the human's existence as in important ways unmoored from the cycles of nature, our troubled existence in time and in the world – even as he disparaged our life in time and in the world – as central to understanding our situation; that is, Augustine understood, unlike Aristotle, that the human is *free* from the world's constraints, so can act in ways which create *real* tragedy, a tragedy which is not rooted in conflicts among the world's powers, but in conflict which opposes forces of nature to some force outside nature – the force, for Arendt, of

---

[57] And I am not the first to note it; see Elshtain 1995a, chapter 4: "Augustine's Evil, Arendt's Eichmann."

[58] Moral realism is a catch-all phrase for those philosophers who argue that concepts such as good and evil are *real* concepts, that is, pick out something in the natural world, which may "supervene" on more "dehumanized" accounts of action but which is not usefully *reducible* to them. For a good introduction to the debates about moral realism, see Sayre-McCord 1988.

[59] For a good discussion of Aristotle and moral realism, see Heinaman 1995. For Arendt's Aristotelianism, see Villa 1996, 3: "Arendt's 'Aristotelianism' is a truism."

human freedom.[60] From the beginning, her work always adverted to the same passage of Augustine (from *De civitate Dei*) when she wanted to reference the human's freedom. "That there would be a beginning, man was created, before whom no beginning existed" (1973, 478–9). The human was, to her, most basically (though not simply) this capacity to begin; and our grasping of that capacity, and our attempts to manage its tragic potential, are, for her, the ultimate point of human life – and it was Augustine's work which began, she thought, to see this (see Chappell 1995). In this way her work offers a vision of tragedy itself grounded in an ontological account of the human that is profoundly Augustinian.

But hers was at least profoundly a *partial* Augustinianism; and it was the partiality of her Augustinianism that led, as we have seen, to her thought's incoherence and failure. Arendt recognized that for Augustine the "outside" force of natality was not ultimately human will, but always human will under the direction of divine providence. She thought that that interpretation of natality was not essential to the structure of willing; so she sought in her own work to "demystify" it, to strip it of its theological pretenses and show it to be solely a human capacity – properly miraculous, to be sure, but not in need of any supernatural powers to back it up. And we have seen that this move – a move which effectively Pelagianizes Augustine – ends up rendering the ontology unsustainable, and the anthropology unintelligible. To recoup Arendt's insights, then, we have had to return to the theological anthropology she thought she could dismiss; upon doing so, we discover that her insights fit very well within a richly Augustinian anthropology.[61]

CONCLUSION

This chapter has argued that Arendt offers the rudiments of a thoroughly ontological and interestingly Augustinian interpretation of the problems that evil sets before us. Arendt's work helps us meet the ontological concerns about the Augustinian concept of "evil as privation" formulated in chapter two. The character of her argument, both implicitly in its overall

---

[60] For an argument that Aristotle's conservativism influences his understanding of tragedy and moral conflict, see Lear 1998, 167–90.

[61] See Wetzel 1992a, and Mathewes 1999. James Wetzel (in private correspondence) provocatively suggests that Augustine differs from Aristotle not ultimately (as Arendt thought) because he has a more robust concept of human freedom (as if we could be free of our good habits as well as our bad ones), but because he has what Aristotle lacks, namely, a doctrine of grace. Augustine's account of grace allows him to acknowledge the value of human life as lived in time and in the body in a way far more profoundly affirmative of it than can Aristotle, despite the latter's putatively more "naturalistic" psychology. In these remarks and in much more, Jim Wetzel's advice has been inestimable.

structure, and explicitly in many of its details, follows the contours of Augustine's *privatio* account even as it develops that inheritance to meet the material and methodological challenges of her own day. By describing the center of the human condition in terms of the free creation of a public "world" in and through which individuals gain their identities and value, her vision of human life and its purposes entails an essentially affirmative and communal "being-towards-natality," in contrast to Heidegger's fatalistic and individualistic "being-towards-death." Furthermore, she appeals both (shallowly) to Augustine's philosophy of the will, and (more profoundly) to his overarching ontology, to underpin her divergence from Heidegger's picture of our primordial attunement. And her critique of Nietzsche's elitist gnosticism implicitly affirms an Augustinian world-affirming populism, which permits her to uncouple Nietzsche's account of modernity as life-denying asceticism and nihilism (which she employs) from his radical solipsism (which she deplores). She uses this account as a lens to interpret modernity, employing it both generally to diagnose modernity's nihilistic anomie and specifically to understand the character of evil's challenge in modernity – especially as it is manifest in its most extreme form, world-denying totalitarianism.

Hence Arendt's work is well understood as an attempt to apply the Augustinian tradition's account of evil as *privatio boni* in a way that is hermeneutically illuminating and morally (and politically) helpful. And we have seen that it is at its weakest where it departs from Augustine's thought most explicitly and fundamentally – that is, in its essentially Pelagian account of agency. To recoup her insights, we should move in a more Augustinian direction than she herself did. And we should more deeply appreciate how her argument about "the banality of evil" is not the importation of an essentially foreign Augustinian influence into an otherwise fundamentally non-Augustinian framework; both in the details and in the strategy of her argument, Arendt was deeply influenced by, and appropriated, Augustinian insights from the start.

So Arendt's account is in many ways a helpful development of the Augustinian tradition, and a development helpfully distinct from that of Reinhold Niebuhr. But are their developments of Augustine *too* distinct? Can we reconcile the Augustinian insights that Niebuhr and Arendt offer, their developments of the tradition's account of sin as psychologically *perversio* and evil as ontologically *privatio*? Given that the several challenges put to the Augustinian tradition can be answered individually, can the tradition synthesize those responses in a single unified perspective? The final chapter aims to do just that.

PART III

The challenge of the Augustinian tradition to evil

CHAPTER FIVE

Demythologizing evil

The question why there is evil is not a theological question, for it presupposes that it is possible to go back behind the existence that is laid upon us as sinners. If we could answer the question why, then *we* would not be sinners. We could blame something else. So the "question why" can never be answered except by the statement "that" which burdens humankind so completely.

The theological question is not a question about the origin of evil but one about the actual overcoming of evil on the cross; it seeks the real forgiveness of guilt and the reconciliation of the fallen world.

Dietrich Bonhoeffer 1997, 120

We have seen that, despite many critics' claims to the contrary, a broadly Augustinian interpretation of and response to evil's challenge remains viable and indeed of considerable use to contemporary theology and ethics. The Augustinian commitments developed by Niebuhr and Arendt work to promote social practices and individual attitudes which respond to evil, collectively, by deepening our worldly participation – not just as a response to evil, but as constitutive of human flourishing *simpliciter*. And we saw that this understanding of evil derives from an essentially positive theological ontology, one built around an essentially "incarnational" core.

But some critics will remain unconvinced. "Sure", they will say, "you've managed to show how the components of the Augustinian account of evil can be said to meet the particular conceptual challenges you identify; but you've not put the conceptual pieces together in an integrated practical whole. Furthermore, and connected to this, you've done nothing to quiet the root worry that all our conceptual misgivings attempt to express, namely, that the practical effect of this vision, irrespective of its conceptual coherence, is profoundly inimical to healthy human life. The real problem with Augustine's account of evil is its essentially 'mythological' character: whether it is anesthetically consoling or guilt-inducing, it succumbs to the charms of a mythologized concept of evil, and retreats from worldly realities into an 'other-worldly' system. In defending the details of the Augustinian tradition's program, you've missed the forest for the trees; and your 'provisional' re-operationalizing of its conceptual framework of privation and perversion only momentarily holds off our ultimate suspicion that the Augustinian tradition is essentially a mythologized form of wish-fulfillment. And the last thing we need is more mythology, more obfuscation, about evil; what we need is to *act*."

Here we reach the deepest level of the suspicions regarding the Augustinian tradition, and we can, I expect, feel the tug of their concern. And we ought to admit that we feel that tug, for it expresses genuine moral concerns – a genuine desire to heal the world, to stop suffering. But we cannot make this tug fully intelligible, and therefore we cannot fully endorse it. The hopes which it expresses are deeply misleading; for the truth is, we cannot fix evil, as we moderns have been wont to believe – either now or in the future. Our moral endeavors cannot seek justification by appeal to some teleological achievement – whether imminent or indefinitely deferred – of a world without suffering or cruelty. Furthermore, that tug only partially captures what we ought to affirm. And it does so because of its implications in subjectivism; it is rooted in a basic disposition of *impatience* with the way things are, which is in turn rooted in our basic subjectivist presupposition that we are the primary actors in the world. And that subjectivism is itself an expression of our despair, a reflection of a basic phenomenological experience of abandonment which we feel. Hence the frustrated rage Augustine's critics feel at his seemingly complacent, even smug, conservativism must be seen as in part their expression of desperation at the obvious failure of their own moral hopes, and the desperate fury they feel at the conclusion they imagine to be inescapable once their favored one has been shown to be wrong – namely that, absent progressivism, we must go about acting as if we can do nothing, and simply enjoy the ride. But this is no solution to them; they are thrown back onto their despair. And they worry that Augustinians offer a form of thought that simultaneously tries both to shield us from this truth and to console us whenever that shield breaks down.

The question we must face, then, is: can the Augustinian tradition offer a response to evil which is not funded by perfectionism's fabulous hopes, one fully stripped of all expectations of working towards the achievement of a perfect world? Can such a truly "demythologized" morality not deflate our moral energies? Can it avoid being a counsel of despair?

Indeed it can, and this is the right way to understand Augustine: it is only by appreciating how Augustine's work radically lacks, and is incompatible with, modernity's belief in perfectionism, that we can come to understand his proposal rightly, or feel its force fully. Here the "metaphysical" aspects of his position come to the fore, but only in a way which highlights their connections with other, more "practical" aspects. Only when the metaphysical framework is isolated, and when it is viewed from subjectivism's perspective, does Augustine's account look mythological; but such isolation offers only a partial picture, the theoretical flower plucked from its practical roots – or rather, the theoretical roots, stripped of their practical blossoms; and to improve our vision of this account, we should see how it flowers in concrete practices. The fact is, Augustine's proposal derives not from reflection on distanciated theoretical presuppositions, but from reflection on our "pre-theoretical" responses to conflict, suffering, and evil. Augustine's major "theoretical" claim is that these responses also share a common material root in love, our various loves and the stubbornness with which we hold them; for Augustine all the virtues are "forms of love," and love is thus the central *energia* of the moral life, as well as of God's life (*DeMor.* xxv; see Burnaby 1938, Langan 1979, Rowan Williams 1990). Because of this, responding to the challenge of evil must take the form of informing, reordering, and ultimately reconciling the various modes of love which always guide our actions. Hence Augustine most fundamentally offers not a *theory* but a *therapy*. Understanding is placed in the service of action, and the ultimate criterion of the account's adequacy must be how it helps us inhabit our lives.[1] But it is not a way of fixing evil; indeed Augustine's goal is identical to what Adam Phillips sees as that of psychoanalysis: "not to cure people of their conflicts but to find ways of living them more keenly" (Phillips 1996, 45).

What Augustine (and the tradition descending from him) proposes is a practice of *demythologizing* evil. By properly facing the challenge of evil, we come to perceive it aright; furthermore, we come to see that the Augustinian tradition's proposed practical comportment is a form of eucharistic remembrance and eschatological anticipation, responding

---

[1] I do not mean to discount the cognitivity or referentiality of religious or moral claims; this is not an ontological point but an epistemological one: the kind of cognitivity and understanding manifest here is fundamentally practical. That practical activities are cognitive is one of the points of this book.

and waiting, which takes the form of a loving and grateful delight in the world's basic existence, even as it suffers the tribulations of that existence as we presently inhabit it.

DEMYTHOLOGIZING "DEMYTHOLOGIZING"

It is often said that modernity is a hard-nosed, "critical" era; as Kant put it, "our age is an age of *kritik*" (1965, 9; see Geuss 1981 and Koselleck 1988). While it is hard to specify just what is meant by such codes as "critique" or "doubting" or "the hermeneutics of suspicion" or, most pointedly, "demythologizing," it seems fair to say that such descriptions dominate our era's self-understanding; the critique of the "husk" of dead theological formulas in favor of the "kernel" of the living existential experience, or of "positive religion" in favor of some set of basic deistic propositions, is a move typical of much modern thought, religious or otherwise. But the term "demythologization" hides a kind of hubris, implicit in the assumption that we can *de*mythologize our thought, that we can in some final way get to an absolute language with which to interpret reality.[2] But the truth in "myths" cannot be extracted by a process of critical distillation, for our ordinary language operates on a continuum with mythology, so we cannot escape "myths" without escaping ourselves. Iconoclasm can not only be idolatrous; it can also be nihilating. Hence the practice of demythologizing can itself become a tragedy, can turn against its makers, leaving them trapped in a final, absolute myth, the "iron cage" of epistemic sterility.[3]

One point of this chapter is that this description is false in its attempted arrogation to modernity of this critical "demythologizing" capacity. But I do not mean simply to offer another critique of "critique" as an attitude. I want to do something more; I argue that the legitimate

---

[2] This is not the way that the most famous proponent of demythologization, Rudolf Bultmann, understood the practice; he saw demythologizing as "a demand of faith itself" against all "objectifying thinking" (1984, 121–2). But he wrongly assumed that faith is itself *sui generis* and immune to demythologizing critique; however, there is nothing in the idea of faith that prima facie implies this. Indeed, such demythologizing is a popular project in much modern atheological thought, and stands near the center of the projects of Marx, Nietzsche, and Freud. (For a good [though controversial] recent discussion of some of these issues see Proudfoot 1985.) In any event, one suspects that the project that Bultmann named is a good deal more complex than he himself seems to have thought. Part of the point of this chapter is to suggest that demythologization needs itself to be demythologized.

[3] This is the narrative essence of Max Weber's story of the "rationalization" and "disenchantment" of the world, a process which led finally to its irrational conclusion in the "Iron Cage" precisely because the actors were all-too enchanted with the process of rationalization.

energies – intellectual and practical – that give this picture its superficial
attractions are not in fact unique to modernity, but have been accessible
to (and accessed by) thinkers long before "modernity." We can see this
by looking at how Augustine demythologizes evil in *De civitate Dei*.

Anyone who gives *De civitate Dei* more than a cursory reading cannot
help but be struck by its demythologizing tone. Indeed, its first ten books
do little *but* demythologize, unmasking the ignoble lies upon which
Rome founded itself, revealing its origins in the self-will of the *libido dominandi*, the "lust to dominate" that itself dominates, and deconstructing
the ideology and rhetoric on which its *imperium* was anchored.[4] In this
Augustine gets much support from pagan philosophers, who also cast a
cold eye on the myths of the city. Yet neither are they safe from
Augustine's demythologizing scorn; they are shown to be ridiculous, possessed by extra-philosophical commitments skewing their work, enslaved
by the same prideful self-deception chaining others to the *imperium*. So
the work exemplifies the "demythologizing" capacities of thought in
many ways.

It may seem somewhat more dubious to see Augustine's treatment of
evil as demythologizing. But in fact it is precisely as regards the challenge
of evil that we see Augustine "demythologizing" in the most interesting
and powerful manner. His account attempts neither to dissolve the
problem of evil, nor to insist on evil's insurmountability; instead, it
attempts to specify our intractable difficulties with evil while avoiding
both naiveté and despair. Through doing this, Augustine explains his
opposition to many of his contemporaries' accounts of evil. But his
demythologizing of evil is constructive as well as deconstructive, for by
locating the roots of evil not in the cosmos but in our psyches, Augustine
shows us how evil need lead us neither into spasms of gothic terror, nor
into the doldrums of gnostic despair, but be turned to our benefit. We
can demythologize popular understandings of the Augustinian tradition's practical response to evil by examining its most systematic articulation in Augustine's own *De civitate Dei*. There, Augustine demythologizes
evil by subverting popular mythological depictions of evil to reveal that
"evil" is not a terrifying, unthinkable, and indigestible fetish, but rather a
mundane and banal reality which, while tragic, should not drive us
towards either pessimism or despair (see Forsyth 1987, 439–40). And by

---

[4] As Peter Brown says, "The *City of God* is a book about 'glory' " (1967, 311); its very first word
attempts to subvert and subsume the rhetoric of the *Imperium Romanum*, by taking its central rhetorical idea – glory – and applying it to the church: "*Gloriosissimam civitatem Dei* . . ." See Dodaro
1994, Harrison 2000, 220.

seeing how he does this, we can learn how to carry this project forward for today.

We should be careful here to note some general facts about Augustine's own understanding of how a response can be at once theoretical and practical. As Pierre Hadot and Ellen Charry have suggested, pre-modern thinkers understood their writings, and expected others to understand their writings, not as self-standing adequate *summae* of the Christian life, but as guidelines for "spiritual practices" to be incarnated with others in community, and most fundamentally in the community of the church (see Hadot 1995 and Charry 1997). We lack this background assumption, and must have it explicitly expressed for us, in a way naturally unnecessary for Augustine – in a way Augustine would not have even imagined. Indeed, for Augustine, genuine Christian life is a life of questioning, of ever-deepening inquiry. It is not a static realization of an end. Conversion is not a *finis*, but a beginning. The last word of Augustine's *Confessions* is *aperietur*, or "will be/shall be opened." (Think about ending – and closing – a book on that.) In the *Confessions* it is Augustine's quest to *ask* questions that leads him finally to the church, which exists for him not so much as the answer to his quest as the locale wherein his quest can be undertaken, and his questioning can be unleashed. Indeed, the *Confessions* is a "book of questions," and it is the failure of groups (such as the Manicheans) to allow Augustine to ask questions that reveals their inadequacy to Augustine's desires. (This does not mean that "doubt" or ironic skepticism is the aim; there is a world of difference between pious apprehension of the mystery of otherness as genuinely *other* to the self, and the ironists' self-congratulatory and fundamentally narcissistic knowingness about the limits of their own thinking [see Mathewes 1998].) This means that love is a form of inquiry, and inquiry is a form of love. Love is an interpretation, a construal of the value and nature of some beloved thing. As such a construal it is cognitive – we learn about things *by* and *in* loving them. Of course, this is an insight Augustine pioneered – for him, hermeneutics *is* charity. To inquire into something is to be oriented toward it by a range of interests and commitments which reveal "the importance of what we care about" for guiding our inquiry.

Theologically all this is captured in Augustine's account of use and the ideas of *res* and *signa*. For God, all *things* are literally significant, because God uses things as signs. Hence it makes sense for us to talk about all material realities as potentially spiritually significant, and we ourselves can come to speak God's language, so to speak, and realize things' spiritual significance, by *using* them in a way analogous to God's use. What was merely material, then, becomes for us truly theological. This practice of using is one we most need to use, and can use quite fruitfully, in confronting the hard facts of suffering. Suffering is quite literally "useful" because it *forces* us to move from material or worldly (or "carnal") to spiritual affections; the only way to weave suffering into the narrative of our lives is to invest it with a significance that is not obvious in it. And we must do this, because it is the nature of sin to vex our material existence. Sin, evil, and suffering are signs that something is wrong in the world, and the fact that we can know that shows our transcendence of the world's limitations, our sense that there is something "outside" the appearances of materiality.

Finally, the Augustinian response is a process, one that occurs *in time* – indeed, it is the way we should inhabit time. Many other accounts cannot take history, and temporal duration in general, seriously enough. Theodicists aim to provide an answer *now*, while anti-theodicists say that we ought not to offer that answer, but be with the sufferer in their suffering, again *now*. But suffering does not happen *now*; indeed, in a way suffering is precisely our inability to inhabit now, and our overcoming of it – a long slow process – is a matter of returning to time, to the ordinary.

Given this, we can turn to the concrete practices that Augustine proposes. There are two "limit situations," extremes of evil's challenge to us: when we (or those close to us) suffer apparently unmerited evil, and when we are called upon to involve ourselves in public life in ways which may inflict suffering on others. With each challenge we will see that Augustine's actual proposal is obscured by a myth that has grown up around it, a myth both implausible and pernicious; but when this mythology is dissolved, the actual proposal's powerful attractions become visible. I turn first to the problem of suffering.

SUFFERING PRIVATIVE EVIL

The myth about Augustine on suffering is that he offers an essentially anesthetically consoling, and ascetically sado-masochistic, approach to suffering. For Augustine, this myth says, whatever evil we receive is deserved, part of our punishment for our inescapable and irremediable implication in original sin. But simultaneously, the critics continue, Augustine says punishment hurts only our materiality and so actually works for our betterment by helping us to "die to self and the world" – thus suggesting that punishment is not *really* punishment at all. So, the critics conclude, Augustine damns us in two mutually contradictory ways: our suffering is well deserved by original sin; but we ought not to hurt at all, because it only acts on our undue attachments to the world. It is wrong to resent our suffering, but we cannot feel good about it either.

The challenge, then, is this: can an Augustinian privationist account address the real experience of suffering, or will it rather dismiss or obscure that experience in an essentially consolatory manner? To answer this, we must study Augustine's proposal for how to respond practically to real experiences of suffering. We can orient ourselves by a question posed by a (quite distant) descendant of Augustine, Albert Camus, who argued that the facts of suffering raise the basic existential question of whether suicide is justifiable.[5] Camus's question is an extreme formulation of the basic question that suffering forces us to ask: what, in the face of victimization (our own or others), should our response be? Should we succumb to despair and perhaps ultimately suicide, and, if not, how should we respond to the senseless harms inflicted upon us?

We can begin to uncover this by turning back to Augustine's own original answer, and see what we can take from it. His response to such questions was formulated in a cultural setting which, relative to our own, held an extremely negative opinion of worldly existence, in part because of the experience of suffering. His cultural setting was experiencing a crisis of confidence in the "world." In part it was built around the pervasive presence of mortality. The presence of death was central to ordinary life: in a world without refrigeration, death attended the most quotidian of tasks; as Peter Brown remarks in *The Body and Society*, Augustine's was "a society more helplessly exposed to death than is even the most afflicted underdeveloped country in the modern world" (1988, 6).[6] But mortality was not the only source of this cultural crisis, for the age confronted a conceptual crisis brought on by external perils of a sort unknown to us. The *Imperium Romanum* was not just what we know as the "Roman Empire"; the *imperium* was more broadly the structures of rule, governance, and indeed order upon which that empire was built. Their political experience was not the experience of multiple and competing states, but of a conflict between *the* state and chaos: it was a world not so

---

[5] See Camus 1955, 3: "There is but one truly serious philosophical problem, and that is suicide." Camus wrote his dissertation on Neoplatonism and Augustine.

[6] See also Brown 1972, 122–3, on the "malaise" affecting the upper classes of the late Roman Empire, for largely socio-political reasons. I am grateful to William Schweiker for conversations on these matters.

much with borders as with frontiers, and to many the barbarian hordes signaled not a change in political structure, but the loss of political structure *tout court*. In the face of this chaos, the cultural authorities, and the world which they epitomized, seemed not so much bankrupt as useless, their beauty "the fragile brilliance of glass," providing "a joy outweighed by the fear that it may be shattered in a moment" (*DCD* iv.3, based on 1972 translation, p. 138; see Brown 1995, 16, 23; and 1996, 37, 54–7). Yet despite these larger cultural trends, Augustine became "ever more deeply convinced that human beings had been created to embrace the material world" (Brown 1988, 425; see Rowan Williams 1990). His position grew like a pearl around his central insight: we are part of the world, and must participate in the world's redemption, just as we were the engines of its corruption. Hence the world is critically important, for we are in a way the vehicles of God's love for the world. In meeting suffering, we must find a way to face it that does not unmoor us from that world.

Augustine's most detailed response to the problem of suffering is found in Book I of *De civitate Dei*, in his response to the traumas of victims of rape in the sack of Rome in AD 410. He affirms that this project is one internal to the Christian tradition and not fundamentally apologetic in nature, that, in other words, "we are not so much concerned to answer the attacks of those outside as to administer consolation to those within our fellowship" (*DCD* 1.16, based on 1972 translation, p. 26). He addresses the victims' temptations towards despair, and possibly suicide, and argues that (a) the "violation" is not in fact one that God will hold against them, but that God suffers with them, and (b) the response of suicide is a nonsensical response, not really a response at all, but merely a perpetuation (indeed, an extension) of the evil done unto them. Affirming that "when physical violation has involved no change in the intention of chastity by any consent to the wrong, then the guilt attaches only to the ravisher," he insists that the violation is not a moral fault of the victim, but rather a psychological trauma: the problem is to respond to the traumatic experience in the best possible way (*DCD* 1.18).[7] He knows that such traumatic violations of selfhood and agency may tempt one to

---

[7] It is interesting to note that, in arguing for the moral immunity of victims of rape, Augustine's position was unique for its time, and went against the more ascetically rigorous traditional moralism that he inherited. See Power 1996, 231: "Augustine's uncompromising stand on the innocence of the raped women . . . demonstrates that when his critical faculties were really engaged . . . he was capable of rejecting Roman custom and freeing women from the odium attached to their victimization." But the rhetoric of "really engaged" suggests Augustine was more often asleep at the wheel, an unfair (and false) insinuation.

"finish the job," as it were, to *collaborate* with the attacker and destroy the self. He rejects this; suicide is never an acceptable response. (Indeed so much of the discussion in Book 1 is proscriptive, concerned with his explication of the rationale behind the prohibition of suicide, that some have argued, quite perversely, that its main purpose is negative, forbidding certain kinds of action.)[8] The proper response is not to answer evil with evil, but rather to attempt to transcend it, to seek to reaffirm the good. As a first step towards doing this, victims of such horrendous depredations should think of two things: first, that their actual integrity has *not* been violated by their attackers, and second, that, insofar as they *can* – and here their particular capacities are crucial – they should attempt to see the attack as a further moment in the long and painful process of God's weaning them away from an excessive *amor mundi* (*DCD* 1.28). In sum, Augustine's proposed response to such violations is twofold: suffering does not besmirch your moral character, and you should try, as best you can, to turn this evil into good, as an internal moment in your own process of healing. But, even if you cannot do this, remember that you must not despair and believe that God is somehow turned against you; suicide is never acceptable.

In offering this proposal, Augustine is presenting a form of what we may call "the therapy of suffering," in two senses. The first sense aims to help us overcome suffering by escaping it, typically by attempting to recover a sense of our own agency in the face of evil's privative, agency-negating effects; here we primarily acknowledge the wholly negative character of evil, and seek, however haltingly and partially, to make sense of the sufferings and wounds that we have endured (see Levinas 1988). This practice has as its ultimate *telos* the recovery, on the victim's part, of a sense of wholeness, an achieved agential reintegration. Suffering here appears as a trauma which the victims must try – again, however haltingly and imperfectly – to comprehend, for the sake of their own wholeness. While this is an ongoing and imperfect process, we must always insist that suffering, while real, is not the ultimate truth of our situation. In this sense, "the therapy of suffering" treats the harms of suffering in their negativity, and proscribes an appropriately negative response for them.

The second, more controversial, sense sees suffering as *itself* therapeutic, offering a positive lesson about our release from excessive affec-

---

[8] Augustine argues that, while there were suicides early in the Christian tradition, in particular the martyrs, such suicides were directly commanded by God. See *DCD* 1.26; for discussion of suicide in late antiquity, see Droge and Tabor 1992, esp. 167–83.

tions or wrongly attuned attachments.[9] In seeing it this way, we attempt to recover and reaffirm the agency lost in suffering. It is thus essentially an *empowering* activity: by resisting the temptation towards victimhood, and attempting to recover our agency in the face of suffering, we are attempting to find in suffering God's presence, to which we are called to respond. At times the empowering purpose of this therapy has been pushed beyond asceticism to self-(and other-) destructiveness. Yet there is a difference between humility and humiliation, and selflessness and self-destruction, and this practice should remain available to us. Because of this, we must emphasize that not every person can manage this, and none of us should assume that we can; it should be undertaken with the utmost pastoral tact, not out of apologetic interests but practical therapeutic ones. The worries of anti-theodicists, discussed in chapter one, must be recalled; we are not most basically interested in exonerating God – God's righteousness is presumed here – but rather in figuring out what to do, how to respond to such absurd suffering without appealing to the arid calculus of merit. Nor does this in any way entail a command to search actively for more suffering. Sufficient unto the day is the evil thereof; we need not seek out further suffering, but what suffering we encounter we should seek to use to our advantage.

These two practices are mutually supportive, and still useful today. It is only when we see evil as no longer an immediate threat to our existence that we can begin to think about what good we can make of it; conversely, turning evil to good use is itself a way of overcoming evil, by taking back the power it took from us. Together they constitute what L. Gregory Jones has aptly called "embodying forgiveness": by learning to engage in distinct practices and habits of forgiveness, we both appropriate for ourselves, and manifest to others, the call to transform our lives and to become people of God (Jones 1995).[10] In this task we are engaged in the *imitatio Christi*, by inhabiting the discipleship to which we have been called. But this imitation is possible only because of a deeper participation in God's own Christ-incarnated forgiveness of the world. So we also embody forgiveness in the sense that we ourselves become the medium through which God announces, and in part enacts, God's own

---

[9] Such attachments are typically described in terms of pride or self-love, though they can be about any excessive love – country, family, and so forth.

[10] Of necessity my discussion of Jones's work here is highly compressed; I do not discuss the Triune form this practice takes, among other things. But by ignoring important aspects of this work, I do not mean to dismiss them.

reconciliation with and redemption of fallen humanity. We embody the forgiveness of Christ to the world, and through it we embody the forgiveness of Christ to us; in learning to forgive, we learn to appropriate Christ's forgiveness. This is a difficult task, demanding a certain self-transcendence, an ability to offer up oneself as a gift in loving relationship with others, and that does involve us in a risky openness, a vulnerability to others.[11] Furthermore, this activity is (of course!) never completed, at least in this life: our corruption, and the corruption of the world, means that we can never completely embody forgiveness; it will always be vulnerable to vexation and rejection, both by ourselves and by others. But in faith, hope, and love, we can undertake this process as constitutive of the Christian life.[12]

This sort of "embodying forgiveness" need not be restricted to discrete acts of forgiving other people. While it is primordially interpersonal, there is nothing to stop it from becoming a general mode of existential comportment towards the events of one's life as a whole. Insofar as one can be "angry at the hand" life has given one, one can forgive life for it. Furthermore, such forgiveness need not be something completed now, or even at any time in this life; it can be an ongoing project. As Margaret Mohrmann has argued, "none of the negative aspects of life – sickness and crime and grief and meanness and pain – is absolute in the world. Their elimination is not required for us to be able to live a fully human existence" (1995, 85). Forgiveness, then, is really a mode of love: it is because of our love that we can forgive, and it is in the practices of forgiveness that we manifest and more fully appropriate our love. Forgiveness requires love, and love is made manifest in forgiveness.

One might suspect that this account is, in the end, finally a slave-morality, because it works both to hinder a retributive response on the part of victims, while simultaneously refusing them what appears as the ultimate act of autonomy, namely, suicide – and it does all this on the "rational" basis of a metaphysical doctrine (original sin) of apparently uniform guilt. But in fact the "metaphysical" doctrine of original sin serves as much to forgive as to condemn, for it frees us from anxiety about a putative moral purity which is suddenly, irreparably, besmirched. By so universalizing sin, then, Augustine's "peccatology"

---

[11] As Jones says, "Christian forgiveness involves a high cost . . . It requires the disciplines of dying and rising with Christ, disciplines for which there are no shortcuts, no handy techniques to replace the risk and vulnerability of giving up 'possession' of one's self" (1995, 5–6).

[12] On the "theory-laden" character of Christian life, see Pinches 1987.

works to defuse his culture's predilection to respond to moral failure with panic. The heroic stoicism of the Roman nobility, so idealized in Augustine's time, was profoundly brittle (as most honor/shame systems are); while a person could take quite a lot, they would not take any more, and they would begin to lash out, against others and themselves, in catastrophic ways. It was too simple a morality, which allowed for an excessively clear moral assessment of one's own state. (This is, it seems, the lesson of Lucretia, who usurped the role of judge and condemned herself to death for being raped, which she deemed to be adultery; Romans who idolized her, Augustine says, must choose between affirming that she was right to put herself to death, thus calling her an adulterer, or denying she was right to put herself to death, thus implying she was a [self-]murderer [*DCD* 1.19].) In this context, Augustine's elaboration of the doctrine of original sin worked to move the culture away from a masochistic fixation on particular discrete punishments, by suggesting that the presumption of prior purity on which Roman *virtus* was based was simply a fable; what we should do is interrupt the cycle of bloodletting which this over-simple morality sets in motion.

To see this, one need only look at its effect on the very common practice of witchcraft in his era. As Peter Brown has shown, part of the general effect of Christianity on popular religion was to rather rigorously "supernaturalize" the forces of evil – to make suffering and misfortune the effects of the vagaries of immaterial demons. But popular culture accommodated this "supernaturalizing" within the framework of sorcery which predated Christianity, thereby retaining the zero-sum calculus which ascribed to every misfortune a localizable cause, and thus by extension ascribed to evil and suffering in general a strategy for its total extirpation. In this setting, Augustine's argument that misfortune arises from original sin directed people's attention away from their anxiety about their own moral standing and their concomitant desire to find a particular person responsible for their misfortune (and hence away from any motivation for blood feuds), and encouraged reflection on the flawed and frail state of one's own moral and psychological (though those two categories would not be readily distinguished for Augustine) constitution (Brown 1972, 132–3, 136–8).

This Augustinian practical program is superior to those offered by the critics (when they articulate any alternative at all), for its account of forgiveness stands between an excessively static notion of soul-making, such as John Hick offers, and the slippery idea of active forgetting, such as

Richard Rorty proposes.[13] It suggests that forgiveness is political in Arendt's sense, and that this sense of political involves something like Niebuhr's sense of love as the root of politics; and conversely, that forgiveness, while arising from love, is fundamentally, as Arendt insists, a basic manifestation of our freedom. To see this, it will help to contrast this account with the alternate accounts of Hick and Rorty.

Thinkers such as Hick are really interested in evil for apologetic purposes, in order to answer questions about how or whether belief in God is possible in the face of evil – and their criticisms of Augustine's work are only of value if we think of his project as similarly apologetic. But Augustine was not worried about the existence of God – he was interested in what, given God's existence, we should think and do about evil. And accusations of offering fantastic consolations fit Hick far better than they do Augustine. Hick claims that faith must believe that *all* instantiations of evil will finally be seen as working to fashion autonomous human souls able to love God in an "adult" manner. But because this mathematical demonstration is so distant, Hick's appeal to faith seems designed less to justify God's mysterious providence than to legitimate Hick's system's expansive ambitions.

On Hick's account, evil is primarily to be understood as driving us out of self-centeredness and towards God-centeredness. But in this world evil has only a horrific face, an annihilating face: "We thus have to say, on the basis of our present experience, that evil is really evil, really malevolent and deadly and also, on the basis of faith, that it will in the end be defeated and made to serve God's good purposes" (Hick 1978, 364).[14] Hence, our primary religious response to evil is not forgiveness but faith, and secondarily hope; while we can employ acts of forgiveness in the world, in doing so we are not elaborating a basic pattern of life, but working round its edges. Indeed, forgiveness is not really forgiveness at all, but rather a promissory note, a statement that one believes that one day we will all realize that what was bad was for the good all along; it will be primarily an epistemic transformation, a change in what we know. Hence Hick does not offer a response to evil but rather a consolation in the face of evil, framed classically in the promise of life after death:

---

[13] I do not mean to suggest that the Augustinian tradition can claim exclusive rights to this account of forgiving. I mean merely to say that the Augustinian tradition can claim this account as having a place in its overall project, without claiming exclusive rights to it.

[14] Compare 340: "[w]e must thus affirm in faith that there will in the final accounting be no personal life that is unperfected and no suffering that has not eventually become a phase in the fulfillment of God's good purpose."

If there is any eventual resolution of the interplay between good and evil, any decisive bringing of good out of evil, it must lie beyond this world and beyond the enigma of death . . . the "good eschaton" will not be a reward or a compensation proportioned to each individual's trials, but an infinite good that would render worth while *any* finite suffering endured in the course of attaining it. (1978, 339)

What we see here is not any sort of practical proposal for good or evil, but rather a sheerly theoretical proposal for reconciling ourselves to the reality of evil.[15] This is especially curious for Hick's "soul-making" theodicy, because it would seem especially amenable to discussing practices by which we can see such suffering as refashioning our souls towards "God-centeredness."[16] Thus we exist on two levels, and cannot, for Hick, transform the one into the other – that is God's work. (Hence Hick's concept of "epistemic distance" is simultaneously an ontological distance.) Hick's program is a classically liberal account of a secular worldview welded onto a religious eschatology; his account of forgiveness reveals a vision of the two worlds as parallel, or static; it insists on the present irreconcilability of God's promises and the way the world is, and it cannot imagine that we might work here and now to integrate God's promises with the world through acts of forgiveness. What happens here cannot be transformed until the end time itself. Our primary religious attitude, for Hick, seems to be one of killing time.

For Augustinians, in contrast, forgiveness is not fundamentally passive, manifest in an eyes-clenched-shut "faith," but fundamentally *responsive*, a real act with real and important consequences. This is the "Arendtian" aspect of Augustinian forgiveness, the aspect emphasizing the power of forgiveness as a manifestation of freedom. This forgiveness acknowledges with Hick that our actions will not lead to any sort of progressive Christianization of history or the world; we will have evil among us even unto the end of time. But that fact must not lead us, as it does Hick, to suppose that evil should thus be *accepted* as necessary in any way for the world; rather we must work to transform it here and now. (Indeed

[15] Even Hick's discussion of Jesus as paradigmatic for Christians' understanding of how to respond to evil is not about the practices Jesus engaged in, but about Jesus' submission to the divine will. See 355–7.
[16] Indeed Hick seems at times to equivocate between forgiveness and forgetting: "It may be that the personal scars and memories of evil remain for ever, but are transfigured in the light of the universal mutual forgiveness and reconciliation on which the life of heaven is based. Or it may be that the journey to the heavenly Kingdom is so long, and traverses such varied spheres of existence, involving so many new and transforming experiences, that in the end the memory of our earthly life is dimmed to the point of extinction" (350).

such is the way that our souls are, if not exactly "made" in Hick's sense of the term, at least *refashioned*.)

Other, more secular thinkers seem, like Augustine, interested in practical responses to evil, but appeal only to a reheated variant of Nietzsche's "active forgetting" as the right response to suffering and evil. Such a response ultimately has very corrosive implications to our selfhood – for it compels us, as Nietzsche says, not to become *stuck* to anything, not even to *not being stuck* to "one's own detachment" (1966, 52). Modern liberal political thinkers often appeal to this sort of slippery forgetting of the past as a way of managing to survive the horrors of our time.[17] And certainly we can admit that something like "forgetting" may very well be the most effective, in the short run, "solution" to political hatreds. When confronted with pain and suffering, we do aim basically to stop it; one important mark of a successful program for dealing with such phenomena is that it will help us escape such experiences. But for Augustinians it can never be more than a tactic; for this forgetting involves finally the *perpetuation* of violence in attempting the (quite literally) suicidal annihilation of one's history in an attempt to *repress* the past (for what is "active forgetting" but repression?), and repressed memories are liable at some later date to reassert themselves in unpleasantly surprising ways.

This is visible in the work of Richard Rorty. If Hick's program is fundamentally static, Rorty's project moves far too quickly; it suggests a sort of self-refashioning as a frictionless whirring in a void. Recall that for Rorty, the world (and the individual person) is a "tissue of contingencies" which must be perpetually reintegrated into some sort of more or less coherent self. When it comes to human life, "there is nothing to complete, there is only a web of relations to be rewoven, a web which time lengthens every day," and "we shall be content to think of any human life as the always incomplete, yet sometimes heroic, reweaving of such a web" (R. Rorty 1989, 42–3). This reweaving is nothing more than psychological *bricolage*, the unending jettisoning and rehabilitation of what lies about us, the perpetual "recontextualization" of our past in terms of new events in our lives. Because human life, for Rorty, is thus most basically a variety

---

[17] For an excellent and profound example of this position worked out in its most thoughtful and interesting way, see Ignatieff 1998. Ignatieff builds on Isaiah Berlin's description of liberalism as the toleration of difference, which is in turn premised on our ability to forget the past and "let bygones be bygones" (see 186–90). Modernity, insofar as it is "liberal," then, on this issue is a project of forgetting. I think the premise of this sort of "toleration" is deeply problematic, not so much toleration as mutual indifference, and I think Augustine offers another way of thinking about how to handle difference; for more on this, see Mathewes 1998.

of forms of such a reweaving, such a recontextualization, he does not worry much about how well or ill we can integrate the disparate aspects of our existence; for him, all life is such a reintegration, a way of coping, more or less well, with whatever happens to come along next. There is nothing so central to our lives that it cannot be abandoned, so our lives are spent not in "getting hung up" on things (as if they were skyhooks), but rather in keeping things interesting by floating from one thing to another. This proposal is a descendant of Nietzsche's proposal for "active forgetting": keep your eyes open, and do not allow your vision to be fixed on any single goal. Here there is no forgiveness either, for there is no recognition of the ongoing presence of the past.

In contrast to Rorty's frictionless form of continual reweaving, this Augustinian form of forgiveness entails some sort of stable self whose most basic mode of action in the world is a form of *response*. This is the "Niebuhrian" aspect of forgiveness, the aspect emphasizing the power of forgiveness as rooted in our responsive love for God. Here, language of human "nature" helps us see that the self is not simply reweavings all the way down, but comes to consciousness – indeed, comes to the world itself – with a "past" and a reality with which it is always already in responsive relation: the reality of God. Thus in encountering the world we encounter it as already something within us; in forgiving others we are engaged in the deeper, more primordial activity of embodying our own forgiveness.

Nonetheless, Rorty teaches an important lesson, namely that the past cannot be determinative of our lives, and that our appropriation of it should always be contingent on what use we can make of it in the future. There is then an inevitably "pragmatic" aspect to forgiveness, an awareness of contextual significance that escapes formulation in algorithmic principal terms. As was said above, what is required here is a form of moral, or pastoral "tact" about when one may be able to forgive another in a more active way, and when one is best left to forgive in the sense of getting over the wounds one has suffered.

Augustine does not smother experienced evil's arationality by frosting it with a fundamentally juridical and punitive theology, nor does he promote a masochistic pursuit of further suffering as soteriologically fortuitous; rather, he seeks to help victims (as their servant) to reconstruct their lives after catastrophe – or, better, to help others to help them; victims of suffering should be most directly offered listeners and companionship, not bibliographies. This account of forgiveness refuses both slave-morality and nihilism. Forgiveness is fundamentally responsive, because the self is always engaged with a reality with which it is always already in responsive relation (see H. R. Niebuhr 1963). Forgiveness is not about being *liberated from* or *escaping* the past, but rather actively appropriating it, an appropriation which, by "possessing" it as a good gift, frees us from it as a heavy burden. Our lives are all of a piece, and their painful parts are not best dealt with by expunging them, but by struggling to find a way to reweave the frayed edges around the tear into one another – to render our lives whole once more. Christian beliefs commit us to affirm the significance of our whole lives, our whole histories; our lives cannot be segmented into discrete episodes unconnected by any overarching narrative. Thus the practice of forgiveness is only possible if you possess a history – or, better, if a history possesses you, if the past is in some sense still present. History is neither necessary (though it may be providentially predestined) nor wholly evanescent. For Augustine, the martyrs, like Jesus, retain in heaven the bodily wounds they suffered on earth, the signs of their violation – not in the carnal form they first took, but as marks of glory: "The defects which have thus been caused in the body will no longer be there, in that new life; and yet, to be sure, those proofs of valor are not to be accounted defects, or to be called by that name" (*DCD* XXII.19, based on 1972 translation, p. 1062; see Bynum 1995, 98). Forgiveness works on history and in history by working through history; it does not obliterate, but transforms, the marks of history.[18]

Forgiveness, then, is a manifestation of freedom and love. This is how Niebuhr and Arendt describe it. For Niebuhr, forgiveness stands both beyond and beneath the claims of retributive justice, as "the final form of love" (1962, 63), and thus the source of our longing for justice, as well as its ultimate aim. On the other hand, for Arendt forgiveness is a form of freedom because it liberates us from the past, enables us to act in new ways: "Forgiving, in other words, is the only reaction which does not merely re-act but acts anew and unexpectedly, unconditioned by the act which provoked it and therefore freeing from its consequences both the one who forgives and the one who is forgiven" (1958, 241).[19] So forgive-

---

18 The concept of eternity can also be of great use here: we cannot forget because "forgetting" is a temporal possibility, but God's reality outside of time suggests that the *whole* of history is significant and will be redeemed, and interestingly, that it is not just me-at-the-moment-of-my-death who matters, and who will be judged (however one understands that event), but the me-as-embodied-in-my-entire-life. On this matter I am indebted to conversations with Stanley Hauerwas.

19 Arendt thought that forgiveness, as a *political* reality, is entirely separable from love, which she saw as an essentially "unworldly" and anti-political reality (1958, 242); but we have already seen how Arendt's attempt to distinguish these two spheres is built upon an impossible anthropology.

ness is not only a form of love, as Niebuhr insisted, but also a form of freedom – indeed, in a sense *the* form of freedom, the primordial form which our action as free beings takes. But as such it is, as Augustine says, communal – we need another person or a past to forgive. But, beyond Arendt, and in tune with Niebuhr, this primordial freedom of forgiveness is not found in ourselves, but rather in another, in Christ. We come to *embody* forgiveness (not of course to *incarnate* it) – to allow it to inform and transform our beings at their base, to reshape our relations with the past, the present, and the future. Forgiveness is the form of freedom, and what this means is found in and through the life, death and Resurrection of Jesus Christ.

But forgiveness, by itself, is not enough, either as a way of inhabiting the world or, more particularly, as a response to evil; alongside it we must initiate actions and manifest our active love for and in the world, our "active gratitude" to God for the gift of existence.[20] There is a second way in which love plays a role in the Augustinian tradition's response to evil's challenges. For alongside our acts of forgiveness of others, we are called upon to initiate action in the world, in imitation of God's creative action. Where this issue leads us is the topic of the next section.

DEONTOLOGIZING EVIL: PERVERSELY INFLICTING HARM

So Augustine's response to suffering differs significantly from its mythology. But what of his analysis of action? Here, Augustine supposedly offers quite the opposite of consolation – namely, an account which invariably *blames* agents and thereby immobilizes them with a paralyzing guilt. This "extreme moral conservativism" (Holmes 1989, 144), resisting genuine individual and socio-political change, is not, it is admitted, fully explicit in Augustine, but is latent in the excessively narrow and rigid account of human nature on which his perversion account relies: if humans would simply *not act in defiance* of the norms, Augustine reportedly argues, evil would have no purchase. But the account's focus on *not acting* to pervert one's nature slides all too easily into a "nay-saying," a desire to avoid all possibility of blame by avoiding all action *tout court.* Thus Augustine's vision of bad human action as perversion – and his rigorist account of right human nature deriving therefrom – internalizes in us just the sort of guilt-inducing and immobilizing morality we do *not* need. The deep challenge these criticisms put to those who wish to follow

[20] I borrow the phrase "active gratitude," with gratitude, from my friend Derek Jeffreys.

Augustine, then, is this: can an account which depicts all of humanity as enmeshed in corruption and perversion actually *enable* and inform action, or does it work largely to paralyze it?

But again, when we look at Augustine's actual proposal, and see how it works in practice, things look quite different. For he uses his account of sin as perversion to *motivate* action by freeing us from all pretense to, and anxieties about achieving, moral purity. He is as deeply aware of the need for action as he is sensitive to what that action may sometimes entail. What do we do in a world riddled with tragic conflict and suffering? How far should we go in resisting evil, and how should we proactively respond to it? Here again, Camus formulates the extreme point quite sharply: are there situations in which homicide is legitimate, perhaps even required?[21] To put it in Augustine's terms: given that we ought always to act out of love, can this love be manifest in decisions to harm another person?

Augustine says yes. He provides a good example of what he means in his famous discussion of the judge in Book XIX, the last book of *De civitate Dei* concerned with the "world." Here he asks not about whether Christians should participate in social life – for social life is for him part of the human good – but rather about how Christians should participate therein. To answer this Augustine discusses the hard case, the judge who, as part of the legitimate civil authority, is compelled by "social necessity" to engage in acts of violence, at times even potentially upon the innocent. Because they "cannot discern the consciences of those whom they judge,"

> the ignorance of the judge generally results in the calamity of the innocent. And what is still more greatly intolerable and deplorable . . . is that the judge, to avoid killing an innocent man, out of miserable ignorance tortures the accused, and kills him – tortured and innocent – whom he tortured in order not to kill him if he were innocent. (*DCD* XIX.6, based on 1972 translation, pp. 859–60)[22]

By trying to learn the truth, the judge kills the one person, possibly innocent, at least not obviously guilty, by whom he might have learned that truth.

Augustine takes the tragically paradoxical situation of the judge as a summit from which we may view the whole expanse of the miserable

---

[21] See Camus 1954, 4: "Our purpose is to find out whether innocence, the moment it becomes involved in action, can avoid committing murder . . . We shall know nothing until we know whether we have the right to kill our fellow men, or the right to let them be killed."

[22] I have modified Bettenson's translation in several places where it seemed to over-elaborate Augustine's Latin.

necessities of human society. Should this inevitable complicity in injustice and cruelty serve to excuse Christians from such participation? "In light of such darkness in our social life, should the wise judge dare to sit in judgment?"

> Sit he will; for he is constrained by and drawn to his duties to human society, to desert which he regards as wicked (*nefas*). For he does not think it wicked to torture the innocent in others' cases, or that the accused are overcome and confess falsely and are punished, though innocent . . . All these many evils he does not count as sins, because the wise judge does them not out of a malicious will, but out of the necessity of ignorance, and also, out of consideration of society, out of the necessity to judge. Here therefore we speak not the maliciousness of the judge, but of the sure misery of humanity. (*DCD* xix.6, based on 1972 translation, p. 860)

Sociality is part of our existence, and required for our flourishing; but accepting this may involve us in the unjust imposition of force. In such cases, Christians should accept such duties, for the consequences of their renunciation are, in the end, the collapse of the social order itself.[23] We must accept that, in our sin-riddled world, we may need to *use* violence in order to protect the social goods we share.

Augustine's program here is neither a moralistic escapism nor an amoral realism. Against common pagan complaints about Christians' indifference to the social order, and against deep cultural and philosophical temptations towards renunciation of the world in favor of a life of *otium*, Augustine insists we must inhabit it: we are constitutively part of creation, the locus of its corruptedness, and the site of its redemption.[24] Augustine's "perversion" account of sin serves to *popularize* evil, to implicate all in the struggle with it: as *we* are responsible for the suffering and evil we find in the world, we must confront it.[25] Nonetheless, we must not usurp the role of the Divine Judge, so we can never assume that our judg-

---

[23] The hopes that Christians may be "free riders" only make their complicity indirect (such as when they pay taxes), which is to say that it does not reduce their complicity at all, but may make it easier for them to allow injustice to be enacted in the society at large. It is interesting to note the occasional implication of this non-involvement argument, that somehow it is *better* if *non*-Christians take up the (on this account) damnable tasks of governance and the sword, as if God would forgive *them*, more readily than God would forgive *Christians*, on the day of judgment. From Augustine's perspective, such an indifference to the fate of one's neighbors bespeaks a chilling absence of neighbor-love in those thoughtless enough to express it.

[24] See *DCD* xix.19 for Augustine's defense of the *vita activa*'s "mixed life" of action and contemplation.

[25] Peter Brown has recently suggested that this popularizing of the concept of sin, the achievement preeminently of Augustine but also involving his contemporaries, its suffusion of all aspects of everyday life, led to a considerable bleaching of the character of moral life (1999, 313). This is an interesting suggestion that merits more consideration.

ment is anything more than a temporary solution. As J. Joyce Schuld has provocatively argued, Augustine sees the largest irony of the judicial calling to be that the more one is wise in judging, the less confident one is that one's judgments are correct and fitting (2000; see O'Donovan 1987). We must always judge in fear and trembling, with the knowledge that our judgment is not the *final* one, and so must beware all pretensions towards such ultimacy. But Augustine no more offers a nihilistic renunciation of morality than a quietistic renunciation of the world, for the judge works not for cynically political reasons, but for significantly *moral* ones: it would be "wicked" (*nefas*) for the judge to refuse his duty, for it contributes to the social good.[26] The point is to promote true religion and piety (the only sound basis for moral order) while still admitting that many attempts to promote it – to create, that is, a true commonwealth – are simply too costly, too harmful to the fabric of the social order, to be pursued. This motivation always requires a wariness about itself, and a recognition that it is always a provisional solution: if the dynamic motivation towards greater justice and piety is lost, then the position veers towards a too static liberalism; but if the suspicion of the motivation is forgone, it veers towards a too arrogant theocracy.[27] Augustinians steer a middle course between these two, affirming the necessity and real goodness of the social order, and yet still acknowledging the *provisional* character of that order, our obligation always to seek to transform it into something better (see O'Donovan 1996). The love that motivates us to involve ourselves in society's tragic sufferings is not jettisoned in that involvement, though it is tortured. The authorities may from time to time restrain evil by force; at these moments, our moral abhorrence of violence is trumped by our obligation to resist injustice. But experiencing that moral abhorrence at what we do is appropriate; the good judge will *regret* the necessity of force (not just *his implication* in it), and bewail its necessity to God:

if his necessary ignorance condemns him to torture and punish the innocent, is it a problem if, while he is innocent, he is yet not happy? How much more con-

---

[26] That "moral" fits ill with the judge's real motives supports the argument I will be making in a moment.

[27] On the avoidance of static liberalism, see Wood 1986, 46–8, which suggests that at times Augustine instrumentalized the visible church for the civil peace, when he permitted the violent coercion of schismatics into the Catholic church, not ultimately for the increase of the church, but rather for the stability of the civil order. It was the Donatist schismatics who were the ones who offered an explicitly *religious* warrant for violence; Augustine's acceptance of the necessity of force was anything but ecclesiastically motivated. For a different though congruent account, see Bowlin 1997. On the avoidance of theocracy, see Loriaux 1992.

siderable and worthy is it when he acknowledges our miserable necessities, hates his part in them, and, if he is pious and wise, cries out to God, "from my necessities deliver me!" (*DCD* xix.6, based on 1972 translation, pp. 860–1; see Baron 1988, 271–4)

Sometimes the world does not meet our moral expectations, and we ought not to seek to fit them perfectly together; we must acknowledge that we are caught in between their claims, and accept the need to live in between.

This project of participation is circular: in coming to love the world more fully, we are transforming ourselves, or are being transformed, in ways that enable us to inhabit (and love) the world more fully. This is neither an appeal to any sort of unrestrained fellow-feeling, a naive "all you need is love" doctrine (though Augustine himself notoriously said "love and do what you will" [*IoEp.* vii.8]), nor is it a fundamentally quietistic response. We see this in Niebuhr's sophisticated development of this Augustinian account of love and justice. In our fallen world, a proper love sets limits on its own concern for the other, limits both *positive* – derived from the "respect" love holds for the other's real individuality and humanity – and *negative* – derived from the suspicion in which love holds its own pretensions to innocence. This is not simply an individualist transformation, though it is centrally the transformation of individuals: Augustinians are deeply interested in the public realm, but we must address the social and political problems therein only by demanding a change of heart; without this, "change" is merely a matter of moving guns from one pair of hands into another.[28]

In Augustine's hard-nosed, though not hard-hearted, acceptance of the necessity of violence, and his insistence that engagement in such violence may be held in tension with genuine moral strictures against harm – indeed, may even be motivated by those strictures – we see a precursor of what is known as "dirty-hands" reasoning (cf. Walzer 1974 and B. Williams 1981). He argues that our moral projects are vexed by their fitting ill with the world-as-it-is, and that we lack the "pure agency" we

---

[28] Criticisms of dispositional ethics imply a dichotomy between inner and outer that we should suspect. The charge is that attention to dispositional change is "inner" (note how the word inserts itself here, as if by magic) in a way that disdains or denigrates "the world." But this charge misunderstands both *the method* and *the end* of the moral transformation being proposed. It misunderstands *the method*, for the method is not a sheerly "purificatory" or ascetic *via negationis*, of a denial or annihilation of our loves; it works from our present affections, and seeks to see in them the seeds of their own healing. It misunderstands *the end*, because that end is not one of retreat or withdrawal from the world, but rather an attempt better to inhabit it, to appreciate its goods for what they are and not to be disappointed at their lack of infinite value. Contrary to rumor, for Augustine the world is not just a holding pattern while we wait for heaven. See Yeager 1982.

dream of possessing. We ought not to finesse this fact by attempting to whitewash our actions, loudly declaiming them innocent of their evil consequences through casuistry; this is the moralist's strategy, which seeks basically to avoid blame, and pictures the self as essentially "characterless," without a character-shaping history.[29] But to seek to avoid blame is ultimately to misunderstand yourself; no one is innocent in the first place.

But Augustine's position differs from more Nietzschean critiques of moralism such as that of Bernard Williams. While such critiques insist that morality's claims upon us are relativized by the extra-moral "horizontal" richness of human life, Augustine's critique derives from a wholly different source, namely, his appreciation of the "vertical" relativizing of morality by our obligations which stand, as it were, "beyond" the this-worldly referents of good and evil. For Augustine, experiences of moral conflict do not justify jettisoning our desire for a morally perfected state; on the contrary, such experiences, insofar as we experience them *as* conflict, bear within themselves an inescapable desire for their own overcoming. Experiences of "dirty hands" and moral conflict are not reasons for ceasing to theorize; they motivate us further to seek some relatively adequate intellectual account (see Santurri 1987 and Scheffler 1992).

Still, while this is a transformative proposal, we are not centrally transforming what is external to us; it is we ourselves who need this medicine. Crucial here is the Augustinian understanding of sin as perversion: we must respond to evil by acting in ways which combat its essentially annihilating and "de-ontologizing" character, while still remembering that, as that evil has its basic root within us, we cannot rely simply on our moral virtuosity. While Christians may be tempted to see themselves as world building in a way dangerously close to a Constantinian theocracy, the Augustinian tradition's universalism suggests that corruption on *our* side of the line will inevitably forbid such perfection. In this situation, appeals to a "virtuous" charismatic or expert ethic are insufficient; our actions must be supported and guided by some extrinsic principles formalized into codes, some explicit appeals to duty, which are required to secure the essential stability of the social order – a prerequisite for any greater transformation.

In order to do this, the Augustinian proposal turns to the notion of *duty* as the fundamental language in which to understand our obligations

---

[29] There have been Pelagian appropriations of Augustine's thought on these lines, but such appropriations have been justly critiqued in Pascal 1967 and, more recently, in Anscombe 1981, 58–9.

to others in the world. To talk of duties is the best way to tie together two strands of thought that Augustine wants to retain: first, a commitment to the character of persons, derived from the belief that genuine change must come from individuals' dispositional change; and second, a commitment to the good of the social order as a necessary good for individuals, and an insistence that we cannot abandon that commitment for fear of society's decay. "Duty" links these two concerns, because it insists that there is a place for sustaining the social good, but that those duties do not pass over into the individual's life in some sort of blanket way. (This restriction of the range of "duty" is clearer in Latin, which uses the word *officium* for duties, a word we associate with "officials" or "office.") For Augustine, any "social ethics vigilantism" is unacceptable: apart from specific formal relations (typically governmental and familial) we have no duties or obligations to engage in violent acts – indeed we, as private citizens, are forbidden to engage in such vigilantism; it is only those entrusted with the burdens of government who have such obligations.[30] We must accept certain socially established duties in the service of the fundamentally "re-ontologizing" character of positive action, in response to evil's basically nihilating, "de-ontologizing" effect on the world. This talk about duty is crucial; we do not act "on our own" in the service of advancing God's purposes in the world; we do not understand ourselves as theological pathfinders for Christ. Rather, our positive actions become manifestations, not simply of our own agency, but of God's will. By harnessing our agency within the yoke of a language (and social ordering) of duty, we understand our positive actions in terms of a fundamentally responsive model of obligations. We act transformatively out of a series of duties we have inherited, by inheriting our community; our moral action is understood as manifesting that inheritance, and seeking the community's participation in God's Kingdom.

What matters is that some modicum of social order be sustained, even at the cost – ultimately inevitable in a sin-riddled world – of unmerited and innocent suffering, which will in any case be requited in heaven. (Those who think any injustice is cause for radical revolution are simply blind to the realities of social life.) Nonetheless, the actions Augustine commends are not of the sort that would permit the total abnegation of moral order in the political realm. Some of these duties, which include

[30] While I will not discuss this issue here, this understanding of obligation changes when we enter, as we in the modern world have, into a more populist understanding of government, one in which power rests finally in the populace as a whole. The notion of a "citizen arrest" would be absurd to Augustine.

duties to the social order, entail the violent defense of the community against the wicked; but while such defense may be allowed, its legitimacy is constrained to certain recognizable social offices, and restrained by certain strict limits beyond which it cannot go.[31] The suspension of moral prohibitions against killing are rationalized, for Augustine, by being for the (clear) good of the social order as a whole; but to say that this entails a *carte blanche* on the brute imposition of power is to misconstrue, in the most fundamental manner possible, the tradition's understanding of the necessity of violating the moral order.

This proposal usefully confuses the relation between action and duty in a way interestingly, though inversely, analogous to the relation, discussed above, between forgiveness and freedom. Just as forgiveness, found primordially in the person of Jesus Christ, is the form under which we realize (or embody) our freedom, so our obligations, similarly informed by Christological ends, become our freedom. By understanding one's actions as commanded by duty, evil becomes a deontological matter, a matter of understanding oneself as fulfilling obligations which, in our time, are tragically torturous for us to fulfill, but which, paradoxically, involve us in the *imitatio Christi* and so transform tragedy from a conflict within ourselves to one between Christ and the "principalities and powers" of the world, opposed to God. By deontologizing evil, that is, we Christologize it; we weave our enmeshment in moral conflict into our enmeshment in the history (which is more than the narrative) of Christ's engagement with and final redemption of this sinful world. In our free action under obligation, the necessities we experience in confronting evil are transformed into the necessities which Christ undertook for our salvation. Far from being conservative and restraining, Augustine's perversion account of human wickedness enables political action.

Augustine is followed in this project, again, by both Niebuhr and Arendt, each of whom employed part of the tradition's account of evil to meet the particular aspects of its challenge that they most centrally addressed. Niebuhr, a theologian whose voice was heard in the corridors of power throughout the western world, thought the greatest danger lay in the possibility of the irresponsible exercise of force by those wielding

---

[31] For more on the rationale and limits of punishment, see Augustine, *Ep.* 153. In contrast to Kantian "self-warrant," for Augustine an act has its moral valence in its coherence with or dissonance from the will of God. This does not mean that moral commands cannot have an *absolute* character (think about Augustine on lying), but simply that their absoluteness is never self-warranted (again, think about Augustine on lying). See Griffiths 1999a.

power; thus he imagined evil's challenge as most basically an internal danger, tempting us towards an excessive self-interest. He perennially insisted that those entrusted with power must neither be naive or willfully blind to the partiality of the causes they served, nor be ever resigned to the futility of all political action in favor of a paralytic conservativism; he used the Augustinian account of sin as perversion to accommodate cynical realists' insistence on the pervasiveness of moral corruption without using it as an excuse for amoralism. This argument practically centered on our capacity to *acknowledge responsibility* for our condition, an acknowledgment made in order to turn whatever injustice is necessary towards some larger and relatively just purpose.

Arendt, as a public intellectual, was centrally interested in the obligations of those, like herself and other intellectuals, outside direct political power. She thought that the challenge of totalitarian movements in the modern world was the greatest danger to human flourishing; thus she conceived of evil's challenges not most basically in terms of internal dangers, but rather as an *external* threat, as the possibility of totalitarian encroachment on our free lives (by either explicitly totalitarian governments or by the swift-rising tide of the analogous "social realm"). She accordingly developed and deployed the Augustinian tradition's account of evil as privation, and connected it to a practice of engaging in positive political action as a means of *enacting resistance*, indirect as it must be, to totalitarianism, in opposition to its threat.

These two practices – of *acknowledging responsibility* and *enacting resistance* – specify and develop the two core aspects of Augustine's proposed demythologizing response to evil. Through them we see that the Augustinian tradition's demythologizing is necessarily both practical and theoretical, as much a moral practice as an intellectual method. Thus this proposal ultimately offers not a simply theoretical response to the challenge of tragedy, but rather an eminently *practical* one. The central insight here is the central *demystifying* insight of the whole tradition, the absolutely vacuous "reality" of evil *in se*. In light of this account, Augustinians affirm that the central truth entailed in such problematic action – in engagement with the brutalities and injustices of the world – is, again, the absolute goodness of being and agency, and our attempt more fully to participate in that, and that it may therefore be sometimes appropriate, in order to affirm and secure the good in the face of evil, to act in ways that would usually be considered unjust and evil. This is a complex response; but we cannot expect that our response will be simple in any way, as the character of the challenge we face is not simple. What we see instead is a way of responding to the challenge of tragedy in a way that, as I said above, challenges our putatively pre-theoretical apprehension of evil and *de-objectifies* it, turns it into a practical problem rather than a cosmological one – a difficulty which is political, not metaphysical.

So the critics focus uncharitably on the letter of Augustine's account and hence miss its spirit. Far from traducing the "this-worldly" or "moral" vectors of his biblical inheritance, Augustine urges us to participate ever more fully in the world, and to understand that participation Christologically. Whereas suffering can seduce us into picturing the world – or more precisely our existence in it – as the source of all evil, by interpreting suffering as the loss of existence, to which we should respond by a greater participation in the world, the privationist account of evil can push us towards a fuller incarnation. And whereas the socio-political necessity of violence (and the possibility that that violence is unjustly inflicted) might tempt us to view our moral commitments as finally fantastic and to jettison them *tout court*, the perversion account understands the need for violence in terms of our perverse corruption, and our participation in violence is a form of suffering injustice in Christ, through which we can come to see our moral life as tormented, partly formed by the trope of Crucifixion. In both ways morality opens to theology and the moral life is a life of deepening growth in Christ.

Still, real questions remain as to whether Augustine's program really offers us a "morality" at all (see Milbank 1997, 219–32; cf. Gustafson 1975, and Scheffler 1992). For morality is instrumental to human flour-ishing; morality serves *our* interests. But for Augustine, surely, there is no question that these commitments transcend the merely human realm of morality, and "refer" to God's self-giving in the Trinity. Augustine knows that humans are not simply "social" beings, but creatures of God, part of God's language, the way God speaks God's love; human acts are sig-nificant in themselves as *verba*, expressions of God's plan. In Greek Orthodox terms, it is a *liturgy*, something that "connotes an action through which persons come together to become something corporately which they were not as separate individuals. It means a gathering whose unifying purpose is to serve (minister to) the world on behalf of God" (Guroian 1987, 53). Our end is not contained within a "moral" horizon, and our moral struggles are incomprehensible on their own terms. But then ought Christians to *renounce* morality? And what would such a renunciation entail?

The critics think they know what it entails: catastrophe. So when their specific accusations against Augustine are unmasked as unwarranted, they become exasperatedly vague, claiming that Augustine's account is wrong because it privileges "theory" over practice, the *merely* "theological" over against the *really* important "moral." They rightly recognize the distance separating their account from that of Augustine. But the difference is in the adjectives: for while they aim to rest complacent within an essentially this-worldly moral framework, Augustine goes beyond their subjectivist understanding of moral agency as *ex nihilo* world building, framing it from within the narrative of a living dynamic God, to whom we respond. It is this "dialogical" picture of the world that Augustine's modern critics have a hard time appreciating; and it is this picture that allows Augustine to demythologize morality, both negatively and positively, melting its frozen formulas yet capturing its dynamics.

To see this, we can ask a question: does Augustine's proposal ultimately serve as an otherworldly opiate for the injustices of this world? Or: is Augustine's a *moral* theology? Well, no and yes. Certainly on one reading of "morality," Augustine is no moralist, not if morality is understood *teleologically* – as an attempt to achieve some aim – or *technologically* – as the application of some method. Yet this is just what much moral thought is. Such moral thought is essentially perfectionist; it imagines humans to be perfectible – their natures capable of being fully realized, completed, finished – by some set of moral strategies (see, e.g., Hurka 1993). There is a goal at which we aim, and towards which we understand ourselves as progressing, "making" ourselves better as we go along. This vision tends ineluctably towards a staticism, the presumption that this work will end when the edifice of righteousness is finally completed, a finished representation of some fabulous transcendent template. While the twentieth century has dashed (for the moment) these perfectionist hopes, the formal shape they give to our understanding of morality remains in place. Many thinkers accept that these moral utopias cannot be realized, but still attempt to retain some sort of purity or absolutism for morality. (The recent turn to "character," "narrative," and "virtue" as different foci of ethical reflection typically only alters the vocabulary within which thinkers seek solutions to these problems [cf. Hauerwas with Pinches 1997].) For example, some Christian thinkers argue that we should reconceive our moral commitments in a specifically theological manner, as injunctions put upon us not for their consequences but for how they express God's will for ourselves and the world.[32] But such approaches are really refusals to rethink the finality of morality's claim on us, attempts to retain morality's aroma rather than rethink its purpose and place in our lives. Few try to do that.

But Augustine did. For him, human nature is not captured within finite naturalistic categories, but always ruptures those categories, seeking ever more intimate relation with the God who is the endless end of all human desiring. The consequences of this realization for moral thought are enormous, and Augustine never flinched from drawing them. As Peter Brown says, he

> will demolish with quite exceptional intellectual savagery, the whole of the ancient ethical tradition: "those theories of mortal men, in which they have striven to make for themselves, by themselves, some complete happiness within the misery of this life." He thought of such theories as leading to a closed circle, calculated to deny a relationship of giving and receiving. To this tradition he will oppose an idea that involves just such a relationship: faith, and above all, "hope." He will search hard among the genuine good things which men enjoy, for some hint of what happiness men may yet "hope" for at the hands of a lavish Creator. (1967, 327)[33]

For Augustine, humans are born not simply immature, but positively perverted, and the moral life is not the naturalistic and/or pagan story of moral development, realizing a closed human nature within a finite model of the universe; rather it is a redemption, our return to an infinite gratuitous blessedness. Genuine graced goodness is possible, but he insists, against all teleology, that sin infects us too thoroughly for progressive improvement to be a straightforward ethical guide. Eschatology has a more complicated role to play in Christian ethics than is often acknowledged; too often it is used merely as a kind of ultimate consequentialist trump card, legitimating a willed indifference to "consequences" through appeals to the idea that God will fix everything at the end of time.

While we cannot counter evil with basic negation, neither can our affirming response undertake any kind of simple opposition through rivalry with evil, any project of seeking to construct the good as a sort of competing alternative to evil. No form of progressivist social gospel theology, which attempts to gather all good to its side, and seeks to claim

---

[32] See note 37 below.

[33] Augustine's controversy with the Pelagians is not fully appreciated without attention to it as part of his ongoing critique of the vestigial pagan moral heroism latent in some sections of the Christian community (see Russell 1990).

for itself and its project sole possession of all goods, will work. Any such project will find itself vexed both internally and externally: internally vexed, because no one's motives are pure, and noble ideals are invariably alloyed with base prejudices and covert parochial interests; externally vexed, because the enormous diversity of legitimate goods that humans pursue can and do lead to conflicts for any attempt to organize them into a coherent proposal (see Hampshire 1983). The account ignores our complicity in evil, both directly – in how that complicity often invests our projects with hidden parochial or self-interests – and indirectly – in how it makes us stubborn and blind to the truth that our apprehension of genuine goods is partial, thus leading to a willful refusal to compromise and inevitable conflict among goods. Furthermore (and therefore), this project misconstrues what would count as a proper response to evil, attempting to "rise above" the past in a way that makes it dangerously close to a practice of forgetting. It assumes, that is, that evil is essentially a reality to be overcome or defeated; but in doing so it lets its oppositional and agonistic metaphors get the better of it, and it fails to see that evil must, most fundamentally, be transformed and not simply defeated – most basically, because *we* are what is "evil," or rather evil has no separate existence outside our souls.[34] Such simple visions of a progressive-eliminationist response to evil's challenges are vexed by its too narrow vision of human good, and its shallow understanding of human corruption, of the depths and the darkness of the human soul.[35]

But if we cannot respond to evil directly, either with counter-attacks or by rival construction, should we perhaps *not* respond to the challenge at all? We can call this the isolationist or sectarian response; we "respond" to evil by ignoring it, and working only in acts that are wholly good, or at least strictly commended by obedience to the Gospel message of Jesus. This proposal suggests we take no heed of the presence of evil, and instead affirm that God's triumph in Christ means that evil has no power over us as people of God (however broadly one conceives of that community); our actions manifest our faith in the Gospel, whose whole point is not their efficaciousness in the world but rather as moments of witness to God's triumph.

[34] As H. Richard Niebuhr writes, "every effort of this sort involves a recognition of the power of evil – as though it exists otherwise than as a spirit of self-seeking, self-willing, and self-glorification; as though it can be located somewhere outside ourselves" (1951, 224–5). This is also where the Augustinian tradition parts ways with Nietzschean proposals about an "agonal" morality, though this is not the place to discuss the details of that divergence.

[35] It should be noted, however, that these two are in fact not unrelated; the provincialism of the first derives from, or at least draws for support on, the superficialities of the second.

Because of the essentially negative character of evil identified earlier, this account has considerable plausibility as a response. But it still misses the full significance of the fact that evil is not simply an external fact, a nihilation of reality, but appears equally in sin as a persistent perversion of our affections. This account thus construes evil's challenge as essentially external to us; as such, our positive project of witness can go forward – indeed should and *must* go forward – without even glancing concern for the evils at our heels.[36] It seems to miss this most patently in its depiction of salvation as most basically an escape, or (to avoid the incipient Pelagianism) a *rescue* from evil.[37] The problem with this vision of rescue from evil is that it seems to imply that we are too simply victims and witnesses – in the sense of audience members – to God's struggle with, and eventual triumph over, evil. It ignores the ways in which God operates *in* and *through* us to transform the world: here the assumption is that God calls us simply to *distinguish* ourselves from "the world" rather than to work for God's purposes within it. There is, an incipient dualism here, not of good versus evil, to be sure, but rather of "church versus world" which, when drawn out, tends to focus our attention not on God's call for us to love our neighbors as ourselves, but rather on being not conformed to the things of the world, as the most basic response to evil's challenges.

Such separatists are often accused of a simplistic optimism about the capacities of their own communities to be perfect; but in fact they start on the opposite end, with shock and revulsion at the ways of the world, and despair at its utter "lostness," and then, seeing their shock not heeded by that world, assuming that their own vision of it is in some way distinct. They err, that is, not in presumptuousness but in uncharitableness, not in their insistence on seeing themselves as different, but rather in their refusal to see others as essentially *like* them. The difference may seem only lexical, but in fact it is crucially important: Augustinians and sectarians can agree on the depth of human imperfection, but they

---

[36] I do not want to give the impression that this vision suggests that we ought to be indifferent to the sufferings of others, for many of the commended forms of witness consist of acts of other-regard; but it does mean that our care for others is undertaken in light of this essentially victimizing vision of evil.

[37] This follows the distinction in Yeager 1996 between "substitution" and "conversion" (at 102). I do not mean to accuse those who hold this account of assuming their own "perfection"; even though this was historically the case with the early Radical reformers, such accounts need not entail claims of perfection for their adherents. (The assumptions surrounding a belief in perfectionism lead to a different sort of flawed proposal, as we have already seen above.) Nor am I accusing them most basically of an essentially escapist mentality; though that is implied, I think, by my criticisms, I think the deep root of all this is a misconstrual of the nature of evil itself.

diverge in their differing assessments of the world's capacities for justice and goodness. Sectarians seem more pessimistic about (at least parts of) the "world's" final destiny, while Augustinians seem more optimistic and hence universalistic.

Given the problems vexing each of these proposed accounts, what can we say *positively* about the Augustinian tradition's project? The comment above about "uncharitableness" is a crucial clue, both about the failures of each of the preceding accounts, and about the contours of Augustinian tradition's own practical proposal. From the perspective of this tradition, we can see the failure of each of these accounts as fundamentally a failure of love. This is not to say that these accounts are most basically cold, or entirely without love, but rather that they fail fully to inhabit the basic motive of love, love for God and, through God, one's neighbor and the world.

The flaw of each is its partiality. We are committed to fighting against evil, but in a way that ultimately derives the grounds for that struggle indirectly, from our positive commitments to love of the world, as commanded by God. We ought properly to love the world, and that love leads us towards a revulsion against evil, as an "ascetic nay-saying" morality may teach us. But that revulsion is itself an inadequate response, for, as the perfectionist-progressivist proposal suggests, it does not reach deeply enough into our existence to make sense of why we reject evil. Furthermore, as sectarians affirm, our love of the world is essentially creative, and calls for us to engage the world in the ongoing act of co-creation with God to which we are called. Each proposal reflects some sense of our loves as our ultimate rationale for resisting evil; but all of them harbor hesitations about, or refuse outright, the affirmation of those loves. Their failings are finally, though in a curious way, dispositional: they fail not so much in having the wrong motives, as in not fully following through on their motives. (As such, Augustinians cannot help but see their errors as representative of human sin in general, as manifesting humanity's essential fault.) From this Augustinians draw a moral. Given the sheer negativity of evil, we cannot respond to it directly; we must respond to it through its manifestation as a perversion of our loves. But our loves are also the source of our every attempt at a response; that is, the problem is essentially with *us*, and not directly with anything "external" to us. So our loves are simultaneously the root of the problem and the source of any possible response to the problem.

This project of transformation essentially entails a dual project: ultimately and supremely, we seek the transformation of our loves, our conversion back to rightly ordered love; but more proximately, though finally subordinate to the first, we seek to restrict the further damage that evil, through our sinful wills, can do, even in pursuit of our transformation. These principles are ordered here in reverse: primarily, restrict further harm, then secondarily, promote the good (see Schweiker 1995, 123–34). Our corruption is pervasive, and to be abhorred; but just because it is *we* who are corrupt, we should be wary about what mechanisms we pursue for our improvement. We do seek change; but we cannot whole heartedly, so to speak, seek change, because our hearts are not in fact whole, and will never, in this sinful world, be so. This is why Augustinian tradition argues for a realistic participation in the mess of history. It must be *participation* for ontological reasons, especially because God has created us as participatory beings, creatures whose good is found in community. But it must be a *realist* participation for theological reasons, because our sins must be recognized as a fact about us. Furthermore, this realist participation must be formed by the *imitatio Christi*, and that *imitatio* can take the form of the *via crucis*, the Way of the Cross. Thus this project has deep theological roots; but it is a thoroughly moral project, a practice of engagement with the world through which our loves are transformed into more proper order. Augustinians affirm that we are participants in our own fall; they also insist that we be participants in our own redemption. It is in this way that our love manifests itself in the world.

Thus, Augustinians resist equally (a) progressivist accounts that seek immanent satisfaction of the human's aims in the world, (b) chastened liberal views that try to be content with reducing cruelty, and (c) theologically absolutist accounts that refuse any acknowledgment of "the world" as a source or appropriate home of human longings. Augustinians can do this because they see the world both as a real good and yet as not in itself *the* ultimate good of human existence, but only insofar as it participates in God. But this does not entail that they deny the world any value at all; simply because others cannot conceive of a way to value the world without making the world of exclusive value need not trouble an account which refuses such an either/or. Following Augustine, they do not *renounce* the "this-worldly" positive moral motivations of modernity, but rather detach those motivations from their Promethean progressivist tendencies, and re-describe them as practices of self-transformation and ecclesial participation which only secondarily aim at even the approximation of worldly justice. Augustine is no nihilist: what happens in the world has more than a merely juridical relevance for our lives; what we do in it forms us in ways that make us better or worse people, better or worse lovers, and it is our capacity for loving that determines our ultimate relationship to God (see Tillich 1954). Augustinians cannot ever forget this; the whole purpose of the project is to transform evil into a means for love.

In this we see how Augustine does, after all, offer a "moral" theology. For he affirms and employs the basic energies captured in and expressed by moral categories – although he thinks they are misapprehended when trapped in those categories, just because those categories illegitimately constrict those energies. They typically conceive of morality as essentially reacting against the world's injustice, and ally themselves with that reaction; and they are led by this to despair about the world's deep goodness.[38] But while it is important to say "no" to evil, sheer nay-saying cannot be our most basic response; we must instead respond to evil by affirming something else.[39] Recall that the virtues are all forms of love, all forms of our participation in God's love, so for Augustinians "morality," like "humanity," cannot be complete or total in itself; all are part of God's "speaking," God's gratuitous and endless word of love, and are not rightly understood simply through the categories of creation. The moral life is a pilgrimage, what Peter Brown calls "a 'therapy of distance,' remaining essentially the act of leaving" (1981, 87). Human life is a journey whose end is not yet known.

Here another "demythologizing" becomes available. Evil itself demythologizes; it demythologizes our faith in the moral seamlessness of the world – because it is through encountering evil that we see the essential inadequacy of our moral systems. It does so merely by our attending to it. And this is, for Augustine, as it should be: indeed, one of the most basic points of his thought is that we ought never to be allowed to turn away from the vision of reality towards some interior, merely theoretical or mythological consolations. Evil demythologizes both because it shows us that the coherence we apprehend really is partial, even as it purports to be total (under the guise of "the world"), and because it cannot be "solved," cannot be broken down into component parts and studied, but puts us into question and compels us to respond

---

[38] This is why much contemporary moral discourse is a discourse of victimization and violation; it is hard for us to imagine why something would be bad apart from its effect on someone else.

[39] This suggests an Augustinian-Nietzschean critique of those liberal proposals which "put cruelty first" and define our public morality most basically in terms of our opposition to "ordinary vices." For an exemplar of such a liberal approach, see Shklar 1984. (For a compelling analysis of Nietzsche as a critic of modern morality in terms of its misplaced [and shallow] loves, see Pippin 1997, 351–71.)

to it. Augustine avoids attempting to solve the "problem of evil" not only because he despairs of ever overcoming suffering in this life, but also because he thinks evil serves a purpose for God's plan. God used it to announce redemption, and for Augustine, the sufferings of Christ have not made our sufferings pointless or egregious. The Christian life is lived in the deepening comprehension of suffering's necessity, not in escaping from evil but in the full and terrible confrontation with it. It is not placed down before us to be dissected; it is not a problem we are set in some sort of cosmological exam. Evil demythologizes because, in attempting to respond to it, we find that it has insinuated itself into our very response; while we should seek to resist it, we must not think that we are engaged in a war that we can ever, in any recognizable sense, "win." The problem is essentially with *us*, not with anything external to us. So our loves are simultaneously the root of the problem and the source of any possible response to the problem. We must participate in the mess of history, for God has created us as participatory beings, but our sin makes this participation a painful one. "From my necessities, Lord, deliver me!"

Augustine's program has a piety that his critics cannot comprehend – a piety, in fact, that they have a hard time apprehending as other than nihilistic, insofar as they see no moral alternative to attempting to defeat evil. And those critics, too often, are us: ultimately we still hold out hope for some way of overcoming, by our own self-will, all suffering. Augustine does not; his soteriological expectations are eschatological, not immanent, so he is freed from the burdensome mythology of perfectionism. This may not be wholly consoling, but that is as it should be. Our faith and hope ought not to be placed in some ultimately temporal configuration of reality. On his account, we are not the primary actors in the world, we are responders; we must understand our lives in terms of waiting and patience, and we must seek to understand the world, in goods and evils, as a gift to us from another. For Augustine, real demythologizing begins by, and consummates in, a self-demythologizing, understanding that we are not our own, that we are possessed by another, namely, God. The real myth we need to surrender, that is, is ourselves.

CONCLUSION

Evil cannot be thought; but that is all that it can "be." But this is not because evil is somehow ontologically opaque or impenetrable, some sort of absolute cipher, a code impossible to crack; rather, it is because it is perfectly superficial, totally hollow, *nihil*, vacuous in every respect. Augustinians are often said to meet "resistance" in thinking about the tragic, but that formulation is precisely the opposite of the truth. For it is resistance of any sort which is what we do *not* meet in thinking about evil. On the contrary, evil offers no purchase for reflection; it is wholly frictionless to thought. Evil, tragedy, and sin are in their essence our interpretive constructs, accidental consequences of our necessary interpretive activity in the world, our need of conceptual guideposts to help us negotiate our way through life. But such phenomena have no ontological reality apart from their existence as figments of our interpretation, as half-believed aspects of our mode of being. It is in this formal way that evil is strictly thought. But in terms of content, evil cannot be thought at all – the Augustinian proposal is perhaps most honest when it simply affirms this and leaves it at that. Inevitably it becomes caught up in ornate elaborations, in its attempts to make others see what it so basically appreciates, namely, the sheer negativity of evil. But these elaborations should not distract us from the original insight that the basic character of the world is found in a love that cannot be explained from the perspective of the world, and that our response to evil must not undercut, but rather reinforce, our sinful participation in that love.

It should be admitted, however, that this response is not a "solution" to the problem of evil. But what, we may justly ask, would such a solution look like? And who would want it? Clearly the "problem" will not go away once "solved"; evil is not a puzzle waiting to be figured out, but a reality that perpetually vexes our lives. Perhaps some seek a solution which would reconcile us to this persistence, this stubbornness in evil. But would not such a "solution" really merely leave its adherents mute before the ongoing brute (and brutal) realities of suffering and evil? In contemporary theological and philosophical reflection on evil, we are often commanded to accept that the reality of evil in our lives undermines our affirmations either of the supremacy of goodness or of God's goodness *simpliciter*. But such commandments owe their force more to an excessive intellectual fastidiousness than to any sustained reflection on our encounter with evil in the world. The rhetoric of such appeals is always one of intellectual economy, theoretical tidiness; but no one ever inquires into just what such a revision of our worldview would do *to* us, once it was believed. What exactly is the point of "admitting" that God wills evil or that evil is necessary, except that such an admission relieves a deep tension in the theoretical account we have? And once that tension is relieved, what else of value has gone with it? Rather than succumbing to such siren songs, it is both wiser and more fruitful to see what resources the tradition has for resisting them – for acknowledging that the problems we face in life are not dissolved in thought, but must rather be confronted, and experienced "more keenly."

Conclusion: realizing incomprehension, discerning mystery

> The theology of evil can therefore be derived much more readily from the fall of Satan . . . than from the warnings in which ecclesiastical doctrine tends to represent the snarer of souls. The absolute spirituality, which is what Satan means, destroys itself in its emancipation from what is sacred.
>
> Walter Benjamin 1977, 230

This book has argued for the plausibility of original sin theologically and ethically. But it has also been an attempt to work out the implications of original sin on a methodological level. Indeed I understand an acceptance of original sin to be entailed by the meaning of tradition. In this conclusion I want to say something about what this means; for, typically, appeals to tradition are made to help us see better. In this book, however, our appropriation of tradition has not improved our vision, but clouded it; "tradition" has helped us see that we do not understand; it has helped us realize our incomprehension of evil's roots. And this I take to be a necessary prolegomenon to our discernment of the mystery of our response to evil – a response which, this book has argued, is irremediably theological.[1]

This work has argued that the Augustinian tradition of moral and religious inquiry offers us considerable resources for understanding and responding to the challenges that evil puts before us. This argument is actually a series of arguments, one nested inside another. Most basically, we sought both an adequate interpretive understanding of, and a fruitful way of practically responding to, the challenges of evil, suffering, and tragic conflict. But this inquiry is from the beginning shaped by the conviction that a confessedly Augustinian proposal offers a fruitful avenue of inquiry. As such an Augustinian attempt, it is alert to the sharp

---

[1] Much of the following discussion of "mystery," and indeed much of the reflection constituting this Conclusion, has been shaped by Louth 1983.

challenges to its plausibility leveled at it by various critics; to meet these challenges, we attempted to rehabilitate the Augustinian arguments and thought-forms that those criticisms target, and we did so by showing how two twentieth-century thinkers developed and deployed them in ways that help us meet the critiques. But we saw that those thinkers' particular proposals are inadequate, undercut by subjectivist assumptions; so we reconstructed their formulations, in more thoroughly Augustinian ways, in order to avoid the subjectivist temptations to which they succumbed. In doing so, we saw that this theoretical proposal entails a very fruitful practical proposal for responding to evil through a form of demythologization, which we detailed in terms of the twin practices of "embodying forgiveness" and "deontologizing evil."

The complexity of this proposal should be manifest in the argumentative density of the above paragraph. But in another way the book's project is quite simple. It attempts to do two things. First, it offers what it claims is an adequately comprehensive interpretation of, and fruitful practical response to, the challenge of evil. Second, it offers the above through its rehabilitation of the Augustinian tradition. So the book's two large arguments are almost two sides of the same coin. It is easy not to appreciate the tight connection between these exegetical and constructive arguments, and it may be tempting to dismiss too easily this argument about the relationship between the two claims. But such a dismissal would be unwise.

The work is centrally an act of retrieval: it attempts to recover and rehabilitate a way of thinking that has fallen into disfavor. But it is not only the *content* of this particular retrieval that has fallen into disfavor; the *form* of "retrieval" itself is today suspected of expressing a dangerous nostalgia or a reactionary conservativism. While I think these challenges are wrong, they are not *frivolous*; it is an open question whether a retrieval can avoid succumbing to either a nostalgic escapism or a willfully blind antiquarianism. But this methodological challenge merely recapitulates the work's material challenges. Hence the book's foundational methodological assumption – that our constructive work arises from our active appropriation of our intellectual inheritance – implies a response to this challenge, one analogous to its material argument. *Ex nihilo* theorizing is as deluded as *ex nihilo* acting; we are, in an important sense, tradition-constituted beings, most fundamentally creatures who love, and the fact of our being such lovers entails that we must work from where we find ourselves to transform the situation in ways that transform us too. Nonetheless, our acceptance of tradition does not mean that new thought is forbidden; this says something of the real meaning of freedom, especially in its relationship to our loves, our attachments. The fact that we are beings-who-inherit does not entail effacing ourselves, abrogating our agency or our freedom; it merely orients it. Indeed, that we can know we are constituted by tradition entails that we can reflect upon those traditions, and actively appropriate them for ourselves, in indeterminate ways. We matter in our traditions, precisely as those who receive the traditions and keep them alive as traditions. By thinking both in terms of, and about, what has been handed down to us, we remake for ourselves both the language by which we understand our world, and the practices by which our linguistic understanding is made manifest in our existence in the world. The book's methodology flows from its argument against subjectivism, and its elaboration of moral practices of embodying forgiveness and acknowledging responsibility. It acknowledges its responsibility to the tradition, and for its further development, and yet also attempts to offer forgiveness for the ways this tradition has been handled in the past by those who have handed it on to us. This transformative hermeneutic of charity tacks back and forth between understanding and action: we come to understand and inhabit our world by means of our inheritance, but we come to understand and transform our inheritance through and in understanding and inhabiting the world. We best learn to advance into the future, by returning to and rehabilitating the past.

One might say that the "hermeneutics of charity" used here assumes the recognition of original sin; the tragic complexity of our lives extends even to our attempts to understand our lives. Our attempt to reformulate, for our own context and in our own terms, our intellectual inheritance, is an attempt to respond to a quandary – tragic, in its own, minor way – without thinking we can escape it. In undertaking this, the book manifests how such a retrieval entails an acknowledgment of original sin, particularly insofar as our attempts at retrieval are themselves perpetually implicated in imperfect and partial misunderstandings of what such a retrieval is, and what it is we are retrieving.

A tradition, as I said at the beginning, is an act of forgiveness. We do not receive this tradition innocent of misuse; nor will we, sinful as we are, employ it with perfect ability. By forgiving those who have handed the tradition down to us, we accept that they tried, as best as they saw how, to inhabit the tradition as it came to them. Not only does this forgiveness liberate us from the theatricalized recitation of blame that would otherwise trap us in a stale circle of recrimination; it also provides us with the requisite hermeneutical charity, by which we can best come to see what they were trying to do and how they tried, and tragically failed, to fulfill their hopes. Forgiveness is an act of liberation, both for our ancestors as well as for us. So also is responsibility: through it we accept the freedom we have as the kind of beings we are. We take what we have received, what we have inherited, and transform it into what is properly our own. In so doing, we make it more possible for others after us to forgive us for our partiality and faults, for our flawed vision of what needed to be done and how to go about doing it. Our hermeneutic of charity takes form in our confession of sin, and that of our ancestors; it is a tragic activity, both relying upon, and hence affirming, the past, while also simultaneously critiquing, and hence transforming it.

If this hermeneutics relies on a confession of original sin, it is no surprise that what it finds in the world is equally complex. And yet the complexity that it sees as a virtue seems like a vice to its critics. For today, in our culture, such complexity is not welcome. We want straightforward solutions, answers which provide us with clear lines of demarcation between good and evil, and we are bombarded with proposals which promise us easy answers, quick "fixes" for the predicament we are in. But simplicity is not to be had in our world – at least, not in the first instance; we can have only a simplicity that has passed through the complexities of thought. Without an adequate appreciation of the complexity, one is tempted towards a partial vision which leads one towards either presumption or despair. This explains Niebuhr's persistent insistence on a proper understanding of "hope"; Arendt, too, in *The Origins of Totalitarianism*, made this point when she said that the book "has been written against a background of both reckless optimism and reckless despair. It holds that Progress and Doom are two sides of the same medal; that both are articles of superstition, not of faith" (Arendt 1968, vii). And Arendt was right: Progress and Doom are ways of *not* thinking about the present; they are excuses for turning away from it. It is against all such simplistic superstitions that the Augustinian tradition perennially protests, and it does so by insisting on the profound complexity of our lives. Given this situation, understanding must proceed to attempt, as best it can, to make some provisional sense out of our tragic situation. This attempt is itself an expression of courage. Again, some of Arendt's lines help us understand this:

The conviction that everything that happens on earth must be comprehensible to man can lead to interpreting history by commonplaces. Comprehension does not mean denying the outrageous, deducing the unprecedented from precedents, or explaining phenomena by such analogies and generalities that the impact of reality and the shock of experience are no longer felt. It means, rather, examining and bearing consciously the burden which our century has placed on us – neither denying its existence nor submitting meekly to its weight. Comprehension, in short, means the unpremeditated, attentive facing up to, and resisting of, reality – whatever it may be. (1968, viii)[2]

Note Arendt's language here: understanding does not simply entail acknowledging the ugly realities of our day, but in some important sense *resisting* them too – forbidding ourselves to be hermeneutically seduced into allowing them the final word on what they themselves mean.

"Complexity" here may sound like either a skeptical academic evasion – a refusal to take a stand on some clear position – or merely a justification for conservative suspicion of proposals for change. But we must allow "complexity" its own complexity. The complexity that Augustinians perceive bears within itself a compulsion towards commitment, theorized in and through the tradition's account of love, a compulsion which insists that the complexity goes, so to speak, "all the way down," to the depths of our hearts, and implicates us both in inactivity and in activity. Complexity is irreducible to either a sheerly objective or a sheerly subjective phenomenon. It is not a code word for the chaos of external reality; it differs from the "booming, buzzing confusion" of those who suggest that we fabricate an order in our minds that is not found in reality. Were such the case, the root of our problem would rest in the conflict between our lives with the world, with the inevitable clash between ideality and reality. Nor is complexity due simply to subjective variety or diversity; it is not simply that we are complex people who operate in an otherwise clear world. Were such the case, the root of our problem would again rest in the conflict between our lives and the world, though this time in the conflict between the transient flux of our passions and the inert and uncaring stony earth. Neither of these alternatives is adequate; both accounts, though typical to moderns, promise more than they can deliver – or rather less. Both accounts, that is, offer us partial accounts, partial truths, but tie those truths to larger and restrictively partial programs which, were we to accept either of them, would blind us to the different partial truth found in the other account. To identify evil's challenge with the fact that the world inevitably fits ill with our hopes and desires is to forbid any useful place for the thought that our ideas are amenable to reconstruction and improvement. The first offers

---

[2] For a recent example of the limits of thinking entirely in terms of precedents, see Müller 2000.

us the consolation of immutability, the second the promise of possibility. But we ought not to, and indeed need not, accept one or the other; we need to feel both the balm of consolation and the sting of a guilty conscience.

In a certain way, the account has created more questions than it has answered, questions asking for further specificity about this Augustinian proposal. For example, how should its theoretical account be thickened by being connected more explicitly with first-order Christian doctrines? How is its practical proposal made more definite, or perhaps even materially altered, by an appreciation of our more "populist" political beliefs? Such questions as these are *fruitful* questions, productive of further exploration rather than merely expressing a deep skepticism about the very idea of the proposal. From an Augustinian perspective, this is all to the good; any attempt at a final, conversation-ending demonstration would be fundamentally misconceived, more an aggressive manifestation of human *superbia* than any actual longing for truth. Hence this work's main obligation has been one of perspicuous presentation, a non-defensive, though dialectical, exposition of what it takes to be the rudiments of its constructive proposal about evil.

In this way, then, the book attempts to reach the proper *in*comprehension, the realization that what lies beyond its ability fully to articulate – though not its ability to appreciate – is precisely the account's basic premises, among which are a set of what Augustinians see as "mysteries." Most especially there are two from which the book begins. First, there is the mystery of God's incarnating creation and sustenance of the world: this we may call the tradition's fundamental ontological premise. Second, there is the mystery of our willing dissent from God's will, our willing divergence from God's proper ordering of our world and ourselves: this we may call the tradition's fundamental anthropological premise. Together these two mysteries serve as the basic conceptual premises upon which the Augustinian proposal builds its account of, and response to, evil's challenges.[3]

This conclusion cannot say much more about these mysteries, because it is hard to know what more to say about them, other than that they are there; they are, in some sense, the sources of reflection, primordial to the tradition's account, and "give rise to thought" (Ricoeur 1967,

---

[3] Note that I am not talking here about the full range of mysteries to which the Augustinian Christian tradition is committed; in particular, I make no explicit reference to the mysteries associated with either Christology or the Trinity, though a comprehensive account of the Augustinian tradition would discuss these, of course.

347–57). Most especially, it cannot say much more about the second, about this deepest level of the Augustinian account of evil, apart from saying that the roots of this situation, its origin as the event symbolized as the Fall, is wholly inexplicable – not because the event is somehow "too deep" for us to comprehend, but because, as was the case with Eichmann, there is no "there" there for us to apprehend.

But our recognition of the truths expressed in these mysteries is not in any direct sense the "moral" of this book, the summary conclusion we should take from it. We do not need more *juridical* knowledge; our encounter with it should not leave us with an increased knowledge of our own badness, a heightened awareness of guilt. To think that such increased feelings of guilt manifest an adequate understanding of the Augustinian proposal is fundamentally mistaken, it is not meant most basically to be juridical but, in a somewhat idiosyncratic sense, funda-mentally *pragmatic* and *therapeutic*. It aims ultimately not to provide us with theoretical proofs of our badness, but rather to offer practical guidance about how to respond to the theoretical insight that we are, ourselves, the source of our problem. It means to make us inquire into evil, suffer-ing, and tragedy, not in order to see how deeply sinful we are, but instead to appreciate how even in intellectual activities such as this we are driven inevitably towards affirming the good. It means to offer an account which can bear the phenomenological weight of our complex intuitions about evil's essential emptiness, about our fundamental resistance to it, and about the concomitant primordiality of the good. And it means to do all this in order to endorse, and indeed reinforce, the hope we know we need, and which we already inchoately feel.

One of the largest tasks of theology, one for the most part abandoned in our age, is the iconic task: offering pictures, non-discursive images of what theologians discourse about. Perhaps the most apt image of what I have been explicitly concerned with – evil and sin – is the image of the fall of the rebel angels: a fall downward, to be sure, but more importantly a fall away, away from God and hence away from one's true self. But there is no "away," so this is a fall towards nowhere, or, more literally, towards nothing: the angels, tumbling down a bottomless abyss, never get "anywhere." And as their fall is interminable, it feels like no motion at all to them; so the experience of paralysis, of frozenness, equally well describes their state as does "falling." An infinite fall is an infinite still-ness. Yet still they live, perpetual rebels against reality, with no reason for their rebellion and no hope of recovery by themselves. This is sin: an endless vertigo, hidden, in part, by an awesome self-deception, caused entirely by a refusal to say yes. And this depicts our lives: at our hearts, we are hurt, but it is a self-inflicted wound, a wound which, once made, we cannot repair. Yet it is also the case that our very capacity, however dimmed and distorted, to see the wound at all means that our healing process has already begun – that it began as soon as we fell. Though we have abandoned God, yet God has not abandoned us. Our faith in the possibility of our repair – our hope for that redemption – and our love for our redeemer – is what we finally, if not yet firmly, are.

"The beginning is not what one finds first; the point of departure must be reached, it must be won" (Ricoeur 1967, 348). In our end is our beginning. This book's argument can be charted as a series of movements, forwards and backwards, circling around a basic reality, the reality of mystery, which lies at the center of its vision. It has moved from a false beginning – the noble lie of its reiteration of the "facts" with which it commenced, the givens of revelation and inchoate human intuition – towards a final appreciation of the account's true origins, in explicit recognition of the mysteries it posits at the heart of human existence, mysteries which cannot be demonstrated, but only displayed.

Yet there remains one further thing to say. One point at which these two mysteries do reveal something about themselves is in the further mystery of Christ, the mystery of Christ's Crucifixion and Resurrection. In this mystery the two others are contained and expressed: we see here both the brokenness of the world, and God's refusal to abandon the world. (In *both* Crucifixion and Resurrection, I repeat: the path back up from death to life is no easier than the path down from life to death.) The mystery of evil is implicated not only in the mystery of creation, and vice versa; both find their summation and their most perspicuous presentation in the mystery of Christ, the *mysterium Paschale*. It is fitting, then, that this book, after so many words, must finally appeal to the Word beyond our words, and end itself by pointing towards that mystery: *veni, veni Emmanuel . . .*

Works cited

Adams, Robert Merrihew. 1984. "Saints." *Journal of Philosophy* 81: 392–401.

Allison, Henry. 1996. "The Banality of Radical Evil." *Idealism and Freedom: Essays in Kant's Theoretical and Practical Philosophy*. New York: Cambridge University Press, pp. 168–82.

Anderson, Pamela Sue. 1992. "Ricoeur and Hick on Evil: Post-Kantian Myth?" *Contemporary Philosophy* 14: 15–21.

1994. "Agnosticism and Attestation: An Aporia Concerning the Other in Ricoeur's *Oneself as Another*." *The Journal of Religion* 74: 65–76.

Anscombe, G. E. M. 1963. *Intention*. Second edition. Ithaca: Cornell University Press.

1981. "War and Murder." *The Collected Philosophical Papers of G. E. M. Anscombe*, volume III: *Ethics, Religion, and Politics*. Minneapolis: University of Minnesota Press, pp. 51–61.

St. Anselm. 1998. "On the Fall of the Devil." In *Anselm of Canterbury: The Major Works*. Brian Davies and G. R. Evans, eds. New York: Oxford University Press, pp. 193–232.

Arendt, Hannah. 1957. "History and Immortality." *Partisan Review*, 24: 11–35.

1958. *The Human Condition*. Chicago: University of Chicago Press.

1961. *Between Past and Future: Eight Exercises in Political Thought*. New York: Viking Press.

1963. *On Revolution*. New York: Viking Press.

1965. *Eichmann in Jerusalem: A Report on the Banality of Evil*. Revised edition. New York: Viking Press.

1968. *Men in Dark Times*. New York: Harcourt Brace Jovanovich.

1971. "Thinking and Moral Considerations." *Social Research* 38: 417–46.

1972. *Crises of the Republic*. New York: Harcourt Brace Jovanovich.

1973. *The Origins of Totalitarianism*. New edition with added prefaces. New York: Harcourt Brace Jovanovich.

1977. *The Life of the Mind*, volume I: *Thinking*. New York: Harcourt Brace Jovanovich.

1978a. *The Life of the Mind*, volume II: *Willing*. New York: Harcourt Brace Jovanovich.

1978b. Letter to Gershom Scholem of July 24, 1963. In *The Jew as Pariah: Jewish Identity and Politics in the Modern Age*. Ron H. Feldman, ed. New York: Grove Press, pp. 245–51.

247

1982. *Lectures on Kant's Political Philosophy*. Ronald Beiner, ed. Chicago: University of Chicago Press.

1987. "Labor, Work, Action." In Bernauer ed., pp. 29–42.

1992. *Hannah Arendt/Karl Jaspers: Correspondence 1926–1969*. New York: Harcourt Brace Jovanovich.

1994. *Essays in Understanding, 1930–1954*. Jerome Kohn, ed. New York: Harcourt Brace and Company.

1996. *Love and Saint Augustine*. Joanna Vecchiarelli Scott and Judith Chelius Stark, eds. Chicago: University of Chicago Press.

Aristotle. 1985. *Nicomachean Ethics*. Terence Irwin, trans. Indianapolis: Hackett.

St. Augustine. 1953. *Augustine: Earlier Writings*. John H. S. Burleigh, trans. Philadelphia: Westminster Press.

1972. *The City of God*. Henry Bettenson, trans. New York: Penguin.

1997. *The Works of Saint Augustine*. Part III: Sermons, volume XI: *Newly Discovered Sermons*, Edmund Hill, OP, trans. and notes; John E. Rotelle, OSA, ed. Hyde Park, NY: New City Press.

Baier, Annette. 1994, "Moralism and Cruelty: Reflections on Hume and Kant." *Moral Prejudices*. Cambridge, MA: Harvard University Press, pp. 268–93.

Barber, Benjamin. 1988. *The Conquest of Politics: Liberal Philosophy in Democratic Times*. Princeton: Princeton University Press.

Barbour, John. 1984. *Tragedy as a Critique of Virtue*. Chico: Scholars Press.

Baron, Marcia. 1988. "Remorse and Agent-Regret." In *Midwest Studies in Philosophy*, volume XIII: *Ethical Theory: Character and Virtue*. Peter A. French, Theodore E. Uehling, Jr., and Howard K. Wettstein, eds. Notre Dame: University of Notre Dame Press, pp. 259–81.

Bauman, Zygmunt. 1989. *Modernity and the Holocaust*. Ithaca: Cornell University Press.

Beckley, Harlan R. and Charles M. Swezey, eds. 1988. *James M. Gustafson's Theocentric Ethics: Interpretations and Assessments*. Macon, GA: Mercer University Press.

Beiner, Ronald. 1982. "Hannah Arendt on Judging." In Arendt 1982, pp. 89–156.

1996. "Love and Worldliness: Hannah Arendt's Reading of Saint Augustine." In *Hannah Arendt Twenty Years Later*. Larry May and Jerome Kohn, eds. Cambridge, MA: MIT Press, pp. 269–84.

Benhabib, Seyla. 1992. *Situating the Self: Gender, Community, and Postmodernism in Contemporary Ethics*. New York: Routledge.

1996. *The Reluctant Modernism of Hannah Arendt*. Thousand Oaks, CA: Sage Publications.

Benjamin, Walter. 1977. *The Origin of German Tragic Drama*. John Osborne, trans. London: Verso.

1978. "Fate and Character." In *Reflections: Essays, Aphorisms, Autobiographical Writings*. Peter Demetz, ed. and Edmund Jephcott, trans. New York: Schocken Books, pp. 304–11.

Berkouwer, G. C. 1971. *Sin*. Philip C. Holtrop, trans. Grand Rapids, MI: Eerdmans.

Bernauer, James, SJ, ed. 1987. *Amor Mundi: Explorations in the Faith and Thought of Hannah Arendt*. Boston: Martinus Nijhoff.

Bernstein, Richard. 1992. *The New Constellation*. Cambridge, MA: MIT Press.

Berry, Wendell. 1983. "The Specialization of Poetry." *Standing by Words*. San Francisco: North Point Press, pp. 3–23.

Blumenberg, Hans. 1983. *The Legitimacy of the Modern Age*. Robert M. Wallace, trans. Cambridge, MA: MIT Press.

Bonhoeffer, Dietrich. 1997. *Creation and Fall: A Theological Exposition of Genesis 1–3*. Douglas Stephen Bax, trans. Minneapolis: Fortress Press.

Botting, Fred. 1996. *Gothic*. New York: Routledge.

——— 1998. "Horror." In *The Handbook to Gothic Literature*. Marie Mulvey-Roberts, ed. New York: New York University Press, pp. 123–31.

Bouchard, Larry D. 1988. *Tragic Method and Tragic Theology*. University Park: Pennsylvania State University Press.

Bowker, John. 1970. *Problems of Suffering in the Religions of the World*. Cambridge: Cambridge University Press.

Bowlin, John. 1997. "Augustine on Justifying Coercion." *Annual of the Society of Christian Ethics* 17: 49–70.

Brown, Peter. 1967. *Augustine of Hippo: A Biography*. Berkeley: University of California Press.

——— 1972. "Sorcery, Demons, and the Rise of Christianity: From Late Antiquity into the Middle Ages." *Religion and Society in the Age of Saint Augustine*. New York: Harper and Row, pp. 119–46.

——— 1981. *The Cult of the Saints: Its Rise and Function in Latin Christianity*. Chicago: University of Chicago Press.

——— 1988. *The Body and Society: Men, Women, and Sexual Renunciation in Early Christianity*. New York: Columbia University Press.

——— 1995. *Authority and the Sacred: Aspects of the Christianization of the Roman World*. New York: Cambridge University Press.

——— 1996. *The Rise of Western Christendom: Triumph and Diversity, AD 200–1000*. Cambridge, MA: Blackwell Publishers.

——— 1999. "*Gloriosus Obitus*: The End of the Ancient Other World." In *The Limits of Ancient Christianity: Essays on Late Antique Thought and Culture in Honor of R. A. Markus*. William E. Klingshirn and Mark Vessey, eds. Ann Arbor, MI: University of Michigan Press, pp. 289–314.

Brown, Robert McAfee. 1986. "Introduction." In *The Essential Reinhold Niebuhr: Selected Essays and Addresses*. R. M. Brown, ed. New Haven: Yale University Press, pp. xi–xxiv.

Browning, Christopher R. 1992. *Ordinary Men: Reserve Police Battalion 101 and the Final Solution in Poland*. New York: HarperPerennial.

Brunkhorst, Hauke. 1999. "The Modern Form of the Classical Republic." Louis Hunt, trans. In *Action and Contemplation: Studies in the Moral and Political Thought of Aristotle*. Robert C. Bartlett and Susan D. Collins, eds. Albany: SUNY Press, pp. 27–35

Brunner, José. 1996. "Eichmann, Arendt, and Freud in Jerusalem: On the Evils of Narcissism and the Pleasures of Thoughtlessness." *History and Memory* 8: 61–88.

Bultmann, Rudolf. 1984. *New Testament and Mythology, and Other Basic Writings.* Schubert Ogden, ed. Philadelphia: Fortress Press.

Burnaby, John. 1938. *Amor Dei: A Study in the Religion of Saint Augustine.* London: Hodder and Stoughton.

Burns, J. Patout. 1980. *The Development of Augustine's Doctrine of Operative Grace.* Paris: Institut d'Etudes augustiniennes.

Bynum, Caroline Walker. 1995. *The Resurrection of the Body in Western Christianity, 200–1336.* New York: Columbia University Press.

Camus, Albert. 1954. *The Rebel.* Anthony Bower, trans. New York: Alfred A. Knopf.

1955. *The Myth of Sisyphus and Other Essays.* Justin O'Brien, trans. New York: Alfred A. Knopf.

Canovan, Margaret. 1992. *Hannah Arendt: A Reinterpretation of Her Political Thought.* New York: Cambridge University Press.

Carr, Karen L. 1992. *The Banalization of Nihilism.* Albany: State University of New York Press.

Cavanaugh, William T. 1998. "Disney and Augustine on Coercion." Paper presented at the 1998 American Academy of Religion.

Cavell, Stanley. 1976. "Knowing and Acknowledging." *Must We Mean What We Say? A Book of Essays.* New York: Cambridge University Press, pp. 238–66.

1979. *The Claim of Reason: Wittgenstein, Skepticism, Morality, and Tragedy.* New York: Oxford University Press.

1989. "Finding as Founding." *This New Yet Unapproachable America: Lectures after Emerson after Wittgenstein.* Albuquerque, NM: Living Batch Press: pp. 77–118.

Chappell, T. D. J. 1995. *Aristotle and Augustine on Freedom: Two Theories of Freedom, Voluntary Action, and Akrasia.* London: St. Martin's Press.

Charry, Ellen. 1997. *By the Renewing of Your Minds: The Pastoral Roots of Christian Doctrine.* New York: Oxford University Press.

Cheney, Jim. 1997. "Naturalizing the Problem of Evil." *Environmental Ethics* 19: 299–313.

Christman, John, ed. 1989. *The Inner Citadel: Essays on Individual Autonomy.* New York: Oxford University Press.

Connolly, William. 1993. *The Augustinian Imperative: A Reflection on the Politics of Morality.* Newbury Park, CA: Sage Publications.

Cress, Donald A. 1989. "Augustine's Privation Account of Evil: A Defense." *Augustinian Studies* 20: 109–28.

Dalferth, Ingolf. 1984. "How is the Concept of Sin Related to the Concept of Moral Wrongdoing?" *Religious Studies* 20: 175–89.

Damascene, John. 1980. *On the Divine Images.* David Anderson, trans. Crestwood, NY: St. Vladimir's Seminary Press.

Davidson, Donald. 1984. "On the Very Idea of a Conceptual Scheme." *Inquiries Into Truth and Interpretation.* Oxford: Clarendon Press, pp. 183–98.

Davis, Mike. 1990. "Fortress L. A." *City of Quartz: Excavating the Future in Los Angeles*. London: Verso pp. 223–63.

Delbanco, Andrew. 1995. *The Death of Satan: How Americans Have Lost the Sense of Evil*. New York: Farrar, Strauss, Giroux.

Delumeau, Jean. 1990. *Sin and Fear: The Emergence of a Western Guilt Culture*. Eric Nicholson, trans. New York: St. Martin's Press.

Diner, Dan. 1997. "Hannah Arendt Reconsidered: On the Banal and the Evil in Her Holocaust Narrative." *New German Critique* 71: 177–90.

Disch, Lisa Jane. 1994. *Hannah Arendt and the Limits of Philosophy*. Ithaca: Cornell University Press.

Dodaro, Robert. 1994. "Eloquent Lies, Just Wars and the Politics of Persuasion: Reading Augustine's *City of God* in a 'Postmodern' World." *Augustinian Studies* 25: 77–138.

2000. "Augustine's Secular City." In Dodaro and Lawless, eds., pp. 231–59.

Dodaro, Robert and George Lawless, eds. 2000. *Augustine and His Critics*. New York: Routledge.

Donagan, Alan. 1993. "Moral Dilemmas, Genuine and Spurious: A Comparative Anatomy." *Ethics* 104: 7–21.

Dorrien, Gary. 1995. *Soul in Society: The Making and Renewal of Social Christianity*. Minneapolis: Fortress Press.

Dostal, Robert J. 1984. "Judging Human Action: Arendt's Appropriation of Kant." *The Review of Metaphysics* 37: 725–55.

Dreyfus, Hubert. 1991. *Being-in-the-World: A Commentary on Heidegger's* Being and Time, *Division I*. Cambridge, MA: MIT Press.

Droge, Arthur J. and James D. Tabor. 1992. *A Noble Death: Suicide and Martyrdom Among Jews and Christians in Antiquity*. San Francisco: HarperSanFrancisco.

Edmundson, Mark. 1990. *Towards Reading Freud: Self-Creation in Milton, Wordsworth, Emerson, and Sigmund Freud*. Princeton: Princeton University Press.

1993 "Introduction." In *Wild Orchids and Trotsky*. Mark Edmundson, ed. New York: Penguin, pp. 3–28.

1997. *Nightmare on Main Street: Angels, Sadomasochism, and the Culture of Gothic*. Cambridge, MA: Harvard University Press.

Eliot, T. S. 1970. "Gerontion." *The Collected Poems, 1909–1962*. New York: Harcourt Brace Jovanovich.

Elshtain, Jean Bethke. 1995a. *Augustine and the Limits of Politics*. Notre Dame: University of Notre Dame Press.

1995b. *Democracy on Trial*. New York: Basic Books.

Elster, Jon. 1983. *Sour Grapes*. New York: Cambridge University Press.

Emerson, Ralph Waldo. 1957. *Selections from Ralph Waldo Emerson*. Stephen E. Whicher, ed. Boston: Houghton Mifflin.

Evans, G. R. 1982. *Augustine on Evil*. New York: Cambridge University Press.

Farley, Edward. 1990. *Good and Evil: Interpreting a Human Condition*. Minneapolis: Fortress Press.

Farley, Wendy. 1990. *Tragic Vision and Divine Compassion*. Philadelphia: Westminster/ John Knox Press.

Farrell, Frank B. 1994. *Subjectivity, Realism, and Postmodernism – The Recovery of the World*. New York: Cambridge University Press.

Fish, Stanley. 1967. *Surprised by Sin: The Reader in Paradise Lost*. Berkeley: University of California Press.

Flathman, Richard. 1992. *Willful Liberalism: Voluntarism and Individuality in Political Theory and Practice*. Ithaca: Cornell University Press.

Foley, Richard. 1993. *Working Without a Net: A study in Egocentric Epistemology*. New York: Oxford University Press.

Forsyth, Neil. 1987. *The Old Enemy: Satan and the Combat Myth*. Princeton: Princeton University Press.

Foucault, Michel. 1978. *The History of Sexuality*, volume I: *Introduction*. Robert Hurley, trans. New York: Random House.

Fox, Richard Wightman. 1985. *Reinhold Niebuhr: A Biography*. San Francisco: Harper and Row.

Frankfurt, Harry. 1988. *The Importance of What We Care About: Philosophical Essays*. New York: Cambridge University Press.

Freud, Sigmund. 1961. *Civilization and Its Discontents*. James Strachey, trans. New York: W. W. Norton.

Fukuyama, Francis. 1992. *The End of History and the Last Man*. New York: Free Press.

Gadamer, Hans-Georg. 1989. *Truth and Method*. Revised edition. Joel Weinsheimer and Donald Marshall, trans. New York: Crossroad.

Galison, Peter. 1995. "Theory Bound and Unbound: Superstrings and Experiment." In *The Laws of Nature: Essays on the Philosophical, Scientific and Historical Dimensions*. Friedel Weinert, ed. New York: Walter de Gruyter, pp. 369–408.

Gamwell, Franklin I. 1975. "Reinhold Niebuhr's Theistic Ethic." In Scott. ed., pp. 63–84.

1990. *The Divine Good: Modern Moral Theory and The Necessity of God*. San Francisco: HarperSanFrancisco.

Geuss, Raymond. 1981. *The Idea of a Critical Theory*. New York: Cambridge University Press.

Giddens, Anthony. 1991. *The Consequences of Modernity*. Stanford: Stanford University Press.

Gilkey, Langdon. 1975. "Reinhold Niebuhr's Theology of History." In Scott, ed., pp. 36–62.

Gillespie, Michael Allen. 1995. *Nihilism Before Nietzsche*. Chicago: University of Chicago Press.

Goldberg, Carl. 1996. *Speaking with the Devil: A Dialogue with Evil*. New York: Viking.

Goldhill, Simon. 1986. *Reading Greek Tragedy*. Cambridge: Cambridge University Press.

Gowans, Christopher. 1994. *Innocence Lost: An Examination of Inescapable Moral Wrongdoing*. New York: Oxford University Press.

Graeme, Gordon. 1996. "Tolerance, Pluralism, and Relativism." In *Tolerance: An*

Elusive Virtue? David Heyd, ed. Princeton: Princeton University Press, pp. 44–59.

Graham, Gordon. 2001. *Evil and Christian Ethics*. New York: Cambridge University Press.

Greenspan, Patricia. 1995. *Practical Guilt: Moral Dilemmas, Emotions, and Social Norms*. New York: Oxford University Press.

Griffiths, Paul J. 1999a. "The Gift and the Lie: Augustine on Lying." *Communio* 26: 3–30.

1999b. "How Epistemology Matters to Theology." *The Journal of Religion* 79: 1–18.

Guignon, Charles. 1991. "Pragmatism or Hermeneutics? Epistemology after Foundationalism." *The Interpretive Turn: Philosophy, Science, Culture*. Ithaca: Cornell University Press, pp. 81–101.

Guroian, Vigen. 1987. *Incarnate Love: Essays in Orthodox Ethics*. Notre Dame: University of Notre Dame Press.

Gustafson, James M. 1975. *Can Ethics Be Christian?* Chicago: University of Chicago Press.

1981. *Ethics from a Theocentric Perspective*, volume 1: *Theology and Ethics*. Chicago: University of Chicago Press.

1986. "Theology in the Service of Ethics: An Interpretation of Reinhold Niebuhr's Theological Ethics." In Harries, ed., pp. 24–45.

Gutmann, Amy and Dennis Thompson. 1996. *Democracy and Disagreement*. Cambridge, MA: Belknap Press of Harvard University Press.

Haack, Susan. 1993. *Evidence and Inquiry: Towards Reconstruction in Philosophy*. Oxford: Basil Blackwell.

Habermas, Jürgen. 1983. "Hannah Arendt: On the Concept of Power." *Philosophical-Political Profiles*. Cambridge, MA: MIT Press, pp. 171–87.

Hadot, Pierre. 1995. *Philosophy as a Way of Life*. Oxford: Basil Blackwell.

Halttunen, Karen. 1998. *Murder Most Foul: The Killer and the American Gothic Imagination*. Cambridge, MA: Harvard University Press.

Hampshire, Stuart. 1983. *Morality and Conflict*. Cambridge, MA: Harvard University Press.

Harnack, Adolph von. 1899. *History of Dogma*. Neil Buchanan, trans. Boston: Little, Brown.

Harries, Richard, ed. 1986. *Reinhold Niebuhr and the Issues of our Time*. London: Mowbray.

Harrison, Carol. 2000. *Augustine: Christian Truth and Fractured Humanity*. New York: Oxford University Press.

Harvey, David. 1989. *The Condition of Postmodernity*. Oxford: Basil Blackwell.

Hauerwas, Stanley, with Richard Bondi and David B. Burrell. 1977. *Truthfulness and Tragedy*. Notre Dame: University of Notre Dame Press.

with Charles Pinches. 1997. *Christians Among the Virtues*. Notre Dame: University of Notre Dame Press.

with Michael Broadway. 1997. "The Irony of Reinhold Niebuhr: The Ideological Character of 'Christian Realism'." In Stanley Hauerwas,

Wilderness Wanderings: Probing Twentieth-Century Theology and Philosophy. Boulder, CO: Westview Press, pp. 48–61.

Havel, Vaclav. 1985. "The Power of the Powerless." In *The Power of the Powerless: Citizens Against the State in Central-Eastern Europe.* John Keane, ed. Armonk, NY: M. E. Sharpe.

Hebblethwaite, Brian. 1989. "MacKinnon and the Problem of Evil." In *Christ, Ethics, and Tragedy: Essays in Honor of Donald MacKinnon.* Kenneth Surin, ed. New York: Cambridge University Press, pp. 131–45.

Heidegger, Martin. 1959. *An Introduction to Metaphysics.* New Haven: Yale University Press.

1962. *Being and Time.* John MacQuarrie and Edward Robinson, trans. New York: Harper and Row.

Heinaman, Robert, ed. 1995. *Aristotle and Moral Realism.* Boulder, CO: Westview Press.

Herdt, Jennifer. 1992. "Cruelty, Liberalism, and the Quarantine of Irony: Rorty on the Disjunction Between Public and Private." *Soundings* 75: 79–96.

Hick, John. 1978. *Evil and the God of Love.* Revised edition. San Francisco: Harper and Row.

Hinchman, Lewis and Sandra Hinchman. 1994. "Existentialism Politicized: Arendt's Debt to Jaspers." In *Hannah Arendt: Critical Essays.* Lewis Hinchman and Sandra Hinchman, eds. Albany: State University of New York Press, pp. 143–78.

Hirschman, Albert O. 1977. *The Passions and the Interests.* Princeton: Princeton University Press.

Hollander, Paul. 1997. "Revisiting 'The Banality of Evil': Political Violence in Communist Systems." *Partisan Review* 64: 50–62.

Holmes, Arthur L. 1989. *On War and Morality.* Princeton: Princeton University Press.

Holmes, Stephen. 1979. "Aristippus In and Out of Athens." *American Political Science Review* 73: 113–28.

Honig, Bonnie. 1988. "Arendt, Identity, and Difference." *Political Theory* 16: 77–98.

1993. "The Politics of Agonism." *Political Theory* 21: 520–32.

ed. 1995a. *Feminist Interpretations of Hannah Arendt.* University Park: Pennsylvania State University Press.

1995b. "Towards an Agonistic Feminism: Hannah Arendt and the Politics of Identity." In Honig, ed., 1995a, pp. 135–66.

Howespian, A. A. 1997. "Sin and Psychosis." In *Limning the Psyche: Explorations in Christian Psychology.* Robert C. Roberts and Mark R. Talbot, eds. Grand Rapids, MI: Eerdmans, pp. 264–81.

Hume, David. 1975. *Enquiries Concerning Human Understanding and Concerning the Principles of Morals.* L. A. Selby-Bigge, ed., P. H. Nidditch, rev. Oxford: Clarendon Press.

Hurka, Thomas. 1993. *Perfectionism.* New York: Oxford University Press.

Hurley, Susan. 1989. *Natural Reasons.* New York: Oxford University Press.

Hursthouse, Rosalind. 1996. "Normative Virtue Ethics." In *How Should One Live? Essays on the Virtues.* Roger Crisp, ed. Oxford: Clarendon Press, pp. 19–36.

Ignatieff, Michael. 1998. *The Warrior's Honor: Ethnic War and the Modern Conscience.* New York: Metropolitan Books.

Isaac, Jeffrey C. 1992. *Arendt, Camus, and Modern Rebellion.* New Haven: Yale University Press.

1998. *Democracy in Dark Times.* Ithaca: Cornell University Press.

Jackson, Timothy P. 1993. "Liberalism and *Agape*: The Priority of Charity to Democracy and Philosophy." *The Annual of the Society of Christian Ethics* 13: 47–72.

Jacobitti, Suzanne. 1988. "Hannah Arendt and the Will." *Political Theory* 16: 53–76.

1996. "Thinking about the Self." In *Hannah Arendt: Twenty Years Later.* Larry May and Jerome Kohn, eds. Cambridge, MA: MIT Press, pp. 199–219.

James, Henry. 1987. *Selected Letters.* Leon Edel, ed. Cambridge, MA: Belknap Press of Harvard University Press.

Jameson, Frederic. 1990. *Postmodernism; or, The Cultural Logic of Late Capitalism.* Durham, NC: Duke University Press.

Jaspers, Karl. 1952. *Tragedy Is Not Enough.* Boston: Beacon Press.

Jones, L. Gregory. 1992. "The Love Which *Love's Knowledge* Knows Not: Nussbaum's Evasion of Christianity." *The Thomist* 56: 323–37.

1995. *Embodying Forgiveness.* Grand Rapids, MI: Eerdmans.

Jordan, Mark. 1992. *The Alleged Aristotelianism of Thomas Aquinas.* Etienne Gilson Lecture Series 15. Toronto: Pontifical Institute of Medieval Studies.

Kamitsuka, David G. 1996. "The Justification of Religious Belief in the Pluralistic Public Realm: Another Look at Postliberal Apologetics." *The Journal of Religion* 76: 588–606.

Kant, Immanuel. 1960. *Religion Within the Limits of Reason Alone.* Theodore M. Greene and Hoyt H. Hudson, trans. New York: Harper and Row.

1965. *Critique of Pure Reason.* Norman Kemp Smith, trans. New York: St. Martin's Press.

Kateb, George. 1983. *Hannah Arendt: Politics, Conscience, Evil.* Totowa, NJ: Rowman and Allanheld.

1992. *The Inner Ocean: Essays on Democracy and Individualism.* Ithaca: Cornell University Press.

Kaufman, Peter Iver. 1982. *Augustinian Piety and Catholic Reform: Augustine, Colet, and Erasmus.* Macon, GA: Mercer University Press.

Keenan, Alan. 1994. "Promises, Promises: The Abyss of Freedom and the Fate of the Political in Hannah Arendt." *Political Theory* 22: 297–322.

Kegley, Charles W. and Robert W. Bretall, eds. 1961. *Reinhold Niebuhr: His Religious, Social, and Political Thought.* New York: Macmillan.

Kekes, John. 1990. *Facing Evil.* Princeton: Princeton University Press.

1998. "The Reflexivity of Evil." *Social Philosophy and Policy* 15: 216–32.

Kellerman, Bill. 1987. "Apologist of Power." *Sojourners* 16: 14–20.

Kelly, Henry Ansgar. 1993. *Ideas and Forms of Tragedy from Aristotle to the Middle Ages.* New York: Cambridge University Press.

Kemp, Anthony. 1991. *The Estrangement of the Past: A Study in the Origins of Modern Historical Consciousness*. New York: Oxford University Press.

Kent, Bonnie. 1995. *Virtues of the Will: The Transformation of Ethics in the Late Thirteenth Century*. Washington: Catholic University of America Press.

Kerr, Fergus. 1997. *Immortal Longings: Versions of Transcending Humanity*. Notre Dame: University of Notre Dame Press.

Kideckel, David A. 1993. *The Solitude of Collectivism: Romanian Villagers to the Revolution and Beyond*. Ithaca: Cornell University Press.

Kierkegaard, Søren. 1991. *Practice in Christianity*. Howard V. Hong and Edna H. Hong, trans. Princeton: Princeton University Press.

Kohák, Erazim. 1984. *The Embers and the Stars*. Chicago: University of Chicago Press.

Koselleck, Reinhart. 1988. *Critique and Crisis*. Cambridge, MA: MIT Press.

Kroeker, P. Travis. 1995. *Christian Ethics and Political Economy in North America: A Critical Analysis*. Montreal: McGill-Queen's University Press.

Kuhns, Richard. 1991. *Tragedy: Repression and Denial*. Chicago: University of Chicago Press.

Kvanvig, Jonathan L. 1993. *The Problem of Hell*. New York: Oxford University Press.

Lacey, Michael J., ed. 1989. *Religion and Twentieth-Century American Intellectual Life*. New York: Cambridge University Press.

Lamberigts, Mathijs. 2000. "A Critical Evaluation of Critiques of Augustine's View of Sexuality." In Dodaro and Lawless, eds., pp. 176–97.

Lang, Berel. 1991. "Hannah Arendt and the Politics of Evil." *Writing and the Moral Self*. New York: Routledge, pp. 140–54.

2000. "The History of Evil, The Holocaust, and Postmodernity." *The Hedgehog Review* 2:2: 57–66.

Langan, John P. 1979. "Augustine on the Unity and the Interconnection of the Virtues." *Harvard Theological Review* 72: 81–96.

Lasch, Christopher. 1991. *The True and Only Heaven: Progress and its Critics*. New York: W. W. Norton & Co.

Latour, Bruno. 1993. *We Have Never Been Modern*. Catherine Porter, trans. Cambridge, MA: Harvard University Press.

Lawless, George. 2000. "Augustine's Decentering of Asceticism." In Dodaro and Lawless, eds., pp. 142–63.

Lear, Jonathan. 1990. *Love and Its Place in Nature: A Philosophical Interpretation of Freudian Psychoanalysis*. New York: Farrar Strauss and Giroux.

1998. *Open Minded: Working out the Logic of the Soul*. Cambridge, MA: Harvard University Press.

Levenson, Jon. 1989. *Creation and the Persistence of Evil*. San Francisco: Harper and Row.

Levinas, Emmanuel. 1988. "Useless Suffering." Richard Cohen, trans. In *The Provocation of Levinas: Rethinking the Other*. Robert Bernasconi and David Wood, eds. London: Routledge, pp. 158–67.

Lewis, C. S. 1996. *The Problem of Pain*. New York: Touchstone Edition.

Lindbeck, George. 1984. *The Nature of Doctrine: Religion and Theology in a Postliberal Age*. Philadelphia: Westminster Press.

Loriaux, Michael. 1992. "The Realists and Saint Augustine: Skepticism, Psychology, and Moral Action in International Relations Thought." *International Studies Quarterly* 36: 401–20.

Louth, Andrew. 1983. *Discerning the Mystery: An Essay on the Nature of Theology*. Oxford: Clarendon Press.

Lovibond, Sabina. 1983. *Realism and Imagination in Ethics*. Minneapolis: University of Minnesota Press.

Lovin, Robin. 1995. *Reinhold Niebuhr and Christian Realism*. New York: Cambridge University Press.

Lyman, Stanford M. 1978. *The Seven Deadly Sins: Society and Evil*. New York: St. Martin's Press.

Lyotard, Jean-François. 1984. *The Postmodern Condition: A Report on Knowledge*. Geoff Bennington and Brian Massumi, trans. Minneapolis: University of Minnesota Press.

MacDonald, Scott, ed. 1991. *Being and Goodness*. Ithaca: Cornell University Press.
    1999. "Primal Sin." In Matthews, ed., pp. 110–39.

MacIntyre, Alasdair. 1990. *Three Rival Versions of Moral Enquiry: Encyclopaedia, Genealogy, and Tradition*. Notre Dame: University of Notre Dame Press.
    1998. "Plain Persons and Moral Philosophy: Rules, Virtues, and Goods." In *The MacIntyre Reader*. Kelvin Knight, ed. Notre Dame: University of Notre Dame Press, pp. 136–52.

Mackinnon, D. M. 1968. "Atonement and Tragedy." *Borderlands of Theology and Other Essays*. New York: J. B. Lippincott, pp. 97–104.

Madec, Goulven. 1994. "Saint Augustin est-il le malin génie de l'Europe?" *Petites Etudes augustiniennes*. Paris: Institut d'Etudes augustiniennes, pp. 319–30.

Magnus, Bernd. 1997. "Holocaust Child: Reflections on the Banality of Evil." *Philosophy Today* 41: 8–18.

Mahoney, John. 1987. *The Making of Moral Theology: A Study of the Roman Catholic Tradition*. Oxford: Clarendon.

Markus, R. A. 1990. "Augustine: A Defence of Christian Mediocrity." *The End of Ancient Christianity*. New York: Cambridge University Press, pp. 45–62.

Marx, Leo. 1996. "The Domination of Nature and the Redefinition of Progress." In Marx and Mazlish, eds., pp. 201–18.

Marx, Leo, and Bruce Mazlish, eds. 1996. *Progress: Fact or Illusion?* Ann Arbor, MI: University of Michigan Press.

Mathewes, Charles T. 1998. "Pluralism, Otherness, and the Augustinian Tradition." *Modern Theology* 14: 83–112.
    1999. "Augustinian Anthropology: *Interior intimo meo*." *The Journal of Religious Ethics* 27: 195–221.

Matthews, Gareth. 1992. *Thought's Ego in Augustine and Descartes*. Ithaca: Cornell University Press.
    ed. 1999. *The Augustinian Tradition*. Berkeley: University of California Press.

Mazlish, Bruce. 1996. "Progress: A Historical and Critical Perspective." In Marx and Mazlish, eds., pp. 27–44.

McCann, Dennis. 1981. *Christian Realism and Liberation Theology: Practical Theologies in Creative Conflict.* Maryknoll: Orbis Books.

McCole, John. 1993. *Walter Benjamin and the Antinomies of Tradition.* Ithaca: Cornell University Press.

McCullogh, C. Behan. 1992. "Evil and the Love of God." *Sophia* 31: 48–60.

McDowell, John. 1994. *Mind and World.* Cambridge, MA: Harvard University Press.
1998. *Mind, Value, and Reality.* Cambridge, MA: Harvard University Press.

McLynn, Neil. 1999. "Augustine's Roman Empire." *Augustinian Studies* 30: 29–44.

Mendus, Susan. 1996. "Tragedy, Moral Conflict, and Liberalism." In *Philosophy and Pluralism: Royal Institute of Philosophy, Supplemental Volume 40.* David Archard, ed. Cambridge: Cambridge University Press, pp. 191–201.

Menn, Stephen. 1998. *Descartes and Augustine.* New York: Cambridge University Press.

Merrin, Jeredith. 1990. *An Enabling Humility: Marianne Moore, Elizabeth Bishop, and the Uses of Tradition.* New Brunswick, NJ: Rutgers University Press.

Meyer, Donald. 1988. *The Protestant Search for Political Realism: 1919–1941.* Second edition. Middletown, CT: Wesleyan University Press.

Midgley, Mary. 1986. *Wickedness: A Philosophical Essay.* New York: ARK Paperbacks.
1992. *Why Can't We Make Moral Judgments?* New York: St. Martin's Press.

Milbank, John. 1990. *Theology and Social Theory Beyond Secular Reason.* Oxford: Basil Blackwell.
1997. *The Word Made Strange: Theology, Language, Culture.* Oxford: Blackwell.

Miles, Rebekah. 1996. "Freeing Bonds and Binding Freedom: Reinhold Niebuhr and Feminist Critics on Paternal Dominion and Maternal Constraint." *The Annual of the Society of Christian Ethics* 16: 121–43.

Mohrmann, Margaret. 1995. *Medicine as Ministry.* Cleveland: Pilgrim Press.

Monleón, José B. 1990. *A Specter is Haunting Europe: A Sociohistorical Approach to the Fantastic.* Princeton: Princeton University Press.

Moody-Adams, Michelle. 1997. *Fieldwork in Familiar Places: Morality, Culture, and Philosophy.* Cambridge, MA: Harvard University Press.

Morris, David B. 1991. *The Culture of Pain.* Berkeley: University of California Press.

Morris, Thomas V. 1987. *Anselmian Explorations.* Notre Dame: University of Notre Dame Press.

Müller, Jan-Werner. 2000. *Another Country: German Intellectuals, Unification and National Identity.* New Haven: Yale University Press.

Murdoch, Iris. 1985. *The Sovereignty of Good.* London: ARK Paperbacks.

Murphy, Nancey. 1990. *Theology in the Age of Scientific Reasoning.* Ithaca: Cornell University Press.

Murphy, Nancey and George F. R. Ellis. 1996. *On the Moral Order of the Universe: Theology, Cosmology, and Ethics.* Minneapolis: Fortress Press.

Nagel, Thomas. 1979. "What Is It Like To Be A Bat?" *Mortal Questions*. New York: Cambridge University Press, pp. 165–80.

 1982. "Moral Luck." In *Free Will*. Gary Watson, ed. New York: Oxford University Press.

 1986. *The View from Nowhere*. New York: Oxford University Press, pp. 174–86.

Niebuhr, H. Richard. 1951. *Christ and Culture*. New York: Harper and Brothers.

 1963. *The Responsible Self*. New York: Harper and Row.

 1996. *Theology, History, and Culture: Major Unpublished Writings*. William Stacy Johnson, ed. New Haven: Yale University Press.

Niebuhr, Reinhold. 1932. *Moral Man and Immoral Society*. New York: Charles Scribners' Sons.

 1935. *An Interpretation of Christian Ethics*. New York: Harper and Brothers.

 1937. *Beyond Tragedy*. New York: Charles Scribners' Sons.

 1940. "Greek Tragedy and Modern Politics." *Christianity and Power Politics*. New York: Charles Scribners' Sons, pp. 95–105.

 1941. *The Nature and Destiny of Man*, volume I: *Human Nature*. New York: Charles Scribners' Sons.

 1942. "Religion and Action." In *Science and Man*. Ruth Nada Anshen, ed. New York: Harcourt Brace and Company, pp. 44–64.

 1943. *The Nature and Destiny of Man*, volume II: *Human Destiny*. New York: Charles Scribners' Sons.

 1944. *The Children of Light and the Children of Darkness*. New York: Charles Scribners' Sons.

 1949. *Faith and History*. New York: Charles Scribners' Sons.

 1953. "Augustine's Political Realism." *Christian Realism and Political Problems*. New York: Charles Scribners' Sons, pp. 119–46.

 1955. *The Self and the Dramas of History*. New York: Charles Scribners' Sons.

 1962. *The Irony of American History*. New York: Charles Scribners' Sons.

 1986. *The Essential Reinhold Niebuhr: Selected Essays and Addresses*. Robert McAfee Brown, ed. New Haven: Yale University Press.

 1991. "The King's Chapel and the King's Court." In *Reinhold Niebuhr: Theologian of Public Life*. Larry Rasmussen, ed. Minneapolis: Fortress Press.

Nietzsche, Friedrich. 1966. *Beyond Good and Evil*. Walter Kaufmann, trans. New York: Random House.

 1967. *On the Genealogy of Morals*. Walter Kaufmann, trans. New York: Random House.

 1982. *Nietzsche Briefwechsel*, volume III: *Briefe–Januar 1885–December 1886*. Berlin: Walter de Gruyter.

Nino, Carlos Santiago. 1996. *Radical Evil on Trial*. New Haven: Yale University Press.

Nussbaum, Martha. 1986. *The Fragility of Goodness: Moral Luck in Greek Philosophy and Tragedy*. New York: Cambridge University Press.

 1990. *Love's Knowledge: Essays on Philosophy and Literature*. New York: Oxford University Press.

 1994. *The Therapy of Desire: Theory and Practice in Hellenistic Ethics*. Princeton: Princeton University Press.

Nussbaum, Martha, and Amartya Sen, eds. 1993. *The Quality of Life*. Oxford: Clarendon Press.

Oakeshott, Michael. 1991. "Rationalism in Politics." *Rationalism in Politics and Other Essays*. Indianapolis: Liberty Press, pp. 5–42.

O'Connor, David. 1988. "In Defense of Theoretical Theodicy." *Modern Theology* 5: 61–74.

O'Connor, Flannery. 1971. "Everything That Rises Must Converge." *The Collected Stories of Flannery O'Connor*. New York: Farrar Strauss Giroux, pp. 405–20.

O'Daly, Gerald. 1987. *Augustine's Philosophy of Mind*. Berkeley: University of California Press.

O'Donnell, James J. 1991. "The Authority of Augustine." *Augustinian Studies* 22: 7–35.

O'Donovan, Oliver. 1987. "Augustine's *City of God* xix and Western Political Thought." *Dionysius* 11: 89–110.

  1996. *The Desire of the Nations: Rediscovering the Roots of Political Theology*. New York: Cambridge University Press.

Ortega y Gasset, José. 1932. *The Revolt of the Masses*. New York: W. W. Norton and Co.

Orwell, George. 1981. "Reflections on Gandhi." *A Collection of Essays*. New York: Harcourt Brace Jovanovich, pp. 171–80.

Pagels, Elaine. 1988. *Adam, Eve, and the Serpent*. New York: Random House.

Parkes, Graham. 1994. *Composing the Soul: Reaches of Nietzsche's Psychology*. Chicago: University of Chicago Press.

Parkin, David, ed. 1985. *The Anthropology of Evil*. Oxford: Basil Blackwell.

Pascal, Blaise. 1967. *Provincial Letters*. A. J. Krailsheimer, trans. New York: Penguin.

Perl, Jeffrey. 1989. *Skepticism and Modern Enmity: Before and After Eliot*. Baltimore: Johns Hopkins University Press.

Peterson, Michael L. 1997. "The Problem of Evil." In Taliaferro and Quinn, eds., pp. 393–401.

Phillips, Adam. 1996. *Terrors and Experts*. Cambridge, MA: Harvard University Press.

Picard, Max. 1951. *The Flight from God*. Marianne Kuschnitzky and J. M. Cameron, trans. Washington: Regnery Gateway.

Pieper, Joseph. 1952. *Leisure, the Basis of Culture*. New York: Pantheon Books.

Pinches, Charles. 1987. "On Form and Content in Christian Ethics." *Sophia* 26: 4–14.

Pippin, Robert. 1991. *Modernism as a Philosophical Problem: On the Dissatisfactions of European High Culture*. Cambridge, MA: Basil Blackwell.

  1997. *Idealism as Modernism: Hegelian Variations*. New York: Cambridge University Press.

Pitkin, Hannah. 1981. "Justice: On Relating Private and Public." *Political Theory* 9: 327–52.

  1998. *The Attack of the Blob: Hannah Arendt's Concept of the Social*. Chicago: University of Chicago Press.

Placher, William. 1996. *The Domestication of Transcendence: How Modern Thinking about God Went Wrong.* Louisville, KY: Westminster/John Knox Press.

Plantinga, Alvin. 1974. *God, Freedom, and Evil.* Grand Rapids, MI: Eerdmans.

1992. "Augustinian Christian Philosophy." *The Monist* 75: 291–320.

1993. *Warrant and Proper Function.* New York: Oxford University Press.

Plantinga, Cornelius, Jr. 1995. *Not the Way It's Supposed to Be: A Breviary of Sin.* Grand Rapids, MI: Eerdmans.

Platts, Mark. 1997. *Ways of Meaning.* Second edition. Cambridge, MA: MIT Press.

Porter, Jean. 1998. "'Mere History': The Place of Historical Studies in Theological Ethics." *The Journal of Religious Ethics* 25: 103–26.

Postman, Neil. 1985. *Amusing Ourselves to Death: Public Discourse in the Age of Show Business.* New York: Penguin.

Power, Kim. 1996. *Veiled Desires: Augustine on Women.* New York: Seabury.

Praz, Mario. 1992. *The Romantic Agony.* Second edition. Angus Davidson, trans. Oxford: Oxford University Press.

Prendville, John G., SJ. 1972. "The Development of the Idea of Habit in the Thought of Saint Augustine." *Traditio* 28: 19–99.

Principe, Walter H., CSB. 1982. "The Dynamism of Augustine's Terms for Describing the Highest Trinitarian Image in the Human Person." In *Studia Patristica.* E. A. Livingstone, ed. Volume XVII, pp. 1291–9. New York: Pergamon Press.

Proudfoot, Wayne. 1985. *Religious Experience.* Berkeley: University of California Press.

Pryzwara, Erich. 1957. "St. Augustine and the Modern World." In *Saint Augustine: His Life, Age, and Thought.* Grove City: Meridian, pp. 249–86.

Punter, David. 1996. *The Literature of Terror,* volume II: *The Modern Gothic.* Second edition. New York: Longman.

Putnam, Hilary. 1983. "Convention: A Theme in Philosophy." In *Realism and Reason: Philosophical Papers, Volume 3.* New York: Cambridge University Press, pp. 170–83.

Putt, B. Keith. 1997. "Indignation Toward Evil: Ricoeur and Caputo on a Theodicy of Protest." *Philosophy Today* 41: 460–71.

Quinn, Philip L. 1997. "Sin and Original Sin." In Taliaferro and Quinn, eds., pp. 541–8.

Rahner, Karl, SJ. 1961. *Theological Investigations,* volume I: *God, Christ, Mary, and Grace.* Baltimore: Helicon Press.

Ramsey, Paul. 1970. *Fabricated Man: The Ethics of Genetic Control.* New Haven: Yale University Press.

Raz, Joseph. 1986. *The Morality of Freedom.* Oxford: Clarendon Press.

Reeve, C. D. C. 1988. *Philosopher Kings: The Argument of Plato's Republic.* Princeton: Princeton University Press.

1992. *Practices of Reason: Aristotle's Nicomachean Ethics.* Oxford: Clarendon Press.

Reichenbach, Bruce. 1982. *Evil and a Good God.* New York: Fordham University Press.

Ricks, Christopher. 1993. *Beckett's Dying Words*. Oxford: Clarendon Press.

Ricoeur, Paul. 1966. *Freedom and Nature: The Voluntary and the Involuntary*. Erazim V. Kohák, trans. Evanston: Northwestern University Press.

1967. *The Symbolism of Evil*. E. Buchanan, trans. Boston: Beacon Press.

1974. *The Conflict of Interpretations*. Evanston: Northwestern University Press.

1985. "Evil, a Challenge to Philosophy and Theology." *The Journal of the American Academy of Religion* 53: 635–48.

1992. *Oneself as Another*. Kathleen Blamey, trans. Chicago: University of Chicago Press.

Riesman, David, Reuel Denney, and Nathan Glazer. 1950. *The Lonely Crowd: A Study of the Changing American Character*. New Haven: Yale University Press.

Rist, John. 1995. *Augustine: Ancient Thought Baptised*. New York: Cambridge University Press.

Roberts, Tyler T. 1996. "This Art of Transfiguration *Is* Philosophy: Nietzsche's Asceticism." *The Journal of Religion* 76: 402–27.

Rogozinski, Jacob. 1993. "Hell on Earth: Hannah Arendt in the Face of Hitler." *Philosophy Today* 37: 257–74.

Rorty, Amélie Oksenberg. 1992. "The Psychology of Aristotelian Tragedy." In *Essays on Aristotle's Poetics*. Amélie Oksenberg Rorty, ed. Princeton: Princeton University Press, pp. 1–22.

1997. "The Social and Political Sources of Akrasia." *Ethics* 107: 644–57.

Rorty, Richard. 1989. *Contingency, Irony, and Solidarity*. New York: Cambridge University Press.

1998a. *Achieving our Country: Leftist Thought in Twentieth-Century America*. Cambridge, MA: Harvard University Press.

1998b. *Truth and Progress: Philosophical Papers Volume 3*. New York: Cambridge University Press.

Rose, Gillian. 1996. *Mourning Becomes the Law: Philosophy and Representation*. Cambridge: Cambridge University Press.

Russell, Frederick H. 1990. " 'Only Something Good Can be Evil': The Genesis of Augustine's Secular Ambivalence." *Theological Studies* 51: 698–716.

Saak, Eric Leland. 1997. "The Reception of Augustine in the Later Middle Ages." In *The Reception of the Church Fathers in the West: From the Carolingians to the Maurists*. Irena Backus, ed. Leiden: E. J. Brill, pp. 367–404.

Sandel, Michael. 1996. *Democracy's Discontent: America in Search of a Public Philosophy*. Cambridge, MA: Belknap Press of Harvard University Press.

Sands, Kathleen. 1994. *Escape from Paradise: Evil and Tragedy in Feminist Theology*. Minneapolis: Fortress Press.

Santurri, Edmund N. 1987. *Perplexity in the Moral Life: Philosophical and Theological Considerations*. Charlottesville, VA: University Press of Virginia.

Sayre-McCord, Geoffrey, ed. 1988. *Essays on Moral Realism*. Ithaca: Cornell University Press.

Scheffler, Samuel. 1992. *Human Morality*. New York: Oxford University Press.

Schleiermacher, Friedrich. 1928. *The Christian Faith*. H. R. MacKintosh and J. S. Steward, eds. Edinburgh: T. & T. Clark.

Schuld, J. Joyce. 2000. "Augustine, Foucault, and the Politics of Imperfection." *Journal of Religion* 80: 1–22.

Schweiker, William. 1990. *Mimetic Reflections.* New York: Fordham University Press.

1995. *Responsibility and Christian Ethics.* New York: Cambridge University Press.

Scott, Michael. 1996. "The Morality of Theodicies." *Religious Studies* 32: 1–13.

Scott, Nathan A., Jr., ed. 1975. *The Legacy of Reinhold Niebuhr.* Chicago: University of Chicago Press.

Searle, John. 1995. *The Construction of Social Reality.* New York: Free Press.

Sedgwick, Eve Kosofsky. 1990. *Epistemology of the Closet.* Berkeley: University of California Press.

Shklar, Judith. 1984. *Ordinary Vices.* Cambridge, MA: Belknap Press of Harvard University Press.

Simon, Ulrich. 1989. *Pity and Terror: Christianity and Tragedy.* New York: St. Martin's Press.

Smith, Thomas W. 1995. "The Uses of Tragedy: Reinhold Niebuhr's Theory of History and International Ethics." *Ethics and International Affairs* 9: 171–91.

Song, Robert. 1997. *Christianity and Liberal Society.* Oxford: Clarendon Press.

Sophocles. 1992. *Antigone.* In *The Complete Greek Tragedies,* volume II: *Sophocles.* David Grene, trans. Chicago: University of Chicago Press.

Sperber, Dan. 1985. *On Anthropological Knowledge.* New York: Cambridge University Press.

Stassen, Glen H., D. M. Yeager, and John Howard Yoder. 1996. *Authentic Transformation: A New Vision of Christ and Culture.* Nashville: Abingdon Press.

Statman, Daniel, ed. 1993. *Moral Luck.* Albany: State University of New York Press.

Steiner, George. 1989. *Real Presences.* Chicago: University of Chicago Press.

1996. "Absolute Tragedy." *No Passion Spent: Essays 1978–1996.* London: Faber and Faber, pp. 129–41.

Stocker, Michael. 1990. *Plural and Conflicting Values.* New York: Oxford University Press.

Stone, Ronald. 1980. *Reinhold Niebuhr: Prophet to Politicians.* New York: University Press of America.

Stout, Jeffrey. 1988. "Virtue Among the Ruins." In *Ethics After Babel: The Languages of Morals and Their Discontents.* Boston: Beacon Books, pp. 191–219.

Struever, Nancy. 1992. *Theory as Practice: Ethical Inquiry in the Renaissance.* Chicago: University of Chicago Press.

Stump, Eleonore. 1985. "The Problem of Evil." *Faith and Philosophy* 2: 392–423.

Suchocki, Marjorie Hewitt. 1994. *The Fall to Violence: Original Sin in Relational Theology.* New York: Continuum.

Surin, Kenneth. 1986. *Theology and the Problem of Evil.* Oxford: Basil Blackwell.

1989. *The Turnings of Darkness and Light: Essays in Philosophical and Systematic Theology.* New York: Cambridge University Press.

Taliaferro, Charles and Philip L. Quinn, eds. 1997. *A Companion to Philosophy of Religion.* Oxford: Basil Blackwell.

Tanner, Kathryn. 1988. *God and Creation in Christian Theology: Tyranny or Empowerment?* Oxford: Basil Blackwell.

1992. *The Politics of God.* Minneapolis: Fortress Press.

1993. "A Theological Case for Human Responsibility in Moral Choice." *The Journal of Religion* 73: 592–612.

1996. "Public Theology and the Character of Public Debate." *The Annual of the Society of Christian Ethics* 16: 79–101.

1997. *Theories of Culture: A New Agenda for Theology.* Minneapolis: Fortress Press.

Taylor, Charles. 1979. *Hegel and Modern Society.* New York: Cambridge University Press.

1985. "Interpretation and the Sciences of Man." *Philosophy and the Human Sciences: Philosophical Papers 2.* New York: Cambridge University Press, pp. 15–57.

1989. *Sources of the Self: The Making of Modern Identity.* Cambridge, MA: Harvard University Press.

Taylor, Mark C. 1984. *Erring: A Postmodern A/theology.* Chicago: University of Chicago Press.

Thompson, G. R. 1981. "A Dark Romanticism: In Quest of a Gothic Monomyth." In *Literature of the Occult.* Peter B. Messent, ed. Englewood Cliffs, NJ: Prentice-Hall, pp. 31–9.

Tillich, Paul. 1954. *Love, Power, and Justice.* New York: Oxford University Press.

1961. "Reinhold Niebuhr's Doctrine of Knowledge." In Kegley and Bretall, eds., pp. 36–43.

Torchia, N. Joseph, OP. 1999. *Creatio ex nihilo and the Theology of St. Augustine: The Anti-Manichean Polemic and Beyond.* New York: Peter Lang.

Varnado, S. L. 1987. *Haunted Presence: The Numinous in Gothic Fiction.* Tuscaloosa: University of Alabama Press.

Villa, Dana. 1992. "Beyond Good and Evil: Arendt, Nietzsche, and the Aestheticization of Political Action." *Political Theory.* 20: 274–308.

1996. *Arendt and Heidegger: The Fate of the Political.* Princeton: Princeton University Press.

Wainwright, William T. 1995. *Reason and the Heart: A Prolegomenon to a Critique of Passional Reason.* Ithaca: Cornell University Press.

Walker, Margaret Urban. 1993. "Moral Luck and the Virtues of Impure Agency." In Statman, ed., pp. 235–50.

Walls, Jerry L. 1992. *Hell: The Logic of Damnation.* Notre Dame: University of Notre Dame Press.

Walzer, Michael. 1974. "Political Action: The Problem of Dirty Hands." In *War and Moral Responsibility.* Marshall Cohen, Thomas Nagel, and Thomas Scanlon, eds. Princeton: Princeton University Press.

Ward, Keith. 1986. "Reinhold Niebuhr and the Christian Hope." In Harries, ed., pp. 61–87.

Weil, Simone. 1951. *Waiting for God.* Emma Craufurd, trans. New York: G. P. Putnam's Sons.

Weissbort, Daniel, ed. 1991. *The Poetry of Survival: Post-War Poets of Central and Eastern Europe.* London: Anvil Press.

Wennemyr, Susan. 1998. "Dancing in the Dark: Deconstructive A/theology Leaps with Faith." *Journal of the American Academy of Religion* 66: 571–88.

Westphal, Merold. 1993. *Suspicion and Faith: The Religious Uses of Modern Atheism.* Grand Rapids, MI: Eerdmans.

Wetzel, James. 1992a. *Augustine and the Limits of Virtue.* New York: Cambridge University Press.

1992b. "Can Theodicy Be Avoided? The Claim of Unredeemed Evil." In *The Problem of Evil.* Michael Peterson, ed. Notre Dame: University of Notre Dame Press, pp. 351–65.

Wiggins, David. 1980. "Weakness of Will, Commensurability, and the Objects of Deliberation and Desire." In *Essays on Aristotle's Ethics.* A. O. Rorty, ed. Berkeley: University of California Press, pp. 241–65.

Wilkinson, Jeffrey. 1981. *The Intellectual Resistance in Europe.* Cambridge, MA: Harvard University Press.

Williams, Anne. 1995. *Art of Darkness: A Poetics of Gothic.* Chicago: University of Chicago Press.

Williams, Bernard. 1981. *Moral Luck: Philosophical Papers 1973–1980.* New York: Cambridge University Press.

1993a. *Shame and Necessity.* Berkeley: University of California Press.

1993b. "Pagan Justice and Christian Love." *Apeiron* 26: 195–207.

1993c. "Postscript." In Statman, ed., pp. 251–8.

Williams, Raymond. 1978. *Marxism and Literature.* New York: Oxford University Press.

Williams, Robert R. 1984. "Theodicy, Tragedy, and Soteriology: The Legacy of Schleiermacher." *Harvard Theological Review* 77: 395–412.

Williams, Rowan. 1990. "*Sapientia* and the Trinity: Reflections on *De Trinitate*." In *Collectanea Augustiniana: Mélanges T. J. Van Bavel.* B. Bruning, M. Lamberigts, and J. Van Houtem, eds. Leuven: Leuven University Press, pp. 317–32.

1996. "Reply: Redeeming Sorrows." In *Religion and Morality.* D. Z. Phillips, ed. New York: St. Martin's Press, pp. 132–48.

Wolf, Susan. 1980. "Asymmetrical Freedom." *The Journal of Philosophy* 77: 151–66.

1982. "Moral Saints." *The Journal of Philosophy* 79: 419–39.

1990. *Freedom within Reason.* New York: Oxford University Press.

Wolin, Richard. 1996. "The Ambivalences of German-Jewish Identity: Hannah Arendt in Jerusalem." *History and Memory* 8: 9–34.

Wood, Neal. 1986. "*Populares* and *circumcelliones*: The Vocabulary of 'Fallen Man' in Cicero and St. Augustine." *History of Political Thought* 7: 33–51.

Woolf, Leonard. 1967. *Downhill All the Way: An Autobiography of the Years 1919 to 1939.* New York: Harcourt Brace Jovanovich.

1969. *The Journey Not the Arrival Matters: An Autobiography of the Years 1939 to 1969.* New York: Harcourt Brace Jovanovich.

Wyman, Walter E. 1994. "Rethinking the Christian Doctrine of Sin: Friedrich Schleiermacher and Hick's 'Irenaean Type'." *The Journal of Religion* 74: 199–217.

Yack, Bernard. 1986. *The Longing for Total Revolution*. Princeton: Princeton University Press.

1997. *The Fetishism of Modernities: Epochal Self-Consciousness in Contemporary Social and Political Thought*. Notre Dame: Notre Dame University Press.

Yeager, D. M. 1982. "On Making the Tree Good: An Apology for a Dispositional Ethics." *The Journal of Religioius Ethics*. 10: 103–20.

1988. "The Web of Relationship: Feminists and Christians." *Soundings* 71: 485–513.

1996. "The Social Self in the Pilgrim Church." In Stassen, Yeager, and Yoder 1996, pp. 91–126.

Young-Breuhl, Elizabeth. 1982. *Hannah Arendt: For Love of the World*. New Haven: Yale University Press.

Zillner, Eric A., Molly Harrower, Barry A. Ritzler, and Robert P. Archer. 1995. *The Quest for the Nazi Personality: A Psychological Investigation of Nazi War Criminals*. Hillsdale, NJ: Lawrence Erlbaum Associates.

Zizioulas, Jean D. 1975. "Human Capacity and Human Incapacity: A Theological Exploration of Personhood." *Scottish Journal of Theology* 28: 401–48.

Index

Rose, Gillian, 46
Russell, Frederick H., 83, 230

Saak, Eric Leland, 61
Sandel, Michael, 15, 141
Sands, Kathleen, 92
Santurri, Edmund, 27, 224
Sartre, Jean-Paul, 45
Sayre-McCord, Jeffrey, 195
Scheffler, Samuel, 27, 109, 224, 228
Schleiermacher, Friedrich, 92
Schmidt, Anton, 193
Schuld, Joyce, 222
Schweiker, William, 17, 129, 160, 208, 234
Scott, Joanna Vecchiarelli, 178
Scott, Michael, 39, 40–1
Searle, John, 180
Sen, Amartya, 16
Shakespeare, William, 149
Shelley, Percy Bysse, 44
Shklar, Judith, 235
Simon, Ulrich, 92
sin, 1–3, 10, 18, 47–51, 56–7, 79–81, 86, 107,
    112–15, 117–20, 125–8, 133–7, 201–2,
    212–13, 219–24, 227, 241
  as perversion, 6–7, 60, 80–1, 107, 112–15,
    117–20, 125–8, 133–7
  as second nature, 74, 81, 107
Smith, Thomas, 133
Song, Robert, 53, 128
Sophocles, 29
Speer, Albert, 26
Sperber, Dan 134
Stark, Judith Chelius, 178
Statman, Daniel 27
Steiner, George, 27, 129
Stevens, Wallace, 107
Stocker, Michael, 27
Stone, Ronald, 109, 112
Stout, Jeffrey, 67, 68
Struever, Nancy, 42
Stump, Eleonore, 95
subjectivism, 4–5, 7–9, 14–17, 24, 28–30, 51–5,
    66, 69, 102, 111, 126, 128–32, 152–3,
    174–84, 196, 202, 229, 240–1
  and evil, 4–5, 28–30, 51–5
  and foundationalism, 53
  and freedom, 13–18
  as consumeristic, 16–17
"supernatural," 48, 143–5, 213
Suchocki, Marjorie Hewitt, 92
Surin, Kenneth, 41

Tabor, James, 210
Taliaferro, Charles, 60
Tanner, Kathryn, 53, 68, 109, 142, 147
Taylor, Charles, 12, 15, 53, 61, 173
Taylor, Mark C., 129
Tertullian, 73
theodicy, 36–43, 58, 207
  critical rejection of it, 36–7, 38–42, 207
theory and practice, 37, 40–2, 164, 183, 203,
    206, 215, 227–9, 237–8, 244–5
Thompson, Dennis, 15
Tillich, Paul, 130, 235
Torchia, N. Joseph, 76
tradition, 5–9, 11, 17–18, 60–70, 100–3, 239–46
  admiring and following, 62
  ethnography and archaeology, 68
tragedy, 5, 29, 89–90

Varnado, S. L., 35
Villa, Dana, 158–9, 169, 179, 191, 192, 195

Wainwright, William, 123
Walker, Margaret Urban, 89
Walls, Jerry, 79
Walzer, Michael, 223
Ward, Keith, 119, 139
Weber, Max, 173
Weil, Simone, 98
Wennemyr, Susan, 129
Westphal, Merold, 4
Wetzel, James, 28, 42–3, 76, 83, 196
Wiggins, David, 27
Wilkinson, Jeffrey, 189
Williams, Anne, 58
Williams, Bernard, 25, 28, 85, 88–90, 142–3,
    223–4
Williams, Raymond, 41
Williams, Robert R., 92
Williams, Rowan, 39, 203, 209
Wittgenstein, Ludwig, 26, 157
Wolf, Susan, 53, 183
Wolin, Richard, 166
Wood, Neal, 222
Woolf, Leonard, 22
Wyman, Walter, 92

Yack, Bernard, 69, 172
Yeager, D. M., 155, 158, 223, 232
Yoder, John Howard, 110–11
Young-Breuhl, Elizabeth, 165, 179

Zizioulas, Jean D., 79